DUBLIN

1660–1860

THE FOUR COURTS, from Winetavern Street Bridge.

Maurice Craig

DUBLIN
1660–1860

ALLEN FIGGIS LTD DUBLIN 1980

© Allen Figgis & Co. Ltd, 1980
First published 1952
Reprinted in paperback 1969
This printing 1980

Printed in Great Britain by
Richard Clay (The Chaucer Press) Ltd,
Bungay, Suffolk

. . . the growing splendour . . . of the Age of Reason, the *Eclaircissement*, the *Aufklärung*—that conception of order and truth, of the whole universe governed by law, which rose in the latter half of the seventeenth century like a sunrise of reason over the spectre-haunted Europe, with its romantic literature, its superstitions, its fanaticisms, and its religious wars.

—LOGAN PEARSALL SMITH: *Words and Idioms*

. . . here and there I noticed that smooth, smiling face that we discover for the first time in certain pictures by Velasquez; all that hungry, mediæval speculation vanished, that had worn the faces of El Greco, and in its place a self-complacent certainty that all had been arranged, provided for, set out in clear type, in manuals of devotion or of doctrine.

—W. B. YEATS: *The Trembling of the Veil*

PREFACE

This book has been conceived more as a 'portrait' than as a 'history'. For a portrait, of any school, must at least base itself on the visible features of its subject, whatever else it may succeed in conveying. The historian proper enjoys less licence to select and omit than is commonly demanded by those who employ the æsthetic approach. The reader will, therefore, find little here about political developments, the condition of the poor, or even the more generalised aspects of social and economic history. Here and there he will find a dab or two from that side of the palette; and he may feel that in the interests of purity of colour these touches should have been left out. Perhaps he is right. But if I paint my sitter in a purple tie, that need not imply that he has no others in his wardrobe.

Others may be more seriously disappointed at finding so little mention of certain famous Dubliners, and so much about men of whom he may never have heard before. But I have been concerned with individuals only so far as each one has given something—it may be a building, it may be a legend, or it may be only a bad example—to Dublin or to Ireland. Goldsmith, Richard Brinsley Sheridan, Burke, Shaw, the younger Wilde, have given little to Dublin, whatever they may have drawn from her. They have little place in a book of this kind.

It will seem to some readers that I have treated political questions with a misplaced flippancy, that I have made too little effort to be fair and to give all sides a reasonable hearing. It is best to confess at the outset that I have used political and other utterances without scruple, for purpose of effect alone. I make no claim to be writing history in this sense. I regard the utterances of political or other figures as no more than so many smoke-screens whose purpose is, as often as not, to delude those who put them out. Much the same criticism applies to all written or literary evidence of motive. But buildings and other artefacts seem to me to be much better evidence. I have done my best to get out of the way of the buildings and let them be seen for themselves, relying on a possibly fallacious belief that architecture cannot lie.

M.J.C.

ACKNOWLEDGMENTS

Among the many people whose help and kindness deserve the author's warmest thanks must be mentioned the Staffs of the National Library of Ireland, especially Mr Patrick Henchy, Keeper of Printed Books, the Public Record Office of Ireland, the Royal Irish Academy, the Office of Public Works, especially Mr Raymond McGrath, Chief Architect, the National Gallery of Ireland, especially Mr Brinsley MacNamara, Registrar, the National Museum of Ireland, especially Dr G. A. Hayes-McCoy and Dr W. O'Sullivan, The Central Statistics Office, especially Miss Dorothy Lynd, and the Bank of Ireland, especially its Architect, Mr H. V. Miller and his assistant Miss Olive Young. Mr H. Vernon, Agent to the Pembroke Estate and his assistant Mr F. Biddulph, also gave valuable help.

Individuals to whom he is indebted include Mr R. Chisholm Batten, Senator Miss Eleanor Butler, Mr Howard Colvin, Mr C. P. Curran, Mr John Harvey, Mr Joseph Haughton, Mr John Hayward, Mr Valentin Iremonger, Mr Oisin Kelly, Mr D. W. Kennan, Mr T. H. Mason, Mr Patrick Meehan, Mr C. Morisy, Mr Oliver Murray, Mr John Summerson and Mr H. A. Wheeler. Mr H. G. Leask's continued interest in the book's progress was attested in numerous most profitable consultations and the dedication is an attempt to discharge this debt. The owners and custodians of buildings are too numerous to specify, but they are not forgotten.

The extracts from Fitzwilliam leases are quoted by permission of The Lord Herbert. The maps are based on the Ordnance Survey by permission of the Minister for Finance, and in this connexion Col. Nolan, Deputy Assistant Director, gave valuable assistance.

Thanks are due to the author and publishers for permission to quote a passage from *Seven Winters*, by Elizabeth Bowen (Longmans, Green & Co.).

Plates IV, V, VI, XII, XIV, XV, XXV, XXXIV, LVII and LXVIII were supplied by T. H. Mason & Sons; Plates VII, VIII, XIII, XVI, XLIV, XLVIII, L, LXIII, LXIV and LXIX by the National Library of Ireland; Plates X, XXVII, XXXV and LXXIV by the Irish Tourist Association; Plate XXXVIII by Dr Joachim Gerstenberg; the Frontispiece by the

Irish Press Ltd.; Plates XVIII and XIX are reproduced by courtesy of the Board of Governors and Guardians of the National Gallery of Ireland; Plate XXXIII by courtesy of the National Museum of Ireland; Plate LVI by courtesy of the Honourable the Benchers of the King's Inns; Plate XXX by courtesy of Norman Ashe Studios and Plate XXI by courtesy of The College Studios. Fig. 6 is reproduced by kind permission of the artist, Mr Raymond McGrath, and Mr R. P. Ross Williamson, and Plate XL is from a photograph in possession of the Office of Public Works, reproduced with the consent of the Royal Society of Antiquaries of Ireland. Fig. 7 is adapted from drawings by Mr H. G. Leask, and two of the moulding profiles in Fig. 15 were constructed from data supplied by Mr Oliver Murray and the Office of Public Works respectively. Plate XLIII is reproduced from A. E. Richardson, *Monumental Classic Architecture in Great Britain and Ireland*, by permission of Messrs B. T. Batsford Ltd.

The remaining illustrations are by the author. Plate XVII was taken with the co-operation of the Bank of Ireland authorities.

Finally, the author desires to record his indebtedness to his wife, who made many valuable suggestions and greatly assisted him in the business of proof-reading.

CONTENTS

Ormonde's Dublin

Swift's Dublin

Grattan's Dublin

CONTENTS

Whose Dublin?

FIGURES IN THE TEXT

LIST OF PLATES

CORRIGENDA

Some of the statements in this book have ceased to be true by reason of the lapse of time. Since part of the book's purpose was to record the state of affairs in the year 1950 or so, it has seemed best to leave it as it was. But some of the statements were untrue even then, and should not be left uncorrected. I am grateful to those who have drawn my attention to mistakes. Those of which I know are here set right. In addition, on one or two topics, notably the career of Sir Edward Lovett Pearce, subsequent research has changed the picture entirely and falsified some of my conjectures.

p. 14   The Commissioners of Woods and Forests controlled the Park only from 1832 to 1851.

p. 51   line 21. Petty probably arrived in 1651.

p. 52   line 5. There is some doubt whether Petty was in fact Surveyor-General.

p. 56   line 23. Mountjoy, it seems, succeeded Petty during the latter's lifetime. line 30. The reference should be (MSS. I. 1–2).

p. 58   bottom. Robinson's patent dated from 1670, not 1661.

p. 62   line 10. The same mannerism is found in the arches of Les Invalides and of the Place des Vosges (Place Royale) and at Holyroodhouse, Edinburgh, which is exactly contemporary with Kilmainham.

p. 66   Robinson had nothing to do with James's Fort (Ringrone) which dates from the reign of James I. Charles Fort is in Rincurran Parish.

p. 67   line 2. This Captain Pratt is not the same man as the cartographer, whose name was Henry. line 13. I incline now to the view that the garden-house is by Pearce and therefore of about 1730.

p. 74   bottom. St Mary's was designed by Thomas Burgh and begun in 1702.

p. 75   line 10. I am satisfied that the story about the two western staircases coming from the old library is nothing but an old wives' tale.

p. 79   The Tailors' Hall has now been completely restored.

p. 96   line 9. Dr Elisabeth Kieven has shown reason to suppose that the west front of St Werburgh's may be by Alessandro Galilei.

p. 102   five lines from bottom. Gardiner called Henrietta Street after his daughter.

p. 103   line 5. Numbers 9 and 10 Henrietta Street are by Pearce. Number 9 is a close copy of Lord Mountrath's house in London, by Lord Burlington.

p. 108   line 19. For 'from Dawson of Molesworth' read 'from Dawson or Molesworth'.

p. 109   line 5. This is incorrect. The Coote baronetcy survived a little longer.

p. 118 bottom. Woodlands is probably by Pearce. Its façade is cleverly adapted from one of the end-façades of Coleshill.

p. 120 line 31. *Thoughts on Government in General* is not by Dobbs but was published anonymously in 1728.

p. 125 Pearce's travels in France and Italy are now well documented. See *Architectural Drawings by Sir John Vanbrugh and Sir Edward Lovett Pearce*, edited by Howard Colvin and Maurice Craig, Oxford, for the Roxburghe Club, 1964, in which Pearce's close relationship to Vanbrugh is documented, and his authorship of other buildings established. His part in the building of Castletown (now known to have been initiated by Alessandro Galilei) is clarified in *Country Life*, March 27 and April 3, 1969. Pearce returned to Ireland in 1726.

p. 128 line 13. The connexion between the Parliament House and the British Museum is proved by the fact that James Malton's large print of the Parliament House forecourt had the figures drawn by Robert Smirke the elder, father of the architect, who must thus have known it well.

p. 138 Mr. Denis Johnston has drawn my attention to the fact that, like everybody else, I have slightly misquoted the famous epitaph.

p. 142 penultimate line. For 'nineteenth' read 'eighteenth'.

p. 144 line 24. For 'eighty-six' read 'thirty-six'.

p. 163 The little Phoenix at Parkgate has now, alas, disappeared, bush and all.

pp. 165–7 It now seems certain that the South-Eastern range of Upper Castle Yard, recently reconstructed, is by Pearce. The Knight of Glin has shown the stylistic affinities of the garden front with other work by Pearce, and the central corridor is unmistakably his. It is also overwhelmingly probable that he designed the Genealogical Office and the Bedford Tower, which consists of a tower taken from Kent's *Designs of Inigo Jones* set on top of a transcript of Lord Pembroke's villa in Whitehall by Colen Campbell. Curiously, the resemblance to the Whitehall original was made closer by the nineteenth-century addition of an attic storey. The Dublin Castle design as a whole may probably now be dated to before 1733, and the Ivory attribution dismissed as unfounded. The civil division of the Barrack Board was already known as the Board of Works by 1780 if not earlier.

p. 168 line 8. The Hospital of St Margaret of Cortona was demolished in the 1950's.

p. 171 line 24. The Ewings published at least one book in French in association with a Parisian publisher, with a joint Dublin and Paris imprint.

p. 174 bottom note. The Act of 1729 (Pearce's Act) was chiefly concerned to regulate the conduct of builders' workmen and (to a lesser extent) that of their employers the master-builders, and the size and quality of bricks. Clause 16 provided that no-one, in Dublin or any other town, 'shall lay . . . any . . . timber . . . in any party, front, or back-wall of any house . . . in such a manner that it shall appear through the same, or shall lay it within four inches of the said wall.' The dimension of four inches was borrowed from the English Act of 1707.

p. 182   line 16. The glazing-bars of the Regent House have now been replaced. The Provost's House. More fully treated by the present author in *The Connoisseur*, April 1960, pp. 148–153, and more fully still by Edward McParland in *Country Life*, October 14 and 21, 1976, where the evidence for Henry Keene's authorship is given but the author shrinks, no doubt properly, from pronouncing it as proven.

p. 200   line 9. For 'south-east' read 'south-west'. Note at end of chapter. John Gibbons and his book seem to be among several pure inventions by the late Colin Johnston Robb: hence totally chimerical.

p. 217   end of chapter. My *Irish Bookbindings* 1600–1800, London, 1954, was an attempt to fill this gap.

p. 228   line 6 from bottom. Jonah Barrington's window has now been re-opened.

p. 229   last paragraph. Belvedere House is by Michael Stapleton.

p. 233   line 7 from bottom. What remained of Moira House has since been destroyed.

p. 243   Cooley, Gandon and the Four Courts. Much further light has been thrown on the evolution of the design by Dr E. McParland in a paper as yet unpublished, in part rehabilitating Cooley in the place from which Dr Curran thought to dethrone him.

p. 246   penultimate line. Gandon bought rather than built the house at Canonbrook.

p. 249   penultimate line. For 'half a mile' read 'a mile'.

p. 250   line 27. For 'capitals' read 'abaci'.

p. 254   top of page. One important function of the triangular spaces is to act as very necessary and effective sound insulation.

p. 279   note at foot. Neither of the surviving Gandon drawings for the West front is very close to that actually built. See my annotated reprint of the Gandon *Life*, London, 1969.

p. 280   line 5 sqq. Both the Henry Aaron Baker attributions (taken from Wright's *Historical Guide*) are erroneous. Dr McParland has established that the Rutland Fountain is by Francis Sandys, Sir Patrick Dun's Hospital by Sir Richard Morrison, and the Westmoreland Street and D'Olier Street elevations by Baker, for the Wide Streets Commissioners. See *Bulletin of Irish Georgian Society* XV 1 (Jan–March 1972).

p. 281   line 7. Dr McParland has cast serious doubt on the attribution of Daly's Club House to Francis Johnston in favour of an attribution to his brother Richard.

CORRIGENDA

p. 283   line 11. The Female Orphan-House Chapel (now demolished) was not by Johnston but by William Farrell whose drawings survive in an album now in America.

p. 284   penultimate line. The trees are not cypresses but Irish or fastigiate yews.

p. 287   line 23. Wilkin's Yarmouth column is not really very similar. The Dublin Pillar, as all the world now knows, is no more.

p. 289   line 19. James Savage (Colvin *Dictionary of English Architects*, p. 528) who designed Richmond Bridge, had an important English career and is not identical with either of the other Savages here mentioned. Barrack Bridge is by G. Halpin.

      line 8 from bottom. The Metal Bridge is now known to have been designed by John Windsor, the foreman of the Coalbrookdale foundry.

p. 292   line 4. Adam and Eve's church is by James Bolger, begun in 1834 (McParland).

p. 292   line 11. For 'T. B. Keane' read 'J. B. Keane'.

p. 294   note. See also the more recent article on Byrne by Patrick Raftery in *Bulletin of Irish Georgian Society* VII 2–4 (Apr–Dec 1964)

p. 298   line 19. It is now clear that the handsome north façade of the Theatre Royal was never actually built.

p. 301   line 5. The Broadstone became disused in 1937, not 1931.

p. 302   line 15. The National Gallery. In 1853 the Board of Works was asked to supply a design for the Natural History Museum, for which F. V. Clarendon was architect. For the National Gallery, on the other side of Leinster Lawn, the same elevation was used, but the principal designer seems to have been Sir Richard Griffith, Chairman of the Board of Works, with assistance from Capt. Francis Fowke. The columnar portico and the Northern (now middle) galleries are by Sir Thomas Manly Deane. In recent years the Gallery has been extended Northwards by the Board of Works and doubled in size.

p. 308   King George IV landed at Howth, not at Dunleary.

p. 315   The anomalously named *Dublin Review* has nothing to do with the *Dublin University Review*, and nothing to do with Dublin either. For a short time in the 1950's it changed its name to the *Wiseman Review*, but reverted to its old name though still, as always, published and edited in London.

p. 326   Royal (Collins) Barracks. The middle part which was by Burgh has gone and only the squares to east and west remain.

p. 331   Glasnevin. The important cast-iron Palm House by the Dublin ironfounder, Richard Turner, should be noted.

p. 332   Mespil House has been demolished and its ceilings re-erected in Dublin Castle and Arus an Uachtarain.

CORRIGENDA

p. 333 line 12. The panelled dies in the centre of the blocking course over the wings have now been replaced.

p. 335 line 26. Some of the statues and internal capitals etc. have been worked up into an engaging little folly by Gerald McNicholl in the Beresford Place park, close to the railway bridge.

p. 345 Add Curran, C. P., *Dublin Decorative Plasterwork of the Seventeenth and Eighteenth Centuries*, London, 1967. A greatly expanded version of the same author's *JRSAI* article, with numerous illustrations.

PART ONE

Ormonde's Dublin

CHAPTER I

The Duke Returns

ON THE 29th of May, 1453, the city of Constantinople fell to the troops of Mahomet II. With a dull explosion the Byzantine polity disintegrated, and the roads to Western Europe were, if the verdict of history is to be trusted, packed thick with refugee scholars, each clutching a precious codex, some now and again casting a backward glance to where, above the smoke of the fallen city, the shallow dome of Hagia Sophia, with monumental buttresses like the paws of a lion or a sphinx, still stood in its tenth century of power. A solemn scene, and one. from which the academic mind is prone to date the beginning of modern history.

In due course the smoke dispersed; Constantinople settled down to its long Ottoman repose; the scholars, hospitably received at Western courts, left their manuscripts in the libraries of Rome and Milan. Like a seismic ripple or the last reverberation of a tidal wave, this great Levantine catastrophe spread its rings until, two hundred years later, a little wave washed up the sands of a remote western shore, and James Duke of Ormonde stepped out of his pinnace on to the sands of Dublin Bay. The Renaissance, in a word, had arrived in Ireland. It was July the 27th in the year 1662. The peasantry welcomed him on the shore, dancing and strewing flowers in his path. They sang, in Irish, 'Thugamar féin an samhra linn': 'We brought the summer with us'.[1] The Duke's reception in Dublin 'was, for the splendour thereof, a kind of epitome of what had lately been seen at London upon His Majesty's happy restoration'. The Middle Ages were at last at an end.

The Duke of Ormonde was now fifty-two, the ninth member of the house of Butler to hold viceregal office, and himself an ex-viceroy. He brought back with him memories of his last departure from Dublin twelve years earlier, involved in the defeat of his royal master. He had more recent memories of the opulent grandeur of Louis XIV's Paris, and of his own poverty and humiliation in

3

the lean years of exile. He had seen in France the happy effects of the toleration of Huguenots, and had learnt the lesson which the French King was so soon to forget. He himself had a family background which was partly Catholic, partly Protestant, matching to a nicety the country he was now to rule. Above all, he had absorbed on his travels the conception of the centralised state and the ceremonial capital.

Ormonde's ideal, then, was an Ireland of Protestant and (if possible) Catholic, whose greatest need was peace, and the noblest outward sign of peace, public works. And as charity begins at home, so improvements were best placed where they would make the best showing, in the capital itself. Any measure which would emphasise Dublin's position as the head and front of Ireland was in tune with the new policy. For it must be remembered that only now did Dublin become the capital in any modern sense. It was less than a century since Drogheda had been abandoned as a venue for Parliament. Even more recently, a large quasi-parliament had sat in Kilkenny.* The Dublin Parliament of 1613, only fifty years before, was the first to be in any sense representative of the whole country; and it was also the first, by a natural consequence, in which any serious anti-English opposition was encountered. The ecclesiastical capital was, and still is, Armagh. For many a long year after 1660 there were whole tracts of the country which held little or no communication with Dublin.

But Ormonde's policy, half-consciously inspired by the Parisian example, was permanently successful in this sense: that Dublin became and remained an object of first interest for all important movements from now on. In the recent past, native Irish leaders such as Owen Roe O'Neill had conducted their strategy almost without reference to the capital as such. But even the Gaelic mind was now to learn the urban habit. Dublin, from being merely the chief garrison of the English Pale, was to become an object of pride and of contention to Irishmen of whatever race or creed.

As it stood in 1660, it was hardly an object of pride to anybody. In area it was about one-sixth of the area of mediæval London, being nearly half as long, nearly half as wide, and roughly the same shape.†

---

* The Confederation Parliament of 1649.

† The areas given are those within the walls. By 1660, of course, both cities had spread outside their walls.

4

The area of mediæval London was about two-thirds of a square mile, that of Dublin about one-ninth of a square mile. Like London it was a rectangle with one of the longer sides bordering the river. In the south-west corner the Castle corresponded to the Tower of London. But, as Dublin lay south of the Liffey instead of north of the Thames, the Castle stood on a landward corner, with the miserable trickle of the Poddle river serving as a ditch round two of its sides. The Castle was fairly enough described by one of Ormonde's relatives in 1684 as 'the worst castle in the worst situation in Christendom'.

Round the walls there stood, besides the castle, some seventeen towers and gate-towers, mostly in poor repair. In the centre of the city stood Christchurch Cathedral, also in a semi-ruinous condition, and within the walls there were six or seven parish churches of the Establishment,* as well as an even more indefinite (though probably smaller) number of Catholic churches. The population, by a census of 1659, was under nine thousand[2]; and this included six parishes without the walls. We may therefore infer that a large proportion of the houses were derelict. Few of them, in any case, can have been more than single-storey cabins, and the unsettled times must have discouraged adequate repairs, to say nothing of new building. A handful of three- and four-storey houses dating from Elizabeth's reign and even earlier survived into the mid-eighteenth century, and the one of which a drawing (Fig. 2a) survives shows that in parts, at least, this earlier Dublin was not unlike the London which perished in the Great Fire.

Hardly anything now remains of the Dublin of 1660. The mediæval street-plan, both within and without the walls, is still almost as obvious on the ground as it is on the map. Some of the old street-names have disappeared: though Copper Alley still survives, the famous Smock Alley close by has become Essex Street West; the Blind Quay has been barbarously re-named Exchange Street Lower; Giglots' Hill has become, more excusably, St Michael's Hill. But Fishamble Street, Winetavern Street, Ship Street ('Sheep' Street), survive in both name and fact. Bull Alley and Golden Lane are there in name but in little more; and little but the name survives of Hoey's Court where in 1668 Jonathan Swift was born.

---

* *i.e.* the Anglican Church of Ireland.

Of the actual buildings still less is to be seen. So little indeed that an attempt at a complete catalogue will hardly be out of place. The remains consist, with only one exception, of the military and ecclesiastical structures, stone-built and of mediæval date. There are the Cathedrals, much-restored in the nineteenth century, of St Patrick's and Christchurch. The Archbishop's Palace of St Sepulchre, long converted into a police-barracks. It contains a mediæval vault and a sixteenth-century window. The mediæval church of St Audoen's, three-quarters ruined and the remaining quarter botched. The chapter-house of St Mary's Abbey of Oxmantown, half underground. A long stretch of early mediæval wall, marking the line before the city had even reached the banks of the Liffey, much remodelled but containing a gate—St Audoen's Gate—which is not quite so much of a fake as it appears to be. Another stretch of wall, from New Gate (the western gate) in a south-easterly direction towards the vanished Hanging Tower. Until a few years ago the Corporation carefully protected with a railing a fragment of New Gate itself; but without warning the same agency abolished it overnight. In the Castle itself there remain the stumps or cores of three towers and other walls, either invisible or heavily overlaid with later work. Of the original Trinity College hardly a vestige remains except a recumbent effigy of an early Fellow, of alabaster hideously eroded by damp, and kept (by the dramatic inspiration of some bygone Clerk of Works) in a gloomy triangular yard which sets off its macabre luminosity to perfection. It would be a fitting place in which to take our leave of the mediæval city, picturesque from a distance, with water-meadows and a still unsullied river flowing past the walls, but at close quarters squalid and constricted.

If we wish to revisit it, the simplest course is to go at night to Castle Street or Fishamble Street, St Michael's Hill (Pl. I), Bride Street or Back Lane. The darkness will obscure the fact that the houses have been rebuilt, and the streets will appear narrower and more tortuous than ever. The derelict tenements might, for all we can discern, have been knocked about by Cromwell's Colonels. In the occupied buildings candle-lighting is still usual, and out of the high windows lean Skeltonian women with wispy hair, gossiping with neighbours in other houses. Even the tall blocks of improving flats

6

built by the Iveagh Trust forty years ago remind one at night of the Old Town at Edinburgh. There have been public-houses on some of these sites since long before Ormonde's time, and in their narrow back rooms sit pensive men with hats on, raising from time to time long black pints of porter to long dark faces. The towers and spires of the Protestant churches, chilly, empty and very firmly shut, cluster together to blot the skyline. Darkness softens the elements of restoration and modernity, and is even merciful enough to hide the French Gothic of the Augustinian Church.

History does not record the antiquity of the festivities on New Year's Eve in Christchurch Place, when crowds gather, young and old, drunk and sober, letting off fireworks and dancing in eddying rings as far as O'Connell Bridge, while the Christchurch peal rings out the old. Few, on these occasions, give a thought to the dank vaults of St Werburgh's where Sir James Ware and Lord Edward Fitzgerald sleep, or to those of the roofless and derelict St Nicholas Within, where nobody sleeps at all. Few even noticed that a year or two ago the tall house* bearing the arms of Archbishop Ussher, which had long surveyed the scene, had gone. A few yards down Werburgh Street, at the entrance to Hoey's Court, a bust of Jonathan Swift faces us from a niche in the wall of a public-house. The associations of the place are unending, and to follow up the most notable would lead us well into the nineteenth century.

We may turn instead into St John's Lane, so narrow that the bells are almost inaudible, deadened by the weight of stone above us. But as we emerge into Winetavern Street (Pl. III), the sound drowns thought again, the clanging waves hitting the windows of the old houses in the Crescent and reverberating back upon us. We descend the steep street, lined with tottering tenements shored up with great baulks of wood. The street-lighting is meagre. We have passed through the King's Gate, long extinct, and looking back we realise how forcibly the Cathedral, small in itself but perched on a high and peaty hillock, dominates the walled city. As we reach the river the sound of the bells is reduplicated, struck back again from the housefronts along the Quays. The lamps are reflected in the water, but the shadows are black under the graceful arches of the bridge. Beyond, stretching almost to the next bridge, is the

* No 3 Fishamble Street, in which, also, James Clarence Mangan was born.

7

river-front of the Four Courts, and rising out of it, dim above the glare of the lamps, the gigantic drum and dome. We have come to 1786: we have come, indeed, to 1922.

REFERENCES

[1] Donal O'Sullivan, *The Bunting Collection* (Irish Folk-Song Society) III, 58 (1930). See also *JRSAI*, LXXIX, 93 (1949).

[2] *CARD* IV 560.

CHAPTER II

An Era of Expansion

THERE WAS no finality about Restoration Dublin. Even at the time, it must have been obvious that this was not an end, but a beginning. The frame of mind was exceptional; for post-Reformation Irish history is at almost every point backward-looking, a series of pretences that history has just stopped happening. After the Boyne, after the completion of the Penal system, after the Union, after the Treaty, even after the Declaration of Independence of 1782, there recurs the assumption that here and now is the goal to which all before was but the prelude. The forward glance is a rarity. It is not so much that Irishmen are given to shouting, with the character in Denis Johnston's play, 'Up the Status Quo!': rather that, in Dublin as everywhere else, the status quo is apt to be taken for granted.

But nobody in 1662 could be so insensitive as to take it for granted. The background of recent civil war was a commonplace; but the present and the future were ambiguous. The rewards and penalties of the war were yet to be distributed: nobody knew which would be which. The Commission of Settlement was busy weaving an opportunist and unstable patchwork over the whole country, making a nice distinction between Cromwellian and 'innocent Papist'. The town was swarming with adventurers and enthusiasts in coats of curious cut and colour, some of which had been turned, some of which had silver linings; Sir Hierome Sankey, Colonel Thomas Blood. The Viceroy himself bore an equivocal character in the eyes of Irishmen and Englishmen alike. In their inmost hearts all parties must have wished for a decision, one way or the other. Only Ormonde himself and a handful of scholars, intellectuals and courtiers, held a comprehensive faith for the times and the times to come. For the others, the question was the old one: are we in power or are they? Though for the moment there was no certain answer, the shorter view was justified: the decision came: the ambiguity was banished. The children of this world are in their generation wiser than the children of light.

They do not, however, leave so much behind them for us to thank them for. In the immortal words of a later Irish parliamentarian, 'Why should we do anything for posterity? What has posterity ever done for us?'* It is a philosophy which has never lacked adherents in Ireland, but in spite of it, much remains in which we still rejoice. This could not have been foreseen. We, being posterity, are in a position to give Sir Boyle Roche the lie. We are wise after the event. From our point of vantage we concentrate on what has survived, by whatever chain of chances it may have done so.

The physical analogue to this perspective in time is the fascination of old maps. It is as though we were suspended, filmwise, high in the air over the developing organism. We see the walled city of the invaders, at a safe distance from the sea but with ships berthed along its walls. To the north, across the river, is the Norse suburb of Oxmantown,† with its parish church St Michan's. There is only one bridge. To the south, round St Patrick's Cathedral, is the old Irish quarter in the valley of the Poddle, well supplied with churches dedicated to Irish saints but now in Protestant hands. One of them has a Round Tower. To the west, a long street straggles into the country, passing St Catherine's Church and leading to the viceregal country residence at Chapelizod. East of the town, on a little hillock by the sea, are the Elizabethan buildings of Trinity College and near them the ancient Norse Thingmote and the Long Stone.‡ Beyond it the estuary widens rapidly. There is water at high tide where later will stand the Custom House, two railway stations, many streets and several churches, and the entire Port of Dublin. Far out in the bay the fishing-village of Ringsend stands on the point of a long spit of land, at the base of which is another 'Irish Town'.

All round the edges of the town are the semi-derelict buildings of the monasteries and abbeys, most of them used in part for one

---

* Sir Boyle Roche, see Chapter XXII.
† The town of the Ostmen.
‡ The successor to the Long Stone or Steyne is the fantastic monument to Sir Philip Crampton, erected at the intersection of Hawkins and College Streets, the subject of a famous query in *Ulysses*.

secular purpose or another. From the surrounding country little rills and watercourses catch the sunlight as they flow towards the Liffey. Water- and wind-mills are dotted all around and in the town itself.

Even as we watch, the space between the Castle and the College becomes a long street. Near its eastern end rises the 'Round' Church. Oxmantown expands, becoming a residential district, with rich houses round its Green. The Ormonde Market on the river-bank faces the old town. Soon there are five bridges, and ships are berthed only below the Castle gate. Over the meadows south-east of the city, new streets begin to stretch. They are easily distinguished from the older streets, for already they are much wider and straighter. They culminate in a huge square of twenty-seven acres, two sides of which are rapidly built over by 1685. At the opposite edge of the town we notice a modest collegiate building, the Hospital of King Charles, or Blew-Coat School.* Beyond it there is something like an enormous green balloon, the nozzle towards Dublin and the outer confines lost on the horizon. It is much larger than Dublin; it will remain so for a century. It is the Phœnix Park. As we pass the 1680 mark we notice a bustle and commotion among the ruins of the Priory of the Knights Hospitallers at Kilmainham, a fine site facing across the river from a height towards the Park. They are laying out a large quadrangular building with an internal arcade, a pleasant place to walk already. As the work progresses, we see that it is in rubble masonry with light stone and stucco trimmings. It has dormer windows, a high-pitched roof and stately chimneys, but as yet no tower. At one corner they seem to be re-arranging what looks like a large mediæval window. As we approach closer one of the busy little figures detaches itself from the rest. It is giving directions to the workmen, answering questions, pointing here and there. We recognise Sir William Robinson, busy about the work for which the credit will long be given to Sir Christopher Wren. But we cannot get near enough to see his face.

We may abandon our exalted viewpoint, and borrow the feet and the eyes of a French traveller, M. A. Jouvin,[1] of Rochefort, of whom we know only that he has already been to Italy and Malta.

---

* Nearly always spelt thus in the eighteenth century.

Spain and Portugal, the Low Countries, Germany, Poland, England, Denmark and Sweden. We may reasonably infer that, as an experienced traveller, he will be critical enough. From other indications we may plausibly conjecture that he is a Catholic. He lands at Ringsend one afternoon in 1668, and puts up at the Mitre in Oxmantown. The next day he seeks out a French merchant to whom he has an introduction. Together they visit Trinity College. The Provost, Dr. Seele, impresses him as 'a man of great wit and learning'. He shows them the College Library, even lending the visitor some rare books from it. Dr Seele seems 'astonished that out of mere curiosity I should come to see Ireland, which is a country so retired, and almost unknown to foreign travellers'. M. Jouvin is shown the gardens, with vines struggling vainly against the Irish climate, and a parterre laid out as a sundial: another touch of optimism. He sees the chapel and the tomb of Luke Challoner (which we have already noticed), and the Provost's hospitality is exceeded only by the extent of his information on Irish affairs.

From the College to the other pole of Dublin life: the Castle. He calls it 'the palace of the Viceroy, Monsieur the Duke of Ormont, uncle* to the King, who has a fine court and a suite altogether royal; among them are several French gentlemen'. The buildings he considers very handsome, although very ancient. Across the stone bridge leading to Oxmantown is a 'great quay, where are the finest palaces in Dublin'. From his lodgings, he often goes walking 'in the great meadows by the side of the river, contemplating the country and the situation of this famous town'. It seems as though Dublin is going to obey the almost universal law of fashionable expansion westwards, for beyond New Gate is 'a great suburb, which is at present both the best and largest part of Dublin', and the houses here are 'fine and straight'.

'Dublin, with its suburbs,' he observes, somewhat to our surprise, 'is one of the greatest and best-peopled towns in Europe, and the residence of all the nobility of the kingdom of Ireland.' Food prices, he finds, are low, for 'this kingdom, which is the richest of all Europe in things necessary for human life, is the poorest in money'. In his travels through the country he notes that 'if you drink two pennyworth of beer at a public-house, they will give you of bread,

---

* This is, of course, mistaken.

meat, butter, cheese, fish, as much as you choose; and for all this you only pay your twopence for the beer, it being the custom of the kingdom'. Happily we may record that, in a modified form and at a higher price, this custom still survives in a few establishments in Dublin, though in rural Ireland eating and drinking have long since been utterly divorced.

At a guess, he supposes that one-third of the Irish are Catholics. (The true figure is of course much higher.) 'There are even in Dublin more than twenty houses where mass is secretly said.' For one who had seen so much grandeur elsewhere, Jouvin's account of Dublin is very favourable. But apart from the College, which he describes as 'grand', and his kind words about the Castle, he points to no particular features as having impressed him. We gather from him the feeling of a city in a phase of *laissez-faire* expansion, with a resident nobility embarking on private improvements in response to a more settled order of things. We are made aware, too, for almost the first time, of a large native and Catholic element which has at last taken to urban life in earnest: its presence will forever prevent Dublin from becoming an English city.

But in fact there were, by the time of his visit, public schemes of unexampled grandeur. They were undertaken with a very complete awareness of purpose. 'It is of importance', wrote Ormonde to his son, 'to keep up the splendour of the government'.[2] To this rather dubious political motive the world owes much.

The first and greatest of these undertakings was the formation of the Phœnix Park. From 1618 onwards a house known as 'The Phœnix', standing on the former lands of the Hospitallers of Kilmainham, north of the river, had been a viceregal residence. Cromwell's son Henry had lived in it as lord-deputy and governor-general. Not only had he kept it in order and even added a large wing,[3] but he had entertained here his political opponents as well as his supporters.

When Ormonde returned to power, Lord Orrery, who like his successor Lord Burlington (another of the huge Boyle clan) was an amateur architect, designed a wing to balance 'Colonel Harry's building'.[4] But Ormonde used the Phœnix for only four years, and the house and grounds were even before that swallowed up in the new Park. He and Sir Maurice Eustace, the Chancellor, were soon deep in schemes for the creation of the Phœnix Park as we know it. On the first of December, 1662, Charles II authorised the purchase of over four hundred acres from Eustace to add to the 400 acres of Kilmainham land. Another hundred were added at the same time, at a cost of £3,000. Eighteen months later the king sanctioned a further purchase from Eustace, and any contiguous lands which could be secured. Eustace's motives were quite evidently less pure than Ormonde's. By the end of Ormonde's vice-royalty in 1669 the Park had cost more than £31,000, and before it was finished it had cost half as much again.[5]

The primary intention was to create a royal deer-park (and therefore in practice a public park), rather than a mere demesne surrounding the viceregal residence. From the beginning it was frequented by the local residents. Near the Dublin end it was early provided with artificial water and suchlike amenities, but most of it was and still remains wild country, not so 'natural', indeed, as it looks, yet still in marked contrast to ordered urban gardens. It is a national park rather than a municipal one, and has always been under the control of a national authority, first the Commissioners of Woods and Forests, now the Board of Works. Its vast extent has made this inevitable; and surely no city of the size of Dublin is comparably endowed.

In its first form the Park enclosed over 2,000 acres, but at the founding of the Royal Hospital in 1680 it was reduced to nearly its present extent of 1,752 acres. It remains larger than Regent's Park, Hyde Park, Kensington Gardens, St James's Park and the Green Park, Greenwich and Battersea Parks all put together. Though a number of Lodges, Legations and so forth, with their private grounds, are islanded in its midst, the acreage remaining open to the public is still nearly as great as the sum of these London parks. Those who relish examples of the Irish bull may find them here; thus, of all the entrances it is the one without a gate which is called Parkgate. Similarly, the largest of the open spaces is ludicrously known as The Fifteen Acres, containing as it does over ten times that area. The very name of the Park itself preserves a sophisticated misconception. The 'Phœnix' was almost certainly so called from a spring of clear water—'Fionn Uisge'—flowing nearby. The classical spelling, with its literary overtones, was adopted from the beginning, though it was left to the eighteenth century to give sculptural form to the conceit.

Of all Ormonde's achievements this is, suitably enough, the most enduring. But the project was not realised without setbacks, and the very existence of the park was threatened more than once. It was necessary to enclose it with a wall and the contractor for this work was one William Dodson. This Dodson was the designer and builder of St Andrew's Church, which began to fall down soon afterwards: he also swindled Ormonde at Chapelizod. In the Phœnix Park he excelled himself in large-scale jobbery, demanding enormous sums for work which he farmed out for one-third the price, and which fell down before it was paid for. He was ultimately found out by Ormonde's son Ossory, whereupon he had the effrontery to offer to keep it in repair for £100 a year. Finally part of the wall was newly built by Sir John Temple in exchange for a strip of land adjoining it, so that Sir John had an interest in doing the work well.

Noblemen and gentlemen had an active part in the furnishing and maintenance of the Park. One was sent to England to purchase deer, another to Wales to fetch partridges, while Lord Ossory himself collected pheasants from the Ormonde estates. But the deer escaped through Dodson's walls and got mixed up with the traffic on the Chapelizod road, while the partridges fell victims to the local poachers. These evils abated in time, and though there are no longer any game-birds in the Park, there is a fine herd of fallow-deer. The Park was divided into a Rangership and two keeperships, which offices were held by people of high station, and ultimately were merged in political appointments. Lord Dungannon, the first Ranger, was above reproach, but his successor, appointed after Ormonde's recall, was a creature of Barbara Villiers, Duchess of Cleveland and mistress to Charles the Second. Already the King had proposed to give the Park as a present to Monmouth, who had waived his claim when the resentment in Ireland became evident. Now it was proposed to give it to the Duchess of Cleveland, and the patent was actually made out.[6] But Ormonde and Essex (his successor) managed to have it quashed; and the lady was placated with lands in England (for a wonder); but not before she had hissed at Ormonde that she hoped she might live to see him hanged. The

Duke replied sweetly that for his part he was content to live to see her grow old. When he was again Viceroy, in 1679, there was another threat to give the Park to a royal favourite; but it was never carried out and since then there has been no attempt at expropriation.

None of the buildings now in the Park dates back further than 1734.* The present ensemble retains the impress of Chesterfield's viceroyalty in 1744-7, with a heavy overlay of later history. The associations of the Park are many, and some of them, being well known, will appear in their proper place. In the early years of the eighteenth century, however, a young poet, James Ward, hardly known to fame, was in the habit of wandering in the Park:

> *Here careless on some mossy bank reclin'd,*
> *Lull'd by the murm'ring stream, and whistling wind,*
> *Nor poys'nous asp I fear, nor savage beast,*
> *That wretched swains in other lands infest.*
> *Fir'd with the love of song my voice I raise,*
> *And woo the muses to my countrey's praise,*
> *Hybernia blest from noxious creatures free . . .*

'Shall Cooper's-hill,' he asked with some reason,

> *Shall* Cooper's-hill *majestick rise in rhyme*
> *Strong as its basis, as its brow sublime?*
> *Shall* Windsor-Forest *winn immortal praise,*
> *It self outlasting in its Poet's lays;*
> *And thou O Phoenix-Park, remain so long*
> *Unknown to fame, and unadorn'd in song?*

No indeed: and for two hundred and fifty lines he celebrates its beauties. It is true, he admits, that being in Ireland it is devoid of dryads, satyrs and other Mediterranean fauna. None the less, he goes on to observe, it is very handy for the Dublin lovers, for here

> *Thy fountains weep—thy groves compassion show,*
> *All nature drooping with one lover's woe . . .*

Moreover it is a congenial haunt for poets, for in the Park

> *Uncommon raptures in my bosom glow,*
> *And from my tongue unlabour'd numbers flow.*

He describes with some skill the place where now Lord Chesterfield's Phœnix surmounts its column:

---

* The date of the Magazine Fort, celebrated in Swift's epigram.

16

Now when the centre of the wood is found,
With goodly trees (a spacious circle bound),
I stop my wandering—while on ev'ry side
Glades opening to my eye the grove divide;
To distant objects stretch my lengthened view,
And make each pleasing prospect charm anew.

There is, he notes, a fine view of the Dublin mountains, rising beyond the fertile plains of South County Dublin. Deep in the vale, he continues, old Liffey rolls his tides; and duly responsive come the romantick prospects which crown his rev'rend sides. The Royal Hospital is conspicuous in the foreground, and beyond it to the left is the distant view of Dublin familiar from so many prints:

A Grouppe of buildings in a cloud of smoak,
Where various domes for various uses made,
Religion, revels, luxury, and trade,
All undistinguish'd in one mass appear,
And widely diff'ring are united here.

We need not linger over the remainder of his poem,[7] the passage in which he espies a mound wherein the 'fairy monarch' hoards the lost property of mortals, or the long coda relating St Patrick's banishment of the snakes. The one is merely abortive in its quaintness, while the other is a trivial event in the long process which began with the first Anglo-Irish drama, Shirley's *Saint Patrick for Ireland*, produced in Dublin in 1636.* The movement came to maturity only in the twentieth century; and much of the classical period of Irish history has for background the uneasily felt need for a satisfactory mythology, political, religious and imaginative.

* At the Theatre in Werburgh Street.

REFERENCES

[1] His account is printed in C. L. Falkiner, *Illustrations of Irish History*, 1904, 409 *sqq*.

[2] *Ormonde Papers*, HMC, 2nd ser. VII, 189.

[3] Ball's *History of the County Dublin*, IV, 184, where it is stated to have been designed by Dr Westley.

[4] Falkiner. *op. cit.* p. 51 n6.

[5] *ibid.*, 56.

[6] Carte's *Life of Ormonde*, 1735, II, 276.

[7] See *Pope's Own Miscellany*, ed. N. Ault. 1935.

CHAPTER III

The Municipality's Part

I T WOULD be most misleading to imagine Ormonde imposing his frenchified ideas of order upon a municipality by nature slovenly and chaotic; this, for a wonder, was a marriage of true minds, and the Corporation very soon gave evidence of it. From the moment of the Restoration they had been encouraged to a new self-respect. In 1661 King Charles sent a gold collar of SS* to the Mayor, together with a Cap of Maintenance and the right to have a 'certain sword guilded with gould' borne before him. A year later the Mayor was given the command of a company of foot. All this in recompense for the city's 'chearful and timely evidences of loyalty'. The Corporation, indeed, had, as one might expect from such a body, behaved most circumspectly during those ticklish times. Royal grants of money followed and the right to operate ferries. How far these acts of Royal favour were inspired by Ormonde cannot be known: but he certainly suggested the assumption by the Mayor, five years after the Restoration, of the style and title of 'Lord Mayor', to which he had the right by a charter of Charles I which had been forgotten in the stormy year 1641. The King himself had, pardonably, forgotten it when two years later he wrote to 'the Maior, Recorder &c.'.[1]

Economic necessity has spoiled so many grand schemes for urban improvement that it is refreshing to find it acting as foster-mother to a particularly happy piece of invention. Very soon after Ormonde's arrival, the Dublin City Assembly met to consider 'how that by reason of the late rebellion and long continued troubles of this kingdome the threasury of this cittie is cleerly exhausted and the yearly revenue thereof is reduced to little or nothing'.[2] A common enough complaint, and in modern times too often the omen of another half-crown on the rates. But on this occasion, having taken one look at the miserably decayed spectacle of central Dublin, they seem to have despaired of raising revenue from such a source.

* So called from the shape of the links.

Firmly they turned their backs on it, and faced, not west as in every other city of Christendom, but east to the rising sun. They hoped that 'the outskerts of Saint Stephen's Greene and other wast lands about this cittie, that now addeth nothing att all to pleasure or profitt, may be set for ninetie nine yeares, or to fee farme, and a considerable rent reserved'. They proposed, in short, to turn an ancient common into a municipally-owned square.

To call this measure 'town-planning' is perhaps a little anachronistic. But it was all the more an act of conscious policy because thirty years earlier, during the viceroyalty of Strafford, an attempt had been made to preserve Hoggen Green (the present College Green), Stephen's Green and Oxmantown Green as a 'green belt' 'wholie kept for the use of the cittizens and others, to walk & take the open aire, by reason this cittie is at present groweing very populous'[3] [at that time perhaps nine thousand inhabitants].

Bloomsbury Square, the first to be so called in London, had been laid out by Lord Southampton two years earlier. It seems certain that the dates are too close together for the London example to have had any influence on Dublin. Moreover, the cases are in no way parallel. The basis of ownership was quite different. The Dublin scheme was incomparably vaster, especially in relation to the size of the existing town. Finally, it was not, and never has been called a Square.[4] It has more affinities of evolution with Lincoln's Inn Fields which, like Stephen's Green in Dublin, is the oldest and the largest of the 'squares'. If there is imitation here, Dublin was able to go one better than London, for the Green contains twenty-seven acres* and the plots surrounding it thirty acres. The sides, though not quite equal, averaged nearly a quarter of a mile each. The central part was planted and furnished with a stone wall and a ditch. Round the periphery were eighty-nine lots, distributed by ballot to merchants, aldermen, butchers, tanners, gentlemen, maltsters, brewers, cutlers, masons, vintners, tallow-chandlers, bakers, smiths, and three knights.[5]

From the descriptions of the lessees it is clear that there was at first no plan to enforce a high standard of residential grandeur. Even if we suppose that many of these people were sufficiently prosperous to take their lots for speculative purposes, they were

* Including the roadway.

not required to build. In fact, for twenty or thirty years after this time, most of the south and east sides must have been used for agriculture or grazing. The rents on the south side, one halfpenny per foot of frontage, were only half those on the other three.

The lessees were not required to build; but if they did build, as on the north and west sides they very soon did, they covenanted 'to build of brick, stone and timber, to be covered with tiles or slates, with at least two floores or loftes and a cellar, if they please to digg it'.[6] Whether they built or not, they were required to contribute to the paving and the wall, and, perhaps more important, each lessee was obliged to plant six sycamore trees near the wall, and to see that none of the trees died for at least three years.

Most of the lots were of sixty feet, sufficient for two of the houses of that date. The earliest of these houses must have faced the Green endwise, presenting a gable to the view. On the west side they were, and still are, irregularly disposed, probably because of the underground stream which fed the College Mill. But, because they were the earliest to be built, the west and north sides now present the most modern and on the whole least interesting appearance. The west side, in particular, has lost almost all the architectural character it may have had, except what derives from the scale of the layout.

'The whole designe of all persons concerned', says the Corporation minute relating to the scheme, 'is chiefly for the reputation, advantage, ornament and pleasure of the cittie'. These are the sort of sentiments which suggest that the hand of Ormonde is at work, but there is no evidence of any influence of this kind. It is true that while the Stephen's Green scheme was being carried through, Ormonde let it be known that, though the Mayor for the year had already been elected, he would prefer to see Alderman William Smith installed instead. The elected Mayor stood down without a murmur, making only the condition that he should enjoy the dignity of an ex-holder of that office.[7]

Alderman Smith is worth a notice on his own account. He became Sheriff at the age of thirty-four during the viceroyalty of Strafford. As one of the Masters of the City Works he had been in close touch with the Viceroy's endeavour to control the development of the town. He was Mayor from 1642 till 1646, while four other mayors were elected but did not take office. He finally surrendered the city to the Parliamentary army, serving thereafter as auditor and treasurer. At the Restoration he was sent to England to plead Dublin's cause to the King. He has, with some reason, been called the Irish Whittington. Not only was he, at this juncture, a most experienced man, but he had as clean a copybook as could be wished or found. He was of course elected, not only then but also for a second term in 1664. Nothing could have been more amicable, and yet in the next year Ormonde took steps to strengthen his position still further. An Act was passed empowering the Lord Lieutenant in Council to make rules and orders governing any corporation in the country, at any time during the next seven years. Ormonde himself did not use this power, but both his successors did, making comprehensive regulations designed to ensure that the Corporation behaved itself.

While this open space on the south-west was being developed, another on the north-west was disappearing. The ancient Green of Oxmantown, which adjoined the northern suburb, was partly enclosed early in 1665 and like Stephen's Green was let by lot. But in this case the members of the committee of survey were allowed to draw their lots before any blanks were put in. Furthermore, apart from a 'convenient highway and a large markett place', the ninety-nine lots covered all the ground, though of course there remained a large open space to the west. The 'convenient highway' seems to be Queen Street, and the 'markett place' is the present Smithfield. The street is straight, and points directly towards St Catherine's Church, probably because the latter, though far away across the river, had a tower or spire to act as a terminal feature.

Under the stimulus of these schemes, and of the relatively settled times, Dublin had begun to grow again, and it was not long before growth brought its attendant problems. The population was now perhaps thirty thousand,* and among these were, inevitably, some 'poor and aged', some 'fatherless and motherless children', and some beggars. Worse still, some of these were 'strange beggars that have no title nor right to be maintained here'.[8] The mediæval church was no longer there to provide for such, and Dublin found

---

* Petty estimated it as 58,000 in 1681.

itself caught in the gap between charity and social insurance. A large number of private individuals were ready to contribute to a scheme, if someone would formulate one. The Viceroy's son and deputy, Lord Ossory, had drawn the city's attention to the number of beggars, hinting that any suitable scheme would be supported.

The committee recommended the building of an hospital on Oxmantown Green, and began work on the west side of Queen Street, in 1669. In 1671 the Mayor and Corporation were granted a Royal Charter for the 'Hospital and Free School' which was to be 'a mansion-house and place of abode for the sustentation and relief of poor children, [and] aged and impotent people'. There already existed a Free School belonging to the city, of which the building was ruinous and the mastership poorly endowed. None the less, it numbered among its alumni the great Archbishop James Ussher, and in 1662 an Englishman in Dublin on Government business sent his twelve-year-old son there. His name was Sir Winston Churchill and the boy was the future owner of Blenheim. The prospectus of the new school, published in 1673, said that it was 'not intended to be an Hive for Drones, but a profitable Nursery . . .' containing, however, some 'Old Trees'.

A peculiar fate attended these composite schemes in Dublin. At the end of the sixteenth century, Cary's Hospital, intended as a composite bridewell and free school, had soon become a private house and soon again a law court and was now the Parliament House. The next foundation, after this Oxmantown Hospital, began life as an asylum and workhouse and turned into the Foundling Hospital. The Corporation seems to have been slow to learn that able-bodied beggars, idiots, children and old people were not easily provided for under the same roof. It was the same with the Oxmantown foundation: it did nothing (except perhaps indirectly and in the future) to solve the problem of mendicancy, for it was opened in 1675 to admit fifty-seven little boys and three little girls. The only aged person who seems to have benefited by it was one of its founders, William Smith himself, who, having been Mayor of Dublin for six terms and Lord Mayor for one, came in 1679 to live in the Hospital himself. Though by now impoverished and an object of his own charity, he was charged with 'the government of the house and the trouble of keeping the children in order,'[9] and so continued until he died in 1684 at the age of eighty-two, and was buried in the Chapel.

The Hospital survives to the present day as a modest but reputable public school.* Its semi-official title, 'The Hospital and Free School of King Charles the Second', is generally shortened to the 'King's Hospital'. It is also known as the Blue-Coat School, or, as the older authorities have it, 'The Blew Coat Boys Hospital'. The original building, superseded in 1777, was a low range with dormer windows, a clock-tower and an elaborate gateway with a scroll-pediment and Royal Arms. The Royal Arms still survive. It stood back a little from the street, with a high wall in which the gate was set. On the left was the gable of the Chapel with its east window and on the right another gable, also on the street, but not matched in height. It must have been a rather rough-and-ready ensemble, not without charm. We would hardly exchange it, however, for Thomas Ivory's magnificent buildings, its successor.

Such institutions as these were usually financed by a variety of means. A popular expedient was to assign the proceeds of some tax (as was sometimes done by Parliament in response to appeals), or the fines payable upon failure to accept an office upon election. Ormonde made an Order in Council in which he imitated the action of Charles II with regard to St Paul's in London, by recommending—he could not insist—that newly-consecrated Bishops of the Irish Church should, instead of giving the customary feast, pay over the money to the Hospital. Besides these rather uncertain assets, the Hospital was endowed with the ground-rents of Stephen's Green and its own district of Oxmantown, which it still holds.

The Oxmantown estate was at the time the more promising of the two. It still seemed that Dublin might develop westwards, and there was a tendency for the Oxmantown lessees to be of a higher status than those on the other property, and they were more inclined to build for residential purposes. Among them were Hercules Langford, Richard Tighe, John Preston, Chief Baron Bysse, Lord Dungannon, Lord Massereene and Warner Westenra —all names of some consequence though some had not yet shaken

---

* After the Municipal Reform Act of 1841 it became autonomous and lost its connexion with the Corporation.

off their association with trade. Still more to the point, the Corporation made a grant in 1665 of seven acres of Oxmantown Green to Ormonde, and it was expected that he would build there, though in fact he never did. It was only natural that the nobility and gentry who did not already possess houses in the Hoggen Green district should wish to build near the Viceroy's House.

A glance at the map will show that this development was bound to lead to the erection of a second bridge. The mediæval 'Dublin Bridge', or, as it came to be called, 'Old Bridge', was at the foot of Bridge Street, a little above the present Four Courts, where Whitworth Bridge stands to-day. This was a quarter of a mile downstream from the new suburb. On the other hand there are several reasons why the Corporation as such was not forward in bridge-building. In the first place, anything which tended to make the suburbs easier of access seemed to threaten the interests of those who, collectively or individually, held land within the old walls or near them. Secondly, the Corporation owned the ferries, and saw no reason why it should spend money building bridges which might be long in paying for themselves. Thirdly, and this applied particularly to projected bridges below the Old Bridge, there were vested interests in wharfage and warehousing which stood to lose much if the port of Dublin were to move downstream.[10]

None the less, a new bridge was built in 1670. It was a wooden structure, something over a third of a mile above the Old Bridge, and providing communication between Oxmantown Green and the west end of 'Usher's Island'. It was not exactly the site where a bridge was most needed: perhaps those who built it did not dare to venture too closely under the nose of the Corporation. It is not known who the builders were: indeed, for all the evidence to the contrary, it may have been built by the fairies. It was probably the work of a speculative syndicate. In the Corporation's opinion its erection was 'against the generall sense of this citty'. Some of these guildsmen must have divulged their opinion to their apprentices, for the latter assembled with the intention of destroying the bridge.[11] Twenty of these lads were arrested, but as the military were taking them to the Bridewell, their comrades rescued them, with the loss of four dead. The bridge thus acquired the name of Bloody Bridge by which it is best known. The Corporation expressed their horror at the licentious action of their juniors. They apologised to the Government; but though they punished their apprentices, they had unloosed passions which they could not control, and they were greatly embarrassed by the activities of the bridge-breaking faction.

Another bridge project at much the same time was even less auspicious. The Corporation had farmed out one of its ferries to an Alderman Fowkes. In 1669 he complained[12] that Mr Mabbott and Colonel Carey Dillon were daily stopping and intercepting his boats. The next we hear of this matter is that nearly two years later[13] the Government has put pressure on the Corporation, forcing it to negotiate with a private syndicate of bridge-builders which included these two gentlemen. William Hawkins and Gilbert Mabbott are named in sequence, and this bridge, if it had been built, would have connected the streets called after them, that is to say the extreme eastern suburbs in the neighbourhood of the present Custom House. The city agreed provided that the channel were not interfered with, and that the maintenance of the bridge should be guaranteed. But no such bridge was in fact built for the next hundred and twenty years.

But now there appears on the scene the first important private 'improver' in Dublin history. Sir Humphrey Jervis was a successful ship-owner and merchant, and a freeman of the city, and later Lord Mayor. Yet when he and some associates bought twenty acres of the lands of St Mary's Abbey for £3,000 in about 1674, he did not think of applying to the Corporation for help in building bridges. He knew better. The Viceroy had by this time effectual powers over the Corporation, and Sir Humphrey approached the Viceroy, Lord Essex, in 1676. Sir Humphrey's enemies assert[14] that he told Lord Essex that he would call the bridge Essex Bridge, garnishing it with his lordship's arms. Beyond it he said he would lay out a fine street and call it after the Essex family name, Capel. These tactics succeeded admirably. Lord Essex made an order directing that part of the proceeds of the Dublin customs should be applied by the city towards the building of this bridge. Other city representatives besides Sir Humphrey himself were nominated in the Order to have charge of the building, among them a representative of the Allen family, master-builders. But it is notoriously unwise to

25

entrust an undertaking to a committee of people opposed to its success; and one by one, Sir Humphrey complains, his colleagues backed out of the business. He was left alone to carry on the building, and Lord Essex was recalled early in 1677. He was succeeded by Ormonde who now returned again to power. As we might expect, Ormonde was interested in the scheme, but as state finance was then at a low ebb, he was not able to do more than promise that he would do what he could if the scheme were completed. It was Ormonde, however, who suggested the most important modification. Sir Humphrey's plans showed the reres of the houses and warehouses facing the river without any quay. Ormonde, through the Council, persuaded him to interpose a stone quay. Sir Humphrey did so, calling it Ormonde Quay, which it remains to this day. Behind it he laid out a market with a central rotunda, which, as Ormonde Market, survived until about 1890.*

This suggestion of Ormonde's was of immense importance to the future development of Dublin, because it was this prototype which inspired the whole system of quays in their final beauty. Otherwise Dublin might well have been like so many other towns, through which the river slinks shamefacedly between tall buildings which give it no chance to be seen.

Sir Humphrey was now, by his own account, sadly out of pocket by his activities. The Corporation harried him unmercifully. The bridge was finished in 1678 (it is vis.ble in Pl. vII), but not so its builder's tribulations. The aldermen spread rumours (so he says) that he was insolvent, and the captains of his ships made off while the going was good. His enemies also managed to undermine his credit with the Viceroy and the Council. They were quite outspoken about their motives in this persecution; for, as they themselves said in print some years later, 'the improvement of the north side would certainly, in a great measure, ruin the old city, whose inhabitants were always on their guard to discountenance and prevent it'.[15]

So well did they succeed that, during Ormonde's absence in England, the Council ordered Jervis to be committed to jail. Primate Boyle, who in the Viceroy's absence held the chief power, refused the unfortunate man permission to go to Church on Christmas Day, 1685. The specific cause for which he was committed

* Its place is now occupied by 'Ormonde Square'.

was a complicated matter connected with the guardhouses at the end of the bridge where ships could pass through it, and this matter had by then been thrashed through all the courts in Dublin and half the London courts as well.

But by this time, astonishing to relate, he and his opponents had another bridge to quarrel about. He was of sufficient following to be elected Lord Mayor in 1681 and again in 1682. He was at this time in favour with both Court and Corporation, for he was now knighted. One of his fellow-aldermen, Peter Wybrants, was a resident of the north side and happened to be foreman of the grand jury, which was induced to make a presentment in favour of a fourth bridge. The assessment was on the city, but was apparently never collected. So Sir Humphrey built the bridge, at his own expense, of timber. He alleged that the Chief Justice and the Secretary of State, who were brothers, conspired to obstruct him in the courts, because they wanted to buy the Ormonde Market cheaply while its future was still being disputed. It was during this term of office that the official venue of the City Markets was moved north of the river. The Corporation later alleged that Sir Humphrey had brought this about by intimidation, and they explained that he had been committed to jail in 1685 for administering oaths in such form as they might be acceptable to Catholics.

In fact there was little need for this particular bridge, which he named Ormonde Bridge. It was too near Essex Bridge to be of much advantage; and when it was ruined in the floods of 1802 it was not rebuilt. Its successor, Richmond Bridge, occupies a slightly more westerly site.

But Essex Bridge itself became immediately the focal point of Dublin, remaining so for more than a hundred years. Capel Street, Mary Street and Jervis Street were profitably developed and began to vie with Hoggen or College Green as a fashionable residential area, and Ormonde Quay was extended eastwards as Batchelor's Walk, a pleasant promenade commanding a view across the river towards the College. Sir Humphrey, as owner of the Jervis Estate, was not the loser. He carried his demands for re-imbursement for the bridges to Parliament itself; but Parliament, taking into account the prosperity of his holdings on the north side, made him an award which can only be regarded as nominal.[16] He died in 1708.

REFERENCES

1 *CARD* I, 37; IV, 350–1.
2 *ibid.* IV, 256.
3 *ibid.* III, 303.
4 But see *CARD* VI, 164 (1697).
5 *ibid.* IV, 301 *sqq.* and map in F. Falkiner, *Foundation of the King's Hospital* p. 43.
6 *CARD* IV, 298.
7 *CARD* IV, 261.
8 *ibid.* IV, 459.
9 F. Falkiner *op. cit.* p. 83.
10 *CARD* IV, 309.
11 Gilbert I, 388. *CARD* IV, 537.
12 *CARD* IV, 471.
13 *ibid.* 549.
14 *ibid.* VII, 582 *sqq.*
15 *ibid.* 589.
16 *Irish Commons Journals*, Sept. 21, 1697 (ed. of 1753), II, 929.

CHAPTER IV

Alarms and Excursions

I
T IS time to glance a little more closely at the presiding genius
of the age, the Duke himself. The Viceroy of Ireland was not
usually an Irishman;* but when, as in this case, he was, it was
only fitting that he should be the head of the greatest family in
Ireland. The Geraldines, the only rivals to the primacy of the
Butlers, were at this time lying rather low. But Ormonde's terri-
torial importance in Ireland was equalled by his ability and by his
attachment to the Stuarts, who were never served by anyone more
moderate or more loyal. Consequently his importance is more
than merely Irish, and so, like Lord Wellesley in later times,† he
could be sent back to Ireland in this capacity without incurring any
more than ordinary jealousy.

His father, Thomas, Viscount Thurles, was a Catholic, and the
boy was brought up in that faith by his grandfather, Earl Walter.
But when a succession of deaths in the family brought the child
into the line of succession, James I ordered him to be taken into the
household of the Archbishop of Canterbury and bred a Protestant.
As a result this remarkable child became a convinced Anglican
without feeling any hostility towards his Catholic relatives or com-
patriots. The family estates had been alienated as a result of a feud
with the Prestons, newly Earls of Desmond, and a plot was hatched
to compose this quarrel by marrying him to the Preston heiress.
This was when the children were aged eleven and seven respectively.

He had a remarkable faculty for bowing to the inevitable and
making a virtue of necessity. By the time he was eighteen this busi-
nesslike arrangement was threatened with failure; it seemed that
the deal might be off. But the young man saved the situation by
falling quite genuinely in love. He went even to the length of a
clandestine courtship with romantic trimmings, notes in gloves,

---

* After Ormonde, his grandson the second Duke held the office. Earl Fitzwilliam, though
not an Irishman, had Irish properties.

† See Chapter XXV.

disguise and so forth, and in due course embraced the Lady Elizabeth Preston with the same fervour as the Protestant religion, remaining throughout a long life faithfully constant to both.

His first public appearance was in Strafford's Parliament of 1634. Feeling in Dublin was running rather high at the time, and Strafford issued orders that the members were to deliver up their swords to Black Rod as they entered the House. Young Lord Ormonde refused to do so, and took seat with his sword still buckled to his belt. When Strafford took him to task for this piece of insubordination, Ormonde produced his writ of summons, pointing out that it required him to attend the Viceroy *cum gladio cinctus*. Strafford recognised a man of his own temper, and a firm attachment grew up between them.

After the fall of Strafford and the outbreak of the war, Ormonde was in command of the troops in Ireland. But the Council who held the civil power bungled matters until, when Ormonde was appointed Viceroy in 1644, it was too late for him to save the situation. In 1647 he had to surrender Dublin to the Parliamentary forces, and went to Paris to confer with Prince Charles. Two years later he was back in Ireland, making a treaty with the Confederate Catholics at Kilkenny, and proclaiming Charles II. But Rinuccini and Cromwell were too much for him, and he withdrew to exile in France, leaving his Countess behind in Kilkenny to hold what she could of the family estates.

In attendance on the exiled Court he shared in its poverty. He could not afford a carriage or even a horse, so he went on foot. On one occasion, after staying with a *grand seigneur* at St Germain-en-Laye, he found that he had in his pocket only ten pistoles, his last. These, according to the English custom, he distributed among the servants, and set out to walk back to Paris. He had not gone far when he was overtaken by his host, who greeted him coldly and enquired whether Ormonde had been dissatisfied with his entertainment. Indeed, he said, he had not, and why should his host suppose anything of the kind? He was then enlightened, learning that 'the leaving ten pistoles to be distributed among the servants was treating his house as an inn, and was the greatest affront that could be offered to a man of Quality'. Ormonde was fortunately abundantly endowed with tact: he managed to avoid a duel, and agreed to take back the money, whereupon, as his biographer tells, 'he returned to Paris with less anxiety about his subsistence'.[1]

In 1658 he volunteered to go in disguise to England, where he sounded the prospects of a Royalist Restoration. His companion on this dangerous mission was a certain Daniel O'Neill. During all the time he was in England, he never once went to bed, but slept always in his clothes. On one occasion he sat up all night in an inn playing shuffleboard and drinking warm ale with four Suffolk maltsters. In London he lodged with a landlady 'who had been in her younger days a servant at Court, and could drink sack as well as her husband. He humoured them in their way, and was much securer there than in his former quarters. He went by the name of *Pickering*, and passed for a discarded officer'. It was here that, finding a peruke irksome as a disguise, he tried to dye his hair black, but succeeded only in giving it 'a variety of colours' and scalding his scalp into the bargain.[2]

He returned safely to France, and at the Restoration was loaded with honours. In Ireland it was as much the restoration of the house of Butler as of the house of Stuart. He became Chancellor of Dublin University, Viceroy of Ireland, and the first Irish Duke in history. There have been only three since.* All his Irish estates were restored, and the Irish Parliament voted him £30,000.

He is a unique figure in modern Irish history. Among the Viceroys, only Chesterfield approached him in aristocratic ease, splendour, tolerance, flexibility and common sense. As one who was both Royalist and patriot, he has a distant affinity with O'Connell, but the eras of diplomat and demagogue are far apart. The old aristocracy did indeed erupt again, in the revolutionary movements of 1798 and 1848, associated with Lord Edward Fitzgerald and William Smith O'Brien respectively, and modern opinion is readier to give them credit as 'Irish leaders' than to give such credit to Ormonde. But Ormonde's conservatism was not the result of his aristocracy; it was the natural result of the circumstances in which he resumed power. In Ireland so much had been destroyed in the wars that little remained to conserve, and the conservatism of Ormonde necessarily took on a constructive character.

* Leinster (1691, Schomberg), Leinster (1766, Fitzgerald), and Abercorn (1868). Royal dukedoms such as that of Connaught are not in the peerage of Ireland.

The kind of problem with which he had to deal is well shown in the career of Colonel Thomas Blood. Blood may have been an Englishman,* yet as a political figure he is much more characteristic of Ireland than of England. There have been, unhappily, many more men of his type in Irish history than there have been of the type of Ormonde.

Blood was a Cromwellian adventurer who had been granted large estates in Ireland. But when these were forfeited at the Restoration, he decided to capture Dublin Castle. Ormonde had imported a number of Englishmen to adjudicate in the Court of Claims, as being impartial in the matter. In the opinion of Blood and his friends, they were very much too impartial, favouring the 'innocent Papists' till it seemed that there would be no land left for good Protestants like himself. Unfortunately there were leakages, and Ormonde kept himself well informed of the progress of the conspiracy. The capture of Ormonde himself was to synchronise with a general rising and the attack on the Castle. This was expected about March 9th, 1663, but at the last moment the date was advanced to March 5th. The Duke, however, had wind of this, and made secret preparations to give the attackers a warm reception at the Sheep Street gate. His preparations were not secret enough to escape the knowledge of Blood and his friends. They scattered in all directions, only a few underlings being captured. Blood himself fled to the North, where the Presbyterians of Antrim sheltered him. He also took refuge among the northern Catholics, among whom he passed for a priest. Soon afterwards he was heard of again in Wicklow, and was even supposed to be planning an attack on Ormonde while the Duke was visiting his country house in Kilkenny. He travelled under various names and disguises, and so passed over into Holland.[3]

His next meeting with Ormonde was even more dramatic. By now he had learnt to do one thing at a time. He had been involved in a rising in Scotland, had returned to Ireland but found it too hot for him, and had then for a short time made a profession of rescuing condemned prisoners in Yorkshire. He then (to quote Carte) 'herded among the Quakers, of whose sect he professed himself, till the fame of his exploits made him considered as a fit person to

* Though he is sometimes said to have been born in Co. Clare.

32

be employed in any desperate undertaking, and he was engaged in a design to assassinate the Duke of Ormonde'.[4]

It was just after the Duke's dismissal from the Viceroyalty and he was returning up St. James's Street in London after dining with the Prince of Orange. He was set upon by Blood and his men. Blood and his son took the Duke out of his carriage and set him upon one of their own horses, and away with them down Piccadilly. Fortunately for Ormonde, nothing would satisfy the Colonel but to hang him on Tyburn tree. So he left his prisoner in charge of one of his men, while he himself went ahead to adjust the rope. By the time he came back to collect the victim, Ormonde and the guard were struggling together on top of the horse, which was making off towards Knightsbridge. By the time help arrived, they had fallen off the horse into the mud, where they were rolling over and over together. The Colonel, seeing that the neighbourhood was by now well roused, fired a couple of shots at the Duke (but missed him) and galloped off into the night. Undeterred by this failure, he tried next year to steal the Crown Jewels, and had actually made off with the Crown and Orb before he was caught. Incredible to relate, he was not only pardoned by Charles II but was given back his Irish estates. When he died in 1680, it was rumoured that he was not dead at all, and an anxious world was only reassured by his exhumation and identification, after which the matter and Blood himself were set at rest.

Other figures, only slightly less startling than that of Blood, adorned the Irish scene. Sir Hierome Sankey, divinity student, soldier, college don, officer, and landowner, was successively an Anglican, a Presbyterian, an Independent and an Anabaptist. Sir John Temple, who had had a chequered career in the late wars, and had written an inflammatory 'History' of the 1641 Rebellion, now became a Privy Councillor and was Master of the Rolls; and his son, also Sir John Temple, of Palmerston, Co. Dublin, was temporary Speaker of the Irish House of Commons in 1661. Fortunately, however, many of those who had played more important parts in the recent wars were now living in retirement in the country. Such were Murrough O'Brien, Earl of Inchiquin, 'Murrough of the Burnings' as he was called, who had been at one time or another on every side in the late wars, finally turning Catholic and being taken

33

prisoner by the pirate Algerine, whence he was ransomed to become High Steward to Henrietta Maria in Paris and later in London. After 1663 he lived quietly on his estates in Co. Clare, where he died in 1674. Richard Nugent, Earl of Westmeath, had had a military career as a moderate Royalist, but retired to Fore at the Restoration and occupied himself with church-building. There were many similar figures who took little part in post-Reformation public life, and were presumably hardly ever seen in Dublin.*

Such people were spent rockets and caused the Government no such disquiet as the extreme Protestant party. Of this party Blood and his like were the lunatic fringe, but there was a strong group in Parliament, led by such men as Sir Audley Mervyn, the Speaker, and Sir John Temple the Master of the Rolls, who were almost equally dangerous to the stability of the state. The Duke, indeed, had reason to be grateful to Blood; for when the Speaker made an inflammatory speech against the Catholics, intending to exclude them as a body from any benefits under the Act of Settlement, Ormonde countered the move by producing evidence implicating a number of the Speaker's party in Blood's plot, and suggesting that the Commons might begin by purging the members concerned. Since nobody could be quite sure whether Ormonde might not play this card again, he was even able to secure the passage of the Act of Explanation, in which the Protestant claims were somewhat abated, and a few Catholics, mentioned by name, were even able to benefit.[5]

Ormonde's task was not made any easier by the policy of England, which in 1663 decided to prohibit the import of Irish Cattle. 'It is not a little surprising', says the Duke's biographer, himself an Englishman, 'that a thinking people, as the English are, should not grow wiser by any experience, and after losing such considerable territories abroad by their oppressive treatment of them, should go on to hazard the loss of Ireland, and endeavour the ruin of a colony of their own countrymen, planted in that Kingdom'.[6] It is an old story, often repeated, yet it never ceases to astonish. Ormonde went to England and spent three years, on and off, in trying to delay or prevent the passage of the Bill; but all in vain. The Scotch

* But Lord Lanesborough, a Royalist soldier, was a resident in Dublin at the time (*CARD* V, 245, 362).

34

Parliament followed the English in imposing a similar prohibition. When, in 1666, London was destroyed by fire, Dublin sent 30,000 head of cattle as a free gift. It was impossible to send money, because Ireland was, as usual, hopelessly short of coin. But such was the tyranny of the mercantile theory of economics, that even this charitable gesture provoked the suspicion of the English, who saw in it only a 'politick contrivance' to put a stop to the Bill!⁷ The most that Ormonde could do was to advise owners of cattle to make sure of sending what they could to England before the Bill came into force. He set up a Council of Trade in Dublin to devise ways and means of recovery.*

The Duke's hand was further strengthened by a second abortive Protestant plot in 1666. He had need of every circumstance which might defend him against the suspicion of favouring the Catholics, for, as he himself observed, 'My father and mother lived and died Papists, and bred all their children so, and only I, by God's merciful providence, was educated in the true Protestant religion, from which I never swerved towards either extreme, not when it was most dangerous to profess it and most advantageous to quit it. . . . My brothers and sisters, though they were not very many, were very fruitful and obstinate (they will call it constant) in their way. Their fruitfulness hath spread into a large alliance, and their obstinacy has made it altogether Popish. . . . But I am taught by nature, and also by instruction, that difference in opinion concerning matters of religion dissolves not the obligations of nature; and in conformity to this principle I own not only that I have done but that I will do my relations of that or any other persuasion all the good I can.'⁸ He might have added that these 'obligations of nature' extended to Catholic fellow-Irishmen who had done him and the King service in the late wars.

Ormonde, himself the target of these complaints, is found echoing many of the commonest complaints of Irish history. He found, for example, that there was a tendency to appoint Englishmen to Irish benefices, in spite of the existence of an Irish university for the production of clergy for Ireland. He pointed out that this policy frustrated the intention of encouraging learning and

* The irony is that Dr George O'Brien (*Econ. Hist. of I. in the XVIIth Century,* 1919, p.160) says that the prohibition stimulated the Irish provision trade and actually enabled Ireland to undersell England in dead meat.

discountenancing Popery, for which Dublin University, of which he was the Chancellor, had been founded.[9]

To mitigate the effects of the cattle embargo, Ormonde sought permission for Ireland to trade under licence with countries such as Holland with which England was at war. Though this failed, the rapid growth of the Irish provision trade, and the unlicensed export of wool to the Continent, saved the country and the capital from the full effects of depression. Ormonde, acting through Colonel Richard Lawrence,*[10] imported linen-weavers from the Low Countries, and settled them at Chapelizod just outside Dublin, as well as in his own town of Carrick-on-Suir. But in spite of Parliamentary support, the Chapelizod venture was not a success.

More enduring was Ormonde's foundation of the College of Physicians in 1667. Its first President, Dr John Stearne, was great-nephew of Archbishop Ussher and Regius Professor of Medicine in the University, and had already founded a 'Fraternity of Physicians' which was accommodated in the building called Trinity Hall, one of the external halls or hostels which were then a feature of the University. The new College met in Trinity Hall until 1692, when it gained a new charter, becoming the 'King's and Queen's College', but lost its building. For over a century it met in the house of the President for the time being, who also had custody of the Library left it by Sir Patrick Dun, who died in 1713. We may be sure that the dividing line between Sir Patrick Dun's Library and whatever books of his own the President at any time had, was not very strictly kept, so that the collection spent a century picking up and shedding books, here a little and there a little. This process may still be traced in the composition of the library which has long had a permanent home.

The Duke was cheered in his perplexities by the birth of a grandson in 1665. His favourite son Ossory had in 1659 married Emilia de Beverweert, related illegitimately to the Prince of Orange. The child now born became later the second Duke of Ormonde, but the proud grandfather might have been surprised to know that his successor, after holding the Viceregal office, would spend his last twenty years of life as an exile in France, though indeed he was to be buried in Westminster Abbey. This child was born in Dublin Castle,

* Author of *The Interest of Ireland in its Trade and Wealth,* 1682.

where his father was acting as Lord Deputy in the Duke's absence. When Ormonde returned from England in October 1665, his reception in Dublin was if anything even more picturesque than in 1662. While still six miles away he was met by 'a gallant troop of young Gentlemen, well mounted, and alike richly attired'. They were under the command of 'one Mr. Corker, a deserving gentleman' and a civil servant. At the city boundaries the Sheriffs and the sixteen guilds were in attendance. There were kettle-drums and trumpets, Serjeants-at-Arms and their pursuivants, the nobility and Privy Councillors and the Life Guards mounted. At St James's Gate (where Guinness's Brewery now is) appeared the Lord Mayor and Aldermen, together with 'six gladiators stript and drawn' and his Grace's guard of battle-axes. At the Cornmarket they reached the City Conduit, where 'wine ran in abundance' and there were 'half a dozen anticks' upon a scaffold. But this was only the first of four such scaffolds: on the remaining three appeared in sequence Ceres under a canopy, attended by four virgins, Vulcan by his anvil with four Cyclops asleep by it, and lastly, at the entrance to the Castle itself, the jolly god himself, Bacchus, with four or five good fellows. To these visible delights were added successive volleys of great and small shot, to say nothing of fireworks, with which, says Carte, 'the streets and the air were filled'.[11] The Duke, who had some little experience of ups and downs in Ireland, may have chuckled to himself as he clattered into the cobbled yard of the dilapidated residence of His Majesty's representative.

REFERENCES

[1] Carte's Life of Ormonde, 1736, II, 159–60. Carte also tells a good story about a Scotch exile who had quarrelled with his French host and complained to Ormonde that he had no other resource yet could not go back and face his host. Ormonde advised him to go back and first eat his words and then eat his dinner, a very typical rejoinder.

[2] Carte, op. cit. II, 176 sqq.

[3] ibid. 261–9.

[4] ibid. 421.

[5] ibid. 314 sqq.

[6] ibid. 317.

[7] ibid.

[8] C. L. Falkiner, Essays Relating to Ireland, 1909, p. 64.

[9] Carte, op. cit. II, 340.

[10] Ball, County Dublin IV, 171.

[11] Carte, op. cit. II, 313.

CHAPTER V

Church and State

ALTHOUGH THE Restoration of 1660 had, in Ireland, as in England, been brought about partly by Cromwellian and Puritan officers, and although in Ireland the Catholics had special claims on the gratitude of the Stuarts, there was no question but that Anglicanism was to be the state religion. There were, none the less, Catholic* and non-conformist churches, but these, being for the most part discreetly situated, and often merely adapted dwelling-houses and warehouses, had little if any architectural character and have not survived. There is one exception to this: the Presbyterian church founded by Samuel Winter, the ejected Provost of Trinity College. But as the building in question belongs to a slightly later date, it will be noticed later.

The Restoration of Anglicanism was celebrated in St Patrick's Cathedral in January 1661, when two archbishops and ten bishops were consecrated at one sitting. Among them was Jeremy Taylor, who preached the sermon. Not only was he now made Bishop of Down and Connor; he was already Provost of Trinity in succession to the Presbyterian. On this occasion an anthem was sung in St Patrick's,[1] which sums up the dominant outlook very neatly:

> *Angels, look down, and joy to see,*
> *Like that above, a monarchie;*
> *Angels, look down, and joy to see,*
> *Like that above, a hierarchie.*

But, satisfactory as this no doubt was, the condition of the visible church was far from being equally so. Even as they sang, they ran a grave risk of bringing the roof of St Patrick's about their ears. It had to be taken down seven years later, and the new one was completed in 1671. It included forty tons of Co. Wicklow timber given by Strafford's son who held land in that county. Ten years later the

---

* In 1678–9 we find Ormonde protecting 'mass-houses' from attack by apprentices, and incurring odium by so doing. (*Ormonde Papers* HMC 2nd ser. IV, 340).

choir was given a masonry vault which was painted blue with gold stars.[2] None of this work however survived the restoration by Sir Benjamin Guinness in 1864.

The fabric of Christchurch, though even more unsound, seems to have received less attention in Restoration times. In 1670, however, it got six new bells, as did St Patrick's.[3] But the city and outlying parish churches were, one by one, made partakers of the happy restoration. St Werburgh's, the parish church of the Castle, was rebuilt in 1662 but has been rebuilt since. St Andrew's, one of the nearest extra-mural churches, had vanished shortly before the Restoration, but it was now revived further eastward (further, that is to say, out of town) to act as the parish church of the new suburb near the gates of Trinity College. Though this church too has vanished, it survived, in one form or another, for so long that some description of it may be welcome. The landlords of the north side of College Green and Dame Street, Lord Anglesey and Sir John Temple, were the churchwardens, and the architect was that William Dodson whom we have already seen swindling Ormonde in the matter of the Phœnix Park wall. He produced an elliptical plan, and the adoption of this explains, if it does not excuse, why St Andrew's is so often called 'The Round Church'. The site was an old bowling-green close to the Norse Thingmote or assembly mound. Francis Place, the English topographical draughtsman who visited Dublin in 1698-9, left a drawing of the church which still exists.[4] It shows a building quaint rather than accomplished, with a western porch, a crenellated parapet and a conoidal roof. In the background can be seen houses and gardens standing on that part of the Corporation Estate called 'The Whole Land of Tib and Tom'.

At the same time the mediæval church of St Audoen, near the west gate of the walled city, was undergoing partial restoration. This was in part paid for by the Royal Regiment of Guards, who were admitted as parishioners in return. Some of the work done at this period may still survive in the tower. The Church of St Michael and All Angels close by had a grievance in that every Friday for several years the Royal Regiment had used their church but could not apparently be persuaded to contribute towards its restoration. A very thorough restoration was none the less done, and it is probable that the tower, which still survives as the tower of the Synod Hall, dates mainly from this time.[5]

St John's, Fishamble Street, was also rebuilt (1680–2), but not, it would seem, very securely for it had to be rebuilt again less than a century later. Of more interest is the rebuilding in 1680 of St Peter's, Aungier Street. The interest does not lie in the fabric, though that is still partly there, invisibly embedded in the walls of the modern church, but in its connexion with building developments. Until about 1679 there were two ancient churches side by side, one certainly and the other probably ruined. The former was the chapel of the mediæval leper-hospital of St Stephen (from which the Green takes its name), the other the parish church of St Peter del Hille. They both stood in Stephen Street, which winds in a large curve round the lands of the White Friars. They are shown thus in Speed's map of 1610.

Now these Whitefriars' lands lay exactly between the walled city and the newly-formed Green of St Stephen. Almost at the same moment, in 1679–82, we find the two old churches being abandoned and a new one being built on Aungier Street, a broad wide street which drives southwards straight through the Whitefriars' pocket. The contrast, even on a modern map, is very startling.

Sir Francis Aungier, Master of the Rolls in the reign of James I, had obtained a grant of the Whitefriars' lands and had turned their abbey into a residence. A later Francis Aungier, created Earl of Longford in 1677, turned the family demesne into a building estate, laying out Aungier Street, Longford Street and Cuffe Street to commemorate the Cuffes who were connexions by marriage. He was also largely responsible for the church, giving the site and contributing towards the building.[6]

Other churches rebuilt between the Restoration and the Williamite Wars included St Bride's and St Michan's. They were both without the walls: one an ancient church of the Irish south of the city, the other the church of the Norsemen of Oxmantown. St Bride's was rebuilt in 1684 by Nathaniel Foy, born in York but educated in Dublin. He was a very emphatic Protestant, later becoming Bishop of Waterford and founding Bishop Foy's School which still exists there. While the church was rebuilding, his grateful parishioners presented him with a capacious burial-vault under it, a gesture which might nowadays be considered rather too pointed.[7] St Bride's vanished in 1898, but its fine early organ-case may still be seen, dominating the great hall of the National Museum.

St Michan's was of course the parish church of Sir Humphrey Jervis's new rectilinear suburb on the north side. It is therefore not surprising to find it being rebuilt in 1685–6 by Dr John Pooley, the rector, who later became Bishop of Raphoe and of Cloyne. Yet it is surprising that no visible features of the present church, except the effigy of a bishop, can be shown to be older than this rebuilding. Although the spirit of the Renaissance had infected the plans of streets and even of churches, it had so far had little effect on elevational elements. The towers of St Audoen's and St Michael's, together with that of St Michan's and those of St Matthew's Irishtown and Little St George's, which are thirty years later, form together a curious and rather deceptive family of structures. Their rubble masonry of the local calp limestone, and their crenellations,* give them a spurious mediæval air. But round-headed windows, classical doorways and the absence of the subtle batter found in Irish mediæval work, give the lie to appearances.

It is sad, perhaps, to have to pronounce that the famous corpses of St Michan's, always so ready to shake the visitor's hand, are unlikely to be much older than this. The plan of the vaults in which they lie, however, tallies with the plan of the church, which is a Renaissance plan. There seems to be no escaping the conclusion.

It will be seen that the expansion of Dublin as reflected in the churches had not yet made necessary the creation of actual new parishes. So far we have nothing more than enlargement and in two cases removal of the church site to a more convenient position. There is little if any sentiment about church restoration: if it is done it means only that the revival of an old church is a practical necessity.

It is reasonable to suppose that the new St Michan's was larger than its predecessor, as it was certainly broader. But it did not long remain large enough to serve Sir Humphrey Jervis's prosperous new grid-planned northern suburb. Another church on Oxmantown

---

* Some of the crenellations: e.g. on St Audoen's, have certainly been remade during the nineteenth century.

Green was proposed in 1682.[8] The landlords of the College Green district were, as we have seen, active in the reconstituted St Andrew's. The Anglesey estate and the Temple holdings between Dame Street and the river cover the more or less rectilinear network of streets which were laid out from 1658 onwards and still survive though entirely rebuilt in the eighteenth century. Both estates were leased from the Corporation but developed by the lessees. Lord Anglesey had his own house on College Green, where were also the town houses of the Earl of Clancarty and Viscount Charlemont. Lord Clancarty, a representative of the ancient line of MacCarthy of Desmond, was Ormonde's brother-in-law, and though a Catholic was the Viceroy's closest confidant. The Duke was indeed accused of hearing Mass at Clancarty house, but parried this very neatly by pointing out that for twenty years he had visited his sister only in the afternoons, whereas Mass was and is always said in the mornings.[9] Two of Ormonde's MacCarthy nephews* followed James II into exile. Lord Charlemont, by descent an Elizabethan adventurer, died in this Charlemont house at an advanced age in 1726, while the Anglesey or Annesley family provided a *cause célèbre* of the succeeding century which will be noticed in a later chapter.

Besides these noble houses there was also on College Green Chichester House, originally built as an hospital by Carew, the famous Lord President of Munster. It later became the town house of Sir Arthur Chichester, Lord President of Ulster and Lord Deputy of Ireland under James I. It was now the meeting-place of Parliament, described by its Speaker, Sir Audley Mervyn,† as 'a choice collection of Protestant fruit'. The building itself, being only occasionally in demand for this purpose, was put under the care of the architect, William Robinson, who took a lease of the grounds and gardens and undertook to keep the fabric in repair. He was appointed first Keeper of the Parliament House in 1677.[10]

The streets on the Anglesey estate which are shown as existing by 1685‡ include Anglesey Street itself, and Fleet Street which bounded it on the north. The strand (Aston's Quay) was City land

---

* Justin MacCarthy, Viscount Mount Cashell, Donogh MacCarthy, Earl of Clancarty.

† Mervyn was given to colourful language: see his speech to Ormonde in *I. Commons Journals* (ed. of 1753) II, 252 *sqq.*

‡ In the De Gomme–Phillips map.

42

let to Henry Aston, who appears as a pew-holder in St Andrew's in 1674. West of this was the Temple holding, where Eustace Street and Fownes Street preserve the names of contemporary notabilities, and Temple Lane and Temple Bar enshrine that of the Temples themselves. There is a credible tradition that Fleet Street was so called out of compliment to the slightly earlier Temple Bar, which itself does honour to London and the landlord in nicely-gauged proportion.

The list of those concerned with the new St Peter's casts a similar light on the ruling interests of the south-eastern suburb. Besides Lord Longford, whom we have already noticed, we find 'Squire Cuff' and 'My Lady Cuff', who were married into the Aungier family and survive in the name of Cuffe Street, Ormonde's son Lord Arran, Lady Antrim, and 'Lord Merrion'.[11] This last person must be Viscount Fitzwilliam of Merrion, lessee from the Corporation of what is now the 'Pembroke Estate'.[12] This estate, which shares with the Gardiner Estate the honour of being architecturally the most important in Dublin, belongs to a later chapter in the story, but the ground in question was at this time largely in St Andrew's Parish. The streets lying between Aungier Street and St Stephen's Green appear on the 1685 map very much as they are at present, but they were hardly built upon so soon. Forty years later they bear the agreeable titles of Rapparee Alley, Love Lane and Elbow Lane, but these names, alas, have sobered with the years.

So, by the time of the Williamite Wars, we find that private speculation, guided here and there by viceregal hints and municipal enactments, has extended the urban area in three main directions: north, east and south-east. There is some evidence* that the Aston and Hawkins interests reclaimed a strip of land on the south bank of the river between the Castle and Trinity College. This reclamation was perhaps used for wharves and warehouses. But in general the character of the expansion is upper-class residential.

We hardly expect to find an increase in population so great as that computed by Sir William Petty in 1682, when he arrived at the conclusion that Dublin contained about 58,000 souls.[13] This is all the more surprising in that he thought that ten years earlier the entire population of Ireland was not much over a million.[14] He

* In the Phillips map.

43

estimated that in 1672 there were in Dublin 3,400 houses 'of more than one smoak'. Of these chimneys 125 were in the Castle, a further twenty-seven in Lord Meath's house, and about 2,000 more in 164 houses of more than ten 'smoaks' apiece. The Protestant inhabitants then numbered, he thought, about 28,000, owning 'nine-tenths of all the housing' by value. He also estimated that there were 1,180 alehouses and ninety-one breweries.

In 1682 he thought that in the central, older and poorer parishes there were 3,416 of the total of 6,025 houses in Dublin. We must suppose that a high proportion of these were the 'wretched nasty cabbins, without chimney, window or door-shut, and worse than those of the savage Americans' of which he elsewhere speaks. In these conditions, mostly within the walls and around St Bride's and St Catherine's, the large number of Catholic and other poor inhabitants of Dublin must have lived. There is some reason to suspect Petty's figure of 58,000 as being too high; but even if it is substantially reduced we are left with a picture of appalling congestion in the old city.

With the outbreak of the Dutch War in 1672 the Government began to be alarmed at the vulnerability of Dublin to attack by sea. The Dutch had burned the British fleet on the very doorstep of London. It was, we remember, the era of Vauban and of those gigantic fortifications in the Low Countries, some of which still remain to astonish the tourist. Sir Bernard de Gomme, the British Engineer-in-Chief, a Dutchman born at Lille, was called in to prescribe for Dublin. He was an officer of very wide experience, who had served in the Royalist army in the English Civil War, and had recently fortified Dunkirk, Portsmouth, Plymouth and Tilbury. In 1673 he produced a report[15] and plan for Dublin which may still leave us gasping, so grandiose it is in extent and expense. He proposed to build a citadel on the shore south-east of the town, in the shape of a five-pointed star nearly half a mile in total diameter. It would have stretched almost from Ely Place to Lower Mount Street Bridge, engulfing what is now Merrion Square with ravelins, redoubts and the whole prickly panoply of the engineer's art. The total cost of this prodigious undertaking was estimated by the designer at £131,227 5s. 9d. Needless to say it was never carried out, though the preliminary building of a revetment along the south bank at Lazar's or Lazy Hill was done now or very soon afterwards.

It was the Government's business to worry about invasions, that of the Municipality to provide against storms and other acts of God. The increase in the size of ships made it impossible for many of these to approach the Custom House at Essex Bridge, or even the newer wharfs further down the river. Instead they lay at anchor in the bay a mile below Ringsend, whence their cargo was transferred to shore with great trouble and expense. Even then the cargo had reached only the end of a long spit of land, separated from Dublin by a mile of strand covered at high tide, and much further away by the dry land route.

In 1674 an English engineer named Andrew Yarranton happened to be in Dublin. Like de Gomme, he was a man of wide experience, and like him had served in the English Civil War, but on the other side. His speciality was rendering rivers navigable, and he had already devised a navigation from Stourbridge to Kidderminster. While he was in Dublin a November storm scattered all the shipping lying off Ringsend, and many cargoes and lives were lost. He approached the Lord Mayor, who was ex-officio 'Admiral of Dublin', with a scheme, and being encouraged, he also produced a report and a map.[16]

His idea was to tap the two minor watercourses of the Poddle and the College mill-stream, the former at the Castle and the latter near St Patrick's Well Lane (now Nassau Street), and leading this water eastwards to make a number of cuts northwards to the river, in each of which should be lock gates to keep the level up so that ships could remain afloat at low tide. The distances on his map are unfortunately quite astray of the true distances, but it appears that he intended one of his cuts to pass west of Trinity College, with a new Custom House facing the College, another cut to pass eastwards of it, and the third to pass somewhere near the line of Westland Row. At the head of this cut he provided also for a Citadel, on much more modest lines than De Gomme's. By this means, he said, 'any weak or crazy ship will lye there safe, and receive no damage at all. A boy and a dog in the new harbour will look to a ship [instead of the crew having to stay on board] and the wise and knowing people in Dublin say if the new harbour were made, there would

45

be ten thousand pound per annum advance in the kings customs yearly. . . . If this new harbour were made, no place in Holland [which he had no doubt seen in his continental travels] were answerable to it for its advantage and convenience; and as to the cittadel, certainly none would exceed it, no not Delfsee, that strong fort, being made by the very same advantage as this may be; which is by the little river that comes from Groningen to Delfsee'. His great object, as expressed in the title of one of his books, was to 'out-do the Dutch without fighting'.

In spite of this, and in spite of the fact that his idea of a lock-protected harbour near Ringsend was realised in the eighteenth century when the Grand Canal was brought to the Liffey there, there is no sign that Yarranton's project ever progressed beyond the paper stage.

Apart from the two Greens and the large Aungier and Jervis holdings, the Corporation was the ground landlord of a great deal of urban and suburban land, and the records of the latter years of Charles II's reign are full of memoranda of leases. Among the most interesting of these are those such as the Amory grant of 1674,[17] or the Ellis grant of 1682,[18] which contain stipulations for open quays along the river-bank, in the former case sixty, and in the latter thirty-six feet wide: a policy of remarkable foresight. The Amory grant* was a strip along the north bank immediately south of the Jervis estate, including what is now Ormonde Quay, Batchelors Walk and Eden Quay. William Ellis's holding, also on the north bank, stretched more or less from the Old Bridge to the Parkgate, including Ellis's Quay, Arran Quay and perhaps Inns Quay. This was consciously designed to be 'for the advantage, ornament and beauty of the city'. Even the older and much more congested south bank was not exempt from their attentions, for in April 1684 they provided for the opening of a quay from Essex Bridge to Ormonde Bridge on the river side of the walled city.[19] They were also vigilant in preventing encroachments by 'stalls, porches, staires, posts &c' on the river and streets. They disbursed money fairly regularly to a city pavier, and even considered the question of the 'common sewers'.† It seems that as far back as 1637 there was in

---

* Part of it was later held by the Gardiners from Amory.

† 'It is further ordered that severall hornes be provided for the severall skavingers of the city, whoe are heerby required to wind the said hornes halfe an howre before the said skavingers come to sweepe the said streetes . . .' (CARD IV, 314).

Skipper's Lane a vault 'which hath heretofore beene an auncient jakes, or house of easement'.[20] From the thought of this vault one turns with disgust, hoping that by 1674 better arrangements were in operation.

The deliberations of the City Fathers took place in a building known as the Tholsel, in Skinner's Row, now Christchurch Place. The Tholsel had been here since the time of Edward II. It was added to and repaired in 1670–1, but in 1674 and again in 1676 it was felt to be inconvenient and too small, as well as being 'very dangerously crackt'—and little wonder.[21] Some extra ground was acquired, and in 1676 rebuilding was begun. The new building was nearly a square of about sixty-four feet, and, mainly because of money difficulties, took six years or more to finish. The supervisor of the work was Thomas Graves, and in the absence of other evidence we may call him the 'architect' of the building. He seems to have been a master-builder and contractor, and held the office of bearer of the great mace. When finished the Tholsel contained a court-room, and a room for the Trinity Guild of Merchants, as well as the Corporation offices. The Royal Exchange, which had till now occupied Lord Cork's house on Cork Hill, moved into the Tholsel also (Pl. VIII).

As it survived till the end of the eighteenth century, when it became ruinous and was consequently demolished about 1806, the Tholsel was included in Malton's *Views of Dublin* (1792–7) and may be studied there or in the *Journal** of Thomas Dineley who visited Dublin in 1680. The two drawings agree tolerably well. Like the surviving Tholsel in Kilkenny, its ground-floor consisted of an open arcade, an almost universal feature of 'exchanges'. On the south front it had a projecting frontispiece consisting of two podgy Tuscan columns supporting a balcony, and a very large cornice divided the two storeys. It was typical merchants' architecture, fat and rather complacent, markedly coarser in feeling than any surviving Dublin building. Dineley's drawing shows an elaborate lantern containing a clock, but this had disappeared by Malton's time.

Above and behind the Tuscan columns were niches for two statues, and William de Keysar was commissioned to carve Portland stone figures of kings Charles the First and Second. They were to be

* Reprinted in *JRSAI*, XLIII, Pt. 4 (1913).

six feet high, and the sculptor was to be paid £100 for the pair. But when one statue was nearly finished, the Lord Mayor and Treasurer decided that it was not 'fameous' enough, and ordered De Keysar to remake both statues two feet taller. This seems to have been done, but it appears that the unfortunate sculptor found difficulty in recovering his fee for the work.[22]

The statues may still be seen by the curious in the crypt of Christchurch Cathedral. All authorities from Gilbert (1854) onwards concur in describing them as Charles II and James II; but whoever they may represent, they have at least the distinction of being the oldest surviving secular statues in Dublin. They derive a certain sepulchral grandeur from their present situation.

REFERENCES

[1] Chart, *The Story of Dublin*, 1932, 86.
[2] Bernard, *St Patrick's Cathedral*, 1940, pp. 12–13.
[3] *CARD* I, 266.
[4] See *JRSAI* LXII, 6.
[5] Gilbert, I, 210.
[6] MacSorley, *The Story of Our Parish*, 1917, p. 12.
[7] Carroll: *Succession of Clergy in St Bride's &c*, 1884, p. 16.
[8] *CARD* V 244.
[9] Carte, *op. c.t.* II, 102.
[10] Gilbert: *Parliament House Dublin*, p. 6.
[11] MacSorley, *op. cit.* 12.
[12] See Morgan: *Rental of the Corporation of Dublin*, 1876.
[13] *CARD* V, 603.
[14] *Political Anatomy of Ireland*, 1672. Chap. IV *ad init.*
[15] *CARD* V, 566 *sqq.*
[16] Map in *CARD* V frontispiece; report in ditto, p. 573.
[17] *CARD* V, 58.
[18] *ibid.* 237, 263.
[19] *ibid.* 322.
[20] *CARD* III, 327. For sanitary conditions in 1661, see *I. Commons Journals*, 1661, June 17th. See also *CARD* V, 528 (1691).
[21] *CARD* V, 96 *et passim.*
[22] *CARD* V, 271, 319, 354.

CHAPTER VI

The Intellectuals

THE INTELLECTUAL life of Dublin benefited, like every other civilised activity, from the Peace of the Restoration. Indeed this is perhaps the first occasion when we can point to any well-defined intellectual movement in the capital. There had been writers and thinkers born or resident in Dublin before, but they had little organic relation to Irish life. They had for the most part been Protestants or settlers or both. Perhaps the most distinguished was James Ussher, born in Dublin at 3 Fishamble Street in 1581. The house, with the Ussher coat of arms, survived until 1944. His uncle Henry was Archbishop of Armagh and a founder of Trinity College. He himself was precocious as a theologian and rose early to high position in the Irish Church. His influence, particularly in 1615 and 1634, was important in giving the Irish Church a more definitely Protestant direction than its English sister. Though he defended Episcopacy and Non-Resistance he ended his days more or less unmolested in England, where he happened to be when the Civil War broke out. At his death in 1656 his library was bought by the Crown and presented to Dublin University. The library of a man who had been the friend of Camden, Selden, Bodley and Cotton was worth having.

His cousin Richard Stanyhurst was the son of the Recorder of Dublin and Speaker of the Irish Commons. He contributed the *Description of Ireland* to Holinshed's *Chronicles*, and wrote a book of his own *De Rebus in Hibernia Gestis*. But his undoubted claim to notoriety is his translation of Virgil, dedicated to his brother-in-law Lord Dunsany, and published in 1582. It must surely be one of the most remarkable linguistic oddities in English literature. Stanyhurst turned Catholic and died on the Continent. The diversity of the careers of these two men, so closely related, will serve to show how far Ireland of the early seventeenth century was from providing a common milieu for men of intellect.

The life of Sir James Ware gives some idea of the circumstances in which Irish scholars worked in the generation immediately following. He was born in Castle Street, Dublin, in 1594, went to Trinity College, succeeded his father as Auditor-General in 1632, and married Mary Newcomen, of a Dublin family whom we shall meet again. Ussher encouraged his early antiquarian interests, and from 1626 onwards Ware published Latin treatises on Irish ecclesiastical and literary antiquities. He was M.P. for Dublin University in Strafford's two parliaments, and again after the Restoration. He attached himself to Strafford's party, and in 1644 was sent by Ormonde to report confidentially to Charles I; he was captured, but succeeded in destroying the papers he was carrying, and was imprisoned in the Tower of London. During the siege of Dublin in 1647 he was held as a hostage. He was released when Ormonde surrendered the city, but soon after his return to Dublin was expelled by Jones, the Cromwellian general, and went to live in France. He spent the 1650's in London, in unpolitical research and converse with Selden, Ashmole and others. At the Restoration he came back to Dublin as one of the Commissioners of Lands, and died in his house in Castle Street on December 1st, 1666.

This bald account does little justice to Ware's great services to Ireland. He collected Irish manuscripts and was friendly with Duald MacFirbis the Gaelic scholar whom he brought from Galway to Castle Street and employed on literary work. (Poor MacFirbis was murdered by a drunk while going to Dublin on his inoffensive occasions a few years after Ware's death.) Ware's works, in particular the *Irish Writers* of 1639 and the *Irish Antiquities* of 1654, entitle him to an honoured place among those who have laboured to rescue the monuments of Gaelic Ireland from oblivion. His manuscripts are now in the Bodleian and the British Museum, and Sir James himself lies buried in St Werburgh's close by the site of his own house. His son, Robert Ware, translated and republished his work which attained a wide and stimulating currency; and this in spite of the fact that the son was a Protestant zealot and wrote also a work entitled *The Hunting of the Romish Fox*. Ware's great-grandson-in-law was Walter Harris, the first serious historian of Dublin, and he, too, republished Ware's works on Ireland.

It is a curious fact that Cromwell's wars, so destructive in most respects, should have assisted indirectly in the rebirth of scholarship and letters in Dublin. Gerard Boate, the author of *Ireland's Naturall History*, was a Dutchman who in 1642 subscribed as an 'adventurer' for lands in Ireland. He did not come over until 1649, when Dublin was in Cromwell's hands, but by then had already written his book, 'for the common good of Ireland and more especially for the benefit of Adventurers and Planters there'. The explanation of how he was able to write, without personal investigation, a book which still retains some value, is that his brother Arnold had corresponded with Ussher on Hebrew scholarship, and had been invited over to settle in Dublin, from which he had sent the materials to Gerard. Again, we find the helping hand of Ussher in the background.[1]

Sir William Petty's connexion with Ireland is even more directly the result of the military situation. One of Petty's first claims to notice is that, like a greater than himself, he addressed a Letter on Education to Samuel Hartlib. There must have been considerable cohesion among these Cromwellian intellectuals, for it was Hartlib who saw Boate's book through the press.

Anatomist, musician, economist, inventor, shipwright, statistician, geographer and man of business, Petty was one of the most versatile men of an age rich in versatility. Before coming to Ireland in 1652 as Physician to Cromwell's army, he had studied on the Continent, consorted with Hobbes and perhaps drawn diagrams for his *Optics*, invented a copying machine and raised a hanged woman from the dead. He found that the applotment and division of lands confiscated for the soldiers was being incompetently done, and contracted to do it properly himself, which he performed in thirteen months. The result was the famous 'Down Survey', so called, it is said, for no better reason than that in this series of maps the results were set *down*. It was the first survey of Ireland to retain its value till the present. The maps were preserved in Dublin Castle till 1711, when they suffered in a fire. They were later transferred to the Public Record Office where in 1922 they were still further damaged in the siege of the Four Courts, and little now remains of them. Fortunately, however, early copies exist elsewhere,* and Petty himself issued a small-scale printed atlas of Ireland in 1685.

In the course of the Survey Petty managed to enrich himself with

---

* Notably in the Bibliothèque Nationale, Paris, and the collection of the Marquis of Lansdowne. See Wood: *Guide to the Public Records of Ireland*, 1919, 150.

50,000 acres of land in Kerry, which he developed most industriously. He was also Secretary to Henry Cromwell, and for two years Clerk of the Council. In spite of his record, but no doubt because of his efficiency, he was knighted at the Restoration and became Surveyor-General of the Kingdom. One of his first enterprises was the construction of a double-bottomed ship which plied between Dublin and Holyhead but was soon lost in a storm. In 1672 he conducted a statistical enquiry into the state of Ireland from the economic point of view. Ten years later he directed his attention to a statistical analysis of the Dublin Bills of Mortality.

Petty seems to have been a man entirely devoid of sentiment or of any imaginative attachment to the land in which most of his work was done. In this he stands in sharp contrast to Ware, who was not a physical scientist, and equally to the Molyneux brothers, both of whom had scientific interests. Petty looked on Ireland with the cold eye of a 'sophister, economist and calculator'; he saw it merely as a 'description of square measurement' to which a great Irishman was later to point out that no human being could feel any sentiment of loyalty. He was the first propagandist of Unionism in its final form. This is not surprising from a man who had been a supporter of Cromwell's government, which had abolished the Irish Parliament and put the harp on the Union Jack, whence it was removed by Charles II, who replaced it on the blue ground of the Irish flag. He was contemptuous of the Irish past. He wrote:

> 'There is at this day no monument or real argument that, when the Irish were first invaded, they had any stone-housing at all, any money, any foreign trade, nor any learning but the legend of the saints, psalters, missals, rituals etc., viz. nor geometry, astronomy, architecture, enginery, painting, carving, nor any kind of manufacture, nor the least use of navigation; or the art military.[2]

All forms of Irish autonomy, even for settlers, were to him anathema, for 'It is absurd, that Englishmen in Ireland should either be aliens there, or else to be bound to laws, in the making of which they are not represented'.

In spite of his Cromwellian past, his view of the religious question was cynically erastian. 'As for religions', he wrote, 'we reduce them to three, viz.:

1. Those who have the Pope of Rome for their head.
2. Who are governed by the laws of their country.
3. Those who rely respectively upon their own private judgments.'

With such brief dismissal did Sir William dispose of topics which did not interest him.*

In 1684 Petty was elected first President of the 'Dublin Society', sometimes called the 'Philosophical Society', founded by William Molyneux in imitation of the Royal Society of London, then a little over twenty years old and including Petty as a foundation member. Three years later Petty died, leaving descendants who enjoyed the earldoms of Kerry, Shelburne and Lansdowne.†

Across the table of the coffee-house on Cork Hill where the Society met, the first articulate Unionist faced the first articulate Nationalist on the common ground of science. The Molyneux brothers were thirty years Petty's juniors and of a very different cast of mind. They were fourth generation settlers: their great-grandfather had been Chancellor of the Irish Exchequer, their grandfather Ulster King-at-Arms, and their father Master Gunner of Ireland.[3]

The interest in law, antiquity and useful arts which this ancestry seems to promise appears in the writings of the brothers. The elder, William, was born in New Row in 1656. He suffered from an hereditary affection of the kidneys and was a semi-invalid all his life. His wife, Margaret Domville, whom he married on his return from London where he had been studying law, in 1678, went blind three months later and suffered pain for the remaining thirteen years of her life. In 1684 he was appointed Surveyor-General‡ jointly with William Robinson the architect,[4] and in the following year the Irish Government gave him a grant to study military architecture on the Continent. He returned the following year in bad health. During the Williamite War he lived at Chester, returning to sit as M.P. for Dublin University in William's first Parliament, and dying in 1698 at the age of forty-two.

---

* 'The real distinction', he notes in Chapter VII of the *Political Anatomy*, is between 'vested and divested of the land belonging to Papists *anno* 1641'.

† Kerry or Shelburne House, in Stephen's Green, North, ultimately gave place to the Shelbourne (*sic*) Hotel.

‡ Of the Ordnance, a semi-architectural post. The Surveyor-General of Lands does not concern us.

He had accomplished much in his short life. In his early years he translated Descartes' *Meditations* and corresponded with the astronomer Flamsteed. His first book, *Sciothericum Telescopicum* (Dublin, 1686) was followed later by *Dioptrica Nova* (London 1692), a treatise on telescopes and microscopes. In 1682 he was busy collecting materials for a 'Description of Ireland' for Moses Pitt's *Atlas*; in this he worked with Roderic O'Flaherty and Peter Walsh, who introduced him to Ormonde.

During his stay in Chester he became friendly with Locke, and propounded the celebrated problem whether a person born blind, but being taught to distinguish by touch between a cube and a sphere, would recognise which was which if his sight were given to him. Locke wrote of him as 'that very ingenious and studious promoter of real knowledge, the learned and worthy Mr Molyneux, this thinking gentleman whom I am proud to call my friend'. It is worth recording, however, that Molyneux himself admitted to being unable to understand Newton's *Principia Mathematica*, though this did not prevent him from being elected F.R.S. in 1685.

A few months before his death William Molyneux wrote and published the work by which he is best known, *The Case of Ireland Stated*. It stands first in the succession later continued by the *Drapier's Letters*, and is of great importance as asserting Irish legislative independence on grounds unconnected with race, religion or any separate allegiance. Its full title, 'The Case of Ireland being bound by Acts of Parliament in England stated', reflects the fact that, like the *Drapier's Letters*, it was evoked by a particular act of British policy towards Ireland, the series of laws aimed at the destruction of the Irish wool trade. He himself wrote of it that 'it was done in haste, and intended to overtake the proceedings at Westminster, but it comes too late for that: what effect it may have in time to come, God and the wise Council of England only know'. The English seem to have had some inkling of its importance, for their Parliament had the book burned by the common hangman and petitioned King William to have the author prosecuted as well. But the King, who had already seen the Articles of Limerick abrogated by a panic-stricken Parliament of Irish placemen, was not disposed to vindictiveness towards an Irish spokesman. On the other hand Molyneux's book had very little influence on Irish opinion at this time, except that it must have been read with sad approval by the merchants whose interests in wool were being ruined.

William Molyneux left a son, Samuel, also an astronomer, who married into the Capel family, settled in England and became secretary to the Prince of Wales and died without issue in 1728.

Thomas Molyneux was five years younger than his brother William, and studied medicine at Dublin and Leyden. He built up a good practice for himself in Dublin, became an F.R.S. in 1687, and subsequently State Physician, President of the Royal College of Physicians, Professor of Physics, and in 1730 was created a Baronet. Like so many doctors, he followed archæology as a side-line. His *Familiar Letters* between himself, his brother, Locke and others, appeared in 1708, and he wrote pioneer papers on zoological subjects. The edition of Boate which appeared in 1725 contained as an appendix his treatise on *Danish Mounts, Forts and Towers in Ireland*. Though very enlightened for its day, this book must be saddled with the blame for the 'Danish' heresy which cumbered Irish Archæology for more than a century, and is still a living thing in the minds of the country people.* It is not, perhaps, strictly accurate to reproach Molyneux with having invented this theory, for it had been tentatively suggested by Ware and handed on by Fr. John Lynch, though the latter was an apologist for the antiquity of Irish civilisation.[5] It is easy to see, also, how well it fitted in with the prejudice of Petty already quoted. In 1709 Molyneux was in Iar-Connacht on behalf of the Philosophical Society, and there visited Roderic O'Flaherty, whom he found in 'a very old and miserable condition', having had to sell even his cherished Irish manuscripts.

Sir Thomas Molyneux died in 1733. The house in Peter Street which he had built for himself in 1711 survived until 1943, bearing the family's coat of arms and an inscription. It was a handsome but not very large house, with a central pediment and a fine staircase with barley-sugar balusters. It continued as the family mansion for a century after his death, then fell into the hands of Astley, the circus-promoter, who built his Amphitheatre behind it, and later

---

* In the Irish countryside, ancient ruins are described as having been built by the Danes and sacked by Cromwell. More recent ruins are usually credited to Italian or French architects, and their destruction—with more justice—to 'the boys'.

still was converted into the Molyneux Asylum for Blind Women, while the Amphitheatre was succeeded by the Molyneux Church where Bernard Shaw was a young and reluctant church-goer. It ended its days as a Salvation Army Hostel, and is one of the really regrettable losses Dublin has suffered in recent years.*

There were two sisters also in the Molyneux family—Jane who married Bishop Dopping of Meath, and Mary who married Dr John Madden. Dopping was a stout Williamite cleric, a member of the Philosophical Society, who ventured as far afield as Clonmacnois† in search of alleged Hebrew inscriptions. The fact that Clonmacnois lay in his diocese should not be allowed to rob him of credit for what was in 1684 quite an adventurous journey. John Madden was a Dublin physician, a foundation member of the still existing Dublin Society (now the Royal Dublin Society) and father of the more famous Samuel ('Premium') Madden.‡

Soon after its foundation the Society moved from Cork Hill to 'Crow's Nest', a building in Crow Street where they established a Laboratory, Museum and Botanic Garden. Among the first members were Narcissus Marsh, St George Ashe, and William King; and names well known in Dublin and Irish history also appear, as Baggot, Barnard, Bulkeley, Clements, Cuffe and Dominick. Sir William Stewart, first Viscount Mountjoy,§ succeeded as President on Petty's death. Among the names of the thirty-three foundation members are at least two native Irish names, Houlaghan and Keogh, and the names Foley and Finglass are probably also native. The topics of their Transactions range from Mathematics and Physics through Medical Science (including Zoology and Chemistry) to Polite Literature, History and Antiquities.[6] They also collected topographical accounts of places in Ireland, which remain of great value and are now in Trinity College Library (MSS. i, I, 1-2).[7]

There seems little doubt but that, if political conditions had allowed it, the Society would have pursued a course comparable to that of the Royal Society of London. But the troubles consequent on the accession of James II broke up the precarious convention of

---

* It is recorded in *Georgian Society Records*, Vol. II.
† The famous Early Christian site on the Shannon below Athlone.
‡ For whom see Chapter XI.
§ Of the second creation.

Irish society, and when the Philosophers met again in 1693 they had become more a clique of college dons than a national institution.

Some of the Catholic intellectuals remained in Dublin during Charles II's reign, though many found a more secure career on the Continent and some even preferred London to Dublin. But Thomas Arthur the physician, Charles O'Kelly and Sir Richard Bellings the historians, were sometimes in Dublin and may have mixed with their Protestant colleagues. Among the lawyers were Sir Richard Nagle and Sir Stephen Rice, both of whom came into their own in the following reign. Also prominent in the following reign was Father Michael Moore, who was appointed Provost of Trinity by James II, and saved the Library and the Protestant prisoners from molestation by the soldiery.

No doubt a number of Catholics found Dublin comfortable enough in Restoration times.* But the insecurity of their position is shown by the fact that between 1680 and 1692 two Archbishops of Dublin died miserably in prison, while an Archbishop of Armagh was taken to London, falsely accused, and executed at Tyburn. It is only fair to Ormonde to say that he does not seem to have persecuted the Catholic clergy more than was absolutely necessary to avoid suspicion of being concerned in a 'Popish Plot' himself.

* A certain number were admitted as freemen in Dublin, especially in 1672 and 1676 (Mac-Lysaght *Irish Life in the Seventeenth Century* and *CARD* V 131).

REFERENCES

[1] *Bibliographical Society of Ireland Publications* III, 5, by J. deW. Hinch.
[2] *Polit. Anat. of I.* Chapter V.
[3] Gilbert, III, index, under Molyneux.
[4] Lascelles: *Liber Munerum Hiberniae.*
[5] See T. J. Westropp: Presidential Address to the Royal Society of Antiquaries of Ireland, 1916.
[6] Gilbert II, 177. The Minute Book of the Society is in the British Museum (Add. MSS. 4811). Dr Allen Mullen dissected an elephant in Essex Street in 1681 (Gilbert II, 147). The poor animal was accidentally burned while on exhibition. See also Gilbert II, App. II.
[7] *JRSAI* XXIX, 429

CHAPTER VII

Robinson and the Royal Hospital

THE MOST conspicuous monument to the viceroyalties of Ormonde (if we except the Phœnix Park which can hardly be called conspicuous) is the Royal Hospital, Kilmainham. Happily it may still be seen, but unhappily only with difficulty or at a distance. The visitor who seeks information about it from guide-book or gossip will probably be told that it is an Irish copy of Chelsea Hospital and was designed by Wren. Neither is true. It would be much nearer the truth to say that Chelsea is an English copy of Kilmainham, bearing in mind that both are copies of the Invalides.

In about 1675 the Earl of Granard, Marshal of the Garrisons of Ireland, began to be seriously perturbed about the problem of the old soldiers of the Irish Army. Many of them had no homes to go to, and in the forts and garrison-towns of Ireland they were a nuisance and in time of trouble a potential danger. Towards the end of Essex's Viceroyalty the scheme for a Hospital began to take shape, but still not very seriously.[1]

It was not till 1679, two years after Ormonde had returned to the sword, that on the receipt of a King's Letter, the site was chosen in that part of the Phœnix Park which lay south of the river. The highest point of this ground, rather to the east of the ruins of the Priory of the Knights Hospitallers, was selected for the new building—a magnificent situation, dominating the whole district and facing high across the river to the open lands of the Park. The building was financed by a small deduction from the pay of the army.

In spite of Professor Richardson's opinion that 'the design could not have been produced by any other hand'[2] than Wren's, there is no doubt that the architect was William Robinson, Surveyor-General since 1661. Wren was the holder of that office in England, but it was the Irish Surveyor-General who was asked to produce a 'draught' or 'model' and an abundance of references to Robinson as the architect in the Ormonde papers at the time of the building, puts the matter beyond dispute. Though Robinson is known to have been responsible for other buildings in Dublin, this, his greatest work, is the first* of which we have any information.

The first stone, at the north-west corner, was laid by Ormonde on April 29th, 1680, and the second by Francis Aungier, Earl of Longford, as Master-General of the Ordnance. The building was fairly complete by 1684, though the Chapel was not ready for consecration till early in 1687,[3] and the Tower was not added 'as it was first intended to be finished' till 1701. An account of the cost has survived, by which it appears that it was built for just under £24,000. While it was being made ready, a few pensioners were accommodated in a building in Back Lane,[4] but the Hospital itself seems to have been occupied by 1684. As early as 1682 Robinson was sending a bill to the Government for £600. He retained Ormonde's confidence, and the Duke wrote of him as 'well acquainted with the rates of work and materials and the value of ground'.[5] A pamphlet published in defence of Ormonde in 1690 says that his enemies reproached him with 'Cheating the Army in building the Hospital, and that Robinson the Architect had enriched himself by it: when indeed not to lessen any thing of his due Character, Robinson shewed the parts of an Excellent Artist in the Contrivance, and of an Honest Man in the Charge, as men of Value and Experience in Building affirm'.[6]

Robinson chose a closed courtyard plan with a ground floor loggia round three of the sides and part of the fourth. This internal court is 224 feet square, and the external dimensions, taking in the extra depth of the north range which contains the Hall and Chapel and the Master's Lodging, are 306 feet (East and West) by 288 feet (North and South). It was designed to accommodate 300 pensioners on its three floors. It is thus very much the largest surviving building of its period in Ireland, and the earliest secular public building in the country (Pl. IV).

It is an eloquent building, the most eloquent Dublin was to see till the coming of Gandon. The north front, of calp stone with limestone, granite and plaster dressings, has a wide and deep central projection treated as a portico with pilasters, and the twelve tall

* Except his part as consultant in Jervis's Essex Bridge (CARD VI 597).

round-headed windows give a strong vertical emphasis. The Renaissance love of symmetry is already very influential: while the tall windows in the centre and left correspond with Hall and Chapel respectively, those on the right conceal the two storeys of the Master's lodging. But it is still early enough to permit minor departures from strict symmetry, as in the absence of dormers over the Chapel, or in the necessarily uneven spacing of the chimneys in this, the principal front* (Fig. 8).

The chimneys, rising from the ridge of the steep continuous roof, are almost the most important elements in the other three elevations, which are treated frankly as two-storey compositions with dormers and low central pediments but no columnar features. The stacks are tall with panelled faces and strong cornices, marching across the skyline in a very stately manner.

Though there are small breaks marking pavilions at the corners, both cornice and roof are continuous and take no account of the breaks, which do not correspond to any internal division. The north front, indeed, seems deliberately to mask rather than to reveal the internal disposition, but the façade to the courtyard does express the plan. The four external doorways have very fine carved wooden tympana,† the northern and southern of heads and garlands, and the eastern and western of trophies of arms. These are now unfortunately thickly covered with brown paint. Broken pediments and scroll-pediments are sparingly used to mark the centres on the first floor. The window cases are simple and emphatic, with plaster architraves, some sandstone and limestone and granite sills. They and the string-course are now painted cream in strong contrast to the grey-blue stucco.

It was formerly believed that all the walling except the north front was of brick, and picturesque analogies were drawn between the red-brick and sandstone of the building and the red coats and pipeclay of the venerable pensioners. But recent research has established that the coat of protective stucco applied about the middle of the nineteenth century covered rubble walling of the local calp, as in the north front.[7]

---

* The dormers over the Chapel are shown in Francis Place's drawing of 1698, and may have disappeared in the restoration of c. 1889.

† They are illustrated in Childers and Stewart, *The Royal Hospital, Kilmainham*, 1921.

At the north end of the east front (that towards Dublin) is the great east window of the Chapel, with its semicircular head rising over the main cornice. This feature shows strong signs of deriving from the great round-headed feature at the Invalides in Paris.* Some of the stone tracery and glass in the Kilmainham window is alleged to have come from the Priory of the Knights. There is fairly good contemporary evidence for the stonework, and the glass in the upper part of the window is certainly not modern.† The wooden tracery in the other large windows is nineteenth-century, replacing the classical work shown in Malton's print.

The large windows of the north front are striking in that they have no impost mouldings, an omission which imparts a flavour as of the last ghostly persistence of the Gothic spirit. Even the keystones are worked separately on the inner arch rings only, leaving the outer rings smooth. Another curious feature is that the Corinthian pilasters of the portico spring straight out of the earth without bases, and seem always to have done so. Over the north door is a magnificent achievement of the Ormonde arms in stone.

Finally, the tower and spire, the character of which Professor Richardson admits to be 'at variance with Wren's usual ideas of cupolas and clock turrets'. This feature sits directly on the pediment roof. It was allowed for from the beginning, for Francis Place's drawings, done in 1698,[8] show a pyramidally-roofed stump which later became the tower's base. It rises to about 125 feet; a square stage with scaled-down replicas of the great windows, a cornice and solid balustrade with four great pillow-shaped ornaments at the corners, then a slenderer clock-stage with re-entrant corners and another cornice, finished off by the octagonal copper spire with its weathercock. It is now painted yellow and the spire, covered with copper, is bright green. It is a very conspicuous landmark in the district and has an odd trick of appearing to be sunlit even on dull days. At the base of the spire are eight graceful appendages in the form of open consoles, which look rather like handles but seem to be the product simply of a happy fantasy of the designer.

The internal courtyard, though small of scale in comparison

---

* Sill lowered about 1850.

† That in the lower part was presented by Queen Victoria in 1849. All the glass has been stored for safety since about 1940.

with Chelsea, has a unique charm. The loggia surrounds a green grassy space, over the Hall entrance is a pediment, a sundial and a balcony; the whole thing is sensitively adapted to its purpose. The provision of covered walks is much more generous than at Chelsea, and the closed plan makes it much less draughty than its English counterpart. It is the only building in Ireland which recalls the atmosphere and setting of a Cambridge college, a point which has struck influential observers at various times from the date of its erection till the present day. One wonders, none the less, who was responsible for the economy of stopping the impost-mouldings abruptly in space, flush with the back-arches and thus saving the expense of extra work.*

The great Hall, 100 feet by 50, had a compartment ceiling with a large clock-face in the centre, but this is now obscured by a later insertion of open joist-work. Until 1927 the walls were covered with armour and large portraits, but the Hall is now used as an overflow store of the National Museum, and like the rest of the building is not normally open to the public. The latest tenant of the Hall is Queen Victoria in bronze from Leinster House, whom I found glaring out at me through a window the last time I visited the Hospital.

The chief glory of the Chapel is the contemporary coved and compartmented ceiling of stucco, the work of an unknown artist. Foliage, fruit, flowers, shells and winged heads hang in riotous tumult from their dizzy height. Unfortunately in 1902 it not only looked dangerous but was so; and the present ceiling is an undetectable facsimile in papier mâché. It is the earliest surviving plaster ceiling in Dublin, and even in a city so rich in plaster it must take a high place, as well as being unlike any other local example, unless we include the later and more modest work at St Werburgh's.† At the angles of the sanctuary is some excellent wood-carving, the work of James Tabary, a Huguenot admitted to the freedom of the city in 1685. At the west end fluted Corinthian columns support a small gallery containing the canopied pew of the Master (who was always the Commander-in-Chief in Ireland for the time being), and in front of the door is a pair of beautiful wrought-iron gates

---

* Especially as these mouldings are of plaster on a projecting course of bricks.
† See Chapter X.

bearing the arms of Queen Anne and therefore somewhat later than the rest of the fittings.

The early years of this great building's life were chequered, and it seemed at times that it might be put to other purposes than those for which it was built. As early as 1682 Sir Francis Brewster observed what we have already noticed, 'that it would make a magnificent college', and wrote to Ormonde suggesting that Trinity and the Royal Hospital should exchange buildings.[9] This scheme would have had the obvious advantage of removing the young men from such close contact with the varied attractions of the capital. Two years later, during the absence of both Ormonde and Robinson, a disastrous fire* occurred in the Castle, which only just failed to detonate the magazine of powder kept there. When Robinson returned he arranged to move this powder to the Royal Hospital, using one wing as a magazine. Ormonde also returned, and finding that his own apartments in the Castle were uninhabitable, wrote to his son, 'I have thought that I might have some conveniency in the Master of the Hospital's lodgings for a short time, especially if the Hospital be not completely filled', and proposed to consult with Robinson about it.[10]

The Chapel was consecrated, after many delays, on January 19th, 1687 (new style). But two years earlier Charles II had died a Catholic, and his brother was determined on Ormonde's recall. Almost the Duke's last act in Ireland was to proclaim James II. His old adversary Richard Talbot was made Earl of Tyrconnel and Commander of the Forces in Ireland, though not yet Viceroy. Ormonde began to be seriously alarmed for the future of the Hospital, which 'would, he foresaw, be made a nest for Hornets, which to prevent, as well as possible, he sate several days with the Council and Judges in private, in the Castle, and there made all the provision that could be made for it, against the imminent Storm . . . At the aforesaid Hospital he appointed a Dinner for all the Officers of the Hospital, and the Officers of the Army then in *Dublin*; which being over, he took a large Glass of Wine in his hand, bid them fill it to the brim, then stood up and called to all the Company: Look here, Gentlemen, they say at Court, I am now become an Old Doating Fool, you see my Hand doth not shake, nor does my Heart fail,

* A similar fire had occurred in 1671, also nearly causing an explosion (*CARD* I, 266).

63

nor doubt but I will make some of them see their mistake, and so drank the King's Health . . .'[11]

After his recall things went, from the Protestant point of view, from bad to worse. Let us look at the events of the next few years through the eyes of a certain Mr Colles, who kept a diary from 1685 to 1690.[12] In July of the former year the Papists 'burned a manikin' for Monmouth in Thomas Street. A few months later Lord Galmoye and Lord Ikerrin (Catholic Butlers) appear drunk in St Werburgh's church. In January 1686 Ormonde's son, Lord Arran, dies and Clarendon arrives as an ineffectual stop-gap between the great Duke and Talbot-Tyrconnel. In May some mysterious trunks arrive at the Custom House, and rumour has it that they are passed without opening by direct orders from King James himself. They are supposed to contain 'Popish Bishops' robes' and similar impedimenta. Clarendon goes back to England. Only two months after the consecration of the Royal Hospital Chapel, the Charter of the new Hospital is seized and Mass said in the Chapel. The Catholic jurists attack the legality of the royal conveyance of the Kilmainham lands, and Tyrconnel takes the whole management of the Hospital into his hands and out of those of the Governors. In the streets of Dublin friars appear in habits and are laughed at by the boys, but the Lord Mayor gives them police protection. In October 1688

> Two armies appear in the clouds; seen by several in this city— watch and seamen; went from east to north; they saw them perfectly shoot at one another, and saw some fall dead; saw the very blood; and the seamen repeat they heard the guns; Colonel Justin McCarthy saw it all at sea, and told the Lord Deputy of it; it continued about an hour, with a very bright night above, and clouds and a fog below. About this time a new building in the Castle of Dublin was finished, and the Lord Deputy removed from Chapelizod, for that house [i.e. the 'King's House' at Chapelizod] was so disturbed with spirits they could not rest. On the 23rd some Protestants in the county of Meath made bonfires, which the Papists quenched. The 29th, rabble break the Mass House in Lime Street, while Lord Mayor was at dinner.

Early in December a flood destroys Essex Bridge. Tyrconnel gives public assurances of toleration to Protestants, but few believe him and many flee to England. He installs friars in the Royal Hospital, and in the cold weather at the beginning of 1689 'The poor old men of the Hospital had forty shillings apiece given them, and all turned out of the House, being as it was intended for a garrison'.

The events of the next two years are common knowledge, but are a blank as far as the Hospital is concerned, until twelve hundred sick and wounded Williamite soldiers were accommodated in it after the battle of Aughrim in July 1691. King James had in the meantime come to Dublin, heard Mass in Christchurch (the tabernacle and candlesticks are still shown in the crypt), held a Parliament which reversed the Act of Settlement, lost the Battle of the Boyne and sailed from Kinsale for France, carrying with him the hopes of the Catholic aristocracy.*

The next hundred years and more are without event, till the ghosts of Aughrim raise their heads again. In 1916 the Hospital, being a strong point, was occupied by 2,500 British troops engaged in suppressing the Rising of Easter Week. On July 12th, the anniversary of Aughrim, in 1921, Sir Nevil Macready held an Investiture in the great courtyard. The Hospital lingered on for a few more years, but in 1927 the remaining pensioners were transferred to Chelsea and the last service was held in the Chapel. The building was offered to University College, the Dublin college of the National University, but the offer was, most regrettably, refused. This harmonious scheme has been mooted from time to time since, and perhaps it may yet be carried out. In the meantime the building does duty as the administrative headquarters of the Civic Guard.† But though the occupants respect its integrity and the Board of Works maintain it in much of its former splendour, its inaccessibility is a grievous loss to the public. The roof near the south-east corner was slightly damaged by a fire in the early nineteen-forties, but no great harm was caused.

This brief survey of the Kilmainham Hospital is perhaps the best place in which to take notice of its architect, the first Irish architect of whose career we have any clear particulars.

As we would expect in the period, he was not an 'architect' pure

---

* When King William came campaigning in Ireland he brought with him an 'itinerant house . . . for him to lye in the field' designed by Wren. (Webb, *Wren*, 1937 p. 118) C. T. Bowden, writing in 1791, saw in Dublin 'an old wooden house . . . constructed in Holland, more than a century ago . . . in such a manner as to be taken down and put up at pleasure'. (*Tour Through Ireland*, Dub. 1791, p. 9.)

† Since this was written it has been (1949) vacated owing to its structural condition. Its preservation is a matter of the first importance.

and simple in the modern sense. His appointment was military, and (unless I am confusing him with other holders of his not uncommon name) he had landed interests and was an importer of goods from abroad. The grant of the Parliament House precincts coincided with his first patent as Surveyor-General in 1670, at a salary of £300 per annum. He was associated with Sir Humphrey Jervis and Sir Joshua Allen (a member of the building family) as technical adviser to Essex Bridge in 1676. In 1679 he was re-appointed Surveyor with a new patent and a fifty per cent. increase of salary.*
While working on the Royal Hospital he is also found supervising the two great forts at the mouth of Kinsale Harbour—James's (or Rincurran) Fort, and Charles Fort, which still survive in massive dilapidation.

In 1682 he (or another of the name) is described as 'a merchant and trader to foreign parts' and as such a member of the Ballast (or Port of Dublin) Committee, and takes a lease of the city water supply. It is credible enough that a professional engineer might have such interests. As a gentleman and holder of high government office, he is nominated a foundation Governor of the Royal Hospital. The last official commission which I can trace, after his rebuilding in Dublin Castle (perhaps the rooms 'over a large stone gallery supported by several pillars of stone' of Dunton's description[13] in 1699), was the rebuilding of the Four Courts beside Christchurch in 1659, but both these works have long since vanished. In 1700 he surrenders his patent and is succeeded by Burgh, and is knighted in the following year. From about 1702 onwards he is building Marsh's Library, probably as a favour to the Archbishop. In 1707 he ceases to be a Governor of the Hospital, and in 1712, on November 13th, dies, at what age is not known, but obviously not less than about 65 and probably more.

We know very little of his personality beyond what he put into his buildings. The few entries in the Ormonde papers which are not official matters relate to mishaps: 'Robinson is taken ill of the gout in the country' (1683), 'Mr Robinson is lame, having been overturned in his coach last Sunday' (1685), 'poor Will Robinson is confined with the gout' at Conway on his way to London. In his later years he is a little inclined to squabble: there is some dispute

* He was now paid £450 p.a.

66

about his position in the Parliament House,[14] he is 'in the wrong in making the demand he did', and Captain Pratt (a surveyor and cartographer) 'is a chief occasion of Sir William Robinson's disappointments'.[15]

We are left with his two surviving buildings, two vanished ones, and the liberty to make what attributions we may guess at. Marsh's Library, a charming little L-shaped building beside St Patrick's, with a steep-pitched roof, has been refaced externally in stone and modern brick, but remains within much as he must have left it,* and much like a small college library of the period, with the books arranged in bays between the windows and some good decorative woodwork. One or two of the ancillary buildings to the Royal Hospital may be his, in particular the amusing little gardener's house with cylindrical corner-towers which faces the main portico across the formal terraced garden. The larger house at the eastern end of the terrace may be his also, and so (among surviving buildings) may be the Hall of the Foundling Hospital, built in 1703.

On the strength of the Royal Hospital alone, it seems very likely that he had travelled in England if not further afield. Not only is the detail, with a few curious exceptions, correct, but it is both more correct and much more sensitive than that of his successor, Burgh. We do not even know whether he was English or Irish. But not only does it seem likely that he had seen the Invalides: he had somewhere acquired a feeling for grand scale. It was certainly not in Ireland, and at the time it was perhaps hardly even in England. It is of course pure conjecture, but the basis of such conjecture is fortunately still standing.

* The plaster string-courses on the courtyard sides, built on brick courses like those of the Royal Hospital, have been replaced with flush courses of modern brick in the Guinness restoration, which also added the brick buttresses.

REFERENCES

[1] Richard Colley, *The Charter of the Royal Hospital*, 1725.
[2] In *Sir C. Wren Memorial Vol.* 1923, p. 137.
[3] *Ormonde Papers* HMC, 2nd ser. VII, 463, 486.
[4] *ibid.* 188.
[5] *ibid.* VI, 487.
[6] *The Secret Consults, Negotiations &c.*, Dublin 1690. Copy in Haliday Pamphlets, Royal Irish Academy.
[7] I am indebted to Mr Raymond McGrath, Office of Public Works, Dublin, for information about the structure.

[8] Reproduced in *JRSAI*, Vol. LXII.

[9] *Ormonde Papers* HMC, 2nd ser. VI, 421.

[10] *ibid*. VII, 249–50.

[11] *The Secret Consults*, pp. 45–6.

[12] *Ormonde Papers* HMC, 2nd ser. VIII, 343, *sqq*.

[13] Dunton: *The Dublin Scuffle* 1699. Much valuable additional unpublished material by Dunton about his visit to Dublin was published by Dr MacLysaght in his *Irish Life in the Seventeenth Century*.

[14] See Curran in *The Bank of Ireland*, 1949, p. 426.

[15] *Ormonde Papers* HMC, 2nd ser. VIII, 168 (1705). Robinson apparently failed to keep the Parliament House in proper repair and got into trouble for pretending to be in debt as Deputy Receiver-General and was committed to the Constable of the Castle. *I. Commons Journ*. Oct. 16th 1703.

PART TWO

Swift's Dublin

CHAPTER VIII

'Freedom, Religion and Laws'

W<small>E MEASURE</small> history out in centuries, and it is surprising how amenably history responds to the treatment. Historical watersheds are apt to occur at or near the centennial years. Irish history-books close the eighteenth century at 1800; English more often at 1815 or even 1832; French are perhaps more likely to choose 1789. Does the English eighteenth century begin at the Revolution or at the arrival of the Hanoverian? The answer depends largely on the context.

But in Ireland there can be no hesitation between the dates 1690 and 1714. Nothing of note happened here in the latter year. The country was by then too deeply sunk in complacent torpor, or (if you prefer to put it the other way) too frozen in a death-like catalepsy, for the change of dynasty to make any particular impression. On the other hand, 1690 is the confirmation in harsher terms of 1660, and is the true beginning of the eighteenth century. Protestant Ireland spent much of that century in a slow recovery from the panic of 1689, while Catholic Ireland spent it in a similarly slow recovery from the penal code which was the expression of that panic.

Times of extreme turbulence or civil strife do not usually favour either architecture or social intercourse; and so the Jacobite interlude, exciting as it must have been to the dwellers in Dublin, need not occupy our attention for very long. There was a general exodus of Protestants, though some remained and some even sat in the Patriot Parliament. Sir Richard Nagle, the lawyer who had been extensively employed by Protestants in conveyances of property, used his intimate knowledge of land titles to pounce on the weak points in Protestant holdings and assist the general process of forfeiture. King James minted in Dublin the brass money which is immortalised in the famous Orange toast,* and for this purpose

---

* As given by Barrington (I, 247–8) it runs thus: 'The glorious, pious and immortal memory of the great and good King William: not forgetting Oliver Cromwell, who assisted
[Note continued overleaf

71

either built or commandeered a comely building in Capel Street known for long afterwards as the King James Mint-House, but now long since vanished. Its wide eaves were an unusual feature for Dublin, and it was the birthplace of Thomas Sheridan the younger.*

The Collar of SS presented by Charles II disappeared in the confusion.† In 1697 one of the Williamite Lord Mayors, Bartholomew Van Homrigh, a naturalised Dutchman, procured from William III another such Collar, bearing a portrait medal of his majesty. Van Homrigh is worth more than a passing mention, if only because his daughter Hester later became famous as Jonathan Swift's 'Vanessa'.

Swift himself, born beside St Werburgh's Church in 1667, was apparently in Dublin in 1690–91, aged twenty-three or so, and again three years later. After brief spells at Kilroot (in Co. Antrim) and Moor Park, he is found again in Dublin as Chaplain to Lord Berkeley, in 1699–1700. He became a Prebendary of St Patrick's, and was already so great a man that the University which had only grudgingly given him a B.A. granted him a D.D. But, though he is now known to have written a patriotic pamphlet as early as 1707, the days of his real greatness as a Dubliner had not yet come. Yet because he is incomparably the greatest figure on this stage in the first half of the century, it is difficult not to think of the intervening years as a preparation for his final arrival as Dean of St Patrick's in 1713.

The business to which Protestant Ireland turned its attention after the flight of James II was the undoing of the work of the 'Patriot Parliament'.‡ Unfortunately, and to the lasting shame of those

in redeeming us from popery, slavery, arbitrary power, brass money and wooden shoes. May we never want a Williamite to kick the —— of a Jacobite! and a —— for the Bishop of Cork! And he that won't drink this, whether he be priest, bishop, deacon, bellows-blower, grave-digger, or any other of the fraternity of the clergy; may a north wind blow him to the south, and a west wind blow him to the east! May he have a dark night, a lee shore, a rank storm and a leaky vessel to carry him over the river Styx! May the dog Cerberus make a meal of his rump, and Pluto a snuff-box of his skull; and may the devil jump down his throat with a red hot harrow, with every pin tear out a gut, and blow him with a clean carcase to hell! Amen!'

* Illustrated in *Georg. Soc.* IV, 61.

† J. E. Walsh in *Ireland Sixty Years Ago*, 1847, says that it was customary in the Lord Mayor's procession to call at Essex Gate upon Sir Michael Creagh, Lord Mayor in 1688, as having stolen the collar.

‡ The name given, with some justification, to the Parliament of 1689 which was predominantly Catholic.

concerned, the Protestants displayed much less moderation in their victory than had the Catholics. This was no doubt due to their numerical inferiority in the country at large. (In the corporate towns, and especially in Dublin, they were a majority.) The 'Patriot Parliament' had attainted many Protestant and some Catholic landholders, but during the same period Protestant and Catholic had, for a time at least, sat together in the Dublin Common Council, and only such Protestants as had fled the country were deemed to have vacated their seats.[1] The Lord Mayor of 1688–9, Sir Michael Creagh, was a Protestant though a Jacobite.

After the Williamite victory all this was changed. The toleration which William III had promised to the Catholics at Limerick was disallowed by the Irish Parliament, which instead passed the Penal Laws, rightly described by Dr Johnson as exceeding in malignance the persecutions of antiquity. The Dublin Corporation expressly excluded Catholics from its membership and from the freedom of the city, and carried out a purge of masters found taking papist apprentices. So anxious were they to throw every ounce of Protestant weight into the scales that for a time they even admitted Quakers to the city franchise, though this was soon afterwards revoked.

The Church of Ireland, under the scholarly Marsh and the vigorous though disingenuous William King, embarked on a vigorous policy of erastian consolidation. In 1697 the ancient parish of St Michan's was divided into three, St Michan's itself, St Paul's,* where Berkeley was consecrated Bishop of Cloyne in 1734, to the west and St Mary's, still the oldest unaltered church in Dublin, to the east.

St Mary's was probably the first galleried church to be built in the city, and for the next 150 years all Dublin churches were to be of this form. It was sited on an empty plot in the Jervis street-grid, one of its long sides on Mary Street and the other flanked by the spacious rectangular churchyard, which is islanded between Jervis Street and Stafford Street. Externally the church is unimpressive, only the mouldings of the east window, enriched with scrolls (Pl. XI), and the severe dignity of the west door relieving its plainness. At the

---

* Is the most likely of several possible burial-places of Robert Emmet in 1803, but it was rebuilt in 1824-Gothic.

west there is the usual Dublin feature—an intended tower which never progressed beyond the first storey and still bears the temporary roof put on when it was first built.

The interior however is of remarkable interest. It is narrower and higher than the later classical churches, the gallery running between superimposed orders, the upper of which carries the central plaster vault, aisles and galleries being flat-ceiled. Both outer walls and gallery-fronts curve inwards towards the sanctuary-arch, which is flanked by wooden pilasters twice the scale of the rest. The west end has the usual three-lobby, two-staircase plan, with extremely deep churchwardens' pews in the thickness of the wall. There is an additional gallery above the main gallery on either side of the organ, but it is difficult to believe that this was ever intended for use, as even the charity-children who were usually consigned to such places would have had difficulty in scrambling up to such a perch.

The round-headed windows have quasi-Jacobean tracery such as that in the Royal Hospital Tower or St Ann's Church. All the internal cornices, etc., are richly executed in carved wood, and the organ-case is particularly splendid. It has a frieze in hollow-relief, in which at intervals appear figure-sculptures in early eighteenth-century costume—a most remarkable feature which unfortunately did not escape the attention of some puritan iconoclast, who decapitated three of the figures and probably removed two more.

Nearly all the fittings are original, eighteenth-century or at latest early nineteenth, and in total effect it is the most snug of the city churches. It even retains the pew-doors which turn each window-embrasure into an emergency pew. It was here that the Volunteer Earl of Charlemont and Wolfe Tone were baptized, and John Wesley first preached in Ireland. A modern tablet commemorates the Wesley connexion, and the church's associations with Tone and the United Irishmen (another of whom, Archibald Hamilton Rowan, is buried in the churchyard) were celebrated by a very largely attended service in November 1948.

No architect's name is associated with the church.[2]

Both before and after the Williamite Wars Trinity College had been adding to its small Elizabethan quadrangle, mainly in a westerly direction, bringing the built-up parts of the College nearer to what is now College Green. By the end of the century* they had completed their new west front, a rather ungainly composition which was begun at the north end and only later continued south-wards and given a centre-piece. It was rather similar in style to the old Blue-Coat school already described, but larger, and it survived till about 1755, when the present west front was begun. Behind it were three small squares where Parliament Square is now. But since of all this seventeenth-century building nothing now remains except the old Library staircases, incorporated in Burgh's great Library of 1710 onwards, we need no longer dwell on it. Though it has been suggested that the present building called the 'Rubrics', together with 'Rotten Row' (demolished 1899), dates from before 1700, a slightly later date seems more probable.

From time to time during the later years of the seventeenth century efforts were made to found a Workhouse in Dublin. The subject was even mooted in the Corporation during the Jacobite interregnum in 1688, when it is rather ambiguously alluded to as 'intended to be built and begun neer the cittie'. It was finally the subject of an Act of Parliament in 1703,[3] in which year the Corporation acquired land in St James's Street, not far from the Royal Hospital. The young Duchess of Ormonde laid the foundation-stone of the great Hall in 1703,† and this is still standing, though modified externally by Francis Johnston in 1798, by the addition of wings, crenellated parapet and a typically Johnstonian cupola. The very handsome doorway was later destroyed by the building of an unpleasant little Protestant chapel, but the interior is still rewarding to the visitor who is not deterred by the melancholy institutional atmosphere. It is a lofty and airy hall, very similar to some of the Wren churches in London which have lost their galleries.‡

This Workhouse was in 1727 reconstituted as the Foundling Hospital (twelve years, it may be remarked, before the London Foundling Hospital was founded). Its history as a Foundling Hospital is one of unspeakable horror: those who have stomach to read

---

* On Dec. 3rd, 1698, for example, the Commons Journals record a vote of £3,000 for building, raised by a duty on tobacco.

† Date-stone on the building.

‡ Richard Mills, who was Assistant to the Masters of the City Works at the time, is a possible 'architect', but Robinson is perhaps more likely.

of such things may do so in W. D. Wodsworth's *Brief History*, published in 1876.

It is a relief to turn to a more colourful, not to say comic, feature of Dublin's history, the famous equestrian statue of King William in College Green, remembered by many who are still living, but regretted, it is safe to say, by few. It must be understood that King William, like a Roman Emperor, was virtually deified by Protestant Ireland even during his lifetime. When his birthday first came round after the Battle of the Boyne, Dublin celebrated it with all the splendour it could afford. There were fire-works in College Green, and a hogshead of claret was set out in the street for the people to drink the healths of William and Mary. There was an enormous banquet for the nobility and gentry in Clancarty House, which, being a Jacobite mansion, had been commandeered by the Lords Justices. Guns were fired, bells rung and bonfires lit. By great good fortune the Birthday, November 4th, was immediately followed by the anniversary of the Gunpowder Plot, which gave an excellent excuse for a repetition of the same festivities, with the difference that the hogshead was this time of strong beer, and an ox was roasted whole for the rabble to eat.

This annual ritual continued merrily for a decade, and the Anniversaries of the Boyne and Aughrim (July 1st and 12th) were marked with similar festivities. On July 1st, 1701, great pomp attended the unveiling of an equestrian statue made in London by no less an artist than Grinling Gibbons. It would be tedious to detail the circumstances: suffice it to say that 'the Recorder of the City made a florid speech suitable to the occasion ... expressing their unanimous loyalty and affection to his person and government; which being ended the great guns were fired'. This time 'several hogsheads of claret being ready placed on stilts, with two large baskets of cakes on each, the claret was set running, and the cakes thrown about among the crowds of people that were in the streets'.[4]

It is a most unfortunate thing that the only example of Gibbons's work in this country should have been of so controversial a nature. From the very beginning of its career it was subjected to repeated defacement and abuse, daubed with filth, tarred, robbed of its sceptre, even beheaded. These actions, when they were not the work of the submerged Jacobites and Catholics, were carried out

76

by undergraduates of Trinity College, who resented the fact that King William stood with his back to that seat of learning and faced the Castle instead. In 1710 two undergraduates were fined £100 each, sentenced to six months' imprisonment, and made to stand before the statue for half an hour with placards on their breasts setting forth that 'I stand here for defacing the statue of our glorious deliverer, the late King William'. In the middle part of the century there was a guard-house beside the statue, but this availed it little. After 1795 the formation of the Orange Society brought it renewed attentions, and in 1805, two years after Emmet's rebellion, an intrepid fellow managed to paint it black on the eve of King William's birthday, explaining to the co-operative watchman that he had been sent by the Corporation to do so, and asking the watchman to see that nobody stole his paints.[5]

In March 1836 no less than three attempts were made to blow it up. By this time it had suffered well-nigh every one of the many possible indignities to which public statues so easily lend themselves. Next month, however, it was successfully blown up. In spite of the opinion of William Cobbett that there would never be peace in Dublin till it had been demolished, the royal and equine fragments were collected and restored. The statue, originally of brass, was given a coat of bronze paint by Daniel O'Connell, when he was Lord Mayor in 1842, but even this conciliatory gesture did not preserve it from further outrage.

By this time, as may be imagined, the handiwork of the famous sculptor was something less than recognisable: indeed it was commonly reported that if the left leg of the horse were to be straightened it would prove to be eighteen inches longer than the right one. In these circumstances the final detonation of King William by explosives in 1929 is the less to be regretted. The scattered fragments were collected and preserved from the fury of the mob,* and the whereabouts of the head in particular remains a closely kept secret. The site remained empty till 1947, when it was reserved for an intended statue of Thomas Davis.

One of the few buildings which remain in Dublin from the reign of Queen Anne is the Tailors' Hall in Back Lane, a narrow alley leading from New Gate to Nicholas Street. A massive pedimented

---

* It was finally broken up for smelting in 1949, since this was written.

gateway is sandwiched between and under the houses. Over it, in place of a long-vanished bust, a hanging sign still proclaims the Tailors' Hall, though the Guild of Tailors has been extinct these hundred years. We enter a dark passage, and emerge into a small courtyard to face a red-brick building of faintly collegiate appearance, with a brick parapet and dormer windows, the four tall windows of the hall proper to our left (Pl. XVI).

There are some grounds for supposing that the present front door, which is not central, was originally a window and the entrance was by what is now the basement, where there is a central door.[6] Street levels in this, the oldest part of Dublin, have risen a great deal. The Hall, lit by round-headed windows, is on the present entrance floor. At its west end is a fine carved wooden screen—perhaps a remodelled reredos from an extinct church.* It may have been placed here in 1706, and is probably older. The chimney-piece is of veined white marble, 'The gift of Christopher Neary, master; Alexander Bell and Hugh Craigg, wardens, 1784'. Hugh Craig is found as Master of the Guild in 1792. At the east end, over the door, is a delicate semi-oval balcony, with wrought-iron railings and a dome-shaped sounding-board or hood, opening from an upper room. It is probably later than the chimney-piece.

The staircase, very similar to the now destroyed example at Molyneux House, must date from 1706. It has beautiful barley-sugar balusters, and is built in a projection at the back, extending from basement to attic. The attic rooms, in their clean plastered simplicity, are specially attractive. Richard Mills, the Assistant to the Masters of the City Works, was the overseer and presumably 'architect' of the building.[7]

During the eighteenth century the Hall was used not only by the Tailors, its owners, but also by the Barbers, the Sadlers, the Tanners, the Hosiers and the Curriers. In the early part of the century, as the largest public room in Dublin, it was in demand for assemblies and fashionable parties. In 1792 the general Catholic Committee met here, and was nick-named the 'Back-Lane Parliament'. Almost simultaneously it was the resort of the Grand Lodge of Dublin Freemasons, and of the United Irishmen until in 1794 their meetings were broken up by the Sheriff and his posse.

* As suggested by the Georgian Society's writers.

When the Tailors were threatened with dissolution by the Municipal Corporations Act of 1841, they prudently realised their movable chattels, including portraits of King Charles II, Dean Swift and St Homohon, a Tailor of Cremona, before the act was passed. The Hall became the 'Tailors' Endowed School' for Protestant boys. In 1873, after a narrow escape from being secured by a distiller as a warehouse, it was leased to a Protestant undenominational organisation who used it for temperance meetings, Sunday-schools, workmen's reading- and coffee-rooms.[8] This organisation vacated it in 1948, and its present future is uncertain.* Few buildings in Dublin have seen more varied activities, and few have suffered less alteration in the process.

The derelictions of modern Dublin have opened up a fine view of the rere of the building from Cornmarket. It would not be Dublin if the foreground were not composed of crumbling ruins, hoardings, concrete revetments and great baulks of timber, with ghostly chimney-breasts on the neighbouring gables, high in the open air.

* It has again found suitable tenants.

REFERENCES

[1] *CARD* V, 495, 499.
[2] Wheeler & Craig, *The Dublin City Churches*, 1948.
[3] 2 Anne 1.
[4] *CARD* VI, x.
[5] Gilbert III, 52.
[6] *Georg. Soc. Records* IV, 119, which is, however, mistaken about the date of the building. See next note.
[7] *JRSAI* XLVIII, 42.
[8] Information of Mr D. W. Kennan.

CHAPTER IX

Art and Industry

THE COMPARATIVE lack of incident in the opening years of the eighteenth century gives us leisure to remark the growing signs of intellectual improvement which had been evident since the Restoration.

A theatre, already mentioned, had been opened in Werburgh Street by John Ogilby, the Master of the Revels, as far back as 1637. It had even enjoyed the premières of a by no means contemptible dramatist, James Shirley. But, like the London theatres, it was closed by the Puritans in 1641. Twenty years later Ogilby returned from London and re-opened the theatre, but this time in the famous Smock-Alley,* behind the Blind Quay,† where the church of SS Michael and John now stands. The Smock-Alley Theatre survived till 1701 when, during a performance of Shadwell's *The Libertine*, the gallery collapsed and many of the audience were killed and wounded.‡ Suitable morals were drawn from this fatality by the preachers of the day. Mrs. Katharine Philips, the 'Matchless Orinda', was among the first to write for the Theatre, coming to Dublin for the purpose. The Irish dramatist George Farquhar, author of *The Beaux' Stratagem*, made his first bow as an actor on the Smock-Alley stage, which he left in consequence of having accidentally wounded a fellow-player by using a real sword instead of a blunted foil.§

The Theatre had its ups and downs. During the brief Vice-royalty of Lord Robarts it was closed, for Ormonde and civilisation were temporarily out of favour. Ormonde himself was a patron, and celebrated the marriage of the Princess Mary to William of Orange by attending the Theatre in state and inviting the company to a party at the Castle. It was again closed during the disturbances

---

* Formerly Orange Street and now Essex Street West.

† Now Lower Exchange Street.

‡ A similar disaster took place in 1671, on St Stephen's Day, when three people were killed. The play on this occasion was *Bartholomew Fair* (Gilbert II, 68).

§ Richard Head, author of *The English Rogue*, produced his comedy *The Humours of Dublin* in 1678.

of 1690–91, but in spite of the triumph of the puritanical William-
ites the Theatre was actively encouraged by the Government,
presumably to divert attention from politics.

During Ormonde's second Viceroyalty the Irish Players performed under his ægis as far afield as Oxford, where the Duke was
Chancellor.[1] But we are not to imagine that they represented anything like an 'Irish Dramatic Movement'. Smock-Alley, rebuilt
after the disaster, flourished almost till the end of the century—it
was rebuilt again in 1735*—with the usual quota of riots and com-
motions, the scene of the triumphs of Elrington, Tom Sheridan,
Peg Woffington, Macklin and Mossop; Thomas Doggett, who
later became joint manager of Drury Lane, and left a famous prize
to be rowed for by Thames Watermen, was born in Castle Street
and began his dramatic career in Dublin. The actual building
vanished in 1815; and Sir John Gilbert reports that the present
burial-vaults of the Church 'originally formed the pit of the Play-
House'.† Dublin is a city much given to strange transformations:
but this is surely among the strangest, paralleled only, perhaps, by
the present use of the former City Morgue as the foyer of the
famous Abbey Theatre.

John Ogilby, the founder of the Dublin theatre, divided his
energies between it and the art of printing, of which he was a
celebrated exponent. But it seems that his activities in Dublin were
restricted to the theatre, and that all his printing was done in London.

There existed already by this time a flourishing craft of printers
in Dublin. Printing had been carried on since the middle of the sixteenth century (1551 in English, 1571 in Irish), but little of the work
is of more than historic interest. The Restoration saw a great increase in quantity, but little improvement in the general quality
which was low, though an occasional pamphlet or book may show
an almost fortuitous beauty of arrangement. Merit or interest apart,
anything printed in Ireland before 1700 can be classed as 'rare'.

The first Dublin newspaper was *An Account of the chief Occurrences Of Ireland. Together with some Particulars from England* which

---

* In 1729 Burgh surveyed the fabric and pronounced it sound (Gilbert II, 73).

† A piece of brick walling to the south-west of the church is said to be part of the old
theatre.

was printed by William Bladen in 1659, at weekly intervals. It is not known how long a run it had, but it was probably short. Bladen had been King's Printer to Charles I, and subsequently official printer to Cromwell and Mayor of Dublin. Another newspaper, *Mercurius Hibernicus, or the Irish Intelligencer*, ran for a while in 1663, at the time of Colonel Blood's plot against the Castle. It made a special feature of the daily proceedings in the Court of Claims, and so many interests were involved that the paper must have had a ready sale. It was printed for Samuel Dancer in Castle Street, where a large number of printers and booksellers are found at this time, and for many years afterwards.[2] Among them was a representative of the Crooke family, King's printers during most of the rest of the century.[3] At the Restoration the House of Lords had ordered that the Bibles printed during Cromwell's time by Bladen should have their title pages torn out and new ones crediting them to Crooke substituted. One is reminded a little of the frugal ascription of Heine's poems to 'Anon' during the Third Reich.

The revival of political interest in 1685 coincides with the appearance of the next newspaper, *The Dublin News-Letter*, printed by Joseph Ray in College Green for Robert Thornton at the Leather Bottle in Skinner-row (now Christchurch Place).[4] But the first appearance of a regular newspaper in the modern sense was that of *Pue's Occurrences*, which began to be published twice weekly in 1703. The *Dublin Gazette* followed in 1706, and Faulkner's *Dublin Journal* in 1725. 'Pue' died in 1773, but the other two survived the century, and by 1763 three more were in existence: 'Sleater', 'Saunders', and the famous *Freeman's Journal* which survived into our own time.

The oldest surviving piece of Dublin hall-marked plate is a flagon in Trinity College of 1638, the year after the Dublin Guild of Gold and Silver Smiths was re-incorporated under a Royal Charter. But the Guild itself has been traced back to 1498, and the

---

FIG. 1. The 'Mediæval' map is largely ideal, showing only the city within the walls. The crosses indicate parish churches. The roads converge on 'Dublin Bridge'. The 1610 map is after Speed. 'T.C.D.' is Trinity College. The 1685 map is after the De Gomme–Phillips survey. 'R.H.K.' is the Royal Hospital, Kilmainham. Molesworth Fields is still shown as marshy undeveloped land. The 1728 map is after Brooking. Development has taken place to the south-west (industrial, in the Earl of Meath's Liberties) and to the north-east (residential, on the

FIG. I. THE GROWTH OF DUBLIN

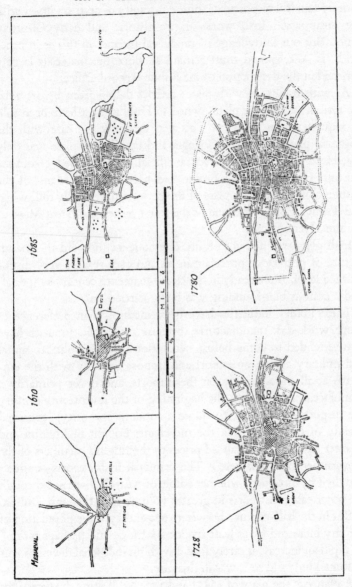

Drogheda-Gardiner estate). Reclamation of the estuary has begun. The 1780 map is after Pool and Cash. The city has now assumed its modern shape, with Quays and Circular Roads.

existence of goldsmiths in Dublin to the twelfth century.[5] It is not entirely fanciful to postulate some continuity of craft tradition with the unsurpassed Irish work of pre-historic and early Christian times. But our knowledge of mediæval Ireland, in this as in other fields, is sketchy and must remain so since the materials largely perished in the destruction of the Public Record Office.

As with books, so with plate; articles dating from before 1700 are rare. Much of the plate owned in Dublin must have been sold or sequestered in 1689-90. This was certainly the case with the domestic plate of Trinity College, and the Chapel plate was only saved by a well-disposed Revenue official, who returned it from the Custom House after the Boyne had been fought.[6] Many of the Dublin churches possess plate of the period immediately following, and Trinity College has one of the finest pieces, the Great Mace of Dublin silver of 1708.

Irish glass was not yet of any consequence, nor did the manufacture of pottery or porcelain in Ireland ever reach a very distinguished level. But already in the late seventeenth century so specialised a craft as bell-founding was being carried on.

These luxury industries have been mentioned in preference to more workaday manufactures, because in Dublin luxuries have always tended to come before necessities. It was a political capital and military centre, an export and import gateway with the emphasis at all times mainly on the imports, and never primarily a manufacturing town. At the beginning of the seventeenth century the imports of Dublin (to quote a modern authority) 'consisted mainly of luxuries which the merchants bought in London and Chester and sold at enhanced prices to the English members of the Government resident here'.[7] The principal Irish exports—animals and their by-products, whether edible or wearable—passed through the other east coast ports in greater volume than through Dublin.

But in the half-century between 1660 and 1710 the population of the city increased by at least five or six times, and perhaps more.* So rapid an increase is rarely found without industrial development of some kind; and so it was in this case.

A glance at the maps of 1685† and 1728‡ will show the directions

* From less than 15,000 to about 75,000.
† Thomas Phillips' map, based on that of de Gomme.
‡ Charles Brooking's map, 1728.

taken by this expansion. It is immediately apparent that, though the town has greatly increased, very little building has taken place to the north-west or the south-east. But to the north-east there is now a good deal of residential development,* the Moore (Drogheda) and Eccles Estates extending eastwards of the Jervis holding, as far as the family mansion of Sir John Eccles and the little Chapel of St George's† built by him for his tenants in 1714. There is also a certain amount of residential building on the south bank between Trinity College and the reclamation wall—Lazar's Hill, Hawkins Street, Moss Street, Prince's Street and George's Street, a district now made hideous with railway-lines and the resultant slums.

This north-eastern development is rectilinear, but diametrically opposite to it, on the south-west, lies the haphazard industrial suburb round Cork Street and the Coombe, lying mostly within the Earl of Meath's estate, the Liberties‡ of Thomas Court and Donore which the Meath family of Brabazon held exempt from the city jurisdiction.

Here, perhaps, we have the clue to the unique eastward tendency in Dublin. After the failure of Ormonde to take up residence in Oxmantown Green, rank and fashion lost interest in the north-western quarter, though a number of noblemen's houses remained there and the Earl of Bective, for example, had his house in Smith-field as late as 1787.[8] This quarter has remained largely unbuilt upon till the present day. Much of it was taken for a congeries of jails, lunatic-asylums, hospitals and the like in the early nineteenth century, and only within the last ten years has suburban building in this direction begun to catch up with developments elsewhere. The large weavers' colony to the south-west put a stop to fashionable interest in that quarter, though indeed the Earl of Meath himself continued to live in a fine house with gardens in the middle of his own estate till the middle of the eighteenth century, and the house and gardens are still there.§

* The population was now about 100,000.

† Of which the tower still stands in Hill Street.

‡ The smaller liberties of St Patrick's, Christchurch and St Sepulchre's were ecclesiastical and also exempt.

§ Said by J. A. Geoghegan (*DHR* VII, 2, 42) to be the house in Mill Street, New-market, which still exists, though altered in 1891. I cannot obtain reliable confirmation of this. The house is now a convent.

So the fashionable-residential could only spread east, and it has done so ever since: first both north-east and south-east, but since 1800 south-east only.

The linen and silk weavers who now became so prominent a section of the population were mostly immigrants. Since before the Revocation of the Edict of Nantes in 1685 there had been a considerable influx of French Huguenot craftsmen into Dublin, and after 1690 they were augmented by Dutch and Flemish Protestants.

FIG. 2a. Old House in Castle Street, taken down 1813.

FIG. 2b. Old House in Marrowbone Lane, 1703, long demolished.

These workers are credited—how justly I do not know—with the introduction of the type of house known in Dublin as a 'Dutch-Billy'. The distinctive feature is that the roof-ridge runs at right-angles to the street, though sometimes a cross-ridge is introduced giving four gables and extra space in the lofts. The front gables, in the most characteristic examples, are masked by quadrants sweeping up to very flat curved or triangular pediments.* These houses were built of brick, and designed to stand in continuous terraces. Very often economy was achieved by the use of corner fireplaces so that

* Thomas Moore's birthplace, for example, No 12 Aungier Street, was till about fifty years ago such a gable-fronted house, and very many other houses have been similarly re-fronted

86

two houses might share a single huge chimney-stack. The returns generally contained a small closet on each floor, and the roof-pitch was steeper than became usual later in the century.

A great many of these houses were built in The Coombe, Cork Street, Weaver Square, Sweeny's Lane, Crooked Staff, Tripilo, Newmarket, Poole Street, Marrowbone Lane and neighbouring streets. They have now nearly all vanished, though groups still

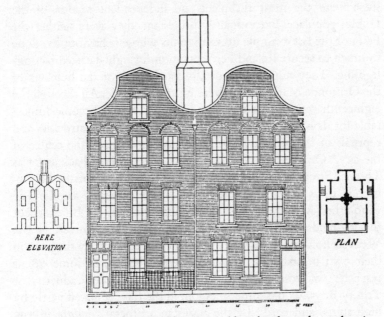

RERE ELEVATION

PLAN

FIG. 3. Pair of Houses in Longford Street, Dublin: the plan and rere elevation are generic and are not based on an accurate survey of these particular houses

remain in Chambré Street, Braithwaite Street, Marrowbone Lane, Hendrick Street★ (off Blackhall Place), Montpelier Hill, Digges Street and Longford Street. These are all in poor occupation now, but a few in Molesworth Street and at least one in Leeson Street† survive in better repair though considerably altered, and must date from the first quarter of the century.

The pair in Longford Street stand just opposite the site of Sir Edward Pearce's Theatre, and seem to have been built before 1728.

★ Three of the nine in Hendrick Street were demolished just as this was written.
† No 11.

They are the only unaltered* examples of curvilinear gables now surviving in Dublin. They were clearly designed as a pair, and the utmost economy of space has been used, the doors, though narrow, being right up against the party-walls. The relieving and flat arches are disposed in a most illogical but not unattractive arrangement. (Fig. 3.)

The 'Liberty-Boys' who lived and worked in houses such as these were the most turbulent and independent section of the Dublin populace. Extravagantly protestant, they were neither the first nor the last example of immigrants whose behaviour has done so much to secure Ireland her reputation for light-hearted faction-fighting. They nourished a deadly hatred against the butchers of the Ormonde Market, who were mostly Catholic. All through the eighteenth century the quays and bridges would become impassable for days on end, as fierce battles, attended with atrocities and reprisals of the utmost barbarity, raged throughout the centre of the city.[9] On one occasion the Liberty Boys, driven back as far as Thomas Street, managed to rally their forces and pursue the Ormonde Boys to the Broadstone, a distance of nearly a mile. The vanquished were treated with incredible ferocity: the Butchers cut the leg-tendons of the Weavers with their long knives, or the Weavers hoisted the Butchers and left them hanging by the jaws on their own meat-hooks. But they were, it seems, to some extent respecters of youth and rank. The College undergraduates, or Trinity Boys, would sometimes join in the fray, actuated partly by high spirits and partly by the augustan aristocrat's delight in low company. It was once rumoured through the town that the Trinity Boys had been captured by the Ormonde Boys and hung on the butchers' hooks. The authorities, who usually allowed these proletarian skirmishings to burn themselves out without interference, became alarmed; and a party of watchmen of sufficient strength was sent to see if this horrid report were true. Sure enough, there were a number of hapless youths in academic costume, slowly revolving like executed criminals, their college gowns fluttering pathetically in the breeze. On closer inspection, however, it was found that the Butchers, pitying their youth and respecting their rank, had only hung them by the waistbands of their breeches.

* The woodwork of the windows, and the doors, have been renewed.

Although a peace was signed between the rival factions, and published in the newspapers in June 1748,[10] it was not permanent, and these bloody outbreaks are reported at least as late as 1790. It is difficult to imagine that the charming and peaceful scene depicted by Tudor in his print of 1753 (Pl. VII), with the Old Custom House in the background, ships and barges moored before its arcades, the towers and spires of the churches on the skyline, Essex Bridge with George I riding in triumph, some ladies being rowed about the river in a canopied boat, another lady idly surveying them from the wall of Ormonde Quay while a coach-and-pair and a brewer's cart pass behind, and two sleepy fishermen ply their rods over the quay wall—it is difficult to imagine that this leisurely scene is not only the heart of a capital, but also the very arena of the bloodthirsty transactions we have just rehearsed.

The truth of the matter is that by the middle of the century the mercantile centre had begun to shift down river. The port of Dublin had always been unsatisfactory: tidal, rocky, very much inclined to silt up, and above all devoid of any unitary control. We have already seen that efforts for its improvement had engaged the attention of both government and city. In 1676 a private individual attempted to start a Ballast Office.[11] By 1688 the river was navigable only at spring tides, and the Corporation resolved to petition for powers to set up a Ballast Office, so that ships could be compelled to take their ballast from the channel of the river and preserve the banks.[12] But the unsettled times prevented this from coming to anything. Two years later a minor naval engagement was fought off the point of Ringsend, and this revived the old idea of a combined fortification and harbour improvement. In 1697 or 1700 one Captain Davison proposed the erection of a lighthouse enclosed in a fort near the Bar of Dublin, together with a Ballast Office.[13] As usual, there were conflicting interests, and nothing more was done till 1707. The city claimed Admiralty jurisdiction, but this was contested by Queen Anne's husband, Prince George of Denmark, who as Lord High Admiral of England claimed that this included Ireland also.

On September 17th, 1707, Thomas Burgh, already well known as an architect, read a paper[14] to the Dublin Society, 'Some Thoughts for improveing the Harbour of Dublin'. 'In the first place' he very pertinently observed, 'it is to be enquired what sort of bottom there is, whether it be sandy, woosey, or rocky . . .' He went on to suggest a weir and sluice within the Bar, so that the river could be kept at high level until low tide, when it could be released to scour out the channel. He also proposed a basin in which ships could lie secure from weather or hostile attack.

Two days after this, the Lord Mayor and Corporation, who had already conceded Prince George's claim without a fight, petitioned him for leave to erect a Ballast Office, offering to pay 'yearley to the Lord High Admirall for ever hereafter, for the said office, a hundred yards of the best Hollands duck sayle cloth as shall be manufactured within the realm of Ireland, which will be a lasting evidence of our holding the office under the admiralties tytle'.[15] This was granted, and by 6 Anne 20 the Irish Parliament passed 'An Act for Cleansing the Port, Harbour and River of Dublin, and for erecting a Ballast Office in the said City'.

From now on the Ballast Office was most industriously occupied in building what are now called the North and South Walls— notably the south wall which stretches for over four miles eastwards into Dublin Bay, unbroken save for the mouth of the little river Dodder. The north wall was much less ambitious and even now is little more than a mile and a half in length. By 1728 both walls were completed as far as Ringsend, a mile or so east of the old river-mouth. They were made by using small sailing-vessels called 'gabbards' to transport 'kishes' or baskets of stones, which were dumped along the line of the intended wall. Later, more regular piling and building consolidated the works. By the middle of the century the modern conformation was virtually complete, and the Poolbeg Lighthouse was begun in 1762.

At first, of course, the slob-lands behind the walls were still overflowed by the sea. But a programme of land reclamation went side by side with the wall-building. Ground behind the line of the south wall had, before 1713, been leased to John Mercer and to Sir John Rogerson, alderman, knight, barrister and ultimately Chief Justice of the King's Bench.* In the panorama attached to Brooking's Map of 1728 we can already see the houses on Sir John Rogerson's Quay (as it is still called), with water behind them at high

* Rogerson appears as early as 1686 (CARD V, 411).

tide. Some of them are still there: notably two public-houses whose names—The Old Post and The Eight Bells—attest the maritime associations. The Old Post must have been a stake set up as a land-mark in the channel. The grant to Jonathan Amory of 1675 exten-ded on the north bank eastwards to where the Custom House now is, and in 1682[16] the Strand north-east of this was surveyed and divided into 152 lots as had been done with the two Greens. This is now the north-west side of Amiens Street and North Strand, including the land on which Aldborough House stands. The list includes all the well-known civic names—Jervis, Deey, Stoyte, Swift, Brewster, Ram, Ransford, Allen, Wybrants, Desmynieres and William Robinson the architect. A few Irish names, such as Boland, Doran and Quine, are also found.

In 1717 the same thing was done with the slob-land behind the north wall. A huge area was surveyed and divided, but it was very long before many of the lots were dry land, and nearly half of it is still unreclaimed.[17] There is a story that in quite recent years the Corporation, having reclaimed some of this land, was success-fully sued by a descendant of one of the original grantees, whose patrimony had spent two hundred years and more at sea. The present East Wall Road represents one bank of the 'Canal' projected to conduct the River Tolka into the Bay, in return for its sinuous and more northerly course. The same thing was done with the Dodder later in the century, as a glance at the map will show. It was not until the nineteen-thirties that the other bank of the Tolka 'Canal' was partly built, and the little river diverted at last. In its new course it has completed the demolition of Clontarf Island, a piece of land form-erly belonging to the Vernons of Clontarf Castle, but carted away piecemeal by industrious sand-seekers during the nineteenth century.

In spite of the rapidity of reclamation, there were times when, even on the south side, the sea claimed back its own for a season. Thus, in January 1792, part of the south wall gave way and the hinterland was flooded. Ringsend was cut off from Dublin except by boat. 'His Grace the Duke of Leinster went on a sea party, and after shooting the breach in the south wall, sailed over the low ground in the south lots and landed safely at Merrion Square.'[18] None the less, all these works confirmed and strengthened the movement towards the east.

Another picturesque by-product of Dublin's commercial expansion may be noticed here. Late in the seventeenth century the 'Ouzel', a vessel owned in Dublin, left Ringsend for the Levant. She became overdue, and finally the underwriters who had insured her in Dublin, paid up in full. But in 1700, when she had long been regarded as a total loss, she suddenly appeared in Dublin Bay, with her own captain and crew still on board. It appeared that while navigating the Mediterranean she had fallen a victim to the pirate Algerine. But the captain and crew had managed to repossess themselves not only of the ship and the cargo, but also of piratical spoils of very considerable value, acquired by the Algerines while they were operating the ship.

The joy of mercantile circles in Dublin was soon turned to dissension. The underwriters and the owners (and no doubt the mariners as well) claimed incompatible shares in the greatly increased value of the cargo. The matter was taken to court, but agreement could not be reached. Finally the dispute was composed by a committee of Dublin merchants to whom it was referred for arbitration. To commemorate this happy result, the Ouzel Galley Society was founded in about 1705. Its objects were to promote the principle of arbitration in commercial disputes, and to encourage conviviality and good-fellowship among its members—or, to speak more strictly, its 'crew'. For the Galley was modelled very closely upon its eponymous Ouzel. It had a 'captain, two lieutenants, master, bursar, boatswain (who had a silver whistle), gunner, carpenter, master's mate, coxswain, boatswain's mate, and carpenter's mate', and it met in taverns. 'The Phœnix', Werburgh Street, 'The Ship', Chapelizod, 'The Rose and Bottle', Dame Street, 'The Eagle', Eustace Street, are among the venues mentioned. The bowl of Irish glass from which new members of the crew and newly-elected officers were required to drain a bumper of claret at a single draught, is still preserved. The Ouzel Galley, during its long life which ended in 1888, settled a great many cases, involving very large interests, and the costs which would in other circumstances have gone to rapacious attorneys, were distributed in charity. When the Commercial Buildings in Dame Street were built in 1796, the serious business of the Galley was contracted there; and visitors may still see over the south door of the courtyard the

Ouzel Galley carved in Portland stone, presiding over the scene where, during the nineteenth century, the annual November gathering of Galleymen was held in the little square.[19]

REFERENCES

[1] La Tourette Stockwell, *Dublin Theatres and Theatre Customs*. Kingsport, Tennessee. 1938.

[2] The only known copies of either of these papers are in Worcester College, Oxford. See Dix in *Procs. of RIA*, 3rd ser. VI, No 1.

[3] See Dix in *Bibl. Soc. of I. Pubs.* II, No 1, pp. 16 *sqq.*

[4] Gilbert, I, 178, calls it mistakenly the first newspaper published in Dublin.

[5] M.S.D. Westropp, *Nat. Mus. Gen. Guide: Metal work: Gold and Silver*, 1934, p. 9.

[6] C. Maxwell, *History of Trinity College*, 1946, p. 82. J. P. Mahaffy: *The Plate in Trinity College*, 1918.

[7] Ada K. Longfield, *Anglo-Irish Trade in the XVIth Century*, 1929, p. 37.

[8] Rotunda Hospital, *List of Sedan-Chair Licensees &c*, 1787.

[9] Walsh, *Ireland Sixty Years Ago*. ed. of 1911. p. 9. J. D. Herbert, *Irish Varieties*, 1836, pp. 83 *sqq.*

[10] *Faulkner's Dublin Journal* June 7–11, 1748.

[11] Falkiner, *Illustrations*, p. 187.

[12] *CARD* V, 480.

[13] *ibid.* VI, 609 *sqq.* See also, for 1698, *ibid.* 205–6.

[14] Printed in *CARD* VI, 613 *sqq.*

[15] *ibid.* 374–5.

[16] A similar scheme, though abortive, had been started in 1664 (MacLysaght, *op. cit.*).

[17] Map reproduced in *CARD* VII. See also V, 331 *sqq.*

[18] *Dublin Chronicle*. Jan. 28, 1792.

[19] Falkiner, *Illustrations*, 203 *sqq.* DHR III, 2. J. M. Hone in *The Bank of Ireland* 1949, p. 478.

CHAPTER X

Burgh and the Gardiners

OLONEL THOMAS BURGH (pronounced 'Birr') is the first architectural name of the eighteenth century, and the first indisputably and unmistakably Irish architect. The family of de Burgo was strongly represented among the Anglo-Norman invaders in the twelfth century. They are now found as de Burgh, Burgh, Bourke and Burke, and the Earls of Clanricarde were the most famous branch of the family. Thomas Burgh was born in 1670, the third son of Ulysses Burgh, Bishop of Ardagh, and himself became a landowner at Oldtown, near Naas in Co. Kildare, within a mile or two of the large but uncompleted palace built by Strafford in 1637.

Thomas Burgh served in the Williamite wars; and in 1700, on Robinson's retirement, succeeded him as Surveyor-General. His first known building is the Royal Barracks (now Collins Barracks), built in 1701-4 on the west of Oxmantown Green. In its early form it was capable of holding four regiments of foot and four of horse; and it has since been greatly enlarged and altered. His next important building has not survived. This was the Custom House (Pl. VII), on Essex Quay, just below Essex Bridge. It was built in 1707, on an arcade, with a grand eaves-cornice and a double-sloped hipped roof with dormers. It was about 200 feet long, and three principal storeys in height. About 1773 the upper part became unsound;[1] and this coincided with the scheme to build a new Custom House further down the river. But it remained in use till the new building was opened in 1791. It then became—sad index of the state of the times—a barrack; and as such acquired a bad reputation in 1798, when the Dumbarton Fencibles were stationed in it. This fact, perhaps as much as the importance of the position, probably influenced Robert Emmet in forming a plan to blow it up or at least seize it in 1803. The old Custom House vanished during the nineteenth century, and its site is now occupied by Dollard's printing house and the Clarence Hotel.[2]

94

Burgh's next large building was the great Library of Trinity College (Pls. XII, XIV), begun in 1712 and opened in 1732, two years after the architect's death. Here also there were three principal storeys, of which the ground floor was originally an open arcade, but with a central wall to help support the superincumbent weight. With its overall length of 270 feet, it must be one of the largest single-chamber libraries in existence.* As in the Custom House, the façade is astylar, being divided simply into twenty-seven bays, five for the centre—broken out but given no other emphasis, and three each for the wings. As originally erected the roof was hidden by the parapet. Since this treatment is unknown in the rest of Burgh's work, it may be the work of another hand after his death. The present double-sloped roof was put on in 1856–62, and the ground-floor loggia enclosed in 1892, to the great loss of college amenities.[3]

Entering the Library to-day, the visitor ascends Cassels's leisurely and ample staircase of 1750, with rococo plaster by Edward Simple. He then finds himself at one end of the Long Room. The visible work of Burgh extends only to the gallery balustrade,† for the semicircular wooden barrel-vault above was a mid-nineteenth-century alteration, replacing a flat plaster ceiling and, by throwing two floors into one, losing a great deal of valuable space. But there is undeniably a certain gain in power and mystery. In spite of a superficial resemblance to Trinity, Cambridge, or Queen's, Oxford, there is little real affinity. Temperament and economic conditions have combined to give the Dublin library the puritanical severity‡ characteristic of Irish architecture.

The unused and open ground storey served the same purpose here as in Wren's library at Cambridge: to insulate the books from the marshy ground. But in all other respects the two buildings are sharply in contrast. Where Wren inflected his façade and gave both centre and wings of his much smaller block a monumental treatment, Burgh went to work in a spirit more akin to that of a designer of a spinning-mill in Belfast. The Library proclaims itself

---

* The staircase and the Fagel Library occupy the west and east ends respectively. The Long Room itself is about 200 feet. The Reading Room of the new Cambridge Library is within a few feet of the same length. The Bibliothèque St Geneviève in Paris (1850) is a little shorter and wider.

† The end walls are also original.

‡ The main entablature, however, is carved with a surprising and little-noticed richness.

a power-house or warehouse of learning. The Dublin granite
glows with no such tints of rose or lemon as one sees reflected in the
waters of the Cam. Only when, on a winter's day, seen from the
top of a tram in Dawson Street across the Fellows' Garden, every
pane of the old crown glass suddenly flashes with orange fire—only
at such moments does this huge building seem to relax its customary
expression of measured reticence. The total cost was about £20,000.

Burgh built the Infirmary buildings of the Royal Hospital in
1711, and St Werburgh's Church in 1715. Both still survive, but one
is of little interest and the other, as we have it now, is largely a
rebuilding of forty years later. His last undoubted work was Dr
Steevens's Hospital (Fig. 11), for which he furnished the plans early in
1719.[4] Dr Richard Steevens was the son of an English immigrant of
the Commonwealth period, who had studied at Leyden and Dublin
Universities, beginning practice in Dublin in 1687. He was a
Fellow and twice President of the College of Physicians, and shortly
after his appointment as Regius Professor of Physics in the University, he died in 1710 at the age of fifty-six, leaving a very considerable estate.

He also left a sister, Grizel, or 'Madam Steevens' as she was always
called. Dr Steevens left his property in trust for her, and after her
death (since she had told him she would never marry) for the
foundation of a general hospital in Dublin. This is the oldest hospital (in the modern sense of the term) in Ireland, and, apart from
three in London (all of mediæval foundation) and one in Bath, the
oldest in the three kingdoms.

Madam Steevens wanted to found the proposed hospital during
her own lifetime, and in 1713 the trustees sent to Queen Anne a
petition and a plan by Burgh. This first scheme miscarried; but
four years later a committee of fourteen of her own appointment,
including Sir William Fownes, Marmaduke Coghill of Drumcondra, Thomas Molyneux, Richard Helsham, Archbishop King
and Burgh himself, had acquired a site near that of the Royal
Hospital. The Trustees, acting sometimes through Burgh, purchased the building materials themselves, and some of the tenders
are still extant. One can hardly leave the list of trustees without
recording that in 1721 Jonathan Swift was added to their number.
The completion occupied over twelve years, and Burgh was

dead before it was opened in 1733. The superintendence had been handed over to his successor as Surveyor, Edward Lovett Pearce. Madam Steevens herself lived in the hospital, in the rooms on the left of the gate. It was widely believed in Dublin that her mother had scolded a beggar-woman and that as a result of the beggar's curse, Madam Steevens had the face of a pig. This presumption was reinforced by the fact that she wore a veil when going about the city on her charitable errands; and it was quite unshaken by her sitting continually at an open window to show the passers-by that she had no snout. She died in 1747 in her ninety-third year.

As a building, Steevens's may be called the last kick of the seventeenth century. If Burgh's authorship were not attested beyond any possible doubt, we should have no hesitation in calling it the work of a sensitive carpenter or mason inspired by the neighbouring Royal Hospital. It reproduces on a smaller scale (about 115 by 95 feet) the courtyard-and-piazza plan of Robinson's building.* All the detail is cruder and less sophisticated, making its effect more by 'quaintness' than by strictly architectural means. Though the general disposition of the east front is accomplished enough, the main doorway with its elliptical arch and segmental pediment cutting through a first-floor window is saved only by the charm of a slight awkwardness and by the delightful wrought-iron which abounds here and elsewhere in the Hospital. The very agreeable little clock-tower with its conoidal hat was not added till 1735-6, and may not be Burgh's work. He was certainly not responsible for the semi-mansard roofs of all but the east range, nor for the squinch arches which cross the angles of the internal court and add still more quaintness to the final effect.† It is a great pity that Steevens' Lane is too narrow to show the Hospital to advantage, and a still greater pity that the ugly red-brick Nurses' Home was inserted in the late nineteenth century between it and Kingsbridge Station, entirely destroying the scale of the ensemble.

The original chapel, placed by Burgh in the south-east corner, was not completed till 1761 and in 1909 was obliterated in favour of a modern chapel on a different site. The chief treasure of the Hospital is the Library, bequeathed by Edward Worth, a trustee

* The walling, as in the Royal Hospital, is calp rubble faced with stucco.
† These are nineteenth-century work.

97

and governor who died in 1733 leaving some four-thousand-odd
volumes, twenty-one of which are incunabula. These remain in the
original Board-room with contemporary fittings. This interior was
probably carried out by Pearce.

The remainder of what is known about Burgh can be briefly
told. He advised the city authorities about the construction of the
new 'Bason' or reservoir, and about the pedestal for King George I's
statue on Essex Bridge.* and, because he had been 'very serviceable
with his advice and attendance, and in regard there may be further
occasion for his advice', a deputation waited upon him to thank him
and to enquire what sort of a piece of plate he would like made, up
to the value of fifty pounds. In the following year, 1724, he published a work on *Right-lined Figures*, a treatise on surveying.†
Soon afterwards his name is coupled with that of Luke Gardiner as
a trustee of the Barracks Chapel,[5] and he is again consulted about
the improvement of the harbour. His last recorded professional
action is to pronounce the fabric of Smock-Alley Theatre quite
safe in 1729. He died on December 18th, 1730.

His status as a designer must remain indeterminate, if only because it is hard to see the same hand at work in the Library and Dr
Steevens'. It is harder still to imagine him the architect of Speaker
Conolly's great house of Castletown, as has been conjectured.
Even between the Library and Castletown the only common
denominators are a preference for immense masses with uniform
and frequent fenestration, and a similar employment of string-
courses. Castletown is the most tantalising problem of attribution
in this period: a work of genius going begging. The mention of
Burgh is prompted mainly by the fact that he was apparently the
only architect of established reputation available at the time and by
the dedication of his book to Conolly. But in spite of certain
difficulties it seems safer to consider Castletown in association with
the work of a greater architect, Captain Pearce.

Of Burgh's private character we know less still. But a Government architect who gave time and attention to the city's concerns,
earning their gratitude and evidently also their affection, must have
had qualities of tact and generosity. We may add moderation and

---

* For which Bishop Berkeley wrote the inscription.
† It is dedicated to Speaker Conolly of Castletown.

common sense: for the city fathers were all set to have King George's pedestal made of polished Italian marbles, black, white and veined, when Captain Burgh came along and persuaded them that Carrickmacross or Portland stone would do excellently well.[6] To moderation we may finally add modesty: for when, as Surveyor-General, he was asked by Parliament to prepare plans for a new Parliament House, he passed the splendid opportunity on to a man only half his age, Edward Lovett Pearce. We have, in the result, a building far beyond what I believe to have been Burgh's powers, and one of the chief glories of Dublin.

There was a growing tendency for the nobility and gentry to spend more time in Dublin than they had in the seventeenth century. The young Duke of Ormonde (grandson of the great Duke) was Viceroy in 1703–7 and 1710–13. Of the other Viceroys from 1700 to 1731, only the Duke of Bolton (1717–21), his successor the Duke of Grafton and Lionel Sackville, Duke of Dorset, who came in 1731,* remain commemorated in street-names. Bolton Street and Dorset Street are names given to parts of the old country road from the north which now became urban, while Sackville Street and Grafton Street are, or were, the two most famous streets in Dublin, known by name to those who know nothing else. Of the nobility who seem to have lived more or less in Dublin during the period, we may mention the Earls of Meath, Fingall, Lanesborough, Anglesey, Ranelagh, Massereene and Blessington, and the Viscounts Molesworth, Allen, Fitzwilliam, Charlemont and Mount Alexander. No doubt there were many others. Parliament sat in twelve of the first twenty-five years of the century, much more frequently than before. Both the Protestant Primate and Archbishop of Dublin lived largely in the capital. The old Palace of St Sepulchre in Kevin Street was still the official residence of the latter. The country, during the frequent absence of the Viceroy, was ruled by the Lords Justices, of whom the Primate and the Lord Chancellor, both very often Englishmen, were the most constantly appointed.†

* Sackville Street is called after Sackville Gardiner, who in turn was called after Dorset. The latter was again Viceroy in 1751. See *Georg. Soc.* III, 76.7.

† Prior's *List of Absentees* of 1729 lists five noblemen, two noblewomen, thirty-nine gentlemen and four ladies of fortune, who were only occasionally absent from Ireland in that year. Of those who 'visit Ireland, now and then, for a month or two', he listed fourteen peers, two peeresses and twenty-six gentlemen. But he does not list those who, like the Earl of Kildare, Mr Conolly and others, are constantly resident, as he himself admits.

These Englishmen varied very greatly in their attitude towards Irish affairs. Thus Sir Constantine Phipps, Lord Chancellor in the reign of Queen Anne, who had defended Dr Sacheverell in London, persecuted nuns in Dublin and Galway but incurred the anger of the Irish House of Commons for not prosecuting a Dublin Jacobite bookseller with sufficient enthusiasm. His successor, Lord Midleton, was an Irishman in the sense that his family had been in the country for a century or so; he was also a Whig and a Williamite. But he supported the English House of Lords against the Irish House in a quarrel of 1718. On the other hand it was he who suggested the inclusion, in an Act for preventing the growth of Popery, of that notorious proposal to castrate Irish Catholic priests, with the result that the humane English Privy Council suppressed the entire Act. As for the bishops and archbishops, it is only necessary to remember Swift's complaint that the English Government always sent us holy and godly men, but by an unfortunate chance they were always waylaid and murdered by bandits on the road to Chester, who took their clothes and letters of appointment and so arrived in Ireland. There is little to command our respect or interest in the public life of the time, till the writings of Swift, Berkeley, Prior and Madden brought practical politics again to life.

Increased security and the revival of economic life brought a new type upon the scene, the self-made financiers and speculators. Time has invested the better-known of them with such an aura of the antique that it is hard to remember how they must have appeared to the more established gentry and nobility of their epoch. Yet William Conolly and Luke Gardiner both seem to have risen to wealth and influence from the humblest beginnings and in a very short time.

Though the Conollys, unlike the Gardiners, have had little to do with urban developments in Dublin, they are too important, too symptomatic of the period and much too interesting to be left out. William Conolly was born in the 1660's, in humble circumstances, probably in Ballyshannon, Co. Donegal. He must have been of native Irish stock, but he was also a Protestant. He was therefore of course a Williamite, and sat in the Parliament of 1692. There is a story that when very young he acted as agent to two maiden ladies who left him their property. He certainly bought a great deal of land from the Trustees of Forfeited Estates after the Boyne. At his death he owned land in ten counties, but practically none of it was urban. He acted in legal matters for the second Duke of Ormonde, and became Chief Commissioner of the Irish Revenue—the post afterwards held by John Beresford. In 1715 he was unanimously elected Speaker; and so remained, being re-elected two years before his death in 1729. And, final triumph of his career, he was a Lord Justice in 1716 and on nine subsequent occasions.

The annual income of this remarkable man was estimated by a trustworthy contemporary[7] at £12,000 or £13,000, which must be multiplied by three or four at least to give its modern value. His political duties made it necessary for him to live in or near Dublin; but, though he had a house in Capel Street where he died, we hear nothing else about it, and a man so fond of building as the Speaker would not have neglected his town house if he had been interested in town houses. On the other hand he began in about 1720 to build, on the lands of Castletown, about twelve miles west of Dublin, a house which is not only the largest but also the most beautiful of the great houses of Ireland. He also bought Rathfarnham Castle, an Elizabethan house, from the Duke of Wharton for £62,000 in 1723. This was much nearer Dublin, though still a country house. There is no evidence that the Speaker used it much, but he probably built the so-called 'Hell-Fire' Club, an exceedingly solid building of stone on the top of Montpelier Hill. It was probably a hunting-lodge; but though its monumental vaulting has withstood time and tampering, all its cut stone has long since disappeared. As for the Hell-Fire Club itself, there is no good evidence that the Speaker ever belonged to it or that it ever met there. It is said to have met mainly in taverns in Dame Street, and to have included such elegant rake-hells as Richard Parsons, first Earl of Rosse, who died jesting in 1741.

Even less is known of the origins of the Gardiners, who appear on the scene only a little later than the Conollys. They had a larger influence on the development of Dublin than any other family (with the possible exception of the Fitzwilliams), and after a succession of worthy and able Gardiners during the eighteenth century they finally flared into fantastic splendour in the persons of the last Earl of Blessington and his wife Marguerite. But if only the end of the story counted, Dublin would have little to thank them for. The earlier Gardiners, though less famous, are perhaps more remarkable.

Luke Gardiner, the founder of the family, was a banker in Castle Street, in partnership with a nobleman's younger son.[8] He married well, a girl related to the Viscounts Mountjoy and Blessington (Stewart and Boyle respectively). At first he seems to have bought land on the south side, behind Sir John Rogerson's Quay, in 1712.[9] But he soon turned his attention to the other bank of the river. His first large purchase seems to have been that of the Moore (Drogheda) holding in 1714. This was part of the lands of Mary's Abbey, and HENRY Street, MOORE Street, EARL Street, OF (later OFF) Lane and DROGHEDA (now O'Connell) Street, attest the rather childish mark which the Moores left behind them. In 1721 he bought more of the Mary's Abbey lands from the Reynell family, as well as encroaching on the eastern tip of the Jervis and Amory holdings.[10] By the time they were sold up in the Incumbered Estates Court in the mid-nineteenth century to pay the debts of Count d'Orsay, the Gardiners owned a very large proportion of North Dublin east of Capel Street, and most of this had been acquired in large unde-veloped chunks, which the earlier Gardiners laid out on a truly magnificent scale. Luke Gardiner the First was Ranger of the Castleknock Walk in the Phœnix Park, and built as a private house what is now Mountjoy Barracks, the headquarters of the Ordnance Survey. He retired profitably from the banking business in 1738, was made a Privy Councillor and Deputy Vice-Treasurer of Ireland, in which capacity he earned the admiration of Primate Boulter, who was never very ready to countenance the advancement of Irishmen in official positions. Mrs Delany speaks of him, a few years after his death in 1755, as 'the famous Luke Gardiner'.

The earliest of his important streets is Henrietta Street, which still contains the oldest and grandest houses on the North Side, though some now fallen, how changed! It was probably called after Henrietta, Duchess of Grafton, and is thus referable to the early seventeen-twenties. It was a broad street, perhaps the broadest yet laid out in Dublin, leading westward from Bolton Street on rising ground towards the Plover Field. The three earliest houses, one of which, being that of the Archbishop of Armagh, gave the street its sobriquet of 'Primate's Hill', disappeared when the King's Inns Library was built in 1827. But Nos 8, 9 and 10 (which was Mountjoy House) are preserved by convent ownership, while No 11 is still in good private occupation. Nos 9 and 10 were built in about 1730 by Richard Cassels, the German architect who enjoyed a large practice in Ireland from 1729 till his death in 1751. No 10, Luke Gardiner's own house, has suffered a good deal of internal and external remodelling, mainly in the mid-nineteenth century, but still shows some fine period decoration, while No 9 has one of the finest staircase halls in Dublin. The street elevation of No 9, five bays wide with a rusticated stone ground-storey, the rest of the façade in warm red brick with a central round-headed window with a balustrade on the first floor, and dormers in the roof, is more attractively individualistic than is usual in Dublin, and shows what this not very inspiring architect could do when he was not being too coldly and monumentally grand.

None of these early houses are so immense as Nos 3, 4 and 5* down the street, lived in later by the Earls of Kingston and Thomond and the Rt. Hon. John Ponsonby. But in the early twentieth century many of them fell into the hands of Alderman Meade, who ripped out the grand staircases and made tenement rooms in their place, and sold the chimney-pieces in London. To walk up Henrietta Street today is a striking and saddening experience. Though it contains only some sixteen houses, they are of so palatial a cast that one easily understands how it remained the most fashionable single street in Dublin till the Union, long after many rival centres of social attraction had been created.†

Near Henrietta Street there lay, almost surrounded by Gardiner property, the lands of the Dominick family, bought by Christopher Dominick before 1692 and left to his son also Christopher Dominick who died in 1743.[11] The most noteworthy street of this estate, Dominick Street itself, was not developed till after 1756, when the Dominick heiress had married Lord St George.

By the time the first Luke Gardiner was succeeded by his son Charles in 1755, he had still further indulged his love of wide

---

* No 5 is now divided into Nos 5 & 6.

† In 1792 the Directory gives one Archbishop, two Bishops, four peers and four M.P.'s (one a peer's eldest son) as living in Henrietta Street.

streets. We may probably ascribe to him the great width of parts of Dorset Street,* an old country road still flanked here and there by huge houses of *c.* 1745 vintage. Though the Gardiners owned some of Great Britain (now Parnell) Street, which had similar origins, they never succeeded in widening it. But Luke Gardiner's greatest achievement was the creation of the Mall which became known as Sackville† Street, and which set the scale for what is now regarded as central Dublin. In the late seventeen-forties he pulled down all the houses in Drogheda Street, and, widening it on the west side till it was 150 feet from house to house, re-let the street in building leases. To examine these houses would carry us beyond the middle of the century; and in any case war and commerce have between them destroyed all but two or three of them;‡ most of the street has now been rebuilt in the neon-classic style.

Down the middle of the street ran a tree-planted walk forty-eight feet wide, called Gardiner's Mall. The great width of the street was not designed, as the casual sightseer today might think, to facilitate the accommodation of six lines of traffic: quite the reverse. In fact Sackville Street, like Portland Place in London which was built twenty years later, was intended as a sort of elongated residential square.§ But, just as Portland Place found itself flooded with traffic when Nash built his Regent Street in the years following 1811, so Sackville Street was vulgarised, first by the creation of Lower Sackville Street in 1784 onwards,‖ and then in 1790 by the building of Carlisle Bridge which carried the line across the river. The process was still further intensified when Westmoreland and d'Olier Streets were made about the time of the Union; and all but completed when the bridge was widened in 1880. But the final transformation was not effected till the fires of Easter 1916 and June 1922 laid three-quarters of the great street in ruins. When it rose again, resplendent with cinemas and ice-cream parlours, it might seem to have moved far from Luke Gardiner's ideas. But at least it

---

* Though the Wide Streets Commissioners had a hand in its widening, somewhat later.

† Strictly, the centre of it was Gardiner's Mall, and the street itself Sackville Street. (Now O'Connell Street.)

‡ In Easter 1916 both sides of Lower O'Connell Street were destroyed: in 1922 the east side of Upper O'Connell Street. The west side had already been largely rebuilt. No 49, a good house, is among the survivors.

§ Not unlike Torrington Square, Bloomsbury.

‖ By the Wide Streets Commissioners.

paid him the compliment of confirming the eastward drive which he had done so much to foster; and the Gardiners, who were always devotees of the drama, would perhaps not have resented the transformation as much as we think.*

* In 1831 G. N. Wright wrote: 'The proprietory is certainly very much changed, but the picture has rather gained in interest by the transition; the solemn silence which generally reigns amid the palaces of the great, has been succeeded by the animation that accompanies a busy commercial scene'.

REFERENCES

[1] Gilbert II, 140.

[2] Mr H. G. Leask tells me that the base of the arcade was found during the excavation for the latter building.

[3] See E. H. Alton, Provost, in *Bulletin of the Friends of the Library of T.C.D.*, 1948.

[4] T. P. C. Kirkpatrick, *History of Dr Steevens' Hospital*, 1920.

[5] *CARD* VII, 285.

[6] *ibid.* 187, 215.

[7] Bishop Nicholson, quoted in. *Georg Soc.* V. 47.

[8] *Georg. Soc.* III, 75.

[9] *CARD* VI, 484. Luke Street, off Townsend Street, perpetuates his memory.

[10] Blessington Rentals of 1846 and 1848 sales from Quit Rent Office, now in P.R.O. Dublin.

[11] McCready, *Dublin Street Names*.

CHAPTER XI

The Tide Flows East

IN ANTICIPATING the end-results of Luke Gardiner's activities we have lost sight of similar developments elsewhere. Though none were so spectacular as Gardiner's all contributed their part.

The largest landlord in Dublin was the city itself. This somewhat unusual circumstance held great possibilities, but after the signal instance of the Stephen's Green scheme, they were little exploited in practice. On the other hand, many of the most important 'landowners', as Trinity College,* the Gardiners and the Fitzwilliams, were in fact tenants of the city.[1] There was no coherent 'Crown Estate' except the Phœnix Park, and the only large fee-simple holding on the London model was the Meath Estate which, as we have already seen, was allowed to develop along industrial lines.

The most conspicuous private enterprise on the South Side during this period was the laying out of 'Molesworth-Fields', a square of land lying between the city lands of 'Tib and Tom' (on the west) and Fitzwilliam of Meryon's land (now Merrion Square) on the east. In 1685 the fields are marked as a marshy patch without even a lane crossing them; since they now contain the part of Dublin most familiar to the moneyed visitor, their evolution is worth examining in some detail. The area is bounded by Grafton Street, Nassau Street, Stephen's Green North and Merrion Street Upper. The eastern part of it belonged to Viscount Molesworth of Swords, the son of a Fishamble Street merchant who had made money in the land market. The Viscount wrote a book on Denmark which was famous in its day, and took some part in European politics. A narrower strip to the west was taken by Joshua Dawson† from Henry Temple in 1705, and includes Dawson Street, one side of

---

* Who sold most of their Fleet Street Estate to the Wide Streets Commissioners before 1799.

† Dawson was Secretary to the Lords Justices.

Grafton Street, Duke Street and Anne Street. The Grafton Street leases begin in 1713, some in Dawson Street as early as 1709, and in Anne Street 1718.[2] Grafton Street, a narrow and miserable thoroughfare which is still palpably a country lane, has lost any distinction it ever had by Victorian rebuilding. Even in 1792 it had almost ceased to be residential, boasting a mere nine Members of Parliament and not a single Peer.* The houses in Dawson Street, origin-

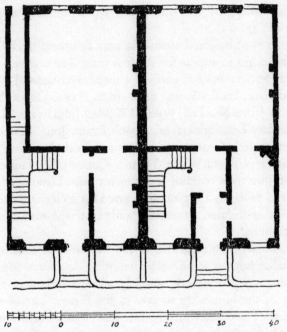

FIG. 4. Sketch-plan of Nos. 20 and 21 Molesworth Street, c. 1730-40.

ally a sort of South Side Henrietta Street, are mostly mid-to-late Georgian, and nearly all have been turned into shops, many being rebuilt in the process. Burgh lived at No 37, now rebuilt.

The Molesworth development was a little later, dating from a private enabling Act of 1725. This time St Ann's Church had been built on ground given by Joshua Dawson, and the Molesworth and Dawson interests seem to have worked harmoniously together, for Molesworth managed to persuade Dawson to pull down four

* Except Lord Donoughmore who lived in the Provost's House.

houses near the church so that Molesworth and Dawson Streets could be linked together.[3] The Molesworth Street houses are the oldest still remaining in this part of Dublin: some of them are of the gabled type described in Chapter IX, though as upper-class residential they have fine spacious timber staircases and wainscoting. No 20, built by Ralph Spring* in about 1730, has one of the most beautiful doorways in Dublin, a severe but not over-correct performance in mountain-granite, doric with triple keystone and a segmental pediment. Many of the others are worth internal inspection, notably No 33.

The names of builder-lessors—we may call them 'architects'† if we wish—begin to appear for the first time. The researches of the Georgian Society have unearthed a number connected with this time and place: besides Spring there are, in Dawson Street William MacGuire, James Mitchell, William Wilde,‡ John Evans, Nathaniel Shaw, Henry Lee, 'bricklayer', Ralph Evans 'Jun.', Ralph Evans 'Sen. bricklayer', George Spike 'Painter Stainer'; and in Molesworth Street William Wilde, Thomas Quin and Benjamin Rudd. Some of these took building leases direct from Dawson of Molesworth, and probably the same men acted for such exalted lessees as the Bishop of Killaloe, to mention only one who took a building lease for himself.

South Frederick Street, also in the Molesworth holding, contains smaller houses, some with interesting doorways and one or two with early plasterwork, possibly added a little later than the building of the houses themselves in the forties. East of this ran 'Coote Lane', so called from the first Lord Molesworth's marriage to one of 'the great and eminently successful stock of the Irish Cootes', military adventurers from Tyrone's wars onwards and premier baronets of Ireland. They deserve a word to themselves. Earls of Mountrath, Barons of Coolooney and Earls of Bellamont, they built Bellamont Forest in the town of Cootehill, which ultimately passed to one member of one of the four illegitimate

* Nos 15 and 16 have the 'weaver' plan, Nos 20, 21 &c have central entrances and staircase halls on left in front, large nearly square rooms at rere. George Spring built houses round the corner in Kildare Street.

† The word 'architector' appears as description of Thomas Lucas, admitted to city franchise as early as 1632. (CARD III, 268).

‡ Ralph Wilde, an immigrant builder from England at about this time, is said to have been the ancestor of Sir William and Oscar (T. G. Wilson, Victorian Doctor).

families of the last Earl of Bellamont. This Earl, failing to secure
the entail of his peerage on another illegitimate son, was consoled
with an English Baronetcy so entailed; but as he omitted to provide
the baronet with enough money, the last holder of the honour died
in poverty in Dublin in 1897, and so ended that branch of the Irish
Cootes. The lane called after them had a more glorious history as
Kildare Street, bought by the Fitzgeralds* in 1744, widened and
renamed. Until 1948 the vista down Molesworth Street led the eye
to the statue of Queen Victoria, not in itself a thing of great beauty
but lent a certain charm by distance. There she sat, festooned by
seagulls and dripping verdigris on to her white limestone outworks,
curiously benevolent in her ugliness, softening the grim impact of
the centrepiece of Leinster House. Her tints of green and bronze
blended agreeably with the orange and green of the Tricolour
flying from the pediment, a reminder that above and behind her
the Irish Parliament sat in the palace of the Dukes of Leinster. But
now she is gone, hoisted ignominiously on to a lorry and taken with
her attendant cherubs to the old soldiers' hospital at Kilmainham.
She is gone; and nothing now mitigates the austerity of Ardbraccan
stone blackened by city soot. The draughts at street-corners seem
a little colder than before. Yet in spite of this and in spite even of
the building in Kildare Street of a huge new block of government
offices, Molesworth Fields remains an attractive, leisurely corner of
Dublin. The difference of character is apparent immediately on
leaving Dawson Street: solicitors, scriveners, obscure but useful
societies, tailors and the Department of Fisheries† set the dominant
tone of the quarter.

Very soon after this we find building spreading even further
afield, out of the south-east corner of the Green along the Donnybrook Road, called in 1728 Suesey Street but soon renamed Leeson
Street after the family which owned its western side and began to
let plots there for building in 1735.[4] Two or three of these houses
still survive.

These Leesons are interesting people. They came to Ireland in
about 1680 and made a large fortune in the brewing business. As

---

* Earls of Kildare and later Dukes of Leinster.

† In a beautiful early house in Kildare Place, formerly occupied, even more fittingly,
by the Commissioners of Charitable Donations and Bequests.

well as their own freehold land in Dublin, they acquired in time extensive interests in the Dawson and Molesworth estates. There were at least two Leeson architects, one in the eighteenth and one in the early nineteenth century,* but they may not, of course, have been closely related. The brewing Leesons became Earls of Miltown and in the forties built themselves an enormously long house in the county Wicklow.

All these developments are shown on Charles Brooking's map of 1728, the first printed map of modern Dublin and the first publication of a representative selection of Dublin buildings. Brooking was given financial support by the Corporation,† and he executed the work in a spirit of celebration which reflects the new self-consciousness of the town about its appearance. Not only is there a panoramic view of Dublin from the north, but all round the map there are twenty views of buildings and other features. Some of these have already been mentioned; others, such as the Corn Market House and the Linen Hall, would not have been thought worth inclusion a few years later when there was much more to make a show. Burgh's work is prominent; there are four of his buildings including St Werburgh's Church with its top-heavy looking wooden tower and dome; and there is another church, St Ann's, which we shall meet when we come to review church-building activity since 1697.

There is also a view of the 'Lord Mayor's House', already then as now the official residence. As London did not provide itself with a Mansion House till well after 1734, Dublin may claim the primacy in this as in several other things. Early in 1713 it was decided that it would be 'for the honour and advantage of this city, and a conveniency to the Lord Mayor' that there should be a permanent Mansion House. Mr Joseph Leeson tried to sell them a house and grounds in the Green, but the first decision was to build on the vacant site of Lord Longford's house in Aungier Street.[5] Though a contract seems to have been placed, little more is heard of this proposal. In 1715 however, Joshua Dawson offered the Corporation a house in Dawson Street which he had built ten years before, explaining at some length that the price he was asking, £3,500,

---

* See below, Chapter XXIV.
† As was Rocque who mapped Dublin again in 1756.

was less than the cost of the house and the extra room which he undertook to erect. He particularises the furnishings which he would sell with the house: 'all the brass locks and marble chimney pieces, as also the tapestry hangings, silk window curtains and window seats and chimney glass in the great bed chamber; the gilt leather hangings, four pairs of scarlet calamanco window curtains and chimney glass in the walnut parlour; the Indian calicoe window curtains . . . in the Dantzick oak parlour' and similar fittings in the 'large eating room'.[6] The house was bought; and the extra room was built on a rather grander scale than Dawson had originally proposed, the city paying the difference. This is now the 'Oak Room', wainscoted in unusually large panels, and still retaining beside the fireplace the bracket for the sword and maces. The exterior of the house gives little promise of riches within, being covered with Victorian stucco and cast-iron enrichments.* Originally it was red brick, a mere two storeys in height without a pediment but having panels with figure-subjects in relief in place of a balustrade above the cornice. The house is still the Mansion House, and happily seems likely to remain so.

Readers of Mr Summerson's *Georgian London* will recall that a 'Fifty New Churches' Act which was passed there in 1710 and amplified by seven explanatory Acts, resulted, over twenty years, in the building of eight churches and some oddments. If this had happened in Ireland an English historian would certainly comment 'how Irish!' The Dublin programme was initiated a little earlier and was much more modest. It began soon after the accession of the active William King to the see in 1703. Within twenty-two years of 1707 four new churches had been built, and three ancient churches rebuilt, not to mention the Chapel Royal in the Castle and the Royal Chapel at Irishtown.† Admittedly the new churches which were intended to have towers and spires hardly ever got them, but Brooking put them into his panorama none the less, so our loss is not so great as it might have been.

To take the rebuildings first. The ancient parish church of St Nicholas Within was rebuilt by an unknown architect in 1707, in black Dublin calp, as a good straightforward classic church. It seems

---

* See a very scathing description by W. B. Yeats in *On the Boiler*: Dublin [1939] p. 10.
† Otherwise St Matthew, Ringsend.

to have had a quasi-gothic tower[7] of a type common in Dublin, but all that now remains to be seen is the three-bay ground storey of the west front, behind which the little church, its vaults emptied, its roof gone, its graveyard overgrown, forms a fantastically inaccessible no-man's-land near the corner of Christchurch Place. One of the earliest incumbents in the eighteenth century was Patrick Delany, best known as his wife's husband and Swift's friend. The church of St James was also rebuilt but has been rebuilt again; and the same applies to the Chapel Royal in the Castle. The rebuilding of St Werburgh's in 1715 has already been mentioned in connexion with Burgh and will recur in connexion with Smyth.

Of the new churches, St Luke's, built soon after 1707 mainly for the benefit of the conformist* Huguenot weavers who overflowed from the 'French Church' in the Lady Chapel of St Patrick's Cathedral, is an economic rectangular box which has now lost all but its western gallery. Only its pleasant situation in a tree-planted garden, some good detail on the organ-case, and a set of early chairs in the vestry, save it from complete dullness. Much the same may be said of St Mark's, built under the same Act† but about twenty years later. The west front is rugged and black, heavily classical with curved sweep-walls‡ and incongruously mediæval slits to light the staircases. The uncompromising bleakness of the side elevation has been rather brutally exposed by the turning of a small lane into a main thoroughfare.

Both the Royal Chapel of St Matthew at Irishtown (built by the Corporation in 1704–6; tower by Richard Mills, 1713),[8] and 'Little St George's,' Temple Street (now Hill Street, built by Sir John Eccles for his Protestant tenantry) have calp-rubble towers of quasi-gothic type. St Matthew's was rebuilt in 1878–9, and St George's demolished in 1894, but the towers of both survive. In St Matthew's one can see perhaps the last authentic persistence of the Irish Gothic tradition of stepped battlements.

The finest surviving church of this period (always excepting St Werburgh's) is St Ann's, built also under the 1707 Act but not

* There were two nonconformist French churches also.
† 6 Anne 21.
‡ Only one of which now remains.

begun till 1720. The architect, Isaac Wills,[9] is presumably the same who worked as master-carpenter under Burgh at Steevens's Hospital. Another Wills, Michael, was Clerk of Works in the building of Steevens's. Isaac is credited by Sir John Gilbert[10] with the design of St Werburgh's, and the fact that Brooking's Map features the two churches very prominently as a pair suggests that there was a close connexion between them. St Ann's west front as shown there is riotously baroque with broken pediments, vast consoles, stone flambeaux and an ornate built-up spirelet in several stages. But this never came to fruition: the west front as built was much chaster, never rose high enough to mask the towering gable, and disappeared in 1868 in favour of the subtly unsymmetrical 'romanesque' frontispiece by Sir Thomas Deane which now commands the view down Anne Street.

St Ann's has continued to be a fashionable church till the present day. This accounts for the re-fronting and also for the fact that the casual visitor entering from the sunny street finds it so dark that he may leave without looking at it. For in Victorian times it was filled with stained glass, nearly all of it execrably bad. But it remains one of the noblest church interiors in Dublin, with gallery carried on square unfluted ionic columns, and a curved apse with magnificent gilt plaster drops, six of them, flanking the three eastern windows. There are also, on either side of the chancel, curved shelves for the bequest of the Rt Hon Theophilus Lord Newtown of Newtown Butler, the father of Lord Lanesborough, who left, at his death in 1723, £13 per annum to be distributed in 5s. worth of bread weekly to the poor. This is still done, though altered money values have made the loaves absurdly small.

So much for the State Church. The largest minority in Dublin was of course the Catholic community, but until the middle of the century Catholicism was so hedged about with restrictions and secrecy that its history has left little tangible trace. But the Catholics did manage, even during the worst period of the Penal Laws, to preserve some sort of parochial organisation, especially in St Michael's and St Audoen's.* In 1746, for example, the latter had a Parish Priest and five curates. There were also the religious Orders

---

* E. Lloyd, the 'Citizen of London' of 1732, says there were then many 'chapels for Mass, for . . . the Roman Catholics have the free exercise of their religion in every parish'. This must be a somewhat sanguine view of the case.

who, unlike the secular priests, were illegal by merely existing. The Catholic churches were back rooms and stables and outhouses, lent by pious and courageous Catholic merchants. The most famous of them was the Franciscan Church still universally known as 'Adam and Eve's' from the fact that the entrance to it was through a public-house which bore that sign. But the present church is much later (1830–32), and not a single architectural trace remains of the Dublin Catholicism of this dark period.

Yet, though the Viceroy, addressing Parliament as late as 1733, alluded to the Catholics as 'the common enemy', it would be a mistake to suppose that this ferocious absurdity was endorsed by all Protestant opinion even in theory, let alone in practice. Thus in 1723 Lord Molesworth proposed in a pamphlet that the priests should be paid by the State. Prebendary Synge of St Patrick's advocated a considerable degree of toleration in a sermon preached before the Irish House of Commons two years later. The Protestant Bishop of Elphin proposed, not only the licensing of 600 priests, but provision for their education in Trinity College without the obligation of attending chapel or submitting to any other religious interference.[11]

But these aspects of the matter are, for our purpose, less important than the fact that there were at this time, in Dublin, no Catholics in 'society'. Though they made up perhaps half of the population of the capital, it was the bottom half. Such a state of affairs may seem difficult to imagine, but it is not far from being paralleled in Belfast at the present moment. The Catholic gentry who by their birth and education would have been qualified to mix with the Protestant rulers of Dublin were in St Germains, Madrid, Vienna, Warsaw or even Moscow, or striking a blow against the usurper at Landen or Fontenoy. On the other hand those of Irish name or stock who were fortunate or prudent enough to be Protestants, were apt to rise rapidly, and such names as Conolly, Delany, Callaghan, Dillon and Donnellan are soon found near the top. By 1751, as we shall see, Mrs Delany is meeting nuns in Dublin and hardly turning a hair.

The Dissenters fared better than the Catholics, especially after 1714. They received an augmented Regium Donum, and considered that the special circumstances in Ireland entitled them to more consideration than was enjoyed by their fellows in England. In this they were perfectly correct; and in spite of the manœuvres of the Bishops led by King, and the fury of Swift, they got a Toleration Act on the Scotch model in 1719.

The one surviving Presbyterian church of early date in Dublin must date from about this time.* It was the home of the Eustace Street Congregation (one of four or five then existing in the city) and it is now a printing works. The façade however survives, with rich segment-headed doors and windows framed in bolection mouldings of strongly English character and suggesting a date somewhere around 1685. The explanation seems to be that these Presbyterians were mostly immigrants from England,† and when circumstances allowed them to build comparatively grandly in a central street, they chose an idiom fashionable in England thirty years earlier. This thirty-year time-lag is almost universal in Ireland: we shall meet it again and again, and indeed we are still meeting it.

* Gilbert (II, 311) thinks the congregation came here in about 1728, but the building must be older.

† Samuel Boyse the poet, who died young after a life of self-induced misery, was the son of a Dublin Presbyterian minister at this period.

REFERENCES

[1] Francis Morgan, *Rental of the Corporation Estates*, 1867.
[2] Miltown Rental, Incumbered Estates Court, P.R.O. Dublin.
[3] *Georg. Soc.* IV, 92.
[4] Miltown Rental, *loc. cit.*
[5] *CARD* VI, 472–3.
[6] *ibid.* 536.
[7] Wheeler & Craig, *Dublin City Churches*, Plate II.
[8] *CARD* VI, 477.
[9] *Georg. Soc.* IV, 104.
[10] Gilbert, I, 32.
[11] Lecky, *History of England and Ireland in the Eighteenth Century*, II, 307 *sqq.*

CHAPTER XII

Drapier and Dublin Society

I N ALMOST every age worth studying there is one great man whose name alone is sufficient to call it to mind. The Duke of Ormonde is the man for the last half of the seventeenth century, and for the first half of the eighteenth a still greater man stands symbol. Many books have been written about Swift, and many of them have combined to fix him in his character as Dubliner and as Dean, as pamphleteer and patriot. He has been the occasion of more nonsense than any other writer except Shakespeare. Happily, there are some signs that the spate of nonsense is abating. It is no longer necessary, for example, to believe in Lord Macaulay's account of the 'apostate politician, the ribald priest, the perjured lover'. Still less need we suppose that Swift's expressions of hatred for Ireland and Dublin are exempt from the cautions usually attendant upon irony.* The great statesmen in London had let him down, and he came back to Dublin soured of politicians but not, as it proved, of politics. After 1714 the only political allies in whom he trusted were the common people of Dublin, and they did not betray him.

'I have ever hated', he wrote to Pope, 'all nations, professions and communities, and all my love is toward individuals'. And again, about Dublin in particular, 'I ever feared the tattle of this nasty town'; and Yeats echoes him two hundred years later, with 'the dull spite of this unmannerly town'. In the meantime Sheridan, a Dubliner born, had written *The School for Scandal* which, though professedly set in London, gives just that feeling of a small capital which enables us to recapture the scale of eighteenth-century Dublin.

* Was Swift, we wonder, ironical when he wrote, to Chevalier Wogan: '. . . I cannot but highly esteem those gentlemen of Ireland, who, with all the disadvantages of being exiles and strangers, have been able to distinguish themselves by their valour and conduct in so many parts of Europe, I think, above all other nations; which ought to make the English ashamed of the reproaches they cast on the ignorances, the dulness, and the want of courage, in the Irish natives; those defects, wherever they happen, arising only from the poverty and slavery they suffer from their inhuman neighbours, and the base corrupt spirits of so many of the chief gentry, &c'?—Hardly.

From Swift himself we get the colour and the detail of the picture. From the beggars to the bishops, from the apple-women and almanack-makers to the attorneys, aldermen and adventurers, dozens of minor figures who would otherwise be totally forgotten, shine in his reflected light. The Sheridans and the Grattans, Delany and Helsham, schoolmasters, parsons, lawyers and physicians, revolve around their primary and come to life as they come in contact. We meet the printers, Faulkner, Grierson and Harding, the poets, Dunkin and Delany, the bluestockings Mrs Constantia Grierson, Mrs Barber, Mrs Sican, Mrs Vesey and of course that egregious adventuress Laetitia Pilkington and her poetical husband Matthew.[1] Matthew Concanen, Murrough O'Connor and James Ward were writing and publishing in Dublin poems descriptive of low life and peasant custom in North County Dublin and even as far afield as Kerry. Yet from the writings of Swift or his circle we get hardly any hint of the submerged three-quarters of Ireland, still clinging to Gaelic speech and poetry and music. Swift was in his lifetime a legend among the common people of Ireland, and fragments of folklore about him may still be picked up in the country, yet there is no sign that he ever met Turlough O'Carolan the famous blind harper, who was his contemporary. Religion was of course the great obstacle, but even that did not prevent Swift from making a spirited translation—based no doubt on a literal prose rendering—of the Irish poem *O'Rourke's Feast*. But though in life they were divided, Swift and Carolan are allied in death, for a memorial erected by Lady Morgan to Carolan faces Swift's monument across the nave of St Patrick's Cathedral.*

The literary culture of early Georgian Dublin was almost exclusively English, like that of Colonial America. The earliest Dublin-printed anthology was *A Select Collection of Modern Poems by Several Hands*, printed for John Henly at the Blackmoor's Head in Castle Street in 1713. It contains poems by Tickell, Lord Mulgrave, Lord Roscommon, Pope, Addison, Denham, John Philips, Dryden and Congreve. The two lords were, it so happens, Irish peers, and Roscommon at least lived a certain amount in Ireland. Denham and Congreve were both born in Ireland, while Addison

---

* Carolan died in 1738. It is not without interest that he composed a song about Wood and his Halfpence. (*Bibl. Soc. of Ireland Pubs.* II. 5. 99.)

and Tickell had official positions in Dublin (as had Namby-Pamby Phillips, though not represented in this book). But none of these authors is Irish in any valuable sense: not as Swift is Irish.

The Sheridans were Irish of the native stock. William was a non-juring Bishop of Kilmore, one of whose brothers founded a Jacobite branch of the family, providing a tutor to Prince Charles Edward. His nephew Thomas was the Cavan Schoolmaster who lived at Quilca, was a friend of Swift, produced a charming transla-tion of Persius printed by Grierson in Dublin in 1728, and died at Rathfarnham ten years later. His son, Thomas the second, was an actor, author, lexicographer (he quarrelled with Dr Johnson), and manager of Smock-Alley Theatre. He migrated to England and was the father of Richard Brinsley. In 1757 he delivered in Fish-amble Street Music-Hall an oration lamenting the practice of sending Irish boys to English schools, which was several times reprinted.

Of Swift's other Dublin friends, the Grattans claim similar notice as being the forebears of another great man. Dr Patrick Grattan, a fellow of Trinity College, had seven sons and was renowned for his hospitality. Of these sons one, a merchant, became Lord Mayor of Dublin. Two others were prebendaries of St Patrick's and one of them, as we learn from Swift's will, was in the habit of chewing a tobacco 'called pigtail'. To the other Swift left a corkscrew and his second-best beaver hat. There was another clerical brother, and the remaining three were respectively Head Master of Portora Royal School, a doctor in Dublin and a landed gentleman. The Doctor's son James was Recorder of Dublin and M.P. for the city, and the father of the great Henry Grattan.

Besides the Grattans proper, another of the clan, their cousin 'Dan' Jackson, will be familiar to readers of Swift. What is less familiar is that his brother Jack, who was Vicar of Santry, built himself in about 1720 an extremely interesting house about five miles to the north of Dublin. Though small, it is noteworthy for its four great chimney-stacks at the angles, and its steep roof rising to a red-brick lantern-gazebo at the apex. It is now known as Wood-lands, and local tradition ascribes the design, absurdly no doubt, to Swift himself, who left the parson his furniture and third-best beaver hat.

When Lord Carteret came as Viceroy in 1724, Swift is said to have asked him whether he had the honour to be acquainted with the Grattans, and when Carteret replied that he had not, 'Then, pray, my lord, take care to obtain it, it is of great consequence: the Grattans, my lord, can raise ten thousand men', a curiously prophetic exaggeration.

Patrick Delany, another clergyman of the Swift circle, was Chancellor of St Patrick's and Rector of St Werburgh's, which he resigned after abusing Baldwin, the provost of Trinity College, in a sermon; but not before he and Dr Synge had paid for the dome and cross on the tower. He, too, was of native Irish race and humble origins. Apart from his friendship with and posthumous defence of Swift, and his marriage to Mrs Pendarves, his chief claim to fame is his house at Glasnevin, at first called Heldelville because he shared it with Helsham, but soon more prudently renamed Delville. It still stands, and according to Mr Curran some part at least of it may be dated as early as 1729.[2] The famous shell-work by the second Mrs Delany is of course later; but the informal miniature gardens must have been laid out long before his re-marriage in 1743, for Mrs Delany writes in the following year a long description of the demesne, then well outside Dublin and commanding prospects 'beautiful beyond all description'. But within the last few years the garden has been levelled and utterly destroyed, even to the Temple with its mocking motto 'FASTIGIA DESPICIT URBIS' under which Swift used to sit, while in the cellar below (which could be explored till a few years ago) tradition has it, not improbably, that some of the more dangerous of the Dean's broadsheets were printed. 'The rurality of it', Mrs Delany wrote, 'is wonderfully pretty', planted 'in a *wild way*' so that 'you would not imagine it the work of art'.[3] Quite apart from its august associations, Delville was noteworthy as being perhaps the first Irish example of the taste for 'wildness' as well as of the genus 'villa'. As such it had numerous progeny.

When we remember Swift in Dublin, we may think of these pleasant places, Delville, Belcamp, Wood Park where Charles Ford lived, or the 'Little House' by the churchyard at Castleknock, with Swift and his friends exchanging rhyming invitations and pasquinades and epistles in pig-latin. Or we may remember him as the hero of that remarkable series of anecdotes retailed by Laetitia

Pilkington in her *Memoirs*: running up and down the stairs of the Deanery for exercise, pinching her for faults of phrasing, flinging open an empty drawer to show her all the money he amassed by being so long in the Church, making her take off her shoes while he measured her. Or we may think of him rather as surrounded by his beggars and apple-women (whose successors may still be seen flourishing in Dublin) to whom he lent and gave money, and for whom he wrote verses. A typical story, the value of which does not depend upon its truth, is that which tells how a large crowd, gathered in the Liberties in expectation of an eclipse, dispersed when Swift sent them a message that the eclipse had been cancelled by his orders. The background of sights, noises, and above all smells, to the portrait of the Dean in his Deanery, can be better imagined than described.

Among Swift's patriotic pamphlets, which more than anything else won him his unique position, was *A Proposal for the Universal Use of Irish Manufacture*. This with Lord Molesworth's 1723 pamphlet on *Promoting Agriculture and Employing the Poor*, ushered in a movement led by Samuel Madden, Thomas Prior, Arthur Dobbs and others. They were all a little younger than Swift: they were Whigs and 'projectors' of the type on which Swift poured scorn in *Gulliver*: Swift had little if anything to do with any of them: none the less they were engaged in the same work for Ireland as he was. The bridge between Swift and this group was George Berkeley.

Thomas Prior was a schoolfellow and lifelong friend of Berkeley. He was a busy economist and practical improver, and in the same year as Swift's *Modest Proposal* he published a *List of the Absentees of Ireland*, which showed the other side of the same medal. In the same year, 1729, appeared an *Essay on the Trade of Ireland* by Arthur Dobbs, the Surveyor-General, a Co. Antrim landed gentleman, and two years later his *Thoughts on Government in General*. He later became Governor of North Carolina, where he died in 1765.

Samuel Madden, perhaps the most remarkable of the group, was born in Dublin in 1686, nephew of the Molyneux brothers. He was a clergyman in Co. Fermanagh, and had leisure there not only to write a tragedy about Themistocles but also to devise the scheme which caused him to be best known as 'Premium' Madden. This, which was first applied to academic learning in Trinity College, and later to agricultural achievement in the country at large, through the Dublin Society, was no more than the idea of giving prizes, but Madden is said to have invented it, and, more to the point, he gave the agricultural prizes at first out of his own pocket. He published his scheme in 1731, and in 1738 published his influential *Reflections and Resolutions proper for the Gentlemen of Ireland, as to their Conduct for the Service of their Country*. In 1739 he proposed in the Dublin Society the extension of the premium scheme to architecture, painting and statuary. Not for nothing did Dr Johnson say that Madden's was a name which Ireland ought to honour.

The Dublin Society, better known, since 1821, as the Royal Dublin Society, and famous in the world for its Horse Show, was founded by fourteen Dublin gentlemen on June 25th, 1731. It has some claims to be regarded as the most illustrious body of its kind in existence anywhere. Thomas Prior was perhaps, more than any other single man, its founder; and old Sir Thomas Molyneux, who dated back to the Philosophical Society of the previous century, was at his elbow. Madden, who was not then in Dublin, joined two years later. Berkeley, though his *Querist* (1735) and his private encouragement helped the Society forward, was never a member: nor was Swift—possibly as the Society's historian suggests, because of personal animosity against some of the early office-holders.

Other early members of the Society were Francis Bindon the architect and portrait painter whose portraits of Swift are familiar: Henry Brooke, author of *The Fool of Quality* and of many pamphlets on economics and manufactures, and a pioneer in toleration of Catholics; Dean Delany and Humphrey French, the 'Good Lord Mayor', whom Swift greatly admired; Lord Orrery, Namby-Pamby Phillips and Thomas Sheridan.

From the outset the Society investigated, experimented and encouraged in every direction the application of practical economics. It lived first in Mecklenburgh Street, where it had an experimental garden. But it had no settled premises till 1756, when it took a house in Shaw's Court, off Dame Street. Ten years later it moved to Grafton Street, where Christopher Myers designed it a new house.* In 1795 it opened its new Botanic Garden at Glasnevin,

---

* Successor to Lord Mornington's house. The Society's house and that of the Navigation Board made a pair: in the latter the Royal Irish Academy first met.

close beside Delville. This little demesne was that occupied by the poet Tickell when he was Under-Secretary for Ireland in the 1720's. Tickell lived here till his death in 1740, but the much-vaunted connexion with Addison is fallacious. The yew-walk beside the Tolka River which bears his name, is, however, none the less worth seeing on that account.

The Dublin Society was, like other bodies, actively supported by the Irish Parliament* and in some measure controlled by it also. The Botanic Garden, like other of the Society's departments at various times, was taken over by the State in 1878.

One of these departments, the Drawing School, is of particular interest to us. The Society took over the private school of Robert West the painter in about 1750. Some years earlier, they had awarded premiums for practical architecture: and in 1759 they engaged Thomas Ivory as Master of the architectural section. James Mannin, a Frenchman, was already there teaching ornament. J. D. Herbert, in his *Irish Varieties*, 1836, gives a vivid and amusing scene with dialogue in this school, at which he attended before becoming an actor. There were about thirty to thirty-five pupils in the architectural school each year, and it was said that 'there was not a working tradesman or mechanic in the building line in Dublin and the chief towns in Ireland who, during his apprenticeship, had not received instruction in it'.† Like the Botanic Garden the Schools were taken over by the State in 1878, though Duncan Ferguson, who retired in 1854, seems to have been the last master of the Architectural School.[4]

The upsurge of intellectual life which gave birth to the Dublin Society was, as I have tried to show, different in kind from that associated with Petty and the Molyneuxs. It was entirely pragmatic and utilitarian: though it had a 'political' tinge it was derived of antiquarian interest. In this respect it is also unlike the intellectual revival of the eighteen-thirties, and finds its nearest parallel in the early twentieth century period associated with the names of Arthur Griffith and A.E., the period, in fact, of Sinn Fein which consciously looked back to Swift.

There was also, during the Swift period, a small school of Irish

---

* Before this, Parliament encouraged projectors with monetary awards.

† From 1749 till 1849 attendance at the Schools was gratis—no fees were accepted.

poets with a flavour peculiar to Ireland: Murrough or Morgan O'Connor, Matthew Concanen, and James Ward whom we have already met. Murrough O'Connor was a Kerryman who published Kerry Pastorals in 1719, 1726 and 1740. Concanen's *A Match at Football*, which is a spirited verse description of the special local game of North County Dublin, appeared in 1720 or 1721, and his *Poems on Several Occasions* in 1722, a desirable volume both in appearance and content. His anthology *Miscellaneous Poems Original and Translated* (1724) represents the whole school: Swift, Parnell, Delany, Brown, Ward, Sterling and others, including Irish low-life pastorals by Brown and Ward, especially the latter's *Smock-Race at Finglass*. Apart from their intrinsic value these poems are noteworthy social documents. Then there were, of course, the Pilkingtons, Matthew and the egregious Laetitia. Matthew's poems, some revised by Swift, were published in Dublin in 1731, and Laetitia's appeared in her *Memoirs*. Another poet who is not to be despised is Swift's protégé William Dunkin, several times reprinted and according to Swift the best Latin poet in Ireland. But for long after Swift's time poetry was by no means Dublin's strongest point.[5]

REFERENCES

[1] Good vignettes of the *minora sidera* of the Swift circle may be found in *Swift and His Circle*, by R. Wyse Jackson, Dublin, 1945.

[2] *JRSAI LXX*, 10.

[3] *Autobiography* &c 1861, II, 315.

[4] Berry, *History of the Royal Dublin Society*, 1915. Strickland, *Dictionary of Irish Artists*.

[5] Some sentences here are expanded from an article by the author in *Bulletin of Friends of Library of T.C.D.*, 1948.

Note to page 119. Delville was demolished after this passage was in proof.

CHAPTER XIII

The Age of Pearce and Cassels

THE IRISH PARLIAMENT, humiliated by the English Declaratory Act of 1720, which asserted its dependence upon England, had recovered some of its self-respect when the Dean, in his character of the 'Drapier', scored a resounding moral victory over the administration. As Delany said, 'No man ever deserved better of his country, than Swift did of his.' For that matter, William Wood and his wretched halfpence were worth their weight in gold to Ireland; for it is difficult to think of any other pretext which would have called forth the very latent patriotism of the members at College Green. We may suspect that some such feeling of self-assertion was behind the decision to rebuild the Parliament House.

There was of course ample practical reason to do so, for Chichester House was falling down, and by 1727 was positively unsafe. None the less, there is a difference between merely rebuilding and housing the Lords and Commons in a building vastly more convenient and above all more magnificent than the Parliament House at London. The first stone was laid with great pomp by Speaker Conolly and the other Lords Justices, early in 1729, and while the new House was building the Parliament sat in the Blue-Coat School. The work proceeded apace, and although the building took in all ten years and young Pearce did not live to see it finished, Parliament was able to occupy it less than three years after the first stone was laid. The building committee were delighted with Pearce's work, and though he had 'charged nothing for his own great expenses, skill and pains', he was twice voted £1,000 by the grateful Commons.[1]

The Parliament House is generally recognised as being the earliest important public building in these islands to embody the full Burlingtonian ideals of correctness.[2] It comes, in time, between Chiswick House (1725) and the Horse Guards (1742). As befits an Irish building, it has none of the frivolity which enlivens Whitehall and St James's Park. Instead it has a monumental grandeur of planning and conception which has influenced at least one large London building of a later age. Pearce's great south colonnade to College Green is one of the most memorable architectural experiences in Dublin, a continual source of delight and refreshment. The strength and clarity of the execution is perhaps unequalled in its period, here or in England.

Edward Lovett Pearce was born probably in 1699, the son of a Major-General and nephew of a Lieutenant-General. His maternal grandfather had been Master of the City works and Lord Mayor of Dublin, and his uncle John Lovett had been concerned with the building of the Eddystone lighthouse. His grandmother Frances Lovett had been an O'Moore before her marriage, a descendant of the famous rebel Rory Og O'Moore of Leix.[3] Pearce became a cornet in Colonel Morris's dragoons at the age of sixteen or seventeen, and soon afterwards visited Italy,* making a number of drawings of buildings in Venice and elsewhere. At about the same time Bishop Berkeley was touring in Italy and making architectural notes, and so was Lord Burlington (another Irishman—of sorts) and William Kent. The date of Pearce's return to, or arrival in, Ireland, is not known. But since his maternal relatives were Irish, and a paternal aunt was married to a Dublin man, and Pearce's own regiment was almost entirely officered by Irishmen, his connexion with Ireland must always have been close.

About 1722 somebody had designed Castletown for Speaker Conolly. On July 29th of that year Bishop Berkeley, then living in Dublin, describes the house in a letter to a friend, leaving no doubt but that, although barely begun, it was already designed as it exists today. 'The plan', says Berkeley, 'is chiefly of Mr Conolly's invention, however, in some points they were pleased to consult me'.[4] In September of the same year Berkeley writes again '... you will be surprised to hear that the building is begun and the cellar floor arched before they have agreed on any plan for the elevation or façade. Several have been made by several hands, but as I do not approve of a work conceived by many heads so I have made no draught of mine own. All I do being to give my opinion on any point, when consulted'.

* Mr Curran doubts this: *Bank of Ireland*, 1949, p. 427.

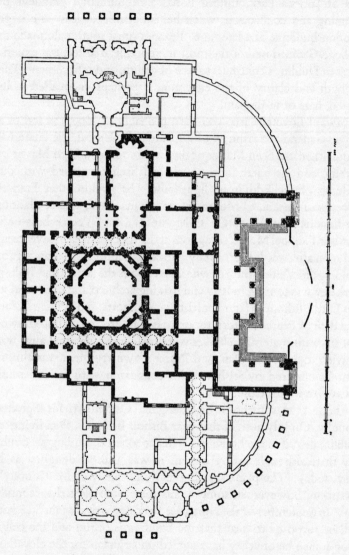

FIG. 5. Plan of the Parliament House. Pearce's work is shown in black: at the top (east) are the Lords' extensions by Gandon, at the bottom the Commons' extensions by Parke and others. Based on the published plans by Bernard Scalé and Thos. Sherrard.

The only contemporary drawing connected with Castletown is a small measured drawing of a section of the coping by Pearce. He could only have been twenty-one or twenty-two when the main block, colonnades and wings, as described by Berkeley, were projected. But if he could design the Parliament House at twenty-eight, why not Castletown at twenty-one? One thing at least is certain, that the general disposition and elevation of Castletown are the work of one mind. Centre and wings are so resourcefully contrasted in mass, colour, texture and fenestration as to predicate, in spite of Berkeley's complaint, unitary control by a talent of no mean order. Pearce's is the only such talent of which we have any record.

Pearce was elected in 1727 Member for the Borough of Ratoath, which apparently belonged to his family. He may have designed Rathnally, a house on the Boyne not far away. His other works include the obelisk still standing at Stillorgan, raised upon an irregular rustic grotto, plans for the palladification of Lord Allen's house at Stillorgan, the theatre in Aungier Street (1733) on the site originally proposed for the Mansion House, and a theatre in Cork on which he was working when he died.

He succeeded Burgh as Surveyor-General on the latter's death in 1730, when the Parliament House was already in progress. He was knighted in the Parliament House by the Viceroy in 1732, received the Freedom of Dublin in the following year, and died suddenly of an imposthume on December 7th, 1733, at his house in Stillorgan. He is buried in Old Donnybrook churchyard, but he has no memorial there. His fame as an architect must have reached England, for Mrs Delany, before her first visit to Ireland, writes to her sister, 'You must send to Capt. Pierce for a plan to build a house, and then I am sure it will be pretty and convenient'.[5] When she came over to Ireland later in 1731 she danced in the Castle ballroom fitted up by Pearce, 'finely adorned with paintings and obelisks, and made as light as a summer's day'[6]—this was in November. A few weeks later he danced with her friend Mrs Donellan at another Castle ball; but he seems to have offended the ladies by yawning or perhaps even dozing off in their company. Who knows what midnight oil he may have burnt in the cause of architecture, or what day-dream-palaces may have been rising before his eyes when he ought to have been dispensing courtesies as a squire of dames?

'Our sleepy lover', she writes, 'was yesterday dubbed a knight, and to-day I have promised to give him the meeting at the Grahams', where I shall dine, but I am afraid *Sir Edward Pierce* will hardly think it worth his while to make up for the neglects of *Captain Pierce!*'[7]

The Parliament House (Pls. XIII, XVII, XVIII and Figs. 5 and 8) is a most original yet unaffected building. Behind the forecourt with its deeply shadowed ionic colonnade, a corridor roofed and lit by little domes surrounded on three sides the great domed chamber, an octagon in a square, in which the Commons sat, and gives access on the east side also to the apsidal top-lit House of Lords. The basic elements of both façade and plan are startlingly similar to those of the British Museum a century later, especially after the younger Smirke had put the domed Reading Room in a position corresponding to the Irish House of Commons. The Parliament House was fully published in plan, elevation and sections in 1767, and Smirke may well have seen these. Some idea of the deplorable ignorance of English writers about Irish buildings may be gathered from the fact that a well-known stand-ard English architectural history illustrates the Bank of Ireland (as the Parliament House became after the Union) labelling it *'circa 1800'* and alluding briefly to it as 'as good of its kind as anything of the Greek revival period'![8]

The building had one defect as a show-piece, that the Pantheon-like Dome of the Commons (nicknamed the Goose-Pie) was too far behind the façade to be visible. Gandon, when working on the Parliament House later in the century, proposed that it should be raised on a higher drum, and always made a point of drawing it so raised whenever he had the chance.* Today, the south front is practically as Pearce left it; so is the House of Lords with its grand plaster barrel-vault and its Diocletian windows; so are the corridors† and many of the smaller rooms. But the eastern apsidal lobby‡ has been remodelled, the Court of Requests has disappeared into Francis Johnston's grand Cash Office (1804), and the House of

---

* *e.g.* in the drawings reproduced in *The Bank of Ireland*, 1949.

† Some of the niches in the corridors have been filled in.

‡ If Mr Ralph Dutton (in *The English Interior*, 1949 p. 111) is correct, this apsidal room is earlier than any English example.

Commons, destroyed by fire in 1792 and meanly rebuilt, has disappeared completely.

One of the earliest of many stirring scenes enacted in the House took place during the first session held in it: the long celebrated episode of Tottenham in his Boots. A dispute had arisen between the Government and the patriotic party, about the control of the National Debt Fund. When it came to a division the numbers were exactly equal. But at the crucial moment in came Colonel Tottenham, the member for New Ross, covered with mud and still wearing a pair of huge jack-boots. He had ridden all through the night, nearly sixty Irish miles, to cast his vote for the patriots. For many a long year after that 'Tottenham in his Boots' was a standing toast in patriotic circles.[9] It may be doubted whether Tottenham's ghost ever clatters into College Green past Grattan's statue on moonlit nights, for when an Irish Parliament sat again in Dublin in the present century it chose Leinster House instead of the Parliament House. The reason was perhaps that Leinster House, standing far back from its own railings and well isolated, was more easily defensible in those troubled times than the Bank building; but whatever the reason it is impossible not to regret the decision.

The other noteworthy architect of the thirties was Richard Cassels, born in Germany—in Hesse-Cassel, in fact—in about 1690. Like nearly all the Irish architects of the time, he was an officer of Engineers. Mr C. P. Curran has shown reason to believe[10] that Cassels may have been of French extraction, and have come to Ireland after other Cassel relatives had already settled here. The same authority traces his artistic ancestry to the French-Netherlandish architectural family of Du Ry, who rebuilt Cassel about the time of our architect's birth and later. In about 1727 Sir Gustavus Hume, a County Fermanagh gentleman, brought Cassels to Ireland to build him a country house on the shores of Lough Erne, and soon afterwards Cassels is found in Dublin with a large and rapidly growing practice.*

For the next twenty years he was the most prominent architect in Dublin, and did a great deal of work in the country as well. The

* The Hume and Loftus families, who intermarried, were both Co. Fermanagh gentry who later in the century developed property in Dublin. Ely Lodge and Castle Hume are side by side near Enniskillen, and Ely Place and Hume Street adjoin near Stephen's Green. Both streets are on the Blue-Coat Estate.

list[11] of his buildings in Dublin alone is longer than that of any other important architect except perhaps Johnston. But he makes his mark by sheer weight of numbers, for though abundantly talented he rarely showed anything more exciting than sober accomplishment. His designs have none of the poetry of Pearce's; his detail, though correct, is rarely sensitive; and he certainly confirmed by his example the Irish preference for large compact blocks of building.

His earliest datable house in Dublin is No 80 St Stephen's Green, built for Bishop Clayton of Killala in 1730. As a house it has vanished, but much of it was incorporated in Iveagh House in the eighteen-seventies. Here Mrs Delany came on her first visit to Ireland in 1731. 'The Bishop and his lady,' she wrote, 'are agreeable, but were never so much so as in their own house, which indeed is *magnifique*, and they have a heart answerable to their fortune.' The front of the house, she says, 'is like Devonshire House. The apartments are handsome, and furnished with gold-coloured damask—virtues, and busts, and pictures that the Bishop brought with him from Italy. A universal cheerfullness reigns in the house. They keep a very handsome table, six dishes of meat are constantly at dinner, and six plates at supper'.[12]

Cassels, as Mr Curran observes, had no particular preferences for one style of internal decoration over another. Thus, though the ceilings in No 80 are compartmented, at Clanwilliam House (No 85 St Stephen's Green), a Cassels house of ten years later, there is a ceiling with rococo arabesques and figure-subjects in the cove, by the Francini brothers. When Cassels remodelled Carton, the Earl of Kildare's country seat near Maynooth, the Francinis decorated the saloon in the same style only more so, with *putti* sitting on the cornice and dangling their chubby legs over the heads of the assembled company. At Clanwilliam House Cassels had some difficulty in adjusting the interior to the façade, and was reduced to playing questionable tricks with the internal window-cases, so that he could make a show outside with a venetian window. He is credited with the introduction of the venetian window into Ireland, and in particular with the use of such windows with a blind centre, as in a pair of houses on the west side of St Stephen's Green.*

---

* There is, so far as I know, no evidence to connect Cassels with these houses. A similar feature occurs in Bellamont Forest, Co. Cavan, which is probably earlier than Cassels's time.

One of the most engaging of Cassels's Dublin buildings is the Printing House in Trinity College, given to the University in 1734 by John Stearne, Bishop of Clogher. This little Doric temple is delicately detailed and has little in common with his usual pedestrian handling. All through the eighteenth century it made an admirable device for the title-pages of the books printed in it, and it still houses the University Press. One of the last books from the Press to bear the old device on its title-pages was, suitably enough, the series of *Georgian Society Records* published between 1909 and 1913. He designed another building for Trinity, the Dining Hall (1745–9), but this began to fall down about ten years later; and it is impossible to tell how much of the present (and very fine) hall represents his work. The tower and dome which he added to the old Chapel of the College have disappeared, but may be seen in old prints.

The great innovation with which Cassels's name is connected was the building by the nobility of great town houses in cut stone. The first of these was Tyrone House (Pl. xx), begun about 1740 for Sir Marcus Beresford, Viscount and later Earl of Tyrone. It would appear that the Beresfords had owned this part of the lands of Mary's Abbey since 1717, through Sir Marcus's marriage with the le Poer heiress who was also the heiress of the Phepoe or Piphoe family, owners of land in North Dublin since mediæval times. Their name is still commemorated in the district of Phibsborough.[13] Marlborough Street, in which Tyrone House stands, had been in existence since at least 1728, and most probably since the epoch of Marlborough's wars. At this time it contained a Bowling Green, successor to the more famous one in Oxmantown, and round the corner in Great Martin's Lane were the premises and Botanic Garden of the Dublin Society.

Tyrone House is a big solid block of a house, seven bays wide, in Irish granite. The main cornice is immediately below the top windows, which is a little unusual in Dublin.* Cassels made a venetian window his centrepiece on the first floor, and the doorway composition was elegant enough; but both these features have now gone. The best feature of the interior is the staircase hall, at the rear, with mahogany balusters and some good plaster. By 1780, when

* Other examples are Nos 21 and 23 Parnell Square.

Pool and Cash wrote their descriptions of Dublin buildings, Tyrone House was 'in the old heavy stile', but they allowed it to be good of its kind.

The connexion between Tyrone House and the famous Beresford ghost story, though fallacious,* is so persistent that it may as well be repeated here. Sir Marcus's mother, Nichola-Sophia Hamilton, had been brought up with the young Lord Decies, and so close was the bond between them that they agreed together that the first of the two to die should return and enlighten the other about the life to come. Lord Decies died in 1693, and duly appeared to Lady Beresford, not, of course, at Tyrone House, but at Gill Hall, Co. Down. He foretold her future life, concluding with her death on her forty-seventh birthday. Mistrusting the spectre, the lady asked for a sign; and after some parley the ghost touched her wrist, which instantly shrank up and withered. For the rest of her life she concealed the wrist with a band of black ribbon. The predictions came true, except that she passed her forty-seventh birthday without incident. But on her forty-eighth she discovered from the clergyman who had christened her that the accepted reckoning was mistaken: she was in fact a year younger. Needless to say, she died a few hours after hearing this news.† Sir Marcus, her son, was a friend of Dr Helsham of Delville, and also built the Dublin house.[14]

In 1835 Tyrone House, like so many other Dublin mansions after the Union, was bought by the Government, and has ever since been the Board of National Education's headquarters. The high wall which concealed it was pulled down, but the façade was altered. Later in the nineteenth century Tyrone House became part of an elaborate symmetrical layout: a replica was built to balance it, and both buildings now frame the domed centre piece of the Central Model Schools to which Bernard Shaw was sent as a child. The Schools are now consecrated to the teaching of all subjects through the exclusive medium of Irish.

The next and largest of the great town houses was Leinster House (Pl. xx) (then Kildare House) begun by Cassels in 1745. The Earls of Kildare, of the great family of Fitzgerald, had a town house in Suffolk

---

* Tyrone House was not built when it happened.
† Sir Walter Scott used this story, as he used the Annesley story.

Street, but this did not satisfy the young Lord Kildare who succeeded in 1744. He bought in that year a strip on the east side of Molesworth Fields—the east side, in fact, of Coote Lane which was henceforward called Kildare Street. On the middle part of this site, facing down Molesworth Street, Kildare House was built.

It was really a country house, both in situation and in planning. There is no 'back': the eastern front, though plainer, is as formal as the western and to many tastes superior. Two well-known stories are told about the building. One, that when a friend observed to the Earl that the site was somewhat remote, he replied 'They will follow me wherever I go' (and of course they did). The other, that the choice of site was dictated by the fact that Cassels wanted a country house and the Earl wanted a town one.

The plan, with a central corridor on the long axis, is that of the usual Irish country house.* So is the relation between entrance-hall and staircase-hall. The former, of two storeys with a deep plaster coved ceiling, is undeniably impressive, as well as being a cunning piece of contrivance.[15]

But Leinster House, magnificent as it is, has never inspired much love or even affection. Even the warmth of its associations has not been enough to thaw the coldness of the architectural expression. The west front is built in Ardbraccan, that hard limestone from Co. Meath which was extensively used in the eighteenth and early nineteenth centuries. It takes fine detail, remaining hard and slowly turning black, and this does not enhance the stodginess of Cassels's western elevation.

Lord Edward Fitzgerald, the most famous resident of the house, disliked it for its melancholy atmosphere, and preferred Carton where the architecture, also by Cassels, is even less distinguished but is at least in the country. His mother, who married the builder of Leinster House, had to spend a season in a rented house in Stephen's Green, in a state of youthful excitement, waiting for her 'charming

---

* One sometimes hears it asserted that the White House in Washington is a copy of Leinster House. Comparison of the elevations lends little support to this belief, but the close similarity of the plans is more suggestive. The main difference is that the bowed projection, which in Leinster House occupies one of the short sides, has in the White House been transferred to one of the long sides. The architect of the White House, James Hoban, was born in Carlow in 1762, studied architecture at the Dublin Society's School where in 1780 he was awarded a prize for 'stairs, roof &c', and in 1792 won the White House competition. He died in the U.S. in 1832.

great house' to be finished. But in the summer she was able to indulge her 'passion for spotted cows' in a small house in the country. The foundation-stone of Leinster House bore an inscription in latin which mentioned the name of the architect—a little unusual, this— and called upon the reader to 'learn, whenever, in some unhappy day, you light on the ruins of so great a mansion, of what worth he was who built it [the Earl, of course, not the architect] and how frail all things are, when such memorials of such men cannot out- live misfortune'.

Leinster House has certainly outlived a good deal of misfortune. Fifteen years after the Union the Duke sold it to the Dublin (now Royal Dublin) Society, who occupied it for over a hundred years. The Society built a large lecture theatre on the south side, and during the second half of the nineteenth century Leinster House became the nucleus of a complex of cultural institutions—the Museums, National Gallery, National Library and School of Art, all in Kildare Street or Merrion Square. This eminently sensible arrangement was reduced to a mockery when in 1921 the new Irish Parliament chose Leinster House as its meeting-place, banishing the R.D.S. to its suburban retreat at Ballsbridge. The Dail (lower house) sits in the Lecture Theatre, while the Senate occupies one of the most attractive rooms in the house, the Saloon in the north wing, some sixty-five by twenty-four feet plus an apsidal recess in one of the long sides, with stucco on ceiling and walls in the late Stapleton manner.*

The remaining work of Cassels in Dublin must be left aside for the moment. Of his country houses Powerscourt and Carton are the nearest to Dublin and the best known, while Summerhill, Co. Meath (twice burned and now a magnificent ruin) is incom- parably the finest, exhibiting in both its general massing and its detail such qualities as to raise doubts of the attribution. In Russ- borough (still intact) and Belan (ruined) he collaborated with Francis Bindon, the Co. Clare architect and painter who is not known to have designed any buildings in Dublin. Like Pearce before him and Davis Ducart after him, Cassels helped to usher in the Canal Age, designing the first stone lock in Ireland, on the

---

* James Wyatt had a hand in a redecoration of Leinster House towards the end of the century (*Georg. Soc.* V. 59).

Newry Canal.[16] Like Burgh, he took an interest in the Dublin water supply, and his only book, published in 1736, is an *Essay towards Supplying the City of Dublin with Water*.

It is recorded of him that, like François Mansart, he was in the habit of ordering work to be pulled down and done again if he was not satisfied with it. He was a successful practitioner, if not a great architect, and he was comparatively well off when he died suddenly at Carton in 1751, and was buried in the church of Maynooth.

REFERENCES

[1] Sadleir in *Kildare Journ. of Arch.* X, 5, 238.

[2] *e.g.* Richardson, *Monumental Classic Architecture*, 1914.

[3] *DHR* III, 54 *sqq.*

[4] Berkeley, *Letters to Perceval*, ed. Rand, 1914.

[5] *Autobiography* &c I, 275.

[6] *ibid.* 309.

[7] *ibid.* 317, 343.

[8] H. H. Statham: *Short Critical History of Architecture* [1912], 529.

[9] Lecky, II, 428. Barrington, *Personal Sketches*, 1827, I, 191. All that need be known about the Parliament House or Bank as a building will be found in Mr Sadleir's article in the *Kildare Journal*, cited above, and in Mr Curran's definitive survey in *The Bank of Ireland*, by F. G. Hall and others, 1949.

[10] Curran, *The Rotunda Hospital*, 1945, pp. 6 *sqq.*

[11] See Sadleir in *JRSAI* XLI, 241 *sqq.*

[12] *Autobiography* &c. I, 288–9.

[13] Fr. Dillon Cosgrave (*North Dublin*, 1932, p. 17) thinks that Phibsborough is named after the Sligo family of Phibbs.

[14] *Georg. Soc.* III, 68 *sqq.*

[15] *Georg. Soc.* IV has measured drawings.

[16] A MS volume on *Artificial Navigation* by Cassels was sold at the Carton Sale of June 1949. Lot 2150. It contained folding illustrations.

CHAPTER XIV

Charity and Entertainment

THE EIGHTEENTH CENTURY was, among other things, the age of charity, using the word in its narrower and by now somewhat repellent sense. A very high proportion of existing Dublin charities were founded between 1715 and 1815, after which the State began to take a hand in the matter.

We have already seen the beginnings in the Foundling and Dr Steevens's Hospitals. The Charitable Infirmary followed in 1721, first in Cook Street, then on the Inns Quay, moving later to Charlemont House in Jervis Street. It was founded by six doctors who seem to have been Catholics.* Soon afterwards Mrs Mary Mercer founded the hospital which still bears her name (1734), and still retains its old façade though surrounded and surmounted by later work.

If we turn from this to the Music-Hall in Fishamble Street we enter on holy ground, and the change of subject is more apparent than real. In the Bull's Head tavern in Fishamble Street, a Charitable Musical Society used to meet. Among those who took part were some of the vicars-choral of St Patrick's Cathedral. When Swift, on the verge of the senile dementia which overcame him at last, heard that officers of his Cathedral were consorting with a parcel of fiddlers in a tavern, one of his last acts as Dean was to condemn this association as derogatory to the dignity of the Chapter.[1] As Swift's illness was relentlessly occulting that gigantic intellect, the Musical Society was building, from Cassels's design, its new Music Hall in Fishamble Street, long the most commodious public room in Dublin. A contemporary poet found some difficulty in reconciling the claims of architectural description and the heroic couplet, but did his best with both, describing it as

* Judging by their names: George Duany, Patrick Kelly, Nathaniel Handson, John Dowdall, Francis Duany and Peter Brennan. (MacGregor: *Picture of Dublin*, 1821.)

Adorn'd with all that workmanship can do
By ornaments and architecture too.
The oblong area runs from east to west,
Fair to behold, but hard to be exprest;
At th' eastern end the awful throne is plac'd,
With fluted columns and pilasters grac'd,
Fit for the noblest President to rest,
Who likes the arms of Ireland for his crest.

$$* \qquad * \qquad *$$

The architect has here display'd his art,
By decorations proper for each part:
The cornice, dentills, and the curious mould,
The fret-work, and the vaulted roof behold;
The hollow arches, and the bold design,
In ev'ry part with symmetry divine . . .[2]

It was opened in October 1741, just before Swift was finally put in the care of guardians.

'Dublin,' as Handel's first biographer remarked, 'has always been famous for the gaiety and splendour of its court, the opulence and spirit of its principal inhabitants, the valour of its military, and the genius of its learned men.'[3] Handel, as the same writer records, 'hoped to find that favour and encouragement in a distant capital, which London seemed to refuse him.' On April 13th, 1742, the *Messiah* was first performed 'for the relief of the prisoners in the several Gaols and for the Support of Mercer's Hospital . . . and of the Charitable Infirmary'. It was a tremendous success; the new Hall accommodated more than seven hundred persons, by dint of the ladies coming without hoops and the gentlemen without swords. Dublin took Handel and the *Messiah* to her heart, and few episodes in her history afford juster grounds for pride.

It was not till the work was performed in England that the King founded the traditional observance of standing for the 'Halleluia Chorus'. But at the Dublin performance Dr Delany was so transported by Mrs Susanna Cibber's rendering of 'He was Despised' that he rose in his seat and exclaimed, with more enthusiasm than tact, 'Woman, for this, be all thy sins forgiven'.[4] The Choirs of both Cathedrals, St Patrick's as well as Christchurch, took part in the performance, which was repeated a few days later.

Meantime, in the Deanery, the Drapier was expiring, 'a driveller and a show'. Mrs Pilkington relates that Handel came to take his leave, and when they had succeeded in making Swift understand who his visitor was, he cried, 'O! A German, and a Genius! A Prodigy! Admit him'. So the author of the *Messiah* came face to face with the author of *Gulliver*: one of the most poignant meetings in recorded history. It was worthy to be added to Swift's own catalogue 'Of Mean and Great Figures made by several persons', though it might be difficult to decide into which category to put it.

The Fishamble Street Music Hall, under the management of John Neal the music-publisher and his son William, throve from its inception, becoming the venue of Lord Mornington's 'Musical Academy' in the fifties and sixties, and the scene of conjuring exhibitions, lectures, political debates, ridottos, masquerade balls, theatrical entertainments, lotteries and the like. It survived into the nineteenth century in occasional use, but the only remains of it now is the entrance on the left of Messrs Kennan's offices.

Swift lingered on for three more miserable years, and died on October 19th, 1745. For two days the people of Dublin filed past his coffin in the Deanery, and he was buried by his own desire, 'as privately as possible, and at twelve o'clock at night'. The inscription, 'in large letters, deeply cut, and strongly gilded' on his black marble monument, was called by Yeats (who translated it) 'the greatest epitaph in history':

HIC DEPOSITVM EST CORPVS
JONATHAN SWIFT, S.T.D.
HVJVS ECCLESIAE CATHEDRALIS
DECANI,
VBI SAEVA INDIGNATIO
VLTERIVS COR LACERARE NEQVIT.
ABI, VIATOR
ET IMITARE, SI POTERIS
STRENVVM PRO VIRILI
LIBERTATIS VINDICATOREM.

A recent writer has said that, for him at least, 'that epitaph would always make our city a place of pilgrimage, even if nothing else of it remained'.[5] Beside it is a bust of Swift, presented in 1775 by the nephew of George Faulkner his publisher. Cunningham, the sculptor, was a brother of that charming poet John Cunningham, of Dublin and Newcastle-upon-Tyne, who wrote this 'Epigraphe' for the bust:

> *Say, to the Drapier's vast unbounded fame*
> *What added honours can the sculptor give?*
> *None—'tis a sanction from the Drapier's name*
> *Must bid the sculptor and his marble live.*[6]

When Swift went mad, Lord Orrery wrote to Deane Swift: 'I have heard him describe persons in that condition, with a liveliness and a horror, that on this late occasion have recalled to me his very words'. His remark on the tree dying at the top, and his quatrain in the verses on his own death, are too well known to need quotation. For the last fourteen years of his life he had been meditating the foundation of an hospital for the insane, and had long been a Governor of Bedlam in London. In *A Short View of the State of Ireland* (1728) he had written: 'I have known an Hospital, where all the Household-Officers grew Rich, while the Poor for whose sake it was built, were almost starving for want of Food and Raiment'. One hopes he had no Dublin hospital in mind.

All Dublin knew that he was leaving his money for this purpose, and when he died the Hospital—St Patrick's Hospital, usually called Swift's Hospital—was built, on land near Dr Steevens's and given by the Governors of that foundation. The architect was George Semple, whose book of drawings and specifications has survived. With the aid of parliamentary grants and legacies, the building, begun in 1749, was opened in 1757. In 1778 it was enlarged by Cooley, but without destroying the architectural character which Semple had given it. The entrance front is a seven-bay astylar façade in mountain-granite, with a central pediment, a dignified and solid design. The little wings are Cooley's, as is the very long extension of both rere wings.[7]

George Semple has another connexion with Swift, in that he designed, also in 1749, the granite spire of 100 feet which surmounts Archbishop Minot's 147-foot fortress-tower placed at the north-west corner of St Patrick's in the fourteenth century. Swift, by obstruction and procrastination, prevented Archbishop King from adding such a spire *in brick* so far back as 1714.[8]

This Semple is the first distinguished representative of the most fecund and ubiquitous of the Dublin building families. They are found in the Gild of Plasterers, Carpenters, Masons etc. from before 1744.[9] In the sixties and seventies there is an Edward, another George, two Patricks and a John, variously described as 'Plasterers and Stuccodores' or 'Bricklayers', while this George appears in Directories as 'Architect and Engineer'. The best known of all the Semples was John the church architect, who flourished from about 1820 onwards.

George Semple built houses in Dublin for notabilities like the Archbishop of Dublin, and at least one country house. He himself lived (in 1776) in Queen Street. His magnum opus was the rebuilding of Essex Bridge, which will be dealt with later.

In the year that Swift died, a young doctor called Bartholomew Mosse opened, in a converted house in George's Lane, the first maternity hospital in the then British dominions. He was a very remarkable man, one who combined in a rare degree the love of architectural magnificence with that of his fellow-men. He was born in Maryborough in 1712, and had travelled extensively in Europe, first as a military man and later in the private prosecution of his medical studies. He was a musician and amateur cabinet-maker, a collector of pictures and patron of sculptors. But above all he had, like Swift, a passionate preoccupation with the wretched condition of the poor and afflicted in Dublin. By the time of his early death in 1759, he had transformed the most fashionable quarter in Dublin, as well as revolutionising maternity services in these islands.

The little hospital in George's Lane was only a beginning, an experiment. It attracted attention, at first mockery but soon emulation, for London paid it the compliment of founding Dr Daniel Layard's Hospital on Dr Mosse's plan, in 1748. Soon Mosse was in a position to move to tailor-made premises, for in the first five years he had raised nearly four thousand pounds by plays, lotteries, concerts and oratorios. The Doctor's excellences were so diverse that we might be tempted to think him an improbable personification of virtue, but for one engaging trait, which rounds off the portrait of this wholly admirable man. He was a great friend of Cassels, and liked nothing better than to sit in taverns with the architect and his musical friends till three or four o'clock in the morning. Mosse had probably contracted this agreeable habit in Germany, where he may have visited the pioneer maternity clinic at Strassburg.[10]

With only five hundred pounds in his pocket, he took a lease in 1748 of a large plot of ground at the north end of Sackville Street, which had apparently escaped the acquisitive activities of the Gardiners. Here, fronting on to Great Britain (now Parnell) Street, he built his Hospital, since famous all over the world as the 'Rotunda'. Cassels gave the design, but died a few months before the building was begun in 1751. At about the same time Luke Gardiner drove a road 72 feet wide (now called Cavendish Row, Parnell (late Rutland) Square, East, and Frederick St North) through the gardens of the Bunch of Keys into the Barley Fields, continuing in a somewhat oblique direction the line of Sackville Street. It is said that Mosse and Cassels intended the Hospital to close the vista up the Mall, but that Gardiner quarrelled with them and made his street instead. The quarrel cannot have been very serious, for Rutland Square as it finally took shape was a joint Mosse-Gardiner scheme, this new street forming the first side of it.

A closer glance at the auspices under which these, some of the most palatial houses in Dublin, were built, will show how the scheme was worked out in detail. Most of the building leases of 'Cavendish Street' to give it its earliest name, date from 1753 and the following few years. Some of the sites were leased by Luke Gardiner or his son Sackville to architects such as John Ensor, Cassels's assistant who executed the Hospital, builders such as Henry Darley, a member of the family of master-masons who owned the Ardbraccan and Golden Hill quarries, Lewis Thomas or Henry Volquartz. Others, such as No 7, were leased to private gentlemen (in this case a barrister) who built themselves private houses.[11] Three houses in the street (only two of which adjoined one another) were built in equal partnership by Dr Mosse, John Ensor and Henry Darley. Yet another house, No 12, was leased as a finished house by Sackville Gardiner to a private tenant. The north and west sides—Palace Row and Granby Row—were 'opened' in 1769 and 1766 respectively, though John Ensor is known to have planned the north side for Mosse as early as 1755, while some sort of a lane or street existed on the line of Granby Row as early as 1728. This could explain why the east and west sides are not quite parallel. Lord Charlemont took the double site in the centre of Palace Row in 1762, and on it built one of the greatest of all Dublin houses.[12] The site next door (No 21) was sold by Dr Mosse's son in 1760 to Simon Vierpyl, the statuary and builder, whom Charlemont brought from Rome in 1756.[13]

When completed in the seventies, the square contained forty-eight numbered houses plus the nine in the part called Cavendish Row. The south side, being formed by Great Britain Street, an ancient thoroughfare leading since time immemorial to the Bridge of Dublin, was and is masked by the Hospital and so is not included. From the acquisition of No 4 by Lord Wicklow in 1754 or so for £3,500, the social success of the venture gathered strength, till in 1787 the Square had a larger number of resident grandees than any other address in Dublin, even including the much larger Stephen's Green.* In 1792 it was the residence of eleven peers, one peeress in her own right, two bishops and twelve Members of Parliament. The Green at the same period had a similar number of grandees— one more to be exact—but a higher proportion were M.P.'s and bishops.

Rutland Square is thus the earliest of the Dublin squares if we except the Green which, as already explained, had a different genesis. It confirmed the eastward drive, and finally marked the division of social Dublin into two quite distinct East (and therefore fashionable) ends: one clustering round Mosse's Hospital, and the other beginning to find its centre in Kildare (Leinster) House. For the rest of the century these two quarters remain quite distinct, separated by narrow and socially impossible streets. They come to be identified, respectively, with the Gardiner and Fitzwilliam (Pembroke) Estates, and continue to be developed in neck-and-neck rivalry into the early years of the nineteenth century. During the nineteenth century they remain astonishingly equal in the numbers of their grandees, differing only by one or two units in a total of

---

* That is to say, that of the 200-odd individuals who paid the private sedan-chair tax for the Hospital's upkeep, thirty-one lived in Rutland Square as defined above, and twenty-four in the Green. Twenty were in Sackville Street, fourteen in Merrion Square, while Dominick Street and Kildare Street tied for the next place with eight each. Others were found as far afield as Broadstone (two), Leeson Street (two), Smithfield (one), Arran Quay (one), Castle Street—not including the Castle itself—(one), Mary Street (two) and Westland Row (two).

about a hundred resident peers and bishops. Considering that the North Side was smaller in area (and of course younger) than the South, it is remarkable how well it held its ground. Indeed, being smaller but so closely matched in numbers, it must have been socially more exclusive. It is only in the twentieth century that its final downfall has taken place, and even that is not complete, for Parnell Square has gone to offices rather than to the slum of its surroundings.

So far we have said little of the Rotunda Hospital itself. Externally it is stodgy enough, a huge block of a building which looks not unlike Leinster House with a three-storey tower and cupola perched on top of it, not very convincingly integrated with the substructure. There are many more graceful towers and domes in Dublin, but it must have made more of a show as originally surmounted with a cradle, crown and ball, which cost Mosse a hundred pounds in the making and a further thirty-seven for gilding.[14]

This is only a minor instance of the lavishness with which Mosse set about his project. But it was not, as it might seem to be, a misapplication of charitable funds. For the core of the project was to harness social ambition and aristocratic gaiety to his humane purpose. Even before the lease was signed Mosse had already begun, with his gardener Robert Stevenson, to plan the centre of the square as a fashionable resort. The site was admirable, southward-sloping and therefore warm. Behind the Hospital, above a steep bank, was a terrace, behind that again a large green with a serpentine walk at its eastern end, then an amphitheatre or exedra half-surrounded by a 'wilderness' of little walks, and finally, in front of Charlemont House, the terrace called the 'Orchestra', designed by Ensor and carried out by Vierpyl, whence the music was discoursed. Even at the beginning there were temples of refreshment and assembly-rooms, though the main development in this direction dates from after Mosse's death.

Long before the new hospital was opened the Gardens had proved their social and financial success. But even Mosse had enemies, and these had their moment of triumph when the Doctor, returning from London, was arrested at Holyhead for an alleged debt of £200. But he managed to escape from custody and made his way back to Dublin, and no more is heard of this trouble. He imported Castrucci and other celebrated musicians, and in addition to concerts there were illuminations and every other kind of fashionable money-raiser. In music, indeed, the history of the Gardens is virtually that of Dublin for the rest of the century. An English visitor of 1764, John Bush,[15] considered the Gardens well worth comparison with those of Vauxhall.

When, after Mosse's death, the Rotunda was built, and the New Assembly Rooms added a generation later, the close alliance between obstetrics and entertainment was permanently cemented. At the present moment, the Lying-in Hospital, the Gate Theatre, the Rotunda Cinema and a dance-hall are all to be found under the same roof, the last three occupying the Supper Room, Assembly Room and Ball Room of the eighteenth century. Only the outdoor activities have entirely ceased. In the centre of the Gardens the Nurses' Home has been built in recent years: a pleasant enough building but in this position an affront to tradition and good sense alike.

With the aid of the receipts from the Gardens and grants from Parliament, the Hospital was opened in 1757. Its supreme artistic treasure, the Chapel, was among the last items to be executed. To reach it, one enters the large flagged hall in the centre, very typical Cassels, low but spacious, with busts of Dr Mosse and other benefactors. The staircase, lit by a venetian window overlooking the Gardens, is an ordinary enough Dublin rococo piece. The Chapel, to which it leads, is in startling contrast. It is a square of eighty-six feet, thirty feet high, occupying the whole centre of the front above the Hall. Its ceiling is without parallel in Ireland, and would be hard to match much nearer than Germany—a full-blooded baroque treatment with figures in whole relief, cherubs, terms, bunches of grapes and ribbands of text flying out from the cove. Groups in the round, emblematic of Faith, Hope and Charity, occupy large niches in the cove, while over the organ two angels, one with a trumpet, display the Tables of the Law, and over the altar the Lamb is enthroned under a canopy, adorned by winged figures kneeling on the cornice of the 'east' window, and cherubs bear aloft the plaster folds of the curtain. The whole work was designed and executed by Barthelemy Cramillion (of whom practically nothing is known), and Mosse paid him five hundred guineas for it.

Mr C. P. Curran (to whose work on the Rotunda's architecture this account is heavily indebted) has rightly pointed out that the Chapel as a whole is only half-hearted baroque in that the galleries and floor plan, though richly executed, are rectilinear and take no account of the undulating octagon and other curvilinear elements in the ceiling. Only the altar-rail swells out in a faint echo of the rhythm above. But this contrast may be held to enhance the value of the baroque element. Certainly it is difficult to imagine the Chapel with (as was originally intended) about three times as much gilding as it has already, and the compartments of the ceiling filled with chiaroscuros by Cipriani, for which Dr Mosse was negotiating at the time of his death in 1759 at the age of forty-six.

Mosse was the first Master of the Rotunda, and was succeeded in the mastership by Sir Fielding Ould, whose name is still famous in the annals of his art.* As Mr Curran has finely said of Mosse 'the amenity of the arts . . . must be regarded as no more than a by-product of his charity and ancillary to its purpose. His primary and more lasting exertions were, and in the hands of his successors still are directed to the stuff of life itself'. The further development of these ancillary arts, in the building of the Rotunda proper and the Assembly rooms, must be left till we come to deal with the architects of the mid-century and later.

> * Sir Fielding Ould is made a knight
> He should have been a Lord by right,
> For then the ladies' cry would be,
> 'O Lord, good Lord, deliver me!'

REFERENCES

[1] Wyse Jackson, *Jonathan Swift, Dean and Pastor*, 1939, 156–7.
[2] Gilbert, I, 72.
[3] [Mainwaring] *Life of Handel*, 1760, pp. 131–2.
[4] Julian Herbage, *Messiah*, 1948, 21.
[5] Arland Ussher in *Irish Times*, May 8th, 1948.
[6] *Poetical Works of J. Cunningham*, Bell's Poets, 86.
[7] See *The Legacy of Swift*, ed. M. J. Craig. Dublin, 1948.
[8] Wyse Jackson, *op. cit.* 115–6.
[9] See Curran in *JRSAI* LXX, 52 sqq.
[10] *Encyclopaedia Britannica*, 11th ed. *s.v.* 'Obstetrics.'
[11] *Georg. Soc.* I, 28, 9; III, 99 sqq.
[12] For which, see my *Volunteer Earl*, 1948.
[13] Curran, *Rotunda Hospital*, 29.
[14] *ibid.* p. 9.
[15] *Hibernia Curiosa*, Dublin & London, 1766.

PART THREE

Grattan's Dublin

CHAPTER XV

Social Symptoms

I T IS NOT the intention of this book to recount in detail the circumstances of life in eighteenth-century Dublin. In most respects Dublin was like any other European capital: the dirt, the gaiety, the cruelty, the smells, the pomp, the colour and sound so remote from anything we know—all were to be found in much the same proportions from Lisbon to St Petersburg. There would be no great gain in attempting to describe the Dublin background as though it were unique.

None the less it seems that in certain respects Dublin is an extreme example of tendencies generally diffused. The eighteenth-century nobility were nowhere remarkable for their community of interest with their inferiors, but in Ireland, where land confiscations and penal laws were the inescapable conditions, this cleavage was more violent. On the other hand the existence of strong internal tension in any society sets up a curiously intimate relationship between the interests involved. Immigrants who, had they stayed in England, would have behaved like normal Englishmen, found in Ireland an almost rootless society of speculators and go-getters. Many individuals adopted a violent habit of behaviour which brought them closer to the dispossessed helots than might have seemed possible. Dublin society had something in common with the Calcutta described by William Hickey, and for much the same reasons. The immigrant Dubliners, like the immigrant New Yorkers of a later era, often adopted the gangster mentality as a rule of life in struggle. Men who would in happier circumstances have been English gentlemen, drifted into the habit of surrounding themselves with roughs and plug-uglies: the sensitiveness of their touch upon the environment round them took the form of the trigger-finger. There was a plentiful supply of roughs among the dispossessed: simple peasants who had been corrupted and in their turn were able to corrupt. The proscription of the Catholic Church which would have been the moral sheet-anchor of the floating urban riff-raff, helped to ensure demoralisation. In many parts of Europe deism had begun to shade into diabolism, and Dublin, which had burned John Toland's book* in 1697, had its secret sects of blasphemers and satanists.

By the end of the century the half-mounted gentlemen described by Sir Jonah Barrington, the petty squireens and middlemen, were beginning to be old-fashioned when the violent events of 1798 gave them a new lease of life, and almost a last chance to run riot in the country. But in the early period the characteristic habit of violence took form more in the pursuit of personal ends than in the prosecution of political advantage. The famous Annesley peerage case, heard in Dublin in 1743, is a classic instance.

Arthur Annesley, first Earl of Anglesey, whom we have already seen developing his estate between Dame Street and the river, had a son, Lord Altham, whose nephew Arthur Annesley succeeded as the fourth Lord Altham in 1701. This Lord Altham married a natural daughter of the Duke of Buckingham. He deserted her once, but they were reconciled again in Dublin. In 1715 a child, James Annesley, was born at Dunmaine, Co. Wexford, Lord Altham's country seat. The parents (if parents they were) separated soon afterwards, Lord Altham having custody of the child, while his lady was struck with paralysis and died in London. Lord Altham, with the boy James, lived in Cross Lane† or Cherry Lane;‡ and a Miss Gregory came to solace the father's widowhood. Soon the boy was sent to school at Barnaby Dunn's in Werburgh Street, and Miss Gregory assumed the title of Lady Altham—while, it is said, the real Lady Altham still lived.

Lord Altham had a reversionary interest in the Anglesey estate; and his desire to raise money on these expectations is given as the reason for what followed. To raise money, it was necessary that the existence of his son should be concealed. Miss Gregory, also, wanted the boy's claim discredited. So James was moved to the house of a dancing-master named Cavanagh, there to be kept in the strictest seclusion, while his father and Miss Gregory, who had been living in Phrapper Lane,§ migrated to the suburban peace of Inchicore.

---

* *Christianity Not Mysterious*: London 1696. Burned by order of the Irish Parliament, Sept. 1697. Toland was himself an Irishman.

† Now called Bolton Parade (!). ‡ Off Bolton Street.

§ Now called Beresford Street, off North King Street.

The boy James now made his escape from Mr Cavanagh, and took to wandering the streets of Dublin like many another waif of nine years old. For a short time he was employed as a messenger boy by an undergraduate in Trinity, then he found asylum with Dominic Farrell, a poor linen-merchant and a creditor of Lord Altham's. Farrell reproached the father with neglect, but was put off with the promises that not only would the debt be paid but the child's board also would be made up.

By this time such an unsettled childhood had begun to tell upon the lad, who now ran away from Farrell. One day Farrell and a friend, John Purcel, a butcher of Phœnix Street, were in Smithfield market and saw the boy riding a horse. When Purcel heard who he was, he offered to take him home with him, and the boy was so grateful that he fell upon his knees and blessed him, 'for', said he, 'I'm almost lost'. Purcel's wife 'put a large pot on the fire, got a wedge of soap, and cleaned him, and put on him a shirt and clothes of her son'. The boy took kindly to Mrs Purcel, and called her 'Mammy', and, says Purcel, 'my wife and some people that knew the child would call him my Lord Altham; and he was a considerable while with me, as good a child as ever stood in the walls of a house; and took the small-pox in September . . .'

It was at this point, when the child was just recovering from the small-pox, 'being green' (as Mrs Purcel said) that the wicked uncle appeared upon the scene. This was Lord Altham's brother Richard, who appeared one day with a gun in his hand and a setting dog with him, while Purcel was joking with the child. They sat down together to drink a glass of beer, but the child began to cry because, as he said, 'the sight of that gentleman that is now come in, has put such a dread upon me, I don't know what to do with myself'. Richard Annesley stayed to drink no less than three mugs of ale, catechising the child and promising to Purcel with fair words.

Soon after this Lord Altham died and was buried in Christ Church, while his son ran quickly to the church and cried bitterly. Uncle Richard assumed the title, and sent for James to Purcel's house. James was frightened to go by himself, so he held on to Purcel's coat-tail while the butcher took his stick and went to wait upon Lord Altham, whom he found surrounded by roughs who attempted, at his orders, to take the child from Purcel. But the butchers of the Ormonde Market (whom we have already met) came to the rescue, and foiled this and later attempts to kidnap young James. For a short time the boy was a servant in the house of Dick Tighe, Swift's enemy, who lived in the Haymarket behind Phœnix Street; but finally Lord Altham managed to arrest him in Ormonde Market, with the aid of two constables, for the alleged theft of a silver spoon.

Without any formal accusation or hearing, James Annesley was hustled in a coach to George's Quay, into a boat and so down to Ringsend where he was forthwith shipped to Philadelphia on board the *James*. On arrival in America he was sold into slavery.

Thirteen years later he managed to escape to Jamaica, where he enlisted as a sailor in a British ship, and made himself known to Admiral Vernon, who was cashiered in 1746 and is remembered as the first man to water the British Navy's rum. James Annesley returned to find his uncle in somewhat uneasy enjoyment of his honours and estates. For Richard Annesley's matrimonial adventures were even more perplexing than those of his brother. He had married one wife in 1715, deserted her and 'married' another, abandoned her and lived with a publican's daughter called Juliana Donovan, living with her in Ireland though he is said to have gone over to London and there married yet a fourth lady. When his much-wronged nephew returned, the uncle had just been excommunicated for failing to pay alimony and costs to his second 'wife', and he remained excommunicated for the rest of his days. As a compensation, however, he had succeeded to his uncle's earldom of Anglesey.

At first he proposed a compromise with his nephew, offering to give up the title and estates for an annuity of two or three thousand pounds on which he himself would go and live in France, and to this end he began to take lessons in French. But fate relieved him of this drudgery very soon, for his nephew had the misfortune to kill a man in a shooting accident in England. Exultantly the Earl set about having his nephew hanged, declaring that he would cheerfully pay ten thousand pounds to ensure that happy consummation. He hurried to London, drove to the Court in a coach-and-six, and jumped on to the bench of magistrates where he tried to intimidate and browbeat the witnesses. But all was in vain: James Annesley was acquitted and came to Dublin to prosecute his claim, staying with an apothecary in Jervis Street.

His *modus operandi* (devised no doubt by his lawyer, Daniel MacKercher) was rather indirect. He began by leasing to one James Craig a large portion of the Anglesey estates in the county Meath, whereupon Craig brought a suit for ejectment against Richard Earl of Anglesey. It was heard in November 1743, and the flower of Irish legal talent was engaged on both sides.*

Uncle Richard's defence was that James, far from being the son of Lady Altham, was the offspring of a union between his father and one Juggy Landy, described as 'a clean bright girl'. But the defence failed, and after fifteen days' hearing—one of the longest in the history of the Bar—judgment was given in favour of Annesley.

Needless to say, this was not the end of the story. From 1743 till 1760, for seventeen whole years, the uncle laboured by every obstructive tactic known to the law, to postpone the final surrender; and so successfully that when James Annesley died in 1760, his uncle was still in effective possession of the title and estates. Still excommunicate, the old rascal lingered on for another year until he himself died, after which the remainder of his estate and his titles became the subject of renewed litigation between his issue by his various wives and quasi-wives. The Irish House of Lords finally decided in favour of his son by Juliana Donovan, who succeeded to the Irish honours (Valentia, Mountnorris and Altham). The English House, on the other hand, decided against him, and the English honours lapsed.[1]

Certainly there were ogres in the earth in those days. Not all the violence in high places was so consciously directed towards self-advancement as that of Lord Anglesey. In 1738 young Lord Santry killed a man out of mere bad temper when drunk in a public-house in Palmerstown, and for this he was brought to trial by his peers. He was found guilty but unanimously recommended to mercy, and after obtaining a reprieve and later a full pardon, withdrew to England. The story that his relatives brought this about by threatening to cut off the Dublin water-supply (which ran through the grounds of their seat at Templeogue), seems, alas, to have no

* The Prime Serjeant, Anthony Malone, the Solicitor-General Warden Flood and the Recorder of Dublin, Eaton Stannard, appeared for Anglesey. Annesley was represented by thirteen lawyers including the Second and Third Serjeants.

documentary foundation. Four years later another nobleman, Lord
Netterville, was also arraigned for murder before the House of
Lords, but owing to the death of the two principal witnesses, he
escaped scot-free. Both these trials were conducted with every
circumstance of pomp, that of Lord Santry being held in the House
of Commons, the better to accommodate the crowds of curious
onlookers.

Pure evil, pursued for its own sake, was not without devotees.
The widely celebrated 'Hell-Fire Club' was founded by the first
Earl of Rosse, Colonel Jack St Leger, and a humorous painter
named Worsdale[2] in about 1735, meeting in the Eagle Tavern in
Cork Hill. Cork Hill was of course very much the centre of things,
on the doorstep of the Castle and only a step or two from Essex
Bridge. Just across the road from the Eagle Tavern was the Sta-
tioners' Hall, where one might see such innocent spectacles as 'a
painting by Raphael, and several fleas tied by gold chains'.*

The amusements of the 'Hell-Fire Club' were more sophisticated.
No doubt they resembled the activities of the similar group in
England; no doubt the stories of black masses and so forth have some
basis in fact. As I have already said, it is less certain that the Club
had any connexion with Conolly's shooting-lodge on Montpelier
Hill at the foot of the Dublin Mountains, which is now universally
known as the 'Hell-Fire Club'. It is, of course, possible that the
Club may at times have exchanged the confines of a city tavern for
the larger and more intoxicating air of a romantic hill-top, possible
even that here they performed the notable experiment which
rumour has handed down, of setting fire to the building in which
they were carousing, in order to anticipate with greater realism the
sensations of Hell itself. Two facts give the tale some likelihood:
Tom Conolly of Castletown is alleged to have held converse with
the Devil in the dining-room at Castletown, and if the Hell-Fire
clubmen wanted to set fire to themselves with comparative safety,
they could not have chosen a more suitable building than his
shooting-lodge, for it is vaulted in stone and survived even being
used as a platform for an enormous bonfire in honour of Queen
Victoria's visit in 1849.

* Gilbert II 14–15. In the Eagle Tavern, also, the Duchess of Hamilton, one of the Gunning
sisters, stayed in 1755, when the approaches were made impassable by the vast crowds which
came to see the celebrated beauty.

Lord Rosse, one of the founders of the Club, is the hero of an oft-told tale. When he lay on his death-bed in his house in Molesworth Street in 1741, the rector of St Ann's wrote him a letter begging him to repent of his evil ways while there was yet time. Lord Rosse read the letter with some amusement, and noticing that it began simply 'My Lord', re-sealed it and addressed it to Lord Kildare, well known for his piety and integrity of life. When Lord Kildare received and read it, he naturally sent for the rector. The luckless parson was subjected to an unexpected and unmerited grilling before the true explanation emerged. Lord Rosse, had he been a witness, would no doubt have enjoyed it hugely; but by this time he had passed to another, and perhaps a warmer, climate.

The stories told of the Dublin bucks and rakes are many, and they illustrate the ferocious sense of fun affected in such circles. Buck English, for example, was a convivial fellow notorious for his many sins.* Being one day in the company of his usual associates at Daly's Club in College Green, he became so drunk that he fell asleep. His companions then devised a scheme. When he woke up, they had drawn all the shutters and blinds, and were sitting in pitch darkness, but continuing to clink their glasses and go through the audible motions of playing dice. They kept up this comedy with the utmost solemnity for a considerable time, long enough to convince the Buck that he had been struck blind as a punishment for his misdeeds. His eyes were bandaged, and in a darkened private room he was visited from time to time by mock doctors. It is related, however, that his remorse did not survive the exposure of the trick that had been played upon him, for his fury against the perpetrators knew no bounds.[3]

The career of Tiger Roche is a not uncharacteristic example of the period. He was born in Dublin in 1729, and showed great polish and prominence in his youth, coming under the favourable notice of Chesterfield when Viceroy. But he fell into evil courses, and with some drunken associates he attacked and killed a watchman. Fleeing from Dublin he concealed himself in Cork, thence going to America where he fought on the French side against the Indians. He was accused of stealing a fowling-piece from a brother

---

* See Sir E. Sullivan, preface to *Buck Whaley's Memoirs* 1906, p. xii, n. 2, where it is stated that English once shot a waiter at an inn in England, and had him charged in the bill at £50.

officer, and after conviction and degradation flew at his accuser's throat, fastening his teeth in it. He fought on the English side at Ticonderoga, but found the way to promotion barred by the report of his theft. He returned to Europe, and in London set himself to seek out and punish all who repeated the story of his guilt, attacking them in the street in London and Chester.

In the meantime his accuser in America had left a deathbed confession attesting Roche's innocence. Armed with this vindication, the Tiger returned to Dublin, where his handsome person, his becoming scars, his skill in dancing and his American adventures won him social success, especially with the ladies.

He was soon able to serve the ladies in a more material respect. There flourished in Dublin at this time a class of nocturnal strollers known as the 'pinkindindies', skilled in the art of 'pinking' or slashing their victims with the points of their swords which protruded below the open end of the scabbard.⁴ They used this technique to recoup their gaming losses at the expense of unaccompanied pedestrians. 'The pinking dindies', says Herbert in his *Varieties*, 'made a rule to be well-dressed', and they 'never attacked swordsmen, nor any but single men and citizens, who neither wore fine clothes nor swords'. They were in the habit also of taking ladies from their protectors, 'and *many* females were destroyed by that lawless banditti'.

One evening Roche happened to be on Ormonde Quay when an old gentleman with his son and daughter were attacked by these miscreants. He engaged them singlehanded, wounding some and putting the rest to flight. This stimulated him to form a body to patrol the streets at night, and so give 'that protection to the citizens which the miserable and decrepit watch were not able to afford'.

Unfortunately this spirited service was unpaid and Tiger Roche gravitated to London, where he soon found himself in the King's Bench debtors' prison, having run through his wife's fortune. And now a strange reversal of tendency showed itself in his character. Where before he had been quick to resent a slight, he was now submissive to the point of torpor. When insulted by fellow-prisoners, he, who would formerly have demanded satisfaction in blood, now wept like a child. By a strange accident, Buck English was also confined in the King's Bench, and assaulted the luckless Tiger with a stick, belabouring him cruelly. On the other hand, Roche behaved so badly to his wife that she separated from him.

Such violent changes as this, from elation to depression, are not unknown to medicine. But it is less usual to find them accompanied, as apparently they were in this case, by corresponding changes in their subject's objective situation. Roche was released from prison: a small legacy enabled him to cut something of his old figure, and to indulge all his old impatience of restraint. Once, in a billiard-room, he was playing solo so long that some one suggested to him that he might be preventing other gentlemen from using the table. 'Gentlemen!' said Roche, 'why, sir, except you and me, and two or three more, there is not a gentleman in the room'. He explained afterwards to his friend that such a remark could be safely made, as 'there was not a thief in the room that did not consider himself *one* of the *two or three* gentlemen I excepted'.

The further adventures of the Tiger are more astonishing still. He became as much admired in London as he had been in Dublin. He was nominated for Middlesex against the odious Luttrell* (another Irishman), but declined to stand. He was nearly murdered by two footpads in Chelsea, and captured one of them. When both were convicted, Roche interceded for their lives and they were spared. He captured another heiress, and again for a short time commanded great wealth. When this came to an end he embarked for India as a Captain of Foot, but quarrelled with another captain who was murdered at night outside his lodgings at the Cape. Suspicion fell upon Roche, who fled by night and took refuge among the Kaffirs. A rumour got abroad that the Dutch authorities had had him broken on the wheel, but the truth, we are told, was somewhat different. The Dutch tried and acquitted him of the murder whereupon he went on to India in a French ship, and was arrested on landing at Bombay. After much legal wrangling, conducted apparently by Roche himself, he was tried again at the Old Bailey in December 1775, and again he was acquitted. But the pendulum had swung for the last time: he did not regain the position which he

---

* The Luttrells lived at Luttrellstown, Co. Dublin, and also sometimes in Dublin. Colone Henry Luttrell, who betrayed the Jacobites at Aughrim, was shot in his sedan chair outside his house in Stafford Street in 1717. The assassin was never betrayed.

had twice lost and twice recovered: he sank into obscurity and is never heard of again.[5]

This fantastic world of Bucks, Bullies, Pinkindindies, Sweaters, abduction-clubs and the like, lives on in the popular mythology of Ireland. It may not have been entirely born of the causes I have suggested, but it certainly throve in the presence of these conditions. It appealed to the savage Irish humour which enjoyed (and still enjoys) the two brothers who were called Kilkelly and Kilcoachy because one had shot a man called Kelly while the other had shot his coachman, or the three noblemen known as Hellgate, Newgate and Cripplegate because one had a satanic aspect, another was never out of jail, and the third 'was lame, yet no whit disabled from his buckish achievements'.[6] The half-mounted gentlemen and barbarous squireens remained curiously close to the grand and polite society of the capital: the tradition carries through George Robert Fitzgerald to the incredible half-world inhabited by the Sham Squire Higgins and the rascally Watty Cox, the needy journalists and scabrous informers of Ninety-Eight and Eighteen-Three, till it finally peters out in the cold grey light of Victorian times. Or rather it takes refuge among the middlemen and election-agents of the country districts, and Dublin knows it no more.

These are the symptoms of a society uncomfortably cleft, but happily there were other and more hopeful signs. Mrs Delany's encounter with the nuns of Channel Row is worth recalling. Early in 1751 Mrs Delany (who had, by the by, been reading Carte's life of Ormonde and pronounced the Duke 'the *completest* character of a truly great man I ever read!' 'Such piety, such loyalty, such conduct!')—Mrs Delany entertained to dinner a Miss Crilly.[7] 'And who is Miss Crilly? say you. Why, she is a *nun professed*, and lives at the Nunnery in King Street, Dublin; but nuns in this country have the liberty of going to see relatives and particular friends . . . She is an old acquaintance of D.D.'s, is extremely sprightly, civil, and entertaining . . . After dinner we carried her home, and she entreated me to go in, that some of her sisterhood might gratify their curiosity by seeing me; we drank tea with them, saw their chapel, and I played on the organ: they wear no particular habit, only a black stuff nightgown and plain linen. I should like them *much better in their habit*; Bushe was very droll amongst them all, and said a thousand comical things, which they seemed not at all offended at. They have a handsome parlour to receive their company in, and no grates belonging to them: the chapel is pretty, the altar mightily decorated with candlesticks, gilding, little statues, but terribly bad pictures ...'

And a few months later:[8] '... here flew in *my nun* Miss Crilly: sprightly and agreeable as she is ... she is an agreeable entertaining creature, and seems to have good principles and pretty sentiments. She has been confined with sickness and devotion, and I don't call upon her so often as I should like to do, as people are so offended here if *these nuns* are much taken notice of, that I should be thought *disaffected*'.

It is all there: the kindliness, the sense of strangeness among these French-educated Dominicans, the anxiety of the nuns to appear well in Protestant eyes, the terribly bad pictures, the wish to make no distinctions, but behind it all the fear of social censure—all this has a very familiar ring. But it is a great improvement on the mood which engendered the Penal laws less than a generation earlier. And Mrs Delany, one should never forget, was English.

The circle of Keane O'Hara, Baron Dawson and Lord Mornington shows a much closer fusion of cultures. Music seems to have been the first thing to overcome the religious barrier, for the Channel Row convent (of which Miss Crilly was an inmate) imported Italian musicians and 'many Protestant fine gentlemen' were 'invited to take their places in a convenient gallery to hear the performance'.

Lord Mornington, son of Richard Colley and father of the Duke of Wellington, was the leader of musical Dublin. He lived first in Grafton Street, but moved in 1765 to Lord Antrim's house in Upper Merrion Street, an enormous brick mansion in which the Duke of Wellington was born. It was bought later by Nicholas Lawless, the first Lord Cloncurry, and it is now the offices of the Land Commission.* Lord Mornington shared the Dublin enthusiasm for amateur theatricals, and he composed glees, one of which, 'Here in cool grot', was once widely known. He founded a Charitable

---

* Cloncurry bought it (*Personal Recollections of* [second] *Lord Cloncurry*, 1850, p. 6) for £8,000 in 1791, and his son sold it ten years later, after it had been rented by Castlereagh during the Union period, for £2,500. A few years ago it lost its cornice and now has the usual flat Dublin coping.

Musical Society, and at the age of thirteen, when visited by his godmother Mrs Delany at the family seat of Dangan, near Trim, in 1748, was already 'a most extraordinary boy . . . he is a very good scholar, and whatever study he undertakes he masters it most surprisingly. He began with the fiddle last year, he now plays everything at sight; he understands fortification, building of ships, and has more knowledge than I ever met with in one so young. He is a child among children, and as tractable and complying to his sisters, and all that should have any authority over him, as the little children can be to you'. He was equally amiable when grown up, for he married a girl without any fortune, a few weeks after Lady Louisa Lennox had jilted him and married Mr Conolly of Castletown.

Keane O'Hara was vice-president of Lord Mornington's Musical Academy. He belonged to an extremely ancient Sligo family, and it was in Sligo that he gave hospitality to Turlough O'Carolan the bard, who celebrated this circumstance in the song 'O'Hara's Cup':

> *Oh! were I at rest*
> *Amid Aran's green isles,*
> *Or in climes where the summer*
> *Unchangingly smiles,*
> *Though treasures and dainties*
> *Might come at a call,*
> *Still O'Hara's full cup*
> *I would prize more than all.*[*]

O'Hara wrote a burletta called *Midas* in ridicule of the Italian burlettas then playing at Smock-Alley Theatre. It was produced at Crow Street Theatre in 1762, and being full of Dublin jokes and allusions, was a great success. He wrote a number of burlettas and musical farces, and died in 1782. He was a conspicuous figure in Dublin society, so tall that the last line of a popular Italian song which ended

> *Che no hanno crudelta*

was often sung as

> *Keane O'Hara's cruel tall.*

He had, they say, 'the appearance of an old fop, with spectacles and an antiquated wig' but was none the less 'the very pink of gentility and good breeding'.[*] He also wrote a satirical novel in the manner

* See the satirical portrait-group showing O'Hara, Mornington and others, reproduced as frontispiece to *Georg. Soc.* III.

of Voltaire, and etched portraits. At the first (private) performance of *Midas* he played the part of Pan himself, and even professionals like Michael Kelly were glad to learn from him.*

Keane O'Hara lived in Molesworth Street, only a few doors from Baron Dawson, a bird of similar feather. Dawson, as a Baron of the Exchequer, was one of the judges in the Annesley case, but his chief claim to fame was the celebrated encounter between him and Carolan. Both the bard and the lawyers were the guests of Squire Jones of Moneyglass, Co. Antrim. Carolan, being asked to produce a song in honour of his host, retired, as is the bardic custom, to bed with a bottle of whiskey and his harp. Here he composed the song, both words and music, the words, we are told, not being equal to the air. Dawson, whose room was next door to Carolan's, memorised the air and composed a better set of words himself. In the morning, after Carolan had sung his song, Dawson accused him of plagiarism and forthwith sang his own, to the great amusement of the company and to the fury of the affronted bard. Dawson's song, 'A Bumper, Squire Jones', is still extant: one stanza may serve as a specimen of its spirit:

> Ye lawyers so just,
> Be the cause what it will who so learnedly plead,
> How worthy of trust, you know black from white,
> You prefer wrong to right, as you're chanced to be fee'd,
> Leave musty Reports, and forsake the King's Courts,
> Where Dulness and Discord have set up their thrones,
> Burn Salkeld and Ventris, with all your damn'd entries,
> And away with the claret, a bumper, Squire Jones!

A somewhat similar trick, it will be remembered, was played by the sportive Father Francis Mahony on Thomas Moore.

Dawson, whose reputation as a wit was among the greatest in Dublin, must have been a pleasant character, for a friend of his son records that he 'wandered with us for hours through his wide domains, leaped over ditches, looked for birds' nests, flew a kite, and played at marbles; he might in this respect be compared to that great Roman, who, when called on to serve the Senate, was found toying amongst his children'.[10]

* According to J. D. Herbert, he was the 'laureate' of the 'Kingdom of Dalkey', a burlesque polity abolished in 1798, and author of *Lord Altham's Bull*, the poem in the Dublin dialect printed by Walsh in *Ireland Sixty Years Ago*.

The improvement in the tone of Dublin society which these men exemplify was no doubt partly due to the Viceroyalty of Lord Chesterfield. He was a great exception to the usual run of beefeating, bored and bigoted English nonentities who succeeded each other in dismal and stodgy pomp at Dublin Castle. He was here during the Forty-Five rebellion, and seems to have been the only man who kept his head. Some frantic alarmist woke him one morning in his State Bed with the news that the Papists were rising. 'Rising?' said Chesterfield, and yawned. 'Rising?' (he looked at his watch and yawned again) 'Why, yes, 'tis time for all honest men to rise. Time I rose myself'. Again, he was asked by some Hanoverian busybody were not there many dangerous Papists in Dublin. 'The only dangerous Papist I know in Dublin', was his reply, 'is Miss Ambrose'. Miss Ambrose was a celebrated beauty of the Viceregal Court, one who in later times would have been called a 'Castle Catholic'. She was the daughter of a wealthy Dublin brewer. and married Sir Roger Palmer of Kenure, but not before the male half of Dublin society was at her feet. She lived to be nearly a hundred, dying only in 1818. One First of July she appeared at a ball at the Castle to celebrate the Battle of the Boyne, wearing a corsage of orange lilies, whereupon the Viceroy addressed her extempore:

> *Say, lovely Tory, why the jest*
> *Of wearing orange at thy breast,*
> *When that same breast betraying shows*
> *The whiteness of the rebel rose.*

He also wrote another epigram in praise of her charms, but this unfortunately, is hardly printable by modern standards. The curious may find it in Volume V of *The New Foundling Hospital for Wit* (London, 1786), followed by the anonymous 'Answer', doubtless the work of a Dublin wit:

> *Flavia's a name a deal too free*
> *With holy writ to blend her;*
> *Henceforth let* Nell Susanna *be*
> *And* Chesterfield *the elder.*

Dublin appreciated Chesterfield's wit and tolerance, and his liberality, too, has left its mark. The precise extent of his improvements in the Phœnix Park is difficult to determine, though he certainly planted large numbers of trees in regular patterns, and made a new road, though not, it would seem, the present great avenue through the centre.[11] Many of his tree-clumps were landscaped out of existence by a gardener named James Donnell in the seventeen-eighties. But the Phœnix Column which he erected still stands, though moved a few yards from its original position. The inscription

CIVIVM OBLECTAMENTO
CAMPVM RVDEM ET INCVLTVM
ORNARI IVSSIT
PHILIPPVS STANHOPE
COMES DE CHESTERFIELD
PROREX

IMPENSIS SVIS POSVIT
PHILIPPVS STANHOPE, COMES
DE CHESTERFIELD, PROREX

records the circumstances. The Column is an extraordinarily beautiful object, almost exactly similar to the one which closes the vista at Santry Court. Just outside the Parkgate there is, on top of a wall, another stone Phœnix, but this time without a column. It bears a family resemblance to the other two. A small bush grows round the bird, rooted among the stone flames which surround it, and every spring this Phœnix appears resplendent in miraculous green fire, a pleasing spectacle which would surely delight that admirable nobleman, were he alive to see it.

REFERENCES

[1] This account is condensed from that in Gilbert, II, 321 *sqq.*
[2] Worsdale figures largely in Mrs Pilkington's *Memoirs*; see also Gilbert, III, 256-7.
[3] Gilbert, II, 306-7.
[4] Sometimes called the Pinking Dindies. See Herbert's *Irish Varieties*, 1836, 77 *sqq*, and Walsh: *Ireland Sixty Years Ago*, 1911, 17-18.
[5] This account is condensed from Walsh: *Ireland Sixty Years Ago*, 108 *sqq.*
[6] Walsh. *op. cit.* p. 17.
[7] Mrs Delany, *Autobiography* &c, III, 9.
[8] *ibid.* 38.
[9] Gilbert III, 266 *sqq.*
[10] *ibid.* 263. See also Bunting: *Ancient Music of Ireland*, 1809, p. 26.
[11] C. L. Falkiner: *Illustrations*, 67-8.

CHAPTER XVI

Public Buildings of the Mid-Century

THE YEARS 1745–60 contain an enormous amount of building activity, much more than is usually realised or implied by the generalisation that Dublin is largely the legacy of the later part of the century. Moreover, during this period some of the most important of the lines of later development were laid down. It was not a period of great political activity: except for the year 1753 when Boyle's 'country party' gained a qualified victory over the Castle, it was fairly stagnant. Parliament still met only every other year, and the Viceroy was still largely an absentee. These things were to be altered in 1767, but the town's development had to some extent anticipated the alteration. Such important events as the rebuilding of Essex Bridge, the setting up of the Wide Streets Commissioners, and the rebuilding of the Castle and of Trinity College (the last on parliamentary grants), as well as other developments already mentioned, were obviously the preparation for something. They were, in fact, the preparation of Dublin as a fit vessel to receive the Royal Exchange, the Custom House, the Four Courts, the enlarged Parliament House and ultimately the General Post Office, but nobody, of course, knew this at the time.

Almost the last official building to go up in brick was the Weavers' Hall in the Coombe (1745), an unpretentious old-fashioned building which until recently boasted an agreeable leaden statue of George II by Van Nost in a niche over the door.[1] The statue was originally gilt, but it unhappily disintegrated in process of removal a few years ago. Within there hung a tapestry portrait of the same monarch, inscribed

*The workmanship of John Vanbeaver**
Ye famous tapestry weaver.

The last appearance of brick on the grand scale was the wholesale

* Who also wove the House of Lords tapestries.

164

remodelling of Dublin Castle in the 1750's, which left it much as it stands to-day. It followed, to a large extent, the ground-lines of the mediæval plan, what is now Upper Castle Yard corresponding with the court of the original castle, while St Patrick's Hall is successor to the mediæval hall. Two of the mediæval towers, the Bermingham Tower (SW, base only, rebuilt after a fire in 1775) and the Record Tower (SE corner, crenellations and outer casing by

FIG. 6.

Johnston, 1811 or so) were visibly incorporated in the new scheme, while one of the original northern gate-towers is embedded in what is now the Genealogical Office, and supports the delightful Bedford Tower with its cupola.[2] (Pls. XXI–XXIII)

The total effect, in red brick with cream stone trimmings, seg-ment-headed ground-floor windows and arcades at salient points, is charming in an intimate collegiate fashion, persuading one to forget the evil role of the Castle in Irish affairs. Upper Castle Yard, in particular, evokes to perfection the complacent Hanoverian corruption of that era. It seems to tell us that though every man has his price, the prices are moderate and have all been paid on the nail. Everything is running like well-oiled clockwork, and the clockwork soldiers are changing guard in front of the Bedford Tower.

The authorship of these buildings is obscure. There is evidence that a wholesale re-building of the Castle was in progress as early as 1732,[3] and we know from Mrs Delany that Pearce was then employed on internal decoration at least. Pearce's office (that of Surveyor-General in the Ordnance Department) was held, after his death, by Arthur Dobbs who was a gentleman and a political economist rather than an architect. His successor, Arthur Jones Nevill, came under the parliamentary fire of the Patriot party in 1752-3, was accused of corruption in the erection of barracks, and was not only dismissed but lost his seat in Parliament. Thomas Eyre, who succeeded him, lasted till 1763. During Nevill's tenure his Clerk of Works was George Ensor, and in the absence of any evidence that Nevill was an architect, Ensor is the likeliest candidate for government designs between 1744-51. In 1752 the clerkship is vacant, but when Eyre comes in in the following year he has Joseph Jarratt* as 'Deputy'. In 1763 Jarratt vanishes from the Surveyor's Department but appears as 'Clerk and Inspector of the Civil Buildings' under the Barrack Board. He either died or retired in 1774, and was succeeded as Clerk and Inspector by Thomas Cooley. Thus Jarratt, sandwiched between two known architectural names (Ensor and Cooley), must surely have been an architect.

The departmental history is very complicated,† and can only be reconstructed from the dubious evidence of the Almanacks. But it does seem that what in 1831 became the Board of Works started as the Surveyor-General's department, and was transferred in 1760-3 to the Barrack Board, whose members became known in

* A Thomas Jarratt of Dublin entered three designs for the Exchange in 1769 (see below, Chapter XVIII) and there was another Jarratt as Engineer-in-ordinary. Mr Howard Colvin tells me that a Major Jarratt is said to have designed the Town Hall at Lancaster (1781-3). He may have been an Irish officer.

† There is a strange discrepancy between the evidence of *Liber Munerum* and that of the Directories and Fitzwilliam leases. The former states that Henry Mark Mason succeeded Eyre on the revocation of the latter's patent in 1766. But the Directories and leases give Ralph Ward as Surveyor-General from 1764 onwards.

the sixties as 'Commissioners of the Barracks and Civil Buildings'. The names of the actual architects (as Christopher Myers 1767, Graham Myers 1777, W. Gibson, Cooley, Thomas Penrose) are found as 'Architect' or 'Clerk and Inspector' under these Commissioners. But in 1766 the Surveyor-General's Department was increased by a 'Civil Branch', with a clerk of the works called William Stokes. General Vallancey (who is said to have had some architectural accomplishments*, was 'Director of Engineers', and there was another Jarratt as 'Engineer in Ordinary'.

The authorship of the Bedford Tower and its flanking buildings on the north side of Upper Castle Yard, depends therefore on their dates. The tower itself, which is probably about 1763,† may be by Jarratt, while the two gates and the central block are probably either by him or Ensor. The whole composition has been attributed to Ivory, but there seems no other justification for this than the similarity of detail between the tower and cupola and Ivory's design for the Blue-Coat School some years later.‡

The composition has its faults, notably the awkwardly wide spaces between the columns of the Musicians' Gallery. The attic storey here, as everywhere in the Castle, is an addition of the nineteenth century§ and not an improvement. The two gates, one real and occupying the site of the original gate, and the other dummy, are excellent, with their bold blocking, their broken curved pediments, and the two lead statues by Van Nost, of Justice and Mars. That of Justice has excited sardonic comment in its time: it has been noted that she stands with her back to everything but the Castle itself: worse than this, it was long remarked that rainwater collecting in her scales caused them to dip unequally. It is said that this circumstance so worked on the sensitive Castle authorities that they had holes bored in the bottoms of the pans.

Two anonymous buildings of this period may be mentioned here.

* See p. 288 below

† It is depicted by Tudor in his print of Upper Castle Yard in 1753. Unfortunately Tudor's draughtsmanship is about on a level with his French (as displayed in the ludicrous captions to his plates), and it is impossible to tell whether he was working from a finished building or an office proposal. It resembles the present tower in general outline. I suggest that a tower was intended, perhaps as early as Ensor's time, that Tudor based his print on this information, but that the detail of the tower as erected may be as late as Ivory's time.

‡ Ivory probably arrived in Dublin in about 1759.

§ Note the difference between the Petrie plates in Wright's *Historical Guide* 1821, and *Ireland Illustrated* 1829.

The Charter School at Clontarf (1748), which disappeared some time during the nineteenth century, was an impressive edifice with a portico approached by elaborate steps, and a hemispherical dome. On either side of the centre were circular niches. It stood on the shores of Dublin Bay, and bore a certain resemblance to the contemporary Palladian Villas in England.* The Incurable Hospital in Townsend Street (built as such in 1753, exchanged with the Donnybrook Lock Hospital in 1792, now the Hospital of St Margaret of Cortona) has a pleasant exterior which looks not unlike the work of George Semple. The wings were added by Park† in 1792. It is rather out of the way and rarely seen.

The building of private houses proceeded apace during the fifties, till the failure of three out of six Dublin banks, at the end of the decade, caused a temporary halt in enterprise. (There had been an earlier epidemic of bank failures in 1729 also.) Dominick Street began to be developed, and almost the first house built upon it was the present No 20, whose magnificent interior is one of the sights of Dublin. Robert West, master-builder and stuccodore, built it for himself in 1755, but let it in the same year to the Rt Hon John Beresford, a figure of whom we shall hear more.[4] It is a four-bay house, generously planned with a large entrance-cum-staircase hall. This hall, with its birds (Pl. xxv) standing on hollow consoles sixteen inches from the wall-surface, is one of the finest pieces of plaster decoration in Dublin. Several of the other rooms have fine plaster, notably the Venus room at the back on the first floor.

Plaster decoration had already become a Dublin speciality by this time. Among the more important of the Dublin ceilings already in existence may be mentioned the wonderful Venus ceiling of the La Touche Bank[5] (executed before 1739 and moved in 1946 to the Bank of Ireland, where it may now be seen); the ceiling of the saloon of Clanwilliam House, by the Francini Brothers (about 1740); and the anonymous but quite outstanding ceilings of Mespil House, built by Dr Barry as a country house (though now in Dublin) in 1751.[6]

---

* See plate reproduced in *CARD* X, Plate V. Sir Richard Morrison in his *Designs in Architecture*, 1793, produced another Irish version of the theme.

† Wright's *Hist. Guide* 2nd ed, 1825, p. 255, where the whole building is credited to Park, which is absurd. Drawings of the wings, unsigned, are in the Murray Collection, National Library.

The subject of Irish plaster is a large one, and those who wish to study it may do so in C. P. Curran's authoritative survey. It is enough to remark here that Dublin is astonishingly full of plaster of astonishingly high quality: it was the characteristic form of ostentation or conspicuous waste, though indeed it is only conspicuous when one has entered from the street, or when, on a winter's evening, one can see from the pavement through uncurtained windows into brightly lit interiors. I may perhaps record my own preference, which is for the figured and rococo ceilings and walls of the period 1740–55, such as those I have mentioned.*

The organisation of the architectural profession was at this time rudimentary. There were military gentlemen like Burgh and Pearce, and, a little later, gentlemen-amateurs like Mr Vesey of Lucan or Mr Trench of Heywood. There were also a few whole-time Architects with a capital A, mainly, so far, importations like Cassels or Davis Ducart. But most of the domestic work was done by tradesmen, guildsmen, members either of the Carpenters or of the Bricklayers and Plasterers. Robert West, for example, belonged to the second of these. Many of these craftsmen have names which figure in Dublin guild history for centuries back, and quite a high proportion have 'native' names.

How high a tradesman of this type could rise is amusingly illustrated in the career of John Magill. He was born in 1703, his father a carpenter and his mother a buttermilk vendor. As a child (if we are to believe the hostile but very entertaining *Life and Adventures of Buttermilk Jack*)† he was employed as a 'pickle-herring' by Madame Violante at her booth in George's Lane, when the famous Peg Woffington was making her juvenile debut under the same auspices. Then, after working as a journeyman carpenter, he 'went to Captain P[earce], and offered his Services as an Overseer to the Workmen, and was accepted'. The anonymous author accuses Magill of profiteering on the building of the Parliament House, but in view of the very moderate cost at which Pearce had the work done, this seems unlikely. He next 'ingratiated himself with some men of

---

* Until about twenty years ago, the famous Apollo room from Tracton House (on the corner of Stephen's Green and Merrion Row) was kept as a show piece in the National Museum. But the expansion of the legislature in Leinster House has banished it to some obscure store-room.

† Dublin, 1760.

Rank and Fortune, so as to be appointed Surveyor of their Estates, Estimator of the Prices of Buildings, &c', and became 'Measurer, Surveyor &c. . . . for the G[overnment] also'. In spite of the fact that, according to this author, he was not only given to various sexual delinquencies, but also ran naked round Stephen's Green for a wager, Magill prospered and for £500 bought himself a seat in Parliament. The pamphlet concludes by expressing the hope that the House will soon purge itself of such a rascal.

There is at least this much truth in the *Life and Adventures*, that Magill, after figuring as Comptroller of Works under the Barrack Board, becomes John Magill Esq, and in 1767 is found as one of the Commissioners, thus translating himself into the world of the grandees.*

George Semple's career was less colourful but more representative. 'My Father', he says, '. . . was a Workman about the year 1675, [and] often told me about a method of mortaring harder than stone'.[7] The only book-learning he had 'was acquired within the Compass of six Winter Weeks, in the thirteenth Year of my age', presumably when the frost made building impossible. For the rest of his youth we may suppose that, coming of a family of builders, he was learning his trade the hard way. But he seems to have gone to England some time before 1752, for he speaks of two engineers, Mr Etridge and Mr Preston, as 'my more intimate friends' at this time. They were then building a pier at Ramsgate. Though a practical builder and a craftsman-architect, he was generous in his praise of the academic training given by the Dublin Society.

His great opportunity was the rebuilding of Jervis's Essex Bridge in 1753. Bridge-building was in the blood of the Semples, for one of them later built the great bridge at Graiguenamanagh in Co. Carlow. Summerson describes Charles Labelye (the architect of Westminster Bridge) as 'a man of a professional type which England had not yet learned to produce', capable of achieving a bridge both 'scientific and classically designed'. Labelye, says Summerson,[8] was 'neither mason nor architect': but it would surely be truer to say that, like Semple, he was both. For Semple, who had already

* He also owned a sand-pit beside Sackville Street (*Georg. Soc.* III, 91).

designed work of accomplished classicism, was content to model his bridge very closely on that of the Swiss.

Labelye's magnificent bridge at Westminster was just finished, after eleven years' work, when in 1751 Sir Humphrey Jervis's bridge began to decay. At the end of May, Semple met Thomas Prior at the Archbishop of Dublin's, and was told that the Corporation were already considering projects for the repair of the bridge. Under pressure from Prior, Semple said he could repair it in ten days for 100 guineas. But later in the year the Corporation decided to rebuild on a wider scale. In the meantime Michael Wills, whose jealousy of Semple probably dated from the rejection of a Wills design for Swift's Hospital, published *A Scheme for Enlarging Essex Bridge*,* in which he proposed to widen the bridge in six months, or alternatively to rebuild it altogether. Wills also claimed some experience in bridge-building, while 'Architecture, both publick and private' has, he says, 'been the employment of my whole life. . . . I know it will be said, that I am wanting a jobb. And so let it be, if I can at the same time save the Publick some thousands'. He claims that the Grand Jury had contracted with him for the repair; but it was Semple who got the job in the end. In May 1752 he went to see Labelye, and consulted with other engineers then building a pier at Ramsgate. Back in Dublin in June, he went to see George Ewing the publisher about books on technical problems, and Ewing's son Alexander who happened to be in Paris at the time brought him back the latest works of the French engineers.

In 1753 Semple began to demolish the old Bridge and to build his new one, with his brother John helping and Dr Rutty, the Quaker naturalist, coming to look on and give moral support. Where Labelye had used caissons (huge boxes filled with accurately coursed masonry and sunk into position) Semple preferred cofferdams, enclosures which were pumped dry of water when the foundations were then built inside them. The bridge was ready for traffic by 1755, and was in essence a shorter and wider version of Westminster Bridge, all the infilling stones being laid radially as in the original, and the architectural details (save for the treatment of the centre arch) being exactly copied from the London bridge (Pl. ix). A few comparative figures may be of interest:

* Dublin, 1752.

	WESTMINSTER BRIDGE	ESSEX BRIDGE
Length	1120 feet	240 feet
Breadth	44 ,,	51 ,,
Span of centre arch ..	75 ,,	45 ,,
No of arches	13 plus 2 small arches	7
Cost	£393,189	£20,661

Essex Bridge survived till 1874, when the modern mania for flat bridges caused its supersession by the ugliest bridge in Dublin, called after Henry Grattan who did nothing to deserve this. Semple was employed for the next ten years prospecting in the West of Ireland in connexion with the canal-craze, and suffering from 'excessive colds ... Gravel and Rheumatism'; but enriching us in the process with a valuable contemporary record of travel in the West of Ireland. His book on *The Art of Building in Water* appeared in 1776, and was reprinted (with a few additions) as *Hibernia's Free Trade* in 1780. It recounts the story of Essex Bridge in full constructional detail.*

Out of the rebuilding arose the most important statutory influence on Dublin's growth, the setting up of the Commissioners for Making Wide and Convenient Streets—to give them their full title. They began as an *ad hoc* body appointed by Parliament to make a wide and convenient street from Essex Bridge to the Castle. Semple afterwards claimed that the idea was his own, and so did Gorges Edmond Howard, the contractor who did the work for the Commissioners. He said that one day in 1757 (the date must be wrong) he was dining with one of the Revenue Commissioners at the Sot's Hole (a well-known chop-house very near where the Dolphin is now) when the idea grew out of their conversation. Later, when he had authority to demolish houses and had paid compensation to their owners, he heard that some of the tenants-at-will thought that they were entitled to six-months' respite. Fearing that it would take at least six months before the courts would show

---

* Towards the end, there is a delightful passage about a nobleman making an ornamental canal.

that they were entitled to no respite at all, he sent workmen at night to unroof the houses concerned. The result was, of course, an alarm of a French invasion and a good joke for some time afterwards.*

The problem had in fact received serious attention as early as 1751, for in that year a map of the district was engraved, and in 1753 a companion map showing a new street forty-six feet wide (as built it was fifty-two).[9] In January 1756 the city petitioned in the matter, and the following year an Act[10] set up the Commissioners, twenty-one grandees including the Lord Mayor being named. One of the names, 'Aland Mason', presumably stands for Eland Mossom, a long-forgotten poet. They were empowered to purchase houses and site by compulsion, and the first street they made, opened in 1762, was named Parliament Street, and so remains. Seven years later it became a superb approach to the new Royal Exchange which faces down Parliament Street, across the bridge and up the 550-yard vista of Capel Street to the north.

The Wide Streets Commissioners were regulated by further Acts in 1759, 1767, 1778, 1782, 1783-4, 1786, 1787, 1790 and 1797, and lasted till the Corporation Reform Act of 1840, when their functions devolved on the Dublin Corporation.† Their achievements in the eighteenth century are set forth in their Report of 1802, and include the widening of Dame Street and opening up of the Quays west of Essex Bridge (1768); further widening of Dame Street (1777-84); the grand scheme of Lower Sackville, Westmorland and D'Olier Streets—their most spectacular legacy (1782);‡ Lower Abbey Street (1784); the improvement of Rutland Square and its approaches (1786-90); Foster Place (1787); and the two quays east of Carlisle Bridge (1798). By the end of the century they were spending £25,000 a year. It was they who achieved the articulation between the two independent and privately sponsored fashionable quarters. A cognate development was the Paving Board, set up in 1773 for 'paving, cleaning, lighting, draining and improving'

* Gilbert II, 24-5.

† By 30 Geo III, 19, XIX, they were empowered to approve or disapprove of all new streets made by private individuals or other authorities, and to make up to proprietors the difference between the cost of ordinary buildings and the special standards imposed for Dame Street.

‡ Date of scheme, not of execution.

the streets—all except Sackville Street and Marlborough Street which had similar statutory Boards* of their own, though oddly enough no Gardiner was named as a member of either.

These enactments show a very high degree of enlightened planning, and were well in advance of their time. They left us a Dublin the breadth of whose streets still astonishes the stranger: Lower O'Connell (Sackville) Street 154 feet, Westmorland Street 96, Upper Merrion Street 102, Baggot Street 100, Gardiner Street 85, Dominick Street 74 and so on. Where the Commissioners failed to tackle a problem, as occasionally they did—Merrion Row, for example—the obstruction is still there and still giving trouble. Long before Regent Street or Kingsway were thought of, our Commissioners were driving their ample thoroughfares in all directions, demolishing all before them. They are the very embodiment of unsentimental utility; and that we should feel so sentimental towards them is a typical irony of the historical process.†

It is a very odd thing that the Irish statute book contains no Building Acts: nothing analogous to the English Acts of 1707, 1709 and 1774. The first two English Acts banished the wooden cornice and the flush-framed window from London. The timber eaves-cornice was never very popular in Ireland,‡ but the flush-framed window disappears from Dublin in about 1740, duly obedient to the Thirty Years Law, without special legislation§ to help it on its way. There are, of course, a good many Acts dealing incidentally with building matters, paving and lighting, projections and nuisances, spouts and downpipes and the like. Of more interest

---

* Abolished 1786 and put under the Paving Board.

† This is how J. D. Herbert felt about them:

'In Lunnon what crowds in the streets,
    Such bustle, and here and there driving,
A porter upsets all he meets,
    To get forward every one striving.
Now, in Dublin we've no such obstructions;
    We've policemen, and we've parishioners,
Peace-officers skilled in destruction,
    With wide and convenient omissioners.
                Ritol lol &c'

The whole poem, *Paddy's Return*, would be well worth quoting if space allowed.

‡ Moira House (1752) had one.

§ Except Clause 16 of 3 Geo II, 14 (1729). In 1766 a Dublin Building Bill was read once, but petitioned against by the building trades, both masters and journeymen, and dropped. See *I. Commons Journ.* 1766 (ed. of 1771), pp. 201, 213, 215, 216, 237, 242, 245, 247.

is the prohibition in 1772 of the burning of bricks within two miles of the public lamps, the reason given being that the fumes have caused the death of weakly persons. There were brickfields just beside Sackville Street and Baggot Street, and later the bricks of Dolphin's Barn and Sandymount were used. These were grey stock bricks: the beautiful red facing bricks which predominate are Bridgwater bricks, brought as ballast by ships plying on the Bristol trade.[11] It is a pleasant thought that Dublin, originally a colony of Bristol, should have continued to draw her life-blood from that city at so late a date. The burning of lime was also prohibited within the public lamps by two Acts in the seventies.

The want of legal standards in housebuilding was supplied by the covenants in building leases. Thus, a Corporation lease of a site in Aston's Quay in 1761 obliges the lessee 'to leave the quay forty feet wide, and to rebuild the houses in the following regular and uniform manner ... at least three storeys high, besides cellars, the first or shop storey to be nine feet high, the second or middle storey to be ten feet high, and the third or garret storey to be eight feet high. The front and rere walls to be fourteen inches thick and built with brick cemented with lime and sand. The window stools and copings to be of mountain stone, and the top of every house to be of an equal height and range with each other'.[12] This brief specification embodies two of the main principles of Georgian street design: the importance of the first floor and the regularity of the skyline. A Corporation lease to Lord Mornington of a site in College Green in 1763 (frontage 151 feet) binds him 'to build thereon a grand and ornamental house for his dwelling, with offices suitable thereto, within the space of five years ... and to lay out on the said house the sum of £3,000, at least, the said lease to be for seventy years and three lives ...' Similar stipulations were made by private landlords.*

---

* The formula in the Fitzwilliam Estate leases of the sixties is that the lessee contracts to build 'one good and substantial dwelling house with lime and stones or with bricks and lime well roofed and covered with slates and not less than N feet wide in the front and three stories and a half high above the cellars at the least and shall and will make an area of eight feet wide at the front of the said house and fix up posts before the same ten feet distant from the said area and lay flaggs between the posts and the front of the said house for a foot passage in like manner as the same is done before the houses in Dawson Street'. Usually there is a three years' time-limit when if no building has been completed an additional rent becomes due. A Merrion Square lease of 1762 (the present No 6) obliges the lessee to pave the whole street in front of the house as far as the railings enclosing the Square itself. (Original documents in Pembroke Estate Office.)

The plans of Dublin houses show great resource and variety. Frontages were long—thirty or thirty-two feet is quite usual—and the plots very deep, much deeper than in London where the pressure on land was greater. There is generally not less than 450 feet between major streets, giving room for a laneway and the long gardens which are so much a feature of the Baggot Street neighbourhood. (The figure for Bloomsbury would be more like 250 feet.) Varieties of plan in adjoining houses are well shown in the illustration of houses in Upper Merrion Street, built between 1752 and 1772. The smallest of these houses would be a 'first-rate' house in London, having nine 'squares' of area, while the two largest had

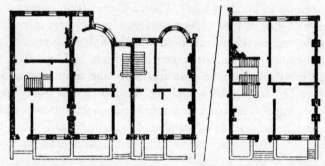

FIG. 7. Plans of Nos. 6, 11, 12 and 13 Upper Merrion Street (now demolished), c. 1760. Based on drawings by H. G. Leask in *The Georgian Society*, Vol. IV.

$14\frac{1}{2}$ and $10\frac{1}{2}$.[13] After about 1780 plans become more standardised on a 'fore-and-aft' pattern, and the really immense houses such as one sees in Dorset Street or the still intact side of Upper Merrion Street, are no longer built. The prosperity of Dublin as a political capital was inducing conditions not unlike those of London, and the architecture, still unassisted by legislation, begins to reflect the increased tightness of space. But the Commissioners, fortunately for us, were still there to provide Wide and Convenient streets.

REFERENCES

[1] See *Georg. Soc.* III, Pl. LXXIX. The Hall is now used as a factory.
[2] H. G. Leask, *Dublin Castle*, Official Guide. Stationery Office, n.d. Essential for visitors.
[3] *CARD* X, 521.

[4] Curran in *JRSAI*, LXX, 31, 36 and *Rotunda Hosp.* 23.

[5] *JRSAI, loc. cit.* 23 *sqq.*

[6] *ibid.* 22.

[7] George Semple, *The Art of Building in Water*, Dublin, 1776.

[8] Summerson, *Georgian London*, 98.

[9] *JRSAI* XLVIII, 140 *sqq.* Several later maps of the district were printed, one is reproduced in John Harvey, *Dublin*, 1949, Plate 58, p. 40.

[10] 31 Geo. II, 19. John Ponsonby the Speaker, and Anthony Malone were among the members named.

[11] Wilkinson, *Practical Geology of Ireland*, 1845, p. 249.

[12] *CARD* XI, 38.

[13] See Summerson, *Georgian London*, 60, 108.

CHAPTER XVII

Piety and Learning

THE POPULATION of Dublin was now (1750) something like 130,000.* Since the beginning of the century it had nearly doubled, and was now between one-fifth and one-sixth the size of London, nor had it any rivals in the Three Kingdoms. Even allowing for the fact that a minority only of these were Protestant, it is remarkable that there was so little church-building. But there are four examples in the mid-century worth some notice. Two are rebuildings of old churches in the mediæval city, one a rebuilding in an unfashionable quarter, and only one a really new church in the Gardiner domain. Fitzwilliam's fashionable quarter managed without any church-building for a whole century, from 1721 till 1825, though in sixty years (1765-1825) it grew from empty fields to be the town's chief residential area. It does seem that there is some truth in the popular view of the eighteenth-century Establishment.

St Werburgh's (Pls. XXVI, XXVII) was reopened in 1759 after the fire of 1754, and this must be the interior we know to-day, the most gracious of all Dublin's churches. The Royal Arms in front of the Viceregal pew, and the upper gallery for the schoolchildren, were inserted in 1767, and John Smith (or Smyth) was architect for the gallery and probably, therefore, of the organ-case also. The tower and spire of 160 feet were added in the following year, and it seems reasonable to credit this also to Smyth. Perhaps he was responsible for the interior as well. The tower, rising by graceful stages to an open-work structure of eight blocked columns on which the spire stood, has a sad history. A church spire fell in Liverpool in 1810, and this gave the Castle authorities, anxious since the Emmet Rising at having so tall a vantage-point overlooking Upper Castle Yard, an

---

* Population figures given in this book are, except where otherwise stated, based on a graph constructed from an average of reputable estimates, as reliable figures before 1831 are not obtainable. The figure in the text is derived from this graph, and is incidentally confirmed by *Memoirs of the City of Dublin* 1757 (RIA Haliday Pamphlets, 272) which gives the figure for that year as 150,000. See Appendix V.

excuse to plot its destruction. They managed to procure seven architects who, doubtless for a consideration, swore that the St Werburgh's spire was unsafe. Though Francis Johnston offered to make it secure, it was taken down, and the tower also was removed twenty-six years later.

Smyth was certainly the architect of St Thomas's,* Marlborough Street (1758–62). It also was a galleried church, the entrance front modelled on Palladio's Redentore, horizontalised and with sweep-walls added. It had a fine interior[1] with a compartment-ceiling, flat-headed windows and wood-carving on the gallery-fronts. Yet, though this was the parish church of some of the most fashionable streets, money was lacking to complete it, and the central pediment was never properly built. Seen from Gloucester Street (down which the church faced) the unlovely mass of the roof rose over the missing pediment. Henry Aaron Baker designed a steeple to hide the roof, but this was never built. In spite of this, St Thomas's was the burial place of the Gardiners, and there they reposed till in 1922 their slumbers were disturbed by the Civil War, in which the church was so badly damaged that it was replaced by a pleasant little modern church† on an island site, and the Gardiners were transplanted to a vault in St George's originally intended for liquor in bond; and there, no doubt, they rest in peace.

Smyth's other church, St Catherine's (Pl. XXIX), has survived intact. It has the finest façade of any church in Dublin, a superbly virile composition in Roman doric, built of mountain granite and facing north across Thomas Street. The tower, which was meant to carry a spire which would have closed the vista down North Queen Street across the river, was, as usual,[2] never built, and the temporary hat placed over the stump is still there, after nearly two hundred years. The interior of the church, though less successful than the façade, is interesting, if only for the experiment of making internal transepts by stopping the galleries one bay short of the east wall.‡

* There was a somewhat earlier St Thomas's on a more southerly site in Marlborough Street, built probably soon after 1749, on the east side where Abbey Street is now. See Rocque's Map of 1756.

† By Frederick Hicks.

‡ Smyth also designed the Poolbeg Lighthouse at the east end of the South Wall, 1768 which though altered, still remains in use.

St John the Evangelist, Fishamble Street, was rebuilt by George Ensor in 1766–9 as an unpretentious little classical temple with a portico of two columns *in antis*, but the only surviving representation[3] of it is so bad that it is impossible to tell whether the order was doric or corinthian. Henry Grattan was baptised in its predecessor. Ensor's church was demolished in 1884, but some of its monuments were put in the north-west lobby of St Werburgh's.

No: it is not to the Church that we must look for examples of conspicuous waste in the mid-century. The University made a more creditable show, and proved that Learning was less disposed than Piety to hide its light.

In 1758 the aged Provost Baldwin, under whom the Library and Dining Hall had been built, who had reigned as a more or less benevolent despot over the College for forty-one years, died and was succeeded by the Rt. Hon. Francis Andrews, the Member for Derry. It was asserted by the gossips of the day that Andrews owed his advancement to his liaison with Peg Woffington, but it is more likely that it was due to his staunch Whiggery and more particularly his friendship with the secretary of the Duke of Bedford (Viceroy 1756–61). Andrews had travelled in Italy and was an accomplished courtier.

The advantages of having a Provost who was also a Member of Parliament soon became apparent, for the rebuilding of the western court of the College, begun in 1752, was paid for by Parliament* and finished in 1759. It remains the most ample piece of collegiate architecture in these islands, planned on the heroic scale in one of the most commanding sites in Dublin (see Fig. 8 and Plate xxx). The architects of the western front are stated to have been Keene and Sanderson of London, that is to say Henry Keene (1726–76) and John Sanderson who was rather older.† It is not absolutely certain that this Keene is the one concerned in Trinity, for he was fully occupied in England at the time, while there is a Henry Keene given as 'Architect' under the Irish Barrack Board from 1763–6 (contemporary with Magill and Jarratt). It is, of course, *possible*

---

* It cost £30,000. Parliament's motives were mainly to avoid the accumulation of a disposable surplus in the Exchequer, about which there had been Castle-versus-Country struggles in 1731 and 1753.

† The supervision of the work was carried out by Hugh Darley. *Commons Journals.* 1759, Nov. 14th, Report, Account No XXXV.

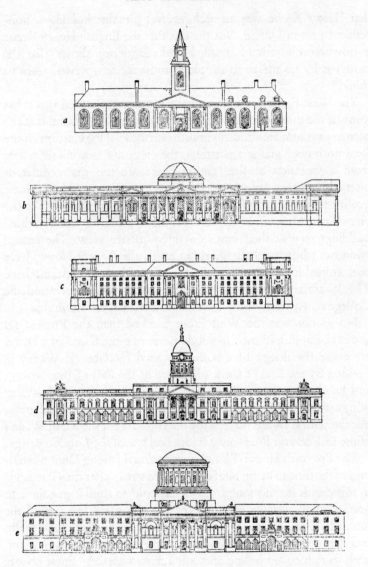

FIG. 8. The Five Major Elevations of Dublin: (*a*) The Royal Hospital, Kilmainham (1680); (*b*) The Parliament House (1729 onwards, now altered, the east curved wall as shown here is not quite accurate); (*c*) Trinity College (1759); (*d*) The Custom House (1781–91); (*e*) The Four Courts (1786–1801).

that Henry Keene was an architectural pluralist holding a non-resident post in Dublin. But the fact that the English Henry Keene is nowhere else found coupled with Sanderson shows that the matter is by no means so simple as most modern writers seem to think.*

The West Front is not an unqualified success. Granted that it has some of the most accomplished fenestration in Dublin, and that the corner-pavilions are almost as beautiful as those of the Custom House (and no higher praise is possible), the elevation as a whole suffers from a weakness at the centre. There are too many different intervals between columns and pilasters, giving an indeterminate quality to the central feature as seen from Dame Street. Like the Fitzwilliam Museum in Cambridge, the West Front is one of those buildings seen at their best in a three-quarter view. The central windows (those of the large room called the Regent House) have been ruined in modern times by the removal of their glazing bars. The Victorian railings, on the other hand, which surround the College on its west, north-west and south sides, are admirable.

No sooner was the West Front finished than the Provost set about re-housing himself in a style becoming the friend of a Duke. He chose the design of a house designed for General Wade† in London by the Earl of Cork (disguised as the Earl of Burlington), and he employed John Smyth to adapt it for him. Single-storey wings were added, and the planning of the interior was different, but the central façade (except for the conical roof shown in Wade's house in *Vitruvius Britannicus*) is identical‡ with the London design.

The Provost's House (Pl. xv) is exceptional among Dublin buildings of the time in being built in imported stone other than Portland: in this case it is sandstone from Liverpool,[4] so similar in colour to granite as to deceive most observers. The great features of the interior are the octagonal staircase with its channelled ashlar walls, and the superb saloon running the whole length of the west front, with its rich coved ceiling and columnar screens, the finest private reception room in Dublin. The Provost's House has a peculiar value to-day as the only one of the great stone mansions of Dublin

* See note at end of chapter.

† Said to be the house of which Chesterfield said that its owner would do best to take a house opposite so that he could look at it without having to live in it.

‡ Except in minute particulars.

still in occupation as a dwelling house—Leinster House being now a parliament-building, Charlemont House an art gallery, Tyrone House offices, Powerscourt House a wholesale warehouse, Aldborough House a stores, Moira House the Mendicity Institution. The Provost's House has something of the grandeur of Lady Isabella Finch's famous house in Berkeley Square, though the Dublin house is much larger and gives up much less of its space to staircases. The modelling of the façade is Lord Cork's doing, but the surprising success of the very low wings, and the internal dispositions, are to Smyth's credit.

Among the treasures of the Provost's House are a very fine Gainsborough of the Duke of Bedford, which hangs in the Saloon, and an extremely prosperous-looking portrait of Andrews himself, done in Rome by Antonio Maroni, which shows him wearing a gorgeous flowered undercoat. Busts of the Emperors Commodus and Caracalla adorn the hall—an odd choice. Among his other achievements was the establishment of a Chair of Music in 1764, Lord Mornington being its first occupant. When the Duke of Bedford was elected Chancellor in 1768, Andrews devised a memorable installation, with speeches, orchestral music provided by Lord Mornington, banquets and dinners and no expense spared.[5] When the Provost died he left his money for the building of Dunsink Observatory, which was not, however, built till 1782-6.

A University which consists of but a single College and is sited in the middle of a capital city enjoys certain architectural advantages (and a few disadvantages). On the whole it may be said that Trinity, largely owing to Andrews, made the best use of these advantages.

From the moral point of view, the blessings of situation were more mixed. We have already seen how the College Boys took part in the fights of the Weavers and Butchers. The habit of violence was not easy to eradicate, and one of the town's many brothel-quarters was on Trinity's very doorstep, in Fleet-lane.* Riots were frequent, and in 1734 one of the Fellows was murdered by some sportive undergraduates. Five were expelled, and prosecuted in the civil courts by the College, but without success. Good society in Dublin (which was Tory) was scandalised at 'so cruel a persecution

---

* Long vanished into Westmorland Street.

against the sons of gentlemen', who were 'suspected only of a frolick', and was most incensed against these Whig dons, who, being, after all, only a sort of glorified schoolmasters, were middle-class at the best.[6] In 1747 five more undergraduates were expelled for a riot in which they tried to storm the Marshalsea Prison. One of these young men was Oliver Goldsmith, who now stands just outside the front gate with his back to his *alma mater*.

One of Trinity's greatest advantages during the eighteenth century was the wide social range of its members. It contained not only the sons of the Irish Peerage, but also those of shoemakers, distillers, butchers, innkeepers, surgeons and even builders and architects. After the Union the peers began to send their sons to Oxford and Cambridge,* very likely because at home they might be reproached with the parts played by their fathers in the promotion of that measure. None the less, Trinity is still a creditable stronghold of social equality.

The College Gibs (as the undergraduates were called) had the right of entry to the Gallery of the House of Commons. Their gowns were their passports, till they lost this privilege by misbehaviour—excusable misbehaviour indeed, that of cheering a speech of Grattan's after Fitzwilliam's recall in 1795.

It may be doubted whether some of the eighteenth-century Fellows were ideal models of behaviour for their juniors to copy. Goldsmith's tutor is nearly as famous as Gibbon's at Oxford, but for an active, rather than a passive reason. His name was Dr Theaker Wilder, and on one occasion while crossing a muddy street he found himself face to face with a pretty girl, so that one of the two, to pass, must walk in the mud. He gazed at her for a moment, then took her face in his hands and kissed her, remarking 'Take that, miss, for being so handsome'. Less pleasant, but perhaps more amusing, is the story of his passing one day through one of the college courts where the undergraduates were ducking a bailiff under the pump. 'Gentlemen, gentlemen,' said Dr Wilder, 'for the love of God, don't be so cruel as to nail his ears to the pump'. The hint was not lost on his hearers, and the unfortunate bailiff was left

* See, on this point, Cloncurry's *Personal Recollections* 1850, pp. 6–7, and p. 4: 'We were not then sent to learn absenteeism and contempt, too often hatred, for our country, in the Schools and Colleges of England'. He overlooked the fact that many Irishmen have learned, at English schools, little but a preference for their own country.

bleeding and shrieking with pain, with one of his ears transfixed with a tenpenny nail.

Dr Wilder is said to have been a good mathematician, and on the whole it seems that the Fellows of his day had a respectable enough standard of scholarship, whether they imparted it to their pupils or not. It was probably in a later day that the legend grew up that the Fellows of Trinity made up in bad manners what they lacked in learning. At all periods, of course, they were, like all dons, proverbially eccentric: Jacky Barrett, who became a Fellow in 1778 and was Vice-Provost and Librarian, living well into the nineteenth century and remaining a lively memory to-day, was the most eccentric of them all: a miser, an astrologer, dirty, slovenly, witty, good-natured and abusive, minute of stature, slithering about the College in carpet-slippers, a figure, as Charles Lever who knew him in old age, said, 'of indescribable meanness'. But a formidable scholar, a linguist who could speak every language but his own, the discoverer and editor of an important New Testament codex. One day an undergraduate shouted 'Sweep! Sweep!' after him. Jacky summoned him before the Board: 'I will chastise him for *scandalum magnatum*, for sure amn't I the vice-provost?' The culprit denied that it was Jacky after whom he had been calling. 'How can that be?' said Jacky, 'For look you, there was no other sweep in the court, only myself'. He rarely ventured further than the Bank of Ireland across the street, where he used to lodge immense sums saved by paring candle-ends. But he once saw the sea at Clontarf, and described it thus: 'A broad flat superficies, like Euclid's definition of a line expanding itself into a surface, and blue, like Xenophon's plain covered with wormwood'. Dining once with the Provost, he was given an ice to eat, and ran from the dining-room shouting 'Look you, I'm scalded!' and holding his face.

A good many stories are told of him which are also told of others. Perhaps the best of these is that when an undergraduate dazzled him with a mirror—an old schoolboy trick—Jacky accused him of 'casting reflections on his superiors'. Yet another episode has a familiar ring: a scholar, reading grace in hall, traded on Jacky's deafness, and instead of repeating the Latin formula, said 'Jacky Barrett thinks I'm saying grace Jacky Barrett thinks I'm saying grace Jacky Barrett thinks I'm saying grace ...' 'May the devil admire me, but Jacky Barrett did *not* think ye were saying grace'.*

I have heard this story told in all seriousness about a living Fellow of Trinity. Jacky Barrett really belongs to a later chapter: my excuse for enlarging on him here is that these stories have, many of them, probably as long a history before his time as they have certainly had after it.

* Further Barrettiana may be found in Chapter VI of W. R. Le Fanu's *Seventy Years of Irish Life.*

REFERENCES

[1] Wheeler & Craig, *Dublin City Churches*, Plate XV.
[2] From RIA Haliday Pamphlets 387 (1775) it appears that there was an enquiry into this question of unbuilt Dublin steeples.
[3] Wheeler & Craig, *op. cit.* Pl. III.
[4] G. Wilkinson, *Practical Geology of Ireland*, 1845, p. 246. Personal inspection has left the question still doubtful.
[5] C. Maxwell, *History of T.C.D.* 1946, p. 117.
[6] *ibid.* p. 112.

Additional note to page 182. Mr. Howard Colvin has since kindly confirmed (from the Dashwood Papers in the Bodleian Library) that the two Henry Keenes are identical, and that he did come over to Ireland, if only for a short time in 1762.

CHAPTER XVIII

Estates and Academic Architecture

I T WAS SOME TIME before Lord Kildare's prophecy, that the grandees would follow him across the river, came true. East of his house he had leased a strip of ground from Lord Fitzwilliam of Meryon. This was and is Leinster Lawn, and it forms one side of Merrion Square. The sixth Lord Fitzwilliam, born in 1711(?) began in about 1750 an orderly scheme of development which went on coherently for at least a hundred years, making what is now very much the 'best' quarter of Dublin. The Fitzwilliams outstripped the Gardiners by about 1820, and though both Fitzwilliams and Gardiners died out at about the same time (1816* and 1829 to be exact) the later history of their estates is very divergent. The Gardiner Estate was broken up, following an Act of Parliament in 1846 and two sales in that year and 1848, in the Incumbered Estates Court.† What was left of it was sold in 1874 to the Hon Charles Spencer Cowper for £120,000.‡ Lord Blessington's (Charles Gardiner the last's) income from Irish ground rents, mainly in Dublin, was said to have been £30,000 per annum. These ground rents were bought up by individual buyers in the Incumbered Estates Court, and all§ vestige of benevolent control disappeared. The Fitzwilliam Estate, on the other hand, passed to the Earls of Pembroke, who still guard its fortunes in an exemplary manner. After the Union Dublin could not afford such a vast acreage of 'good' property: the 'good' tenants simply were not there to live in it all: and even the truly incredible numbers of lawyers who moved

---

* The last Viscount Fitzwilliam, a brother of the second-last, did not own the Dublin estates.

† Strictly speaking, the Incumbered Estates Court was not set up for general purposes till 1849.

‡ Fr. Dillon Cosgrave: *North Dublin*, p. 49, where it is stated that 'all the Gardiner property in Dublin, except Henrietta Street, was sold in one lot'. This cannot be correct, for the earlier sales had comprised freeholds in at least 37 streets.

§ Not quite all. The Rotunda Hospital Estate, the Mountjoy Square Commissioners (set up in 1802) and the Eccles-Archdall Estate remained.

in to the 'good' streets on the north side,* were unable to hold it up for ever. As things turned out, it was a walk-over for the Pembroke interest; but it is interesting to speculate what would have happened if they had had a rival comparable to themselves.

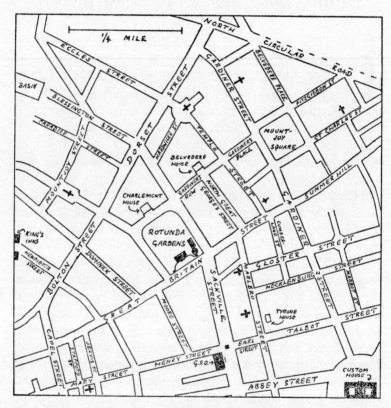

FIG. 9. The North-East Quarter, the Gardiner-Beresford sphere of influence. Ideal date, about 1825.

Fitzwilliam began much as Gardiner had done, by building one broad short street of very magnificent houses, Upper Merrion Street, containing Mornington House already mentioned, and the

* The 1850 Directory lists about 1175 barristers, of whom about two-thirds had addresses in Dublin, and about 1680 attorneys nearly all with addresses. This includes the names of firms as well as individuals, but the figures are still astonishing. Doubtless the Incumbered Estates Courts provided plenty of work for them.

now demolished houses of which plans are given.* The land was a wedge-shaped tract widening as it got further from the mediæval city. As in the case of the Gardiner Estate, there already existed ancient roads converging on Dublin Bridge (the bridge above the

FIG. 10. The South-East Quarter, the Fitzwilliam sphere of influence, with the adjacent Blue-Coat, Leeson, Kildare and Molesworth estates shown in part. Ideal date, about 1830.

Four Courts). And, as in the Gardiner Estate, these ancient roads remain with the renaissance grid crossing and recrossing them. In both quarters the ancient roads give radial articulation and induce a curvature expressed as a deflection of straight lines, though this

* The west side was demolished in *c.* 1910 to make room for Sir Aston Webb's opulent College of Science. Some of the houses were built by Wm. Fitzwilliam under lease from his brother.

189

is more marked on the North side than on the South. Present conditions should not blind us to the fact that, of the two, the Gardiner Estate shows the more imaginative conceptions of street-planning: it has more variety and is less rigidly imposed on the topography.

Fitzwilliam's ground lay between the old road to Merrion 'the Artichoke Road' (St Patrick's Well Lane, Denzil Street and Grand Canal Street) and the old road to Donnybrook (Leeson Street). In the middle, bisecting the angle, was Baggotrath Lane (Baggot Street) leading out of one corner of the Green towards Ball's Bridge. The parallel with Dorset Street, Great Britain Street and Abbey Street is very close.

In 1762 Fitzwilliam lured John Ensor away from the north side and got him to plan* a square, Merrion Square, of which the north side by-passed the old Merrion road. At about the same time he developed Denzil Street,† Clare Street and Holles Street, called after Denzil Holles, Earl of Clare, who was a cousin. The north side of Merrion Square began to go up in 1762, thirty-four houses, built by builders taking two or three lots each, Thomas Keating, coachbuilder, John Wilson, bricklayer, Timothy Turner, iron-monger, Robert Pries, Joseph Keane, Clerk of the Ordnance, Matthew Body and Ralph Ward, the Surveyor-General.[1] John Ensor himself built Antrim House at the eastern end in 1778.‡ These houses are much more varied than those on the other sides of the Square, and most of them have channelled ashlar entrance-storeys. In this respect they recall (as well they might) those of Rutland Square, but their doorways are nearly all more modest, as well as showing more variety.

The original intention was to make the Square even longer than it is: about 1,500 feet or nearly 1/3 mile, as against 1,150 feet or rather more than 1/4 mile.[2] (The breadth is about 650 feet.) This immense echoing space, with the trams sailing up and down its northern side, was not complete till the end of the century, when

---

* There is no evidence that the Estate at any time employed a permanent 'Surveyor' or Architect'.

† Now Fenian Street. It is part of the old Artichoke Road.

‡ *Georg. Soc.* IV, 81. The house was possibly built earlier, as the Georg. Soc. entry about Nos 29–32 is incorrect, ignoring the fact that there was a building lease to George Ensor as early as 1766, renewed in 1780 in respect of houses already built.

the south side, the highest and most regular* was finished. Most of the west side, being Leinster Lawn, was never built over. Many of these houses have fine plaster, particularly gorgeous being the staircase of No 12, and some of the cognate houses in Clare Street have notable interiors.†

On its western side the estate was co-ordinated with the Leeson holding already begun to be developed in the 1730's. Of the three ancient highways involved, Leeson Street is the only one to be so thoroughly widened and straightened as to appear a new street altogether. This must have been done by agreement between the Fitzwilliam and Leeson interests,³ for in 1759 we find the Earl of Miltown (Leeson) letting five plots on the corner of what is now Hatch Street, to John Hatch. Hatch Street itself was not made till about forty years later,‡ continuing Pembroke Street and working round by small angles to accommodate itself to the curvature of Dublin as a whole. The result is one of the pleasantest streets in this neighbourhood.

Close by is the longest intact Georgian street in Dublin, and perhaps anywhere. More than half a mile long and ninety-one feet wide and dead straight,⁴ it goes by various names: Merrion Square East (where it was begun about 1780 by Samuel Sproule), Fitzwilliam Streets Upper and Lower, Fitzwilliam Square East, and finally Fitzwilliam Place, which was not built till the eighteen-thirties. The vista is closed at one end by the mountains, and at the other, since 1934, by the 252-foot gasholder on Sir John Rogerson's Quay. Its only rival in Dublin is Gardiner Street, with its vista from Mountjoy Square to the Custom House, but this is not quite so long nor so broad.

Here, more strikingly perhaps than anywhere else in Dublin, the effects of local fenestration-technique may be appreciated. The 'patent reveal', a thin plaster lining round the windows, which projects about three-quarters of an inch beyond the brickwork and is usually painted white or near-white, whatever the colour of the sash- and glazing-bars, is here seen in all the brilliance of its

---

* The Act (31 Geo III, 45) of 1791, enclosing the Square and setting up the Commissioners, gives a list of occupants and shows how many houses were then built. The east side begins at Bond, the south at Christopher Deey, the west at Mrs Earbery.

† Especially No 29, formerly the Leinster Club house.

‡ Date-stones, 1810.

light-catching and reflecting effect. Down the whole length of this street the light ripples in gay vertical streaks, varied within modest limits and disappearing, as cheerful as ever, into the anonymous distance.

Baggot Street, the middle one of the three ancient roads, was widened but not straightened and laid out with smaller houses.* With its organic shape and its row of trees down the middle, it gives just the touch of variety to set off the rectilinear grid. Denzille Street, though well built, never rose very high and was later killed by the nearness of the railway. By 1787 the Fitzwilliam venture had prospered to the extent that thirty-one of the 'upper two-hundred' lived in streets on his estate, six of these in Holles Street.†

The urban part of both the Gardiner and Fitzwilliam estates was delimited by the making of the Circular Road in 1763 onwards.‡ The total length is about seven and a quarter miles, three on the north side from the Park to the North Wall, and four and a quarter on the south side from Islandbridge to the mouth of the Dodder. This confined central Dublin into an oval shape about two and a half miles long by two and a quarter broad, equivalent, in London, to the distance from Grosvenor Square to the Mansion House in one direction, and from King's Cross to Westminster Bridge in the other. It will be seen that the planners of Dublin were thinking on a scale of which London would not have been ashamed. This great work was kept going for years as a relief scheme to employ labour, financed partly by toll-gates. Though the northern part of it has long ceased to be the fashionable promenade it was in

* Widening map approved by Wide Streets Commissioners, 1791, now in Pembroke Estate Office. It gives the width as eighty-four feet: it is in fact rather more.

† In 1792 fifteen out of ninety-eight peers and bishops, and thirty-five out of about 200 M.P.'s, lived on Fitzwilliam land. A map approved by the Wide Streets Commissioners in 1791 shows Fitzwilliam Square as already projected; and Payne's *Universal Geography* (Dublin 1793: Vol II: page 194), mentions Fitzwilliam Square and says the ground of it 'is all taken for building under penalties to be completed in three years'. It was not, in fact, completed for more like thirty years.

‡ An Act of 1763 (3 Geo III 36) set up Commissioners for making the Circular Road. Lord Palmerstown and Henry Monk had objected to the Bill and it was provided that the new road should not pass through the lands of either of them without their consent. Further Acts, in 1775-6 and 1777-8, regulated the Commissioners' activities. By the second Act (15 & 16 Geo III 28) it was decided that the road should run further north than originally intended, and on the south-east side should link up with a 'circular road' already made by Lord Fitzwilliam. This road, as appears from the Act and from maps in the Pembroke Estate Office, was what is now called Mespil Road and Haddington Road, described as 'Circular Road' on maps as late as 1868. Clause 31 of the third Act (17 & 18 Geo III 10) has stringent regulations about building on the Circular Road.

the seventeen-eighties, its more permanent blessings are with us still. These were further increased in the seventeen-nineties when the two Canals, the Grand on the south and the Royal on the north, were brought in round the town, outside and parallel to the circular roads, to connect with the Liffey at the mouth of the Dodder and the North Wall. If the pattern is no longer quite so satisfactory in reality as it is on the map, this is the fault of the nineteenth century which failed to implement it in the original spirit.

Dublin was thus divided into four quarters, the two to the east rich and fashionable, that to the south-west poor, and that on the north-west more or less empty.

In the meantime John Ensor, though employed for Lord Fitz-william, had not entirely deserted the north side. Three years after Merrion Square, he laid out Gardiner's Row, leading out of the Rotunda Gardens towards the future site of Mountjoy Square. In the previous year he had built the Rotunda itself, which gives the Lying-in Hospital its familiar name.

This Rotunda was undoubtedly inspired by Jones's Rotunda at the London Ranelagh, and thereby hangs a curious and some-what confusing tale. The Jones family took their title from Rane-lagh in Co. Wicklow, and though they lived for a time in Dublin they moved in the early eighteenth century to London where they built themselves a house at Chelsea. This naturally became known as Ranelagh House, and was later turned into the famous Ranelagh Gardens (1742), in which William Jones (no relation) built a Rotunda. In 1766 one Hollister, of a family which had been build-ing and tuning church-organs in Dublin since at least 1719, started a pleasure-garden at Cullenswood, just outside Dublin, and called it Ranelagh Gardens. So the name of Ranelagh returned to Ireland. More than that: it gained currency and supplanted the older name of Cullenswood, while the name of Ranelagh in London gradually faded from the popular mind.

Ensor's Rotunda, eighty feet in diameter, was not quite so large as the London one, but as a *tour-de-force* it far surpasses it, for the flat ceiling has no supports whatever except the outer walls.[*] Externally it is a frustum of a cone, and the framing of this roof

---

* The London one had a central column.

supports the great expanse of ceiling.* As at first built by Ensor the outside was unsightly: the roof was very prominent and the outer wall was of brick. In 1786 Gandon raised and stuccoed this wall, partly concealing the roof, and adorning it with a frieze and plaques in Coade stone by Edward Smyth. The interior, which became a cinema in about 1910, has been barbarously treated,† but enough remains to make it well worth visiting. It has been the scene of many memorable happenings, of which two may be singled out: the Volunteer Convention of 1783, and the opening scene in James Joyce's story *A Painful Case*, when Mr Duffy attended a concert there and 'the house, thinly peopled and silent, gave distressing prophecy of failure'.

A new standard of sophistication was set in Dublin architecture by the Royal Exchange Competition of 1769, which arose indirectly out of the making of Parliament Street. The Tholsel was 'in a decayed condition, particularly the Exchange, the flags whereof are supported chiefly by old rotten timbers'. In 1754 repairs were directed to be done 'in the most frugal manner',[5] and it is not surprising that this merely postponed the problem.

At the head of Parliament Street the demolition of old Cork House and Lucas's Coffee-House left a space where it was originally proposed to put the statue of George I which had stood, like that of Henri IV in Paris, on Essex Bridge itself. There was good precedent for putting the Exchange here, for in 1670 'an exchange place was made in the garden of Cork House . . . very convenient with buildings erected on pillars to walk under in foul weather, where merchants and others met every day at the ringing of a bell to treat of their business'.[6] The next idea was to put a new Chapel Royal with a cupola at the head of the street, but this also was abandoned.[7]

The story goes that the newly-appointed Taster of Wines in 1763 tried to levy a tunnage fee to which he was, or believed himself to be, entitled. The merchants banded together and raised a large sum for their defence against this tax, so large a sum, in fact, that when the case was over they still had a large balance in hand.

---

* This structure, of timber, was renewed in steel in 1932, the copper centre and old slates being replaced. The present plaster ceiling was substituted at the same time.

† The bottoms of the pilasters have been shaved off flush with the wall, producing a ludicrous effect.

It sounds unlikely, but apparently it is true.[8] They then, with the aid of the patriotic Dr Charles Lucas, one of the Members for Dublin, bought the site, 100 feet square, from the Government, and raised some forty thousand pounds by lotteries. The design was offered to open competition between the architects of Great Britain and Ireland, one of the first occasions on which this method was used, though it later became very common in England also.

Sixty-one designs were sent in, of which twenty-four came from thirteen named Irish architects, three who gave initials only, and three pseudonyms. Thomas Jarratt sent in no less than three designs, Thomas Ivory, Oliver Grace and William Barber (all of Dublin) two each. It was rumoured that some of the Irish architects, fearing that the committee might on principle prefer the imported article, had their designs sent over from London pseudonymously. But it did not avail them: the first prize of £100 went to Thomas Cooley, who carried out the building, the second, of £60, to James Gandon, and the third, of £40, to Gandon's friend Thomas Sandby, all of London.[9]

Cooley came to Dublin and settled here, dying in 1784. Very little is known about him, except that he had been a carpenter and was born in 1740. A mason called William Cooley, who was working in London in the 1730's, may have been his father,[10] and Thomas Cooley himself was a pupil of Robert Mylne who built Blackfriars Bridge. The name Cooley sounds as though it might be Irish, but we cannot claim him on the strength of that. He had already exhibited designs and won prizes in London, but no buildings of his in England seem to be recorded.

He made the most, from the monumental point of view, of the hundred-foot-square site of the Exchange (see Pls. XIX, XXVIII, LV and Fig. 11), putting a ring of columns forty-six feet in diameter in the centre, free-standing with circulation-space stretching out into most of the rest of the square. Over this is a deep entablature, a drum full of windows and a coffered dome. Staircases on either side of the portico lead to the upper rooms, of which the Coffee-Room, over the entrance, had a fine ceiling till it was accidentally destroyed by fire in 1908.[11] When the building became the City Hall in 1852 the free space beyond the circular colonnade was

partitioned off, and much of the effect was destroyed. But otherwise the interior is as Cooley left it*—fortunately, since the other
and greater domed hall, that of the Four Courts, was so badly
damaged in 1922. The door-cases under the north and west
porticoes were injudiciously remodelled by John S. Butler in 1867,[12]
and the windows have lost their glazing-bars. Though it is an

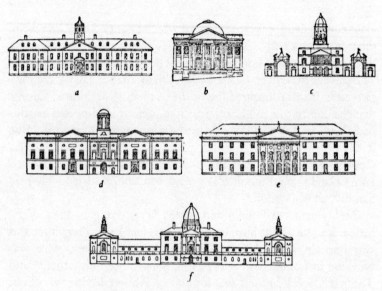

FIG. 11. Six Minor Elevations of Dublin: (a) Dr Steevens's Hospital (Thomas
Burgh, 1721–33); (b) The Royal Exchange (now the City Hall, Thomas Cooley,
1769–79); (c) The Bedford Tower and Gates, Dublin Castle (c. 1750—c. 1763,
architects uncertain); (d) The King's Inns (1795–1816, James Gandon and Henry
Aaron Baker, wings mid-nineteenth century); (e) The General Post Office (Francis
Johnston) 1814–18; (f) The Blue-Coat School (Thomas Ivory, 1773–80, central
cupola modern).

accomplished building, there is something a little cold about the
City Hall: its best points are its site, the excellence of the detail, and
the grandeur of the central hall. It does not inspire much affection.

During the eighties it was much used for Volunteer rallies, when,
we are told, 'from the clang of arms the vibrating dome caught the
generous flame, and re-echoed the enlivening sound of liberty'.[13]

* Except of course for the paintings round the frieze.

During the Rising of 1798 it was used as a barrack and torture-chamber by the government troops. There is a story that a gentleman who was passing during that grim period paused to look up at the Exchange, no doubt to admire Cooley's mouldings, and was tapped on the shoulder by Major Sirr,* who told him that if he did not immediately lose interest in the building he would rapidly find himself inside it.

The present stone balustrade on the front of the steps is not original, for a large concourse of persons who assembled there in the year 1814 to watch a criminal being whipped, so moved the wrath of heaven that the iron railings gave way and nine of them were killed and many more wounded. Until the Irish currency was abolished in 1826† the Exchange was still used for buying and selling bills on English banks, but afterwards it fell into disuse until the Corporation bought it in 1852 and it became the City Hall.

In addition to much work outside Dublin, Cooley did a great deal of work in the capital during his fifteen years' residence: the Hibernian Marine School (1770–3);‡ the Chapel of the Hibernian Military School (1771); the new Prison in Green Street (1773 onwards); additions to Swift's Hospital (1778); and the Public Offices on the Inns Quay (begun 1779). He also enlarged the Linen Hall. From 1775 till his death he was Clerk and Inspector of the Civil Buildings, apparently subordinate to Myers.

The Marine School (Pl. XXXI) is a striking feature in Malton's print of Dublin from down river, and the elevation may be studied in Pool and Cash.[14] What is left of it may be seen by anyone who goes down Sir John Rogerson's Quay; for after a fire in the eighteen-seventies it was abandoned and turned into a warehouse and it is now an ice factory. Within the last few years it has become practically invisible: a pity, because it was a handsome building. The Chapel of the Military School is free-standing in leafy surroundings in the Park, unspoilt externally, towered and boasting a Borrominesque cupola, but the interior is disappointing. New Newgate Gaol (the old one

---

* Town-Major of Dublin: a very famous character during the 1798 period, who captured Lord Edward. He also collected pictures and was interested in the Irish language.

† The Dublin Corporation, however, continued to keep its books in Irish currency till 1829.

‡ This has been attributed to Ivory, but seems more like Cooley's work.

had been New Gate itself★) was inspired by Dance's masterpiece in London. It had drum-towers at the corners, and was entirely built in black calp, a suitable enough choice, except for the pedimented centre-piece (Pl. xxxiii) in granite, a powerful piece of terroristic architecture with an iron balcony on which the condemned stood for public executions. 'The cells for those under sentence of death,' says a contemporary account, 'are gloomy mansions indeed! they compose the cellarage of the east front, and are nine in number'.[15] Though the prison was built in accordance with Howard's principles, it seems to have been a monument of inhumanity, for the prisoners in irons were forced to climb to the top floor to attend the chapel. Oddly enough, it was not considered 'either well situated or strongly built, the blocks of stone not being cramped as they are in the county-gaol [i.e. Kilmainham]. Few prisoners, however, have ever been able to effect their escape, without the connivance of the turnkeys'.[16]

The Turnkeys, before the reforms of 1808, were as corrupt a set of miscreants as could be found, in any capacity, in any gaol. The poorest prisoners were kept in one side of the prison which had no windows save tiny loopholes, and from these they suspended bags to beg alms from the passers-by, so that they might pay garnish money to the gaolers and so be moved to more salubrious quarters. Life in the Dublin prisons presented scenes of incredible depravity and riot. The coffins of the condemned were, by the kindness of the authorities, sent to them a day or two before the execution, and it was quite common for the malefactor to sell his body to the surgeons before death. With the proceeds he then bought a large quantity of drink for himself and his friends, and using the coffin as a table, spent his last night playing cards, attended by his 'widow'. The hangman wore a grotesque mask, and on his back a hump formed by a large wooden bowl, and after the execution he would use this bowl to fend off the stones with which the crowd pelted him, while the widow slanged or 'dusted' him according to a well-established convention. Her next task (if the body had not been already sold), was to expose it on straw in the streets, 'with or without a head', the breast bearing a plate on which

★ In 1775 the prisoners in Old Newgate offered the turnkey some mulled claret containing aqua-regia and rat's bane, but he saw through their stratagem and, singlehanded, relieved them of their firearms.

was a halfpenny to encourage sympathisers to add their mites to pay for a good funeral. The widow and children crouched around, providing a wailing obbligato. The witticisms of the hangman were much quoted and relished. One, Tom Galvin, would almost cry with disappointment if anyone got a reprieve, exclaiming: 'It's a hard thing to be taking the bread out of the mouth of an old man like me'. On another occasion, when a felon named O'Brien lingered over his devotions, Galvin said: 'Mr O'Brien, long life to you, make haste wid your prayers; de people is getting tired under de swing-swong'. The ballad-literature of Dublin prison-life, written in a strange patois now entirely extinct, is well known: in addition to the famous *The Night Before Larry was Stretched* there is *The Kilmainham Minit*, i.e. minuet, and *Lord Altham's Bull*.[17]

It may seem a far cry from Leinster House to Newgate, but here, in 1798, the best-loved of the great house of the Geraldines died in delirium from the wounds inflicted by Major Sirr, with Lady Louisa Conolly and Lord Henry at his bedside, while Lord Clare, of all people, stood with his face to the wall and wept.* Newgate was demolished in the eighteen-eighties, but the footings of its outer walls are still there, forming the boundaries of St Michan's Park, where children play and old men nod and doze on the benches in the sun.

Cooley's coming confirmed the new status of the architect *pur sang*, as distinct from the builder-architect. Other factors conspired to foster the growth of the academic approach, notably the establishment of the Dublin Society's Schools of drawing, ornament and architecture.† As far back as 1745 the Society had offered prizes for plans of houses with two to eight rooms on a floor. Cassels was the judge, and George Ensor, then a clerk in a surveyor's office, was awarded the first place. Eight years later George Faulkner, Swift's publisher, issued proposals for a work to be entitled *Vitruvius Hibernicus*, 'containing the plans, elevations and sections of the most regular and elegant buildings, both public and private, in the kingdom of Ireland, with variety of new designs, in large folio

---

* Lord Aldborough was also imprisoned here for six weeks in 1798.

† In 1767 (by 7 Geo III 1), Parliament voted £500 to Thomas Conolly, Thomas Lyle, Redmond Morres and George Paul Monk and Colonel William Burton, or any three of them, to be applied towards the building of an academy for painting, sculpture and architecture. But nothing seems to have come of this.

plates, engraven on copper by the best hands, and drawn either from the buildings themselves, or the original designs of the architect'. It was to have been printed on Irish paper, with descriptions of the buildings in Latin, French and English.[18] This tantalising project was, alas, still-born.

The first work on architecture to be printed in Ireland was John Aheron's *General Treatise on Architecture*, which appeared in Dublin in 1754. Aheron was a builder of country houses in the south and south-east, and a little later he was employed to draw elevations of Dublin buildings for monthly publication in the *Dublin Magazine*. He died in about 1761.* Though not strictly relevant to urban building, another Irish copy-book of the period may be mentioned here: *Twelve Designs of Country Houses* by the Rev. John Payne, published in Dublin in 1757 but written in 1753. Tudor's series of six views of Dublin appeared in the latter year, Harris's *History and Antiquities of Dublin* of 1766 has folding architectural plates, and in 1767 came Bernard Scalé's magnificent series of five engravings of the Parliament House, after drawings by Rowland Omer. At the same period the Dublin Society's school was using *'Gibbs' Architecture*, Loudon's *Art of Building*, Hopper's *Architecture*, Halfpenny's *Builder's Assistant*, Price's *British Carpenter* and *Jesuit's Perspective*'—the last presumably Andrea Pozzo's treatise on that art.[19] It is a sobering reflexion that the Society purchased all these books for five pounds. Very soon the students of the school were able to see examples of the latest English Palladianism in Chambers's work at Charlemont House and the Clontarf Casino; but neither of these buildings had any appreciable influence on the Dublin style.

* A book by John Gibbons on *Building in Stone and Lime* was apparently published in Dublin in 1760 (*Irish Builder*, 1946, p. 532).

REFERENCES

[1] *Georg. Soc.* IV, 79 *sqq.*

[2] See maps reproduced by Miss Eleanor Butler in *Country Life*, Nov. 1st, 1946, p. 812, and Mr Harvey, *Dublin*, 1949, Pl. 135.

[3] See a map of 1812 in Pembroke Estate Office.

[4] It is shown on the 1762 map reproduced by Miss Butler, *loc. cit.* See also Ferrar, *Ancient and Modern Dublin*, 1796, p. 73.

[5] *CARD* X, 133.

[6] Gilbert II, 8.

[7] *ibid.* 55.

[8] *ibid.* 56-7 and *JRSAI*, XLVIII, 143.

[9] *Anthologia Hibernica.*

[10] Information of Mr Howard Colvin. See also Curran in *Bank of Ireland*, 1949, p. 438, and *JRSAI*, LXXIX, 20.

[11] Illustrated in *Georg. Soc.* III, Pl. LXXXI.

[12] Drawings in author's possession.

[13] Gilbert II, 60.

[14] Pool and Cash, *Views of the Public Buildings in Dublin*, 1780. The first illustrated description of the capital. Very well done.

[15] *ibid.* p. 57.

[16] Wright, *Historical Guide.* 2nd ed. 1825, p. 112.

[17] See Walsh, *Ireland Sixty Years Ago*, 1911 ed. Chap. VIII.

[18] Gilbert II, 36-7. For another abortive project in 1871, see *Irish Builder*, 1871, p. 191.

[19] Berry, *Hist. of Roy. Dub. Soc.* pp. 114, 117.

CHAPTER XIX

Printers, Poets, Politics and Patronage

THE RAPID ADVANCES in material culture which took place during the middle third of the century (*i.e.* from about 1733 to 1766) are not exactly paralleled in the culture of the mind. Prosperity and enterprise can much more easily call into existence an improved agriculture, a canal system, waterworks, public buildings, useful charities, and even a school of sculptors, stuccodores and silversmiths, than it can summon a national literature out of the limbo of unbegotten things. What enterprise alone can do is to print books: and this, to judge from the surviving bulk of their work, the Dublin printers did in enormous volume during the period. Irish booksellers were legally entitled to reprint any English book they liked, or even to print it, as sometimes happened, before it came out in England.* There is some reason to think that the great proliferation of Irish editions was in part directed towards satisfying a demand from the American colonies, but most of them were produced for the home market; for if Ireland could not yet produce a school of writers, she was beginning to produce readers in much larger numbers than ever before.

There is in this respect a great contrast between the first third of the century and the years which followed. In the earlier period we find that more than half the most important works of George Berkeley, a writer of European and indeed world importance, were first published in Dublin. Much the same is true of Swift: thus, though *Gulliver* was first printed in London, it is the Dublin edition of 1735 which presents the earliest 'good' printed text of that masterpiece.[1] But after Swift and Berkeley there are no Irish writers of even remotely comparable stature. It is true that Dublin gave birth to Burke in 1729 and Sheridan in 1751, and that Burke and Goldsmith were both at Trinity in the forties. But all three left the country as soon as possible. Though there are contemporary

* The most famous case is that of Richardson's *Grandison*.

Dublin editions of all three, they are just the ordinary Dublin editions of English books. None of them, except perhaps Sheridan, took any further interest in Ireland. The stars of literary Dublin were such people as Richard Pockrich,* John Winstanley, William Dunkin, Samuel Shepherd, Laurence Whyte and Samuel Whyte: none of them without merit but all very small men. It is no accident that the printers and publishers such as George Grierson and George Faulkner are to-day better remembered, for in their day they enjoyed a reputation and a social position which most poets would have envied, if envy were part of the make-up of poets. Faulkner was the friend of Lord Chesterfield, and a familiar figure in the streets of Dublin and London, with his wooden leg (called by the Dublin wits his wooden understanding). He lived in Essex Street, in a house which, according to Jephson,[2] was accidentally built without any stairs, where he dispensed a liberal hospitality, being witty at the expense of gentle and simple alike, dispensing 'good meat and claret in abundance', and himself swallowing 'immense potations with one solitary strawberry at the bottom of the glass, which he said was recommended to him by his doctor for its cooling properties'. This description of him is from the dramatist Richard Cumberland, who adds that 'he never lost his recollection or equilibrium the whole time, and was in excellent foolery', maintaining, for example, that he had lost his leg in flying from the fury of an enraged husband. He was full of reminiscence about Swift, telling a number of entertaining stories. Clearly he partook of the characteristic Irish sense of humour, for Cumberland records that when he dined at Faulkner's two of the guests were a man who had been sentenced to death but reprieved, and the judge who had sentenced him.[3] One is reminded a little of the man who found Fielding one evening dining on cold mutton and a hambone, in the company of a blind man, a whore, and three Irishmen.

George Grierson, the King's Printer, was even more prosperous, for he lived in a huge house at Rathfarnham and he or his grandson built other houses in the Dublin and Wicklow mountains.† His

* The inventor of the Musical Glasses. See D. J. O'Donoghue: *The Poets of Ireland*, and F. E. Dixon in *DHR*, X, 1 (1948).

† Handcock: (*History of Tallaght*, 1877, p. 81.) says that Grierson owned Mount Venus, of which George Moore left such a wonderful description in *Hail and Farewell*. But Gandon (Mulvany, p. 121) says James Cullen lived there. Mount Venus has now almost disappeared.

wife Constantia, the celebrated learned lady, had already been mentioned as a friend of Swift's. Her son George Abraham was a friend of Dr Johnson, but he must have inherited his mother's constitutional weakness, for he died in Dusseldorf at the age of twenty-seven. George the elder, who died in 1753, sank a lot of capital in type-founding,[4] whereas Faulkner had been content to use imported types. His son Boulter Grierson succeeded him in the business, and the third George, when Boulter died shortly before 1779. He got £100,000 compensation at the Union, but the family held the office of King's Printer until at least the middle of the nineteenth century. The earlier folio Bibles and Prayer Books of the firm are very fine, and they did work of all kinds and in all formats. Other Dublin printing families were the Powells (a Powell had been the first printer in Dublin in the mid-sixteenth century), and the Ewings, who did a great deal to restore printing standards after the coarsening of quality induced by the mass-production of the sixties.[5]

The most famous of the Dublin engravers was John Brooks of Cork Hill who produced a great many excellent portraits and topographical plates, but left the country in 1746 after the poor response to his scheme to engrave by subscription a number of the country seats within thirty miles of Dublin.[6] This, like the Faulkner scheme, is most tantalising: if either had been carried out we should know a great deal more than we do. Brooks went to London, where, with Henry Delamain, another Dublin emigré, he invented transfer-printing on pottery. The Dublin mezzotint school of this period was second to none: yet one by one, Luttrell, Charles Spooner, Brooks, Gwinn, Ford, MacArdell, they were drained away from Dublin and set up in London where they prospered. But Andrew Miller, of Hog Hill (St Andrew Street) remained here till his death in 1763.[7] The engravings of the second half of the century are, in general, below the standard of the earlier period.

The newspapers became more numerous and voluminous, but still contained little enough news, especially Irish news. The pamphlet literature gives, perhaps, a more vivid picture of the times. Pamphlets of all kinds—poetical, political and nondescript, poured from the Dublin presses in inexhaustible profusion, as indeed they had in Swift's day. Every political occasion produced a crop of them: Lucas's war with the city authorities in 1741–8; the war of Henry Boyle, Anthony Malone and Lord Kildare with Primate Stone in 1752–4; Lucas's return to Ireland and the fray in 1760 and the agrarian disorders of 1763. And every now and then there were rumours of the threat of Union, as in 1759 and 1773, to prevent politics from stagnating completely. It is remarkable, by the way, how seriously the ragged Dublin populace took these political squabbles—squabbles which, the historians tell us, were nothing but the bickerings of oligarchical factions. Lord Kildare, for example, was so popular that it took him an hour to get from the House of Lords to his own house through the cheering mob, while the town blazed with bonfires. What, one may ask, was the Earl to them, that they should cheer for him? The rumour of Union in 1759 produced even more startling eruptions of popular feeling:* the jacquerie broke into the Parliament House, placed an old woman in the Speaker's Chair, rigged up a gallows and threatened various dignitaries with death, stopped the carriages of the members, killed their horses and forced the occupants to swear they would vote against the measure, pulled off Lord Inchiquin's periwig and red ribbon, pulled Sir Thomas Prendergast by the nose out of the House of Lords and rolled him in the kennel, sent for the Journals of the Commons and were about to burn them when the Clerk pointed out that if they did they would be destroying the only record of the defeat of the English interest in 1753, at which they changed their intention and sought for the Master of the Rolls to hang him. They were finally dispersed by a troop of horse who killed fifteen or sixteen of them in the process.[8] Lecky[9] alleges that this was a Protestant mob: but how this could have been established by any means other than that of questioning each member of it as to his religion, does not appear very clearly.

There are worse ways than this of ensuring that the legislature is kept in touch with public opinion. No doubt the individual members of this mob had their economic or social aspirations which were in some obscure way reflected in this action. But it was mainly a matter of sentiment, and expressed the principle largely lost sight of in our time, that the chief use of politics is to act as a safety-valve

* This was expected for some days previously. See I. Commons Journals. Nov. 24th, 1759 which speaks of 'gaming or other disorders in the court of requests', and 'an unusual concourse of disorderly people gathered about the House'.

for the emotions of the masses. It is worth pondering that in the same year as Parliament, to ensure that the Crown should have no disposable surplus, was voting large sums of money for projects of such magnificence as the West Front of Trinity College, the front of the Parliament House itself should have been penetrated by this rude invasion. English readers should pause before they forget that Dublin in the eighteenth century witnessed no popular turmoil seriously comparable to the Lord George Gordon riots in 1780.

The year of the great invasion saw also the election to Parliament of two men, Henry Flood and John Hely Hutchinson, both, in their ways, celebrated: one as the chief author and the other as the chief butt, of two of the best-known satirical volumes of the period: *Baratariana* and *Pranceriana*. *Baratariana*, written largely by Flood and Sir Hercules Langrishe,* appeared in 1772, and was aimed at the administration of the Viceroy Townshend (1767–72). 'Barataria' in it signifies Ireland, Townshend appears as 'Sancho', Provost Andrews as 'Don Francisco Andrea del Bumperoso', Hutchinson, who was Prime Serjeant and Alnager, as 'Don John Alnagero', Lord Loftus (later Earl of Ely) as 'Count Loftonso', his lady's niece the celebrated beauty Dolly Monroe as 'Donna Dorothea del Monroso', Primate Stone (posthumously) as 'Cardinal Lapidaro', and one Surgeon Cunningham as 'Don Alexandro Cuningambo del Tweedalero'. This foolery is obscure enough nowadays: but we should not leave Barataria without following the career of 'Don Ricardo'. This gentleman, in real life Richard Power, Third Baron of the Exchequer, is alleged to have attempted to take the life of Black Jack Fitzgibbon, Lord Chancellor Clare, with a loaded pistol. Unfortunately failing in this laudable endeavour, he set off to Irishtown to commit suicide by drowning, which he did. It was remarked by witnesses afterwards that, as the day was wet, he took an umbrella.

The occasion of *Pranceriana* was the appointment in 1774 of Hely Hutchinson as Provost of Trinity. As a barrister and a politician with

---

* It was, of course, Langrishe to whom Burke wrote the celebrated *Letter*. The best-known of Sir Hercules' witticisms is his reply to Earl Fitzwilliam, when that Viceroy asked him to recommend a history of Ireland that came down to the present time. It would be found, Sir Hercules answered, in a continuation of Rapin. The best part of the joke is that there really was such a book.

a sketchy academic background, he was resented by the dons. He innovated in a terrifying manner, establishing Professorships of French and German, and Italian and Spanish. Worse than this, he proposed to engraft upon the mediæval curriculum of the University instruction in the arts of riding, fencing and dancing. Naturally the Fellows were almost inarticulate with rage. Almost—but not quite. They nicknamed Hutchinson 'The Prancer', and several of them collaborated to produce *Pranceriana*, a libretto of shrill denunciation. Their good work was carried on by an abusive Orange boor named Duigenan in *Lachrymae Academicae* (1777). Duigenan later deserted academic life for the politico-legal sphere so much better suited to his talents, while Hutchinson survived the storm and was at least as good a Provost as Andrews. Though he remained a politician, he was on the whole a sound one; though ambitious for his family he managed to serve the University as well; and he was an economist of some stature. His enemies prophesied that, being a family man, he would fill the College courts with nursemaids and squalling brats; but in the event his family activities led to nothing more disastrous than the Earldom of Donoughmore. In any case, some of the Fellows were themselves married in violation of the College Statutes, and Hutchinson, by consenting to connive at this abuse, was able to bring them to heel.

In 1767 the Octennial Act[10] was passed, 'whereas a limitation of the duration of parliaments may tend to strengthen the harmony and good agreement subsisting between his Majesty and his people of Ireland, and may be productive of other good effects to his Majesty's subjects there ...' Though it did not strengthen 'harmony and good agreement' it certainly was 'productive of other good effects', for it speeded up the tempo of life in Dublin, first in the political but very soon in every other sphere. After 1771 Parliament sat every year, and the Viceroy was more or less constantly resident. He was also in constant difficulty over the maintenance, by jobbery and influence, of a majority in Parliament. The almanacks of the day list an imposing array of offices, and a most melodious recital they make: the Jerquer, the Craner and Wharfinger, the Taster of Wines, the Prothonotary, the Cursitor of the Court of Chancery, the Clerk of the Crown and Hanaper and the Clerk of Entries and Errors, the Clerk of the Pipe and the Comptroller of the Pipe, the Philizer and the Deputy Philizer, the Exigenter and the Filacer, the Alnager of Ireland, the Summonister and Clerk of the Estreats, the Clerk of the Out-Entries, the Clerk of the Essoins and the Clerk of the Pells, together with Tide-Waiters, Land-waiters and Supernumerary Gaugers by the dozen. No doubt many of these functionaries were as useful as they were picturesque, but many such places were given to the cousins, brothers-in-law and nephews of Honourable Members in return for support in the House. And, as well, there was the long list of pensions on the Civil Establishment, which served the same purpose. The Viceroys Townshend and Harcourt deployed this formidable array most industriously, and the ding-dong of controversy and pamphleteering resounded ever more merrily.

Ten years earlier the recreations of the Dublin reading public had been more leisurely and less sensational. Hurd's or Lyttleton's Dialogues, the poems of Waller, John Philips or Shenstone, or the latest number of the *Dublin Magazine* which chose the easy way out by feeding its readers on the distant battles of the *North Briton*, and reprinting the political satires of Charles Churchill. True, it also printed the Addresses of the Irish Houses and the Viceroy's speeches, but without much evidence of excitement. Here one might read 'The Portrait of a good Senator' and 'The picture of a wicked Senator', a description of Mr Randall's new-invented Seed-Plow, or an improved method for raising Cucumbers. Among the useful articles were the remedies of Mr Theobald, for every known disorder, including (sandwiched between Looseness and Measles) the remedy for Madness: 'Take forty drops of tincture of Black Hellebore in a glass of water, two or three times a day'. Much the same remedy is specific for Green Sickness. Besides the inevitable serialised 'History of Kamtschatka'—for some reason a constant favourite in the eighteenth century—the magazine ran an instructive series of articles on Irish topography, as well as illustrated articles on Irish and other buildings, from the Parliament House to an 'Essay on Convenience, Strength and Beauty in public and private buildings' by John Morrison, by way of commentary on his own elevation for a Mayoralty-House in Cork. One might read of the prize-winning numbers in the State Lottery,* of a fire in

---

* The twentieth-century 'Irish Sweep' has a long ancestry.

Aungier Street or an explosion in Lower Castle Yard, causing 'a scene of terror and distress, which, for so much, can only be equalled by the earthquake at Lisbon'. Some Red Indians arrive in Dublin and are minutely described: 'Unencumbered with breeches, they, now and then, discover the natural complexion of their skins, which are of a brown colour'. There are brief reviews of new books: 'his language is very well adapted to his subject, and is far from being reptile or inflated'. Finally one may quote the epitaph of a notable drinker, written by himself,

> *Than whom no man*
> *Took more pains*
> *To quench his thirst;*
> *Than whom no man*
> *Was more constantly thirsty.*

> *   *   *

> *He decanted this life*
> *On the 4th day of*
> *November, 1762,*
> *Performing a libation to that*
> *Glorious anniversary.*

> *Go thy way, reader!*
> *Drink and be merry,*
> *For death*
> *Will take off the heel-taps,*
> *And not leave thee a sky-light.*

The emphasised words were at that time in common use among drinkers. This particular drinker was Clerk of the Faculties and Errors.

English visitors found Dublin conspicuously lacking in hotels or even passable inns: a defect which has been long since remedied. But the hospitality of individuals was lavish to the point of embarrassment, especially in the matter of claret, which was then the national drink of Ireland. The best cost 2s. 6d. a bottle, and a 'middling drinker' would drink four bottles without showing any effects. According to John Bush, who visited Dublin in 1764,[11] no man was seriously considered a drinker who could not 'take off his gallon coolly', yet 'I believe it may be said with a great deal of truth, that the Irish drink the most of any of his Majesty's subjects with the least injury. 'Tis hardly possible, indeed, to make an Irishman, that can in any sense be called a drinker, thoroughly drunk with his claret: by that time he has discharged his five or six bottles, he will get a little flashy, perhaps, and you may drink him to eternity he'll not be much more'. But Bush considered the Dublin claret, though good, inferior to that of London, and as for what he calls 'the ridiculous vanity of pretending to speak better English' than would be heard in London, he dismisses this claim with contempt and it has been left to that distinguished Dubliner Mr Bernard Shaw to carry this warfare into the enemy's camp. It is only fair, however, to remark that the literary evidence seems to suggest that the corruption of English as spoken in England is of comparatively recent growth.

English tourists who published offensive books when they got home were summarily dealt with. When Philip Luckombe came to Dublin in 1779 he found that, though there was still a shortage of inns, some hotels had recently been opened, fitted with every modern convenience, notably chamber-pots on the bottoms of which the countenance of one Richard Twiss was to be seen, 'with his mouth and eyes open ready to receive the libation'. A 'Twiss' indeed, says Luckombe, was the name commonly used for these vessels, and so Twiss was requited for the illiberal reflexions he had published about this country in his *Tour in Ireland* of 1776.[12] The same method was used in more recent times to express Irish opinions on the late Lord Balfour, and the manufacturer in this case is said to have made his fortune.

Drinking and duelling go together in the popular mind, and Arthur Young, that pudding-fed economist and calculator who toured Ireland in 1776-8, thought that the recent decline in heavy drinking had caused a decline in duelling also.[13] If this was so, it was soon offset by political causes, for the intoxication of parliamentary oratory has cost more lives than the intoxication of claret. When both intoxications concur, as for many years to come they continued to do, the duel was often the only way out.

But there were other counter-influences undermining the duelling habit. Half-way through the century a society had been formed called the 'Friendly Brothers of St Patrick', whose members bound themselves to abstain from settling differences in this way. This club prospered and still exists as a social club with its headquarters in St Stephen's Green and branches, or 'knots' as they are called, elsewhere through the country. It seems likely, too, that the acceptance of trading and commercial men in good society further reduced the popularity of duelling, for business men are commonly almost as careful of their skins as of their shop-windows.

Brewing, always one of Dublin's main industries, became respectable very early on, and the brewers leavened the polite society of the capital.* We have already seen how Miss Ambrose, a brewer's daughter, shone at Chesterfield's court and married a baronet, and how the Leesons left their brewery behind them and became Earls of Miltown. But it soon became possible to move in good society without having to give up trade. In 1773 the House of Commons examined three brewers on the condition of their industry: they were George Thwaites, Master of the Brewers' Guild and later of soda-water fame, Mr Andrews, 'a considerable brewer', and Mr Arthur Guinness, 'another considerable brewer'. The Guinnesses had at this time been established in Dublin for fourteen years, and Thwaites for more than twice as long. Brewing in Dublin was suffering from unfair English competition, and they sought and obtained some protection. In 1790 the English traveller C. T. Bowden dined with the 'most eminent' of the Dublin brewers, Mr James Farrell, who had his brewery in the Black Pitts but his dwelling-house in Merrion Square East. Bowden was introduced to Farrell's brother-in-law, Mr Byrne, another eminent brewer, and reports that he 'was never more elegantly entertained in [his] life'. Both gentlemen, he adds, were 'held in the highest estimation by all ranks for the most exalted virtues'. They improved the occasion by pouring into Bowden's ear a catalogue of the disabilities under which the Irish brewing trade was still restrained by an obtuse legislature.[14] This, it should be remembered, was before the Union, and it is a little surprising. After the Union, of course, all sorts of residents, but still mainly lawyers and doctors and a few minor peers and gentry, began to live in the Squares.

* The first Cloncurry was a woollen-draper, and his wife the daughter of Valentine Browne, a rich Catholic brewer. Both turned Protestant.

Banking was another activity which was by no means incompatible with high social position. The Gardiners, it is true, sold out of banking before they became peers, but the great Huguenot family of La Touche,* intermarried with the Grattans and the Marlays, with grand houses in Stephen's Green (Nos 15, 45 and 85), Ely Place (No 11) and Merrion Square (No 44), with large country houses at Marlay, Co. Dublin, and Bellevue, Co. Wicklow, busy everywhere with philanthropic activities—the La Touches carried on their private bank till 1870 and one of them was the first Governor of the Bank of Ireland in 1783. Four of them sat in the House of Commons and voted against the Union. On the other hand Newcomen's Bank, on the other side of the street from La Touche's, was found on the other side of the house on that memorable occasion, and Sir William Gleadowe Newcomen, Bart., got away, as Sir Jonah Barrington says, 'with a peerage, the patronage of his county, and the pecuniary pickings also received by himself';[15] but not without provoking the revenge of the printsellers, who published a view of his very beautiful Bank building, with the caption

Though many years I've lived in Town
As New-Come-In I'm only known.

Even aristocratic place-holders with ample incomes engaged in banking—for example one of the detested Beresfords, John Claudius, son of John and nephew of Lord Waterford, alderman and Member for Dublin. He carried on his banking business in Beresford Place, opposite his father's Custom House; and in 1798 the infuriated canaille gathered there and ceremonially burned large numbers of his promises to pay, ejaculating the while 'What will he do now? his bank will surely break'. These sentiments did them credit, but disclosed a most unfortunate and pathetic incomprehension of the principles of finance.

Even tobacconists became sufficiently prosperous to build themselves grand houses and move in good society towards the end of

---

* For the La Touches, see Gilbert, I, 20 *sqq*, and Hone in *The Bank of Ireland*, 1949, pp. 475 *sqq* and 496 *sqq*. A confidential Castle notebook of 1773 has this amusing note on David La Touche the younger: 'He is a Banker and accounted the safest in Ireland he would willingly serve Government: but but ['*sic*'] he has an eye to popularity as it might be of use to his shop'. *Procs of R.I.A.* August 1942 p. 205. The La Touche Bank financed the building of Queen's Bridge in 1764 (*CARD* XI, 247).

the century. The famous firm of Lundy Foot & Co. began in 1758 in the Blind Quay selling 'Bristol Roll, Common Roll, Pig-tail, High and Low Scotch Snuff, St Vincent, Strasbourg, Bergamot, Spanish, Brazil, Irish Rappees and Superfine Pig-tail for Ladies'.[16] It moved to Essex-Gate in 1774 and later to Westmorland Street. In about 1780 Lundy Foot built himself a fine house called Holly-park in the Dublin mountains (now St Columba's College), while his brother Jeffrey built Footmount (now Orlagh College) also in the mountains a few years later. Lundy was a well-known figure in Dublin, and the most familiar story of him is that which relates how he asked his neighbour John Philpot Curran, the celebrated legal wit, what motto he should inscribe on the doors of his carriage. 'Quid Rides' was Curran's reply. Lundy was a magistrate, and a few years after the Union was active in hunting down three brothers who were publicly executed for conspiracy to murder in 1816. Lundy Foot, who had a country seat in Co. Kilkenny, was riddled full of slugs there by persons unknown. He recovered; but in 1835 while planting some trees on his Kilkenny demesne, he was stoned and hacked almost to pieces. But the fame of his snuff survived him, and while snuff-taking was still general, Foot's establishment, with a branch in London, was second to none.

Lundy Foot's tobacco has long since dissolved in smoke, and it would be difficult now to test the quality of his snuff. The exact nature of the liquor brewed by Mr Arthur Guinness at this date cannot now be determined by the most conscientious of personal experiments: we know little more of it than we do of the song the Sirens sang. We can, it is true, read the books printed by Grierson or Powell, Byrne or Chambers or Graisberry and Campbell. We can read them if we want to; but few of them, unfortunately, are in keen demand as reading-matter today. Of all the articles produced in the heyday of Dublin craftsmanship, it is perhaps only the furniture, the silver and the glass which is now useful as well as valuable (buildings, of course, always excepted).

We saw that Trinity College had its mace made in Dublin as early as 1708. The House of Commons had its Mace of 1765 made in London,[17] but when the Lords were getting theirs in the following year they supported home industries and bought it from Isaac D'Olier for £286 9s 4¾d.[18] It was made by William Townsend in

Dublin, in silver gilt, and is now in the National Museum, which has, as is only fitting, an excellent collection of Irish silver including examples on loan. The Commons' Mace was taken away by Speaker Foster at the Union and remained in the possession of his descendants at Antrim Castle until sold at Christie's in London in 1937. It was bought by the Bank of Ireland and may now be seen, somewhat illogically, in the House of Lords.

Silver was made in several of the provincial towns, notably Cork, Limerick, Galway and Kinsale, but nowhere on such a scale as in Dublin. In the late seventeen-eighties the Dublin output averaged 85,000 oz. per annum,[19] more than three times what it was at the beginning of the century. Certain types of piece are peculiarly Irish: the dish-rings sometimes erroneously called potato-rings, or the two-handled cups with the handles of the so-called 'harp' shape. Apart from this, the character of the chasing is often enough to satisfy an expert that a piece is of Irish or Dublin make.

Some of the cups in the National Museum's collection were presented on interesting occasions. One, of 1781, was given by the Booksellers' Company to John Exshaw (proprietor of the well-known *Exshaw's Magazine*—the *Gentleman's and London* to give it its official title) for his services as Secretary to the Company. Another, of 1798, was given by two ladies to a married pair in Wexford 'as a testimony of the grateful sense they feel of the benevolence and humanity which they experienced from them while prisoners in their house during that dreadful period in which the Rebels held possession of the Town of Wexford in June, 1798'. Among the items on loan is the fine series of snuff-boxes presented by various grateful bodies to Henry Grattan in token of his exertions for Irish trade, and recently purchased by Messrs Guinness, and, among the gold objects, the 'Rutland Salver', lent by a private owner.

It appears, from an anecdote told by J. D. Herbert, that the articles now generally called 'coasters' were at this time only called so in Ireland. Herbert, who had been in London where he had been rather irritated by having to adopt English usages and pronunciation, was serving behind the counter in his father's hardware shop, when an English gentleman asked to see some 'bottle-stands'. Herbert answered 'We have no such article, Sir'. When the customer pointed them out, 'Oh, I beg your pardon, Sir,—we call these bottle coasters'. 'Coasters! Coasters! they are called bottle-stands all through England'. 'That is just as it should be, Sir; but the bottle never stands in Ireland. We, therefore, call them bottle coasters!' So Herbert lost his customer but had his joke.[20]

Nobody seems to have made any political capital out of the English origin of the Commons' Mace, for the seventeen-sixties were a little early for this kind of sentiment to have come to full flower. But the case of the two State Coaches is another matter. When Black Jack Fitzgibbon became Lord Chancellor in 1789, he ordered himself a grand coach from London. In the same year the Lord Mayor, John Rose, ordered one from William Whitton of Dominick Street, after a competition among the Dublin coach-builders. Fitzgibbon's coach, which is said to have cost nearly £7,000, was landed in Dublin on September 15th, 1790, and by its owner's orders was available for public inspection at his stables in Baggot Street. Incredible numbers of people came to visit it; but among these were not a few whose hatred of the Lord Chancellor was their motive for coming; so that special precautions had to be taken to preserve the coach from injury. In the meantime Mr Whitton of Dominick Street, aided by the prayers and blessings of the patriotic party, was working away for all he was worth. A few days before the landing of Fitzgibbon's vehicle, the Dublin papers reported that 'the new City State Coach building by Mr Whitton is in such forwardness as to enable that ingenious mechanic to launch it from his yard on the 4th November next'. But this, like most artificers' promises, was delusive. The arrival of the Chancellor's coach had upset matters: the City Fathers, previously (though somewhat grudgingly) committed to the expenditure of a paltry £1,200 on their State Coach, took one look at the English coach with its ormolu trimmings and threw caution to the winds. Mr Whitton was instructed to spare no expense, he redoubled his efforts and at length, on November 4th, 1791, it took the road.

The reader will doubtless have noticed the prominence of the date November 4th in this narrative. This is no accident. The birth-day of William III, that unlovely monarch who of all recent Eng-lish rulers has, I suppose, the least affectionate appeal to the people of England, was still dutifully observed in Dublin. This particular November 4th was a round century after the Battle of Aughrim, and that battle was, in a manner of speaking, fought again as the two coaches, the honest Irish coach of the good Lord Mayor, and the ostentatious coach of the detested Chancellor, lumbered creakily round King William's statue in College Green, then up Grafton Street and round King George II in Stephen's Green, pursued by the alternate cheers and hisses of the populace. It was decided by the best judges that the Irish coach was the grander of the two. At this distance of time we can perhaps afford to be neutral about their artistic qualities. Both coaches still exist, and may be inspected by the curious. The cynical will derive some amusement from the fact that on Fitzgibbon's coach 'the arms of Ireland are supported by the Genii of Immortality', in view of Fitzgibbon's decisive role in destroying the Kingdom of Ireland nine years later.[21] The whole subject, indeed, is instinct with irony, for Fitzgibbon (by then Earl of Clare) went in this coach to the Union debates in the House of Lords preceded by the Lords' Irish mace, while Foster, the Speaker, who was equally strong on the other side of the question, walked into the Commons behind the London bauble.

We cannot leave this brief review of some of the Dublin crafts without some mention of the bookbinders, whose work was among the most illustrious done in the period. Unlike the other crafts, decorative bookbinding seems to have been confined to the capital; at least, in the present rather unsatisfactory state of knowledge, it seems to have been so. But it was more distinctively Irish than perhaps any other craft, with the possible exception of plasterwork. It sprang into existence, apparently without antecedents, in the early eighteenth century, and by the end of the century it flowered in a school of extraordinary loveliness, distinguished by morocco inlays of various colours including white, in panels based mainly on the lozenge shape. The manuscript journals of the two Houses of Parliament, preserved in the Record Office until the appalling disaster of its destruction in 1922, formed what Sir Edward Sullivan called the best 'pictorial representation of development'[22] in binding available in any country; for the Journals themselves contained the records of the bindings paid for to different craftsmen, and they were not uniform, but bound year by year in the style favoured by the binder at the time. There were 149 of these volumes: the early examples crude and evidently the work of Irish craftsmen learning for themselves and by themselves. The Lords' Journals until 1707 resembled, in Sullivan's opinion, the English work of the period. But thereafter the series presented the majestic progression of work by Joseph Ray, Samuel Fairbrother, Nicholas King, Abraham Bradley and Abraham Bradley King his grandson, exercised on all the plenitude and splendour of tall folios.* Very few Irish binders signed their work before the nineteenth century: but the binders mentioned also bound the printed sets for the Members, so that a printed set with a reasonable pedigree—and such are not uncommon—should provide the student of binders' tools with a starting-point. When we add to that the reflexion that any book printed in Dublin and bought second-hand in or near Dublin is most likely to have been also bound in Dublin, it is clear that the materials exist for a study which would be very rewarding and is very badly needed.

* Happily, rubbings of many of these bindings are preserved in the National Museum, together with some good photographs.

REFERENCES

[1] First accorded full recognition by Mr John Hayward in his Nonesuch edition of Swift, 1934.

[2] *A Familiar Epistle to Gorges Edmond Howard Esq*, Dublin 1771. This entertaining work purports to be by Faulkner himself.

[3] Gilbert II, 51.

[4] Strickland in *Bibl. Soc. of I. Pubs.* II, 2.

[5] See article by the author in *Friends of Lib. of T.C.D. Bulletin*, 1948.

[6] Gilbert II, 18.

[7] *ibid.* III, 318.

[8] Gilbert, *Parl. Ho. Dub.* 56.

[9] Lecky, II, 435.

[10] 7 Geo. III, 3.

[11] *Hibernia Curiosa*, Dublin, 1769.

[12] P. Luckombe, *A Tour Through Ireland*, Dublin, 1780, 39–40.

[13] Young, *Tour in Ireland*, Dublin, 1780, II, App. p. III.

[14] Bowden, *Tour in Ireland*, Dublin, 1791, 47 *sqq*.

[15] Barrington, *Rise and Fall of the Irish Nation*. Duffy ed., 282.

[16] Gilbert II, 120.

[17] Curran in *Bank of Ireland*, 1949, 448.

[18] Westropp, National Museum Guide: *Metal Work*, 34.

[19] *ibid.* 15.

[20] Herbert, *Irish Varieties*, 1836, 224.

[21] Strickland in *JRSAI*, LI, 49 *sqq*.

[22] Sullivan: *Decorative Bookbinding in Ireland*: Ye Sette of Odde Volumes: *Opuscula* LXVII, 1914. Illustrated. See also the same author's Preface to *Buck Whaley's Memoirs*. And see Addenda to List of Authorities, below.

CHAPTER XX

Ivory and some Great Houses

THE MOST distinguished Irish-born architect of the Cooley era was Thomas Ivory who, though an older man, died at about the same time, and shared the public building plums with Cooley until the coming of Gandon. Ivory (who is not to be confused with the Thomas Ivory of Norwich who was a contemporary and, to confuse matters still further, took part in the Dublin Royal Exchange Competition) was born in Cork in about 1720. He is said to have been a carpenter, like so many other architects of the period; but from the delicacy of his detail one would suppose that 'cabinet-maker' would be nearer the mark. At some period, probably before he first came to Dublin, he designed the graceful and picturesquely sited bridge over the Blackwater at Lismore, probably for that Duke of Devonshire who had married Burlington & Cork's only daughter and so inherited the Lismore property of the Boyles, in 1753.[1]

Ivory next appears in the employ of a Dublin gunsmith aptly enough named Alderman Truelock, for whom he made gunstocks. He studied drawing under 'Mr Bell Mires' (presumably one of that Myers-Meyers family of architects) and became the best architectural draughtsman in Dublin. In 1759 he was appointed Master of the Dublin Society's Architectural School, and so remained till his death in 1786. He was also Surveyor of the Revenue Buildings until his death, and built some country houses of which one at least can be identified.[2]

His name has been attached to both the Bedford Tower (probably about 1763) and the Marine School (1768–75), but both these attributions lack support. His first well-authenticated building in Dublin was a Market-House in Oxmantown Green for which he won a competition in 1768, but as he was paid £50 'compensation' in the following year, it was probably never built.[3] But his connexion with Oxmantown Green was only now beginning.

The haphazard old building of the Blue-Coat School, where old

William Smith had lived and died, where, during the building of Pearce's masterpiece the two Houses of Parliament had sat, was now 'only kept together by patchwork'.[4] With the expectation of Parliamentary assistance a Building Committee which included Ivory's old master, Truelock, decided to rebuild on a more westerly site. Ivory produced a very magnificent plan, and the first stone was laid in what was soon named Blackhall Place in June 1773, by the Viceroy Harcourt, walking between 'two rows of the children, very clean and neatly dressed, who made a most pleasing appearance, and sang psalms in a most harmonious manner'.[5] The work went on, with Vierpyl in charge of the stonework, Semple the bricklayer, Thorpe the plasterer, Cranfield the carver, Chambers the wood-worker, until 1779. But the Parliament, unmindful of past hospit-ality or even of the sweet voices of the children, failed to vote the necessary sum to provide a cupola for them to sing under. The Governors raised money by private subscription, and, by way of a hint that the Royal assistance would not come amiss, they presented Ivory's twelve beautiful drawings bound in morocco to George III in 1776. (George IV later gave them to the British Museum where they are now.)

In 1779 Ivory was told to cut down his scheme,[6] and to abandon the arcaded quadrangle at the rear when only the Dining Hall (on the south-east corner) had been built. A picture by Trotter in the boardroom shows Ivory and Vierpyl receiving these distasteful instructions. Ivory remained long enough only to finish his façade and boardroom,* and resigned in 1780. The central tower with its lofty lantern was never completed beyond the stage of its main order, and the furnishings of (for example) the Chapel which occupies the north wing were severely simplified.

None the less, the Blue-Coat School (see Pl. xxxii and Fig. 11), though the least familiar of Dublin's major buildings after the Royal Hospital, is one of the most beautiful and, in its way, original. Ivory loved smallness of scale, and small variations of scale in a single design. He loved shallow curves, slender lanterns and lace-like balustrades. Yet he was able to unify these elements into a whole quite strong enough to stand a searching analysis. But his planning, like most eighteenth-century planning, is primitive. The building

---

* The ceiling of which, damaged by fire in recent years, was renewed in facsimile.

was 'finished' by John Wilson, an architect and a Governor; but it was not until 1894 that the unfinished tower colonnade was taken down and the present rather dumpy copper cupola substituted by R. J. Stirling. The streets round the School—Blackhall Place* in which it stands and Blackhall Street down which it faces—were laid out under Ivory's direction on a generous plan, and in Blackhall Street especially large fine houses were built, which are now decayed or decaying. Thus disappeared almost the last vestige of Oxmantown Green.

The year after his resignation from the Blue-Coat, Ivory was called upon to design Newcomen's Bank (Pl. XXXIV) in Castle Street, on a corner site with great possibilities, facing the Royal Exchange and the Castle Gate. The result is the only building in Dublin which looks as though it might have been designed by one of the Adams. The main and entrance front was the south, facing the Castle. The other front, to the east, was three narrower bays wide with a decorative feature of niches and swags surrounding the one first-floor window. Some time between 1850 and 1868[7] this front was extended northwards by duplication in facsimile (save that the ornaments are of compo instead of Portland stone), and a new entrance made with a porch between the two halves.

The south front (though somewhat pitted by machine-gun fire) is a most sensitive piece of work, with Ivory's beloved window-balustrades, a fluted impost-frieze on the *piano nobile*, and the main frieze enriched with swags and medallions. The east front shows some influences from Cooley's design for the Public Offices. The windows recessed in shallow arches are a somewhat Adamite feature not usual in Dublin. Both fronts are entirely in Portland stone, silvery and elegant with delicate cabinet-maker's mouldings, a delicious contrast with its neighbours, the Palladian City Hall and the Wren-like Upper Castle Yard. The building later became the Hibernian Bank and later still was acquired by the Corporation as offices. The oval staircase in the south front is well worth seeing.

Ivory is described by Herbert, who was taught by him in the Dublin Society's school, as 'a gentle urbane character'; and this description exactly fits his two most important buildings. He died in 1786, having lived long enough to see Gandon begin work on

* Named after the chairman of the Building Committee.

his vast commission for the Revenue Board to which Ivory was official architect.* The author of the *Anthologia Hibernica* article on his career (whom some think to have been Gandon) opined that 'it's scarce worth the attention of an ingenious person to pursue and study the profession of an architect, unless he becomes mercenary and unites that disgraceful and illiberal one of a contractor or builder', which Ivory did not do. The anonymous author of the anti-Gandon *Letters to Parliament* (supposed by some to have been James Malton) seems to hint that Gandon's influence in high places had prevented public money being voted to finish the Blue-Coat School. Certainly the extraordinary deafness of Parliament to repeated appeals at a time when money was being spent lavishly on other buildings, is suggestive: but all we know of Gandon is against such a suspicion. He mentions Ivory and Cooley as the two architects of reputation when he himself first came to Dublin:[8] in fact, understandably enough, he overdoes the picture of a Dublin where corruption and political ambition were strangling the fine arts until his own pure-souled patron John Beresford changed all that. Ivory and Gandon were professionally connected in that Ivory's apprentice H. A. Baker became Gandon's pupil and partner after Ivory's death, and succeeded him as Master of the Society's School.

Very few indeed of the greater Dublin houses of this period have since disappeared. They are nearly all there still, and some are in good hands. To consider a few of them together with their builders or occupants is perhaps as good a way as any of seeing the period in a true perspective.

Let us begin with No 86 Stephen's Green, South, next door to Clanwilliam House and, since 1908 part of University College. This granite house has one of the most handsome fronts in Dublin, five bays wide, virile and well-proportioned, with an admirable lion couchant over the door. Its only fault is that it clashes in scale with Clanwilliam House which was there first.† Internally it is equally admirable, spacious planning and flowing plasterwork bespeaking the hand of Robert West, its probable designer and builder in about 1765.[9] Though extremely palatial, it was built for a commoner, Richard Chapell Whaley, M.P. for Co.

* It appears, curiously enough, that Gandon never held this or any other official post.
† This is said to be intentional on the owner's part, which is quite likely.

Wicklow, who died in 1769, leaving, among other children, a son
Thomas, the famous Buck Whaley who made the celebrated journey to Jerusalem. Richard Chapell Whaley was commonly called
Burn-Chapel Whaley, and was a magistrate and a notorious priest-
hunter. But the Dublin tradition that he swore no Papist should
ever darken his threshold, has doubtless been preserved, if not
created, by the circumstance of Cardinal Cullen's having bought
the house in 1853, after which it was for many years the Catholic
University of Ireland. He is also renowned for having written a
cheque in rhyme in favour of his wife:

> Mr. La Touche,
> Open your pouch,
> And give unto my darling
> Five hundred pounds sterling:
> For which this will be your bailey,
> Signed, Richard Chapell Whaley.

His son the Buck is much more famous. He entered Parliament
at the age of eighteen in 1785, but he seems to have spent much
more time gambling in Daly's Club in College Green, than in the
House next door. The story of his leaping for a wager[10] out of a
first-floor window and over a standing coach is sometimes placed
here and sometimes in Stephen's Green, but he himself places the
incident at Dover on his way to or from the Continent. It is a very
typical Dublin Buck exploit. His renowned journey to Jerusalem
to win a wager incurred at dinner in Leinster House is perfectly
authentic: indeed he left an amusing account of it in MS, which was
printed in 1906.[11] It was also the subject of contemporary Dublin
balladry:

> Buck Whalley lacking much in cash,
> And being used to cut a dash,
> He wagered full ten thousand pound
> He'd visit soon the Holy Ground.
> In Loftus's fine ship
> He said he'd take a trip,
> And Costello so famed,
> The captain then was named.

The journey took him from 1788 till the summer of the following
year, and cost him £8,000, leaving a net profit of £7,000 from the

wager, 'the only instance in all my life before, in which any of my projects turned out to my advantage'. In spite of his wild reputation, the account shows him to have been an observant traveller and even something of a scholar.

In Dublin he was known as the boon companion of the Sham Squire Francis Higgins and John Scott (Copper-Faced Jack), Earl of Clonmell: as rascally a pair as could be found anywhere. These three were frequently to be seen promenading in the Green, whether on Leeson's Walk (their own side) or the more fashionable Beaux Walk (Stephen's Green, North): Whaley the Buck, Higgins the gutter journalist and government informer, and Scott, the obese and unscrupulous Chief Justice of the King's Bench. Whaley's sister married Fitzgibbon, and he himself married, a year before his death, the sister of Valentine Browne Lawless, second Lord Cloncurry.*

Buck Whaley's gambling debts finally became so embarrassing that he withdrew from Dublin and ended his days in the Isle of Man, where he wrote his Memoirs in a spirit of commendable contrition. He built a large house there known as Whaley's Folly, subsequently the Fort Anne Hotel, which is said to have been built on Irish earth imported in shiploads sufficient to underlie the whole mansion to a depth of six feet to satisfy a wager—a typical part of the Buck Whaley legend. His last patriotic action was to accept a bribe of £4,000 from the Grattan party to vote against the Union. He died at a coaching inn in Cheshire on November 2nd, 1800, at the age of thirty-four.

The façade of Charlemont House (Pl. xx) is by no means so startlingly different from that of 86 Stephen's Green as one might expect from the dissimilarity of the respective lives led behind them. True, one is of granite and the other of limestone: and, though built at almost the same time, they are at opposite ends of the town. Whaley's house is the more robust, Charlemont's the more refined; and this is a weak reflexion of the immense gulf which separated their occupants. Such was the power of eighteenth-century architectural manners that both houses could with propriety have stood in the

* Cloncurry's politics were liberal, not to say revolutionary. He was imprisoned by Pitt in the Tower of London for two years without trial, and later became an ally of O'Connell. He added the wings of his house at Lyons in about 1810, in a severe grecian manner, and died there in 1853, aged eighty-three.

one street. Such was the weakness of the social cement that, as events were to show, there was no room in Ireland for such variable standards of political morality.

Charlemont was a gentle, cultivated and patriotic nobleman whose chief interests were architecture, scholarship and a version of patriotic whiggery at once gentlemanly and dogged. After travelling on the Continent he devoted his prime to building in or near Dublin: this house and the enchanting Casino at Clontarf, both designed for him by his friend Sir William Chambers. Of all the building grandees in Dublin, Charlemont was the one most seriously interested in architecture. Charlemont House is the centre-piece of Rutland (Parnell) Square, North, and is therefore an integral part of the design of Dublin. The exterior, with its unfortunate modern porch, the entrance hall (slightly altered) and the grand staircase are almost all that now remains to be seen of Charlemont House, after its use as the General Register Office from 1870 onwards and its remodelling in 1930 as the Municipal Gallery of Modern Art. It was the last of the great town houses of Dublin to be lived in by its noble owners. The Casino, two miles outside Dublin in the Earl's demesne of Marino, is one of the most beautiful buildings of its kind anywhere, but has little relevance to Dublin except as being a work by Gandon's master.[12]

Charlemont's patriotism involved him, in middle age, in the Volunteer movement of 1779, and as Commander-in-Chief of the Volunteers he is known to history. Wholehearted as he was in upholding his sober brand of Whig Nationalism, one cannot help feeling that building, literature and the concerns of the Royal Irish Academy (of which he was virtual founder in 1785-6) were more congenial occupations. The Earl died in 1799, shortly before the passing of the Union which, with the Duke of Leinster and a few more aristocratic idealists, he resisted and so much dreaded.

The Royal Irish Academy now occupies Northland House in Dawson Street, a brick house built in about 1770 for the Knox family of Dungannon, and much resorted to by Wolfe Tone who was very attached to the Hon. George Knox, Lord Northland's son, a prominent anti-Unionist. The architect is unrecorded, but may have been John Ensor.[13] Though of brick, it was given some prominence by stone coigns, string-courses, window-cases and a cornice, but the plan and essentials of the elevation are similar to ordinary Dublin houses. It is remarkable internally for its elaborate plaster in a distinctive style showing 'Chinese' influence—white on a green ground. It passed through various hands before the Academy took it over in 1852, and was then extended over the garden in libraries and meeting-rooms. It is fortunate in being used for such a purpose.

Much grander than this was the house in William Street (Pls. XXXV, LVII) built by the third Viscount Powerscourt in 1771. The Wingfields were a respectable opposition family rather of the Charlemont type, though indeed a Castle dossier notes opposite this Lord Powerscourt: 'Wanted to be an Earl,—hitherto in constant Opposition', implying that if he were made an Earl he might cease to oppose. His elder brother, whom he succeeded at his early death in 1764, had been Charlemont's friend from youth. The family already had a large country mansion in Co. Wicklow designed by Cassels and built in 1731, which they still occupy.

Powerscourt House was designed by Robert Mack and built under his supervision. Little else is known of Mack except that, like Ivory, he produced designs for the Four Courts which were not used.[14] He was also an entrant in the Royal Exchange Competition, and there is an almost contemporary account of Essex Bridge which says that Mr Robert Mack, 'a skilful mason', executed Essex Bridge, but was 'a considerable loser by a mistake in the contract'. This Robert Mack worked for the Barrack Board and was also concerned in the building of the 'Rialto' bridge over the Grand Canal for the Corporation in 1769.[15] By 1780 he is quite definitely called 'Robert Mack, Architect'.[16]

Powerscourt House is extremely imposing with its frontage of 130 feet, its great height* crowned with a tall blind attic, all in so narrow a street that it is impossible to see except slantwise. The detail is coarse, and some tastes might find the composition too crowded and overpowering, but there is a daring about the conception which compels admiration. The attic, with its immense consoles, is said to have been intended as an observatory.[17] When the Commissioners of Stamp-Duties bought the house for £15,000 in 1807 they built three ranges of additional buildings round a

* About seventy-three feet.

225

court-yard, which cost them a further £15,000. In 1835 it was bought by Messrs Ferrier Pollock, wholesale drapers, who keep it in admirable order and courteously show it to visitors. The powerful granite exterior is in sharp contrast to the interior. Like other great houses, it was decorated internally in successive stages, the hall and staircase being done by James McCullagh while the main reception rooms upstairs are by Michael Stapleton in his style which is the Irish analogue of Adam. One room is especially beautiful with a shallow dome ceiling meeting the walls in graceful segments, a treatment which Stapleton applied also to No 17 Stephen's Green, now the University Club.[18]

Clonmell House in Harcourt Street, finished soon after Powerscourt House, brings us back to Copper-faced Jack Scott, whose somewhat precarious dignity it was designed to support. He had risen in the world with discreditable speed, running through the offices of Solicitor-General, Attorney-General and Prime Serjeant to Lord Chief Justice in ten years. The origins of his wealth were, according to a good authority,[19] tainted with particular odium, for he held lands in trust for Catholics who, till 1778, could not legally hold lands, and he dishonoured the agreements under which he did so. He spent most of his life in office in waging war upon the freedom of the Press, which, understandably, he held in peculiar abhorrence. On the Bench and in the House he was a typical 'friend to Government': he disposed of £400 a year for his brother, two Supernumerary Gaugers and a Stamp Inspector of the Courts, and was noted as 'grateful and punctual'.[20] But he had an uneasy conscience. Shortly before his death he told the patriotic young Cloncurry: 'My dear Val, I have been a fortunate man in life; I am a Chief-Justice and an Earl; but believe me, I would rather be beginning the world as a young sweep'.[21] His family—one cannot imagine why—printed his diary after his death, and this reveals him as pitiably caught in the mesh of his own wickedness, perpetually making good resolutions but never keeping them. Six years after his appointment as Chief-Justice, he resolves '*seriously* to set about learning my profession'. Elsewhere he intends 'to establish a complete reform from snuff, sleep, swearing, sloth, gross eating, malt liquor, and indolence'. Not all his resolutions were good: 'Last month I became a Viscount; and from want of circumspection in trying a cause against a printer, I have been grossly abused for several months. I have endeavoured to make that abuse useful towards my Earldom'.* He got the Earldom four years later.

The printer was John Magee, proprietor of the *Dublin Evening Post*. In 1789–90 the Chief-Justice, assisted by his creature the bestial Francis Higgins, proprietor of *The Freeman's Journal*, Justice of the Peace and subsequently betrayer of Lord Edward Fitzgerald, conducted a campaign of unscrupulous ferocity against Magee and his patriotic paper. Magee was in and out of prison for months on end, but after ventilation in the House of Commons the case went in the prisoner's favour. After his release Magee happened to come into a large sum of money. He settled £10,000 on his family in case of accidents, and the remainder, £4,000, he advertised that he intended 'with the blessing of God, to spend upon Lord Clonmell'.

Clonmell had a country house called Neptune near Blackrock, and had spent large sums and much loving care on its gardens. Magee bought some land next door, and advertised that he would hold a Grand Olympic Pig Hunt at his own expense. Several thousand people, including (as Cloncurry, who was there, tells us) 'the entire disposable mob of Dublin of both sexes', assembled in Magee's grounds. The festivities—which, by the way, were nominally in honour of the birthday of the Prince of Wales—began with such harmless items as competitions for grinning through horse-collars, climbing poles, sack-races and the like. But Magee had also arranged for a liberal supply of whiskey to keep his guests in good humour, and as the uproar rose in volume the Chief-Justice began to shake in his shoes. Magee then announced that the pig-hunt would begin, and that anyone who could catch a pig might thenceforth possess him in fee-simple. A large number of these animals, selected for their strength and their agility, and

* Elsewhere in the Diary he says 'Play with your books before others are out of bed; play with the world until seven o'clock in the evening, and with your papers until midnight'. He is constantly endeavouring to imitate Ulysses, Cromwell, Edmond Sexten Pery (Speaker of the Irish Commons), Frederic the Great, Henri IV of France and other heroes. 'Yesterday', he notes against a date, 'a beastly turtle feast'. 1793, 6th July, 'Died Lord Mountgarrett, as wicked a malignant selfish monster as ever I knew, a victim to his brutal appetites and thirst for blood, a lesson to vice, and a caution to be civil to all, obliging to many, to serve few, and offend none . . .' 'A civilized state of war', he observes elsewhere, 'is the safest and most agreeable that any gentleman, especially in *station*, can suppose himself in'. He advises for himself punctuality in 'licentious, voluptuous intrigue'. Parts of the diary are extremely funny, but too long to quote here; and other reasons forbid.

carefully anointed with soap, were released among the revellers. Not only did the terrified pigs and their intoxicated pursuers over-run and utterly destroy the gardens of Neptune, but the corpulent Clonmell rang his alarm-bell, was hoisted into his chaise-and-four, and pursued by the yelling mob disappeared in a cloud of dust towards Dublin Castle where he told the Viceroy that South County Dublin was in a state of insurrection, and implored him to summon the Privy Council and suspend the Habeas Corpus.

Clonmell House, which he first occupied late in 1778,[22] is a large brick mansion of 120 feet frontage,* distinguished externally by its size and the beauty of the ironwork. It is the earliest surviving house in Harcourt Street, which was created in 1777 on part of the Archbishop's farm of St Sepulchre's, let by him to Clonmell on a short lease. The gentle curve of Harcourt Street, which gives it such beauty, seems to have been introduced partly for beauty and partly, perhaps, to prevent the new street from approaching too close to the backs of the Houses in Kevin's Port (Camden Street) which were there already. On the east side of the street Clonmell had extensive gardens, and to reach these from Clonmell House he built a tunnel which still exists.[23] The Sham Squire's house in Stephen's Green backed on to these gardens.

Clonmell House has some good internal features, ceilings, mantels, &c, but its exterior is not very remarkable. Since 1830 it has been divided into two, and part of it is now occupied by an advertising firm who display their talent in letters three feet high across part of the façade. The larger section of the house was Sir Hugh Lane's Municipal Gallery of Modern Art until the adaptation of Charlemont House for that purpose, and now it, too, is disfigured by an enormous and unlovely name.

The visitor who looks down Montagu Street will notice that No 14 Harcourt Street has a side bow-window, now bricked up. In this house (then No 12) lived that engaging old rascal and incomparable raconteur Sir Jonah Barrington, whose *Personal Recollections* have immortalised the oddities and extravagances of his period, and not least those of Copper-faced Jack. Clonmell called on Jonah and took him to see his gardens, walking him round and giving him

---

* It originally had wings which have been replaced by later houses, reducing the frontage of Clonmell House to about sixty feet. (Peter: *Sketches of Old Dublin*, p. 66.).

good advice. He told the newly-married barrister on no account ever to give in to his wife. Some time later he asked Jonah whether he had followed this counsel. 'No', said Jonah. 'Why?' asked Clonmell. 'Because', said Jonah, 'a philosopher has an easier life of it than a soldier'.[24]

But Jonah does not tell us the story of the window, which we have from another source.[25] At this time the intervening house had not been built, and Lady Barrington, who had been a silk-mercer's daughter by the name of Grogan, used to sit every day in the window observing the comings and goings in Clonmell's garden. This irritated Lady Clonmell, who caused her husband to remonstrate with Jonah. But the Barringtons declined to abandon their position until it came to their ears that Lady Clonmell had said that 'Lady Barrington is so accustomed to look out of a shop-window for the display of her silks and satins that I suppose she cannot afford to dispense with this'. The Barringtons closed the window, and closed it remains to this day. Such a quip, it may be remarked, came ill enough from Lady Clonmell, whose relatives were woollen-drapers and brewers while her husband's brother was a provincial tallow-chandler.

Clonmell died, very appropriately, on May 23rd, 1798, the day the Rising broke out. His son married Lord Brooke and Warwick's daughter and became an absentee. His gardens were opened to the public as the Coburgh Gardens in 1817, and as such prospered for a while. They were again rescued from neglect to form the site of the 1865 Exhibition, after which they became the Iveagh Gardens attached to Iveagh House. Lord Iveagh presented them to University College in 1939,* and they now form a delightful communication between the main building and No 86 St Stephen's Green.

Belvedere House is another enormous five-bay mansion, with a much more imposing exterior than Clonmell's. It has a dominating site in Great Denmark Street, facing down North Great George's Street. It is hard to pronounce between the two views afforded by that superb street, looking down it from Belvedere House to where the Custom House dome rises over the buildings of Parnell Street,

---

* Strictly, Lord Iveagh presented them to the Government, which in 1941 handed them over to the College.

or looking up it (and it really is 'up') towards Belvedere House itself.

It has been a Jesuit school since 1841, but it still recalls the strange story of the first Earl of Belvedere and his Countess. The Rochfort family, Earls of Belvedere, are well known to students of Swift as the Dean's friends and owners of Gaulstown, Co. Westmeath. The first Lord Belvedere married Lord Molesworth's daughter when she was sixteen. A little later he was anonymously sent a packet of letters purporting to be a correspondence between his wife and his brother Arthur Rochfort. He sued his brother for crim. con. and was awarded £20,000 damages. Arthur Rochfort fled the country but returned seven years later thinking that by now the Earl would have relented. On the contrary, he had him thrown into the Debtors' Marshalsea where he remained till the death of Lord Belvedere in 1774. A similar but more dreadful vengeance was wrought upon the Countess, who was imprisoned by her husband in Gaulstown for nearly thirty years, deprived of all society, while the Earl lived in a new house only seven miles away. On one occasion she escaped to Dublin, but Lord Molesworth refused to harbour her. After her release she continued to live as a recluse. But all this took place before the second Earl built the house in 1786, on land belonging to Nicholas Archdall but developed in harmony with the neighbouring schemes of the Gardiners.*

Belvedere House is undoubtedly well worthy of its commanding position. Like Charlemont House, it is insulated by a few feet from its flanking neighbours. The elevation is strong and harmonious, though impoverished by the introduction of plate-glass windows. The most distinctive feature is the fluted frieze and cornice which replaces the usual flat Dublin coping. The architect was Michael Stapleton, the 'Dublin master of the silver age'.[26] His internal decoration is astonishingly lavish and adorns generously proportioned spaces, entrance-hall, staircase-hall and first-floor lobby being all contained in one enormous L-shaped compartment which the spectator can take in at once from the return landing. Gone is

---

* Archdall bought the Eccles Estate in 1748. (*Georg. Soc.* III, 57.) The Bryan Bolger Papers (P.R.O. Dublin) show Edward Archdall engaged in building-schemes in Gardiner Street, 'Gardiner's' (*i.e.* Mountjoy) Square and Temple Street in the early 1790's. The Archdalls were a Co. Fermanagh landed family, like the Humes who were developing land on the South Side.

the high relief of the Robert West period: instead ceilings and walls are covered with geometric arabesques framing round and oval panels in relief, the whole in brightly-coloured plaster. Stapleton's drawings for some of the rooms have survived, and from them we can reconstruct the original appearance of the Venus room, which lost its centrepiece when the house became a boys' school. The Diana room or Library is untouched, with the mahogany organ and bookcases sold by Lord Belvedere's stepson with the house. The Apollo room also survives, with a ceiling of very original plan.[27] James Joyce, who was here as a pupil from 1893 to 1898, is perhaps the most illustrious of the alumni, but the visitor who enjoys the courtesy of the Fathers will do well to talk of other subjects.

Lord Belvedere died without issue in 1814. He commanded four seats in Parliament, and the Castle dossier from which we have already quoted says that at his father's death he was 'left very embarrass'd in his circumstances, & from his Distress must consequently be dependent on the Crown [i.e. the Castle], likely to quarrel with his Brother Robert, a respectable amiable man'. Although he was active in his county in opposing the Union, he was bribed by Cornwallis to change his mind. Doubtless the building of Belvedere House had increased his 'Distress'.

The last of the great mansions to go up before the Union was Aldborough House, overlooking the Royal Canal on the extreme north-east periphery of the city. Lord Aldborough, whose family name was Stratford, had properties in England also, and twenty years before building Aldborough House he had laid out Stratford Place in London, and built a house at the head of it, known successively as Stratford House, Derby House and (by its late owner) Hutchinson House. They had a Cassels-Bindon country house in Co. Kildare (Belan, now in ruins, though the Temple, stables and two obelisks survive), and two more in Wicklow and Carlow. Their main Irish property was round Baltinglass, and they were intermarried with the local families of Tynte and Saunders. They built a model linen-town, Stratford-on-Slaney, which may still be seen mostly in ruins in the Slaney valley beside the road to Tullow. It is a sad tale of ruin and abandoned purpose, yet it does not do justice to the Earl, who was on the whole an estimable man. True, an anonymous contemporary characterised him as 'a *petit-maitre* and a patriot: equally ready to expire at the feet of a fine lady, and to die with pleasure for his country's good'. And Francis Hardy commented on this, 'Neither the one nor the other—A Poor Creature every way except as to Wealth'.[28] Jonah Barrington tells a number of tall stories about him, and asserts that he made no less than fifty-one wills. In 1798 he was incarcerated in Newgate for contempt of the House of Lords, and remained there for six weeks, part of the time 'without furniture, bed or bedding', and constantly attended by his wife.

It was mainly for his wife's benefit that he built Aldborough House, begun in 1792 and finished probably in 1798.[29] He died in 1801, and his wife remarried in the same year, moved into Aldborough House, but died shortly afterwards. House and title were separated: the house went to his nephew Wingfield-Stratford, a son of Lord Powerscourt, while the title passed rapidly through a ludicrous succession of spendthrift holders, ending with the sixth and last Earl who bred dogs, advertised patent pills, and died at Alicante in 1875.[30]

Aldborough House has a gaunt and melancholy air which derives as much from its architecture as from its forlorn history and its present situation. It has been alleged that Sir William Chambers was the designer, but in spite of a superficial resemblance to Albany in London, it is hard to believe that Chambers would have designed such an unhappily elongated *piano nobile*, or such an ungainly porch. The loss of the balustraded parapet and of the north-wing pavilion has not made it any more graceful.

The main block is of brick, faced on the east front with granite. The surviving wing has Portland stone trimmings and a sphinx and a lion in Coade stone. This wing is supposed to have contained the theatre. Some of the urns and eagles from the pediment, also in Coade stone, languish in the basement of the Clontarf Casino, together with the lion and sphinx from the north wing. The most startling feature of the interior is the astonishing top-lit staircase-hall, like a well-shaft or a mine or one of Mr Howard's model penitentiaries. On the portico is the inscription *RUS IN URBE*, true enough when it was built, and elsewhere are such pious aspirations as *OTIUM CUM DIGNITATE* and *SEGNITIES INIMICA*

GLORIAE. The house had originally a handsome curved double perron giving on to the garden at the rear, but only half of this survives.

Wingfield-Stratford lived in London, and Aldborough House remained empty till 1813, when it was taken by Professor von Feinagle, a Luxemburger who specialised in education by Mnemonics and Methodics, and was encouraged in Dublin. He re-christened the house Luxembourg, and with help from forty guarantors, built many additions of chapel, hall and classrooms. The Feinaglian Institution prospered, having nearly 300 pupils, a preparatory school at Clonliffe (in Buck Jones's house) and a day-school in Kildare Street (in Rossmore House). It seems to have been a genuinely advanced educational experiment, 'severity of any kind being altogether banished from its code'.[31] But the Professor died in 1819, and about ten years later the school was closed. During the Crimean War it was used as a barrack—most large buildings in Dublin have been used as barracks at some time or another—and afterwards it became the Stores Department of the General Post Office, and so remains. Its beautiful gardens are now covered by working-class flats, and the area in which it stands is one of the most depressing in Dublin. As one leaves or enters Dublin by the Great Northern line, Aldborough House is starkly silhouetted against the sky. In the summer of 1941 it narrowly escaped destruction by one of the few bombs which fell on Dublin during the Second World War.

Here we may take our leave of the great houses. There were many more, of course; and of many the associations or the architecture or both are interesting. Such are Langford House in Mary Street (now destroyed: one of the few Irish houses decorated, by remote control, by Adam); Moira House on Usher's Quay (1752), where the patriotic Earls of Moira lived and where Pamela Fitzgerald was when Lord Edward was arrested; Ely House in Ely Place,* built by that extravagant Marquess of Ely who lived in Rathfarnham Castle and built a folly over 350 feet long in the Dublin Mountains and had his books bound with unexampled splendour. In the closing years of the century Dublin had a resident

* Ely Place and Hume Street, on the Blue-Coat Estate, were developed as a result of an Ely-Hume marriage in 1736. The Ely, pronounced with the 'y' as in 'high', is Ely O'Carroll, not, of course, Ely in England.

population of about a hundred peers, besides collaterals and other grandees. They may not, in most cases, have been very estimable people, but they gave Dublin society an animation and pace which it has never possessed before or since. But on the last stroke of midnight, December 31st, 1800, the gaily caparisoned horses turned into mice, the coaches into pumpkins, the silks and brocades into rags, and Ireland was once again the Cinderella among the nations. Dublin was still littered with crystal slippers in the form of unwanted palaces. For a few years some of them lingered on, inhabited by dowagers or the few peers too poor or too patriotic to remove to London. In a very few years even these had vanished, and the greater houses had mostly settled down to their very varied occupations. The future of Dublin lay henceforth with the middle and professional classes.

REFERENCES

[1] The principal authority for Ivory's life is the unsigned article in *Anthologia Hibernica*, 1793, I, 334.

[2] See *Country Life*, July 8th, 1949.

[3] *CARD* XI, 44; XII, 38.

[4] F. Falkiner, *Foundation of the King's Hospital*, 204.

[5] *ibid*. 205.

[6] *ibid*. 211.

[7] Gilbert I, 27 (1854). Ordnance Survey 5-Foot maps. Shaw's *Pictorial Directory*, 1850. Since this was written Mr Leask tells me that it was done in 1858.

[8] Mulvany's *Gandon*, 49, 50.

[9] Curran, *Rotunda Hospital*, 1945, 23.

[10] Barrington (*Personal Sketches*, 2nd ed. 1830, I, 255n.) says that this was a very common practice in the country.

[11] Edited by Sir E. Sullivan as *Buck Whaley's Memoirs*, Lond. 1906, the Preface of which contains most of the information repeated here.

[12] See the author's *The Volunteer Earl*, 1948.

[13] *Georg. Soc*, IV, 64.

[14] Gilbert III, 365.

[15] *CARD* XII, 24.

[16] A William Mack, Stonecutter, appears in the 1792 Directory.

[17] Pool and Cash, *Views &c*, 1780, 113.

[18] Curran in *JRSAI*, LXX, 43.

[19] W. J. Fitzpatrick, *The Sham Squire*, 1895 ed., 104.

[20] Hunt, *The Irish Parliament*, 1775. 1907, 47.

[21] Cloncurry, *Recollections*, 1850 ed., 46.

[22] The Act 17 & 18 Geo III, 46, describes Clonmell as legal occupier and authorises the making of the new street.

[23] Confirmed by Mr H. G. Leask.

[24] Barrington, *Personal Sketches*, 1827, I, 317-8.
[25] Fitzpatrick, *op. cit.* 76-7.
[26] Curran, *Rotunda Hospital*, 23.
[27] The house is fully illustrated in *Georg. Soc*, III.
[28] *Irish Book Lover*, XXX, 6, 128.
[29] Bolger Papers, PRO, Dublin.
[30] *Georg. Soc*, IV, 11-17.
[31] MacGregor, *Picture of Dublin*, 1821, 213.

CHAPTER XXI

James Gandon: the Culmination

JAMES GANDON was born in London on February 29th, 1743,[1] the only son of a French protestant of independent means, who had married a Welsh lady. When he was about seven years old, his father became infected with Rosicrucianism and alchemical pursuits, and filled half the basement of the house with 'furnaces, crucibles, retorts, receivers &c'. When the little boy came back for his holidays from school in Herefordshire, he found the cellars full of his father's Rosicrucian friends, 'most of whom were dressed in the costume of the day, with large flowing wigs, holding gold or amber-headed canes, and awaiting with solemn composure the results of the different experiments'. He used to amuse himself by drawing pictures of these alchemists.

Mrs Gandon died when her son was fourteen, and the elder Gandon, no longer shielded from his own folly by the good sense of his wife, found himself in money difficulties. Depressed by the loss of his mother, the boy penetrated to his father's study, and finding there a number of Rosicrucian books, he opened the window and, exclaiming 'Those books have been my ruin!' flung a great many of them into the street. Afterwards he regretted this act, as many of the books, he tells us, 'were both scarce and curious'.

Realising that he would soon have to earn his living, Gandon applied himself to reading the classics, studying mathematics, and drawing, attending evening classes at Shipley's Academy which was generously patronised by the Duke of Richmond. In about 1758, when he was fifteen, he heard that William Chambers, then recently arrived from Rome, was in need of an assistant or office clerk to make working drawings. With his portfolio under his arm, he set off for Poland Street, and impressed Chambers so favourably that he was soon taken on as an apprentice. During the day he worked for Chambers, and in the evenings at Shipley's. At Chambers's he met Lord Charlemont, then in his youthful phase of residence in London, and his Lordship exhorted him 'to the cultivation of taste, and to those scientific attainments essential to a great architect'. After seven or eight years with Chambers he left and set up on his own.

The first year or two of his independent career is obscure. He may have done some maintenance work for some of the London Livery Companies; he was certainly offered an engineering post in Sumatra: but happily for Dublin some 'intelligent Quakers' advised him not to go East. Instead he hung about waiting for something to turn up, went snipe-shooting in New Oxford Street, and formed a lifelong friendship with Paul Sandby.

At this time the recognised expedient for an aspiring young architect was to publish a book, the taller and grander the folio the better. Gandon and a young Irish architect named Woolfe, a County Kildare man in the English Office of Works, decided to bring the Bible of English Palladianism, Colen Campbell's *Vitruvius Britannicus* (by now more than forty years old) up to date. The first volume of this continuation appeared in 1767, the second and last in 1771. They are sumptuous and in every way worthy of their predecessors. Gandon did not use the opportunity for direct self-advertisement, for he included only one of his own designs, two versions of the Nottingham Court-House, which he built in 1769-70. If, like most architects of the time, he had committed his unrealised projects to print, we should know more about the evolution of his art than we do. It is enough to remark that the Nottingham Court-House, though admittedly not exactly like either of his published designs, shows little promise of the greatness to come.* At the same time he produced his second-prize design for the Dublin Exchange, but of this we know nothing except that one of Gandon's enemies asserted that Cooley, in executing the building, drew heavily on Gandon's design.[2] Otherwise none of his work until the Custom House seems to have survived for inspection in any form. His earliest Irish work, alterations to Ferns Palace,[3] performed *in absentia* for the Rev. Joseph Dean Bourke in 1768, seems to have disappeared when it was rebuilt in about 1790.

From 1771 till 1780 he lived in Broad Street, London. His friend

---

* The interior has been completely altered, and the exterior also seems to have suffered some change. The Gaol, which he also built, has vanished.

Sandby introduced him to Lord Carlow, and Lord Carlow introduced him to John Beresford. This connexion was pregnant with future importance, but at present his life as an artist was frustrated and unsatisfactory.* He won a competition for rebuilding Old Bedlam, and nearly died in the process. 'It was necessary that I should visit every apartment in the original structure, and more particularly those to which the public had not access . . . In these visits I encountered the most deplorable cases of the wreck of the human mind. To this appalling part of my duty I submitted for several days; but at last I experienced sleepless nights, and when I did procure any rest, I was troubled with horrible dreams . . . I was at last attacked with brain fever, and neither my family nor my medical attendants had any hopes of my recovery. But I was mercifully spared, and, through the affectionate care of my wife and the skilful attentions of my medical friend, aided by a strong and vigorous constitution, I gradually recovered'. In such a fragment as this, embedded in the bald narrative of his professional life, we find more than a hint that the unearthly serenity of his masterwork was not cheaply purchased. Though he won the Old Bedlam competition, the job itself, which would have been a big one, was bestowed elsewhere.[4]

At Sandby's Gandon met that remarkable woman Princess Dashkov, who took up a map of the world and, pointing to England, said 'Monsieur Gandon, ven I do look on dis speck called England, and do see its large possessions, I do be astonish'. We do not know how much Princess Dashkov had to do with the departure of Charles Cameron from London to build palaces for Catherine the Great in 1779. But we do know that also in that year, the Princess invited Gandon to Russia to build in St Petersburg, offering him an official post with military rank. He hesitated to accept, for Lord Carlow and John Beresford were already coaxing him to come to Ireland. After more than a year of negotiation (1779– February 1781) Gandon closed with the Irish offer, and Dublin gained what Sumatra and St Petersburg had lost. It is amusing to speculate what would have happened if the roles of Cameron and Gandon had been reversed: to visualise the Agate Pavilion or the

---

* Chambers writes to Charlemont (Jan. 18th, 1777) 'I think he merits encouragement, and wonder he has been so little employed'. This, of course, was before Gandon came to Ireland.

Cameron Gallery rising by the banks of the Liffey, while the Custom House and the Four Courts adorned those of the Neva.

During 1780 Carlow and Beresford arranged a financial guarantee for Gandon, should he come.[5] Everything was done in the most secret and conspiratorial manner: not a word must be said to anybody: Beresford appeared one wintry night at Broad Street and took Gandon's Custom House sketches away with him: Gandon must wait a day or two but all would be well: there were powerful interests on the other side: 'This business must be kept a profound secret, as long as we can, to prevent clamour, until we have everything secured'. No wonder that Gandon's enemies later accused him of having been 'smuggled' over. At length Beresford's mining and countermining succeeded, the order for a new Custom House was secured, and Gandon, leaving his wife and family behind him for the moment, arrived in Dublin on April 26th, 1781.

An easterly Custom House and easterly bridges were bogies which had long haunted the troubled slumbers of the Dublin merchant princes. Continual agitation and petition against such projects had been going on since at least 1750. In February 1774, for example, a well-organised campaign of petition was carried on by the Merchants, the Brewers and the Manufacturers of the Liberties. One of their grounds of opposition, which history has endorsed, was that 'all the Hurry, Croud and Annoyance which necessarily attend Trade, will be brought even to the Doors of our Nobility and Gentry, and many of those elegant Streets in which they now reside, will become the common Passages for Porters and Cars, loaded with the Necessaries of Life, and all kinds of Merchandize, to be diffused throughout the whole City. Wherever the Seat of Trade is fixed, to that Neighbourhood the Merchants, with all their Train, will in Time remove themselves. The Nobility and Gentry are best secured against those Inconveniencies, by continuing the Custom-house in its present Situation'.[6] The weakness of this argument was that some of the most influential of the nobility, improving landowners such as the Gardiners and Beresfords, were quite unappalled by the prospect. On the other side Beresford's unpopularity enabled the merchants to enlist the mob on their behalf.

At first the mob were more picturesque than effective. They assembled in July 1781, fortified with whiskey and gingerbread, for the purpose of filling up the foundation-trenches, but as it was a warm summer's day they amused themselves by swimming in them instead. John Beresford laid the first stone, more or less in secret, on August 8th, 1781. By the next month the rabble were better organised, and, armed with adzes, saws, shovels, &c, and led by Napper Tandy, they broke down the paling round the new works.* Although there were legal difficulties about the title to the ground, Beresford wrote to Gandon that he was not to worry, but to 'laugh at the extreme folly of the people'.

Meanwhile the architect remained semi-imprisoned, on Beresford's advice. He received several threatening letters, and, when he did visit the works, carried 'a good cane sword . . . determined to defend myself to the last'. But the opposition gradually died down, and Gandon was left in peace. Hearing that his wife was ill, he went to London to wind up his affairs there and bring her over to Ireland. But he found her too ill to move, and a short time later she died. In March 1782, bringing his three children and Mr Harman his clerk of works, he returned to Dublin and settled in 7 Mecklenburgh Street.

He found the building well advanced, the east pavilion (that nearest the sea) erected, and the north and south fronts ready to be marked out. The difficulties of the site were prodigious. It was all reclaimed slob-land, and the old quay-wall was simply sitting on the surface of the strand. No praise was too high for Gandon's Irish assistants Henry Darley the stonecutter, John Semple the bricklayer and rough mason, and Hugh Henry the carpenter.† Every available mason in Dublin was engaged in the work, but such a vast undertaking needed even more labour than was available. Some English carpenters and stonecutters were invited over; 'they were very orderly at first', Gandon tells us, 'but in the end more refractory than the natives, more exorbitant in their demands for increase of wages, and worse by far as to drunkenness'.

The north-east corner of the building was soon begun, followed by the foundations of the south (river) portico and dome. Gandon

---

* Gandon's assertion (Mulvany, 57) that the Corporation were officially behind this manœuvre is not borne out by the existing records.

† James Lever or Leaver, the father of the novelist Charles Lever, was also engaged in the work as a contractor. He lived nearby, in Amiens Street. The house, where the novelist was born, has now disappeared into the Station.

decided not to use piling. Instead he pumped out the space in a coffer-dam, levelled it off, laid down a quantity of cut heath, and on top of this a huge grating of Memel timber of section one foot square. He then filled in the interstices with good stock brick in a mixture of pounded roach lime and mortar, and covered the whole with four-inch fir planking. Then came a course of rough mountain granite, embedded in which was an iron chain four inches by two and a half, the collars run with lead and the bars covered with a cement of wax, resin and stone dust. Regular granite courses brought the work up to ground level. Under the rest of the south front the grating was covered with Dublin calp. Time has proved the soundness of Gandon's construction, but during the building he was subjected to some frivolous criticism by amateur architects who came to gape down into the black oily depths, particularly a doctor and speculative builder who delivered his opinions with great sententiousness.

Fortunately some of his visitors were more welcome. His old friend Lord Charlemont had no great love for the Beresfords, but he quite rightly valued architecture above politics, and he used to take sea-baths at the mouth of the Tolka river. He did this on Saturdays, and on his way he would call in on Gandon at Mecklenburgh Street and talk for an hour or so. No doubt he also came on weekdays to see the progress of the work, especially as Edward Smyth, pupil of his own protégé Simon Vierpyl, was brought forward by Henry Darley and commissioned by Gandon to do the wonderful series of fourteen river-gods which form keystones on the ground floor.[7] He also did the statue of Commerce which surmounts the dome, two of the now destroyed statues over the south pediment, the tympanum of that pediment, and the four Arms of Ireland on the pavilions, perhaps the most perfectly architectural sculptures in these islands. He worked, as we shall see, on all Gandon's Dublin buildings, as well as those of Francis Johnston.

In spite of a series of vicious attacks from 'An Admirer of ... necessary Improvements' in the Dublin papers of 1786,[8] the Custom House rose gradually to completion, and was finished in 1791, at a cost (including the docks to the east) of nearly £400,000.[9] Beresford was accused of building a palace for himself under the guise of a public building, one of Creevey's correspondents, for example,

writing in 1805 that it is 'in every respect a noble edifice, in which
there is no fault to be found except that old Beresford is sumptuously lodged in it'.* The first-floor room under the north portico
facing Beresford Place used to be shown as 'Mr Beresford's ballroom'.[10]

Long before the Custom House was finished Gandon had other
schemes on foot. In 1782 a committee of the House of Lords commissioned him to make extensions to the east side of Pearce's Parliament House, and these were finished by 1789.[11] About the same
time he designed an extra library for Charlemont House (now destroyed), and the Court House and Gaol at Waterford and a model
town to be called New Geneva, neither of which concerns us here.
His work for the House of Lords shows that, though like most
architects he was happiest working on an entirely unencumbered site,
a problem of adaptation brought out special abilities. He built a
grand hexastyle portico east and slightly north of the House of
Lords, on the axis of the House of Commons, connecting it with
Pearce's south colonnade by a curved wall containing seven niches
but having no ordonnance or balustrade. His object was to mask
the various compartments within—both his own and Pearce's—
without distracting attention from Pearce's front or his own portico.
The level of Fleet Lane (as it then was) was a good deal lower than
that of College Green, and he had, at first sight, two alternatives,
to raise his columns on pedestals, or the whole frontispiece on a high
plinth with steps. Boldly he chose a third solution, using a corinthian order which, with its taller proportions, brought him down to
earth again.

Internally his resource was equally happy (Fig. 5). He created a
corridor along the north wall of the House of Lords, brought it on
to a rectangular lobby north-east of the apse, escaped back on to his
necessary axis by going diagonally out of the far corner of this lobby,
and so into an exquisite circular hall which, in its dimensions and the
cool lyricism of its treatment, is sister to the first-floor lobby under
the Custom House dome. Adjustment to street-level is by curved
steps which spill out of the circular hall into a long lobby† with

* These sentiments were pretty generally diffused.

† The lobby is now shortened at both ends: it was shut for many years as an entrance and
used for the display of Mr Doolittle's model of the building.

three doors into the street under his portico. In the flanks of the portico he devised rooms some of which have disappeared while others, like the sequence just described, survive almost intact. Gandon was also concerned with extensions of similar scope for the Commons on the west (Foster Place) side of the building, but this complicated story is better left till later.*

His greatest opportunity—or rather, the opportunity which seems to me to have called forth his greatest powers—occurred in 1785, during the Viceroyalty of the Duke of Rutland, 'the only Chief Governor', says Gandon, 'who could find leisure to pay the least attention to the Fine Arts'. The old Four Courts, in a huddle under the wing of the ruinous Cathedral of Christchurch, approached by a passage called Hell, were thoroughly unsatisfactory and had been so for years. In 1762 there was an abortive scheme for moving them to that site which keeps cropping up in Dublin architectural history—the site of Aungier's house, Pearce's theatre and the intended Mansion House of 1710.[12] Later suggestions were that they should be in College Green, opposite the Parliament House, or at least in the College Green neighbourhood, which was already beginning to be the 'centre' of the city. The Inns Quay site, on which Cooley's Public Offices already stood, in part at least, was now decided upon.

Cooley's building stood at the west end of a site which, including that building, was 436 feet long, and 155 feet deep, an area rather smaller than that of the free-standing Custom House.† Gandon incorporated the Cooley building, with additions and some subtractions, in his own. He put the Courts in his central domed block 140 feet square, and on the east built a replica of the altered Cooley building, joining both to the centre with arcades and triumphal arches. The first stone was laid by Rutland in 1786, on March 3rd. Ten years later, on November 8th, 1796, the Courts first sat there, but the finishing touches were not put to the wings and arcades till 1802. It cost in all about £200,000.

The building history was even more chequered than that of the Custom House. His friend Lord Carlow (now Earl of Portarlington) persuaded him not to bring the portico out over the footpath

---

* See Chapter XXIII.
† Which measures 375 feet by 209 feet plus projections.

as he had done in the House of Lords. He was harassed with threats of stoppage, money trickled but slowly from the reluctant Parliament (£3,000 per annum later increased to £6,000), and Gandon became a mere pawn in a political game. A party in Parliament who had nothing against Gandon (they came and told him so in so many words) tried to have the work stopped in order to test the strength of their influence with the new Viceroy, for Rutland had died in October 1787. Gandon was haled before the Commons but answered satisfactorily.[13] Yet another change of Viceroy in 1790 gave pretext for a renewal of the attack. The preposterous suggestion was made that the central block, already largely built, should be taken down and moved bodily back from the quay. The next line of attack, when that failed, was the suggestion that the troops passing with banneret and pennon, trumpet and kettle-drum, every day from the Barracks to the Castle, would disturb the courts. To which the defenders retorted that the troops could quite easily march on the far side of the river as they did already in summer to avoid the sun. And so it went on, one obstacle after another being set up and knocked down, not least of these being the outbreak of the war with France and the resulting urge for economy.

In addition to these official vexations, Gandon's old enemy the 'Admirer of ... Necessary Improvements'[14] kept up a running fire of vilification. In his mean little way, he was quite a master of abuse. After pointing out that the number of unfinished and un-steepled churches in Dublin is a disgrace, he suggests that part at least of the money being spent on Gandon's secular domes could well be diverted to this purpose. 'If we go on at this rate till the Architect's taste for elegant Domes is exhausted ... we shall be doomed to bankruptcy'. He attacks the complex plan of the Four Courts: '... there are so many oblong Vestibules, so many Squares, Octagons, (and other Poligons [sic]) and Triangles, to fill up a cir-cumscribing Square, that one would imagine the Author of it a profest Mathematician, or at least a Geometrician ...' In a foot-note he suggests that Gandon knows little mathematics of any kind, and always changes the subject when mathematics is mentioned! The Four Courts he characterises as 'the most absurdly whimsical Building in the WORLD ...' the purpose of which is 'merely to do the Architect Credit, in a display of his Taste, and magnificence of Design'. He speaks of the 'contemptible Vanity' of the lawyers having 'the grandest Building in Europe, in the World, to plead in, and to walk around . . .', and alleges that the sole purpose of the scheme is to improve the estate of Welbore Ellis (an absentee landlord) as that of the Custom House is to improve that of Luke Gardiner.[15] At one moment he is accusing Gandon of inserting 'puffs' of his own buildings in the papers; at the next he reproaches him with cowardice in not defending himself against attack.

He suggests that Gandon's supporters will, 'to complete HIM, and put the finishing Stroke to *their* Folly, dub him *Sir James Gandon*, (as his most consummate Vanity, and Assurance, expects nothing less) and send him back to England, in Triumph, with 50,000 *l* in his possession, secured, and all sent over safe, before him. Well may he sneer, and laugh outright, at *Irish* folly'. This assertion, which was of course neither provable nor disprovable in 1787, is repeated again. Cooley, the author avers, 'was naturalised to the place, and ended, as he meant, his days here. 'Tis very different with Mr Gandon; he hates the Place, and despises the People, most cordially; being determined to return to England, as soon as they will let him, by ceasing to *cram* Money into his Pocket, of which he will not lay out a single Guinea, again, amongst them, except in the gratification of his sensual Appetites. This is all manifest; has he attempted to make any Purchase? nor *will* he, unless he can make Cent. per Cent. of his Money; it is all remitted over, and bank'd safe, in the Funds at London, which he means to follow, as soon as he *can be spared*'. This is, of course, malicious nonsense, as Gandon died a property-owner in Ireland in 1823, having lived here constantly, save for brief intervals, since 1781. True, he resisted the temptation to use his special knowledge to speculate in land near the Custom House, but this is rather to his credit. The only point in his assailant's indictment which has any substance at all is that Gandon was a little too ready to take at its face-value the assertion of his friend Lord Carlow (then more or less an absentee) that there were no architects worth the name in Ireland. This links up with his contempt for builder-architects; but this attitude, though we may disagree with it, is just what we would expect of a man with his academic training.

As if to conspire with public and private hindrances, and with the labour and contractual troubles attendant upon rumour of stoppage, Nature herself took part against the architect. A landslide at the Portland quarries in 1792 caused delays in the delivery of stone for columns and entablatures, though most of the building, including much fine detail, was Irish granite. By a curious coincidence a similar landslide a century earlier, in 1695, caused interruption at St Paul's Cathedral. The tide turned in his favour when part of the dome colonnade was up, and people began to feel that it would be well worth completing.

The third of Gandon's Dublin buildings (excluding the Military Infirmary) was the King's Inns (Pls. XLV, XLVII, XLVIII). The Four Courts had usurped the old site of the Inns, though indeed the Benchers of the Inns remained, and still remain, proprietors of part of the Four Courts. The Benchers acquired a site[16] at the top of Henrietta Street, extending westwards to Constitution Hill, and Lord Clare laid the first stone on August 1st, 1795. Gandon had produced various designs, to accord with the uncertainties as to how much of the site the Benchers could secure. He closed the end of Henrietta Street with a curved screen and gateway, behind which the long narrow court of the building is on a different axis. The Benchers' Dining Hall is on the right, and on the left the building of the old Prerogative Court, now the Registry of Deeds.* Through the gateway under the clock tower one emerges on to the green park before the main (though not the entrance) front. On either side are Smyth's caryatides, flanking the entrances of the two wings. Security and Law guard the Prerogative Court, while Plenty and a Bacchante preside, no less suitably, over the door to the Dining Hall.†

Similar delays attended the completion of this building, in which Gandon's pupil and partner, Henry Aaron Baker, was associated with him. In 1808 Gandon, irritated by the ignorant interference of Lord Chancellor Redesdale, resigned and left Baker in possession of all his drawings from which to finish it.[17] And now, at the age of sixty-five, he retired from active professional life and built himself a house at Canonbrook, Lucan, where he died in 1823. His other

---

* Note the boat-shaped chimney-stacks: distant relatives of the soup-tureens on the Custom House, which were also used as chimneys.

† The statue of Themis which stands facing the entrance originally held aloft a gas-jet in the centre of the Great Hall of the Four Courts.

work in Dublin comprised the Military Infirmary in the Phœnix Park (executed by Gibson,* 1786, the cupola not by Gandon) and old Carlisle Bridge, 1791-5 (Pl. L). He intended the bridge to have colonnades over the footways, in the Palladian manner, but this was abandoned as too expensive. His drawings showing the colonnades were extant until a few years ago.[18] The bridge as built was very beautiful, with keystone-heads by Smyth on its central arch.† It was rebuilt and nearly trebled in width in 1880, when it was re-named O'Connell Bridge. The new bridge is a great deal flatter than its predecessor, but mercifully not quite flat. All its details are a coarsened but otherwise faithful reproduction of Gandon's details.

There are good grounds‡ for thinking that Gandon designed the elevations for the widened Dame Street in 1785-6: most of this has now been rebuilt or masked by Victorian work. His old enemy says that in 1786 'there was lately exhibited [at the Royal Exchange] a Design for the new Buildings, intended for the continuation of Sackville-street, to the River, and signed J. Gandon, (which redounds so little to his credit) in which, Shops were introduced, an absurdity so very gross, that it needs no comment on it; the best, and most spacious Street in Dublin, inhabited, chiefly, by the first Nobility in the Kingdom, to be continued, and the Continuation to be occupied by Shopkeepers'. We seem to have heard this argument before. But the same author describes a treatment of recessed arches and pilasters on the corner houses, facing Carlisle Bridge, which was certainly not carried out. On the other hand the two large buildings on the corners respectively of D'Olier Street and Burgh Quay, and of Westmorland Street and Aston's Quay, look (especially the former) as though Gandon had had something remotely to do with them. Westmorland and D'Olier Streets were made in about 1803,§ and designed as shops, with a uniform pilas-tered treatment of the ground storeys in granite which still survives

---

* W. Gibson, architect to the Board of Works. The centre of the front has been altered in quite recent years, and the ornamental plaques destroyed.

† They are now in the Tropical Fruit Co's building on Sir John Rogerson's Quay. The heads on the present bridge are mediocre reproductions.

‡ *Letters to Parliament,* 1787, pages 3, 30. See also pp 67, 80-4. The Wide Streets Commis-sioners, for whom Gandon was evidently working, were empowered to require uniformity in new elevations, and to make up to individual owners the difference in cost, where they imposed a more formal treatment.

§ Date-stone, 1800, on D'Olier Street corner building.

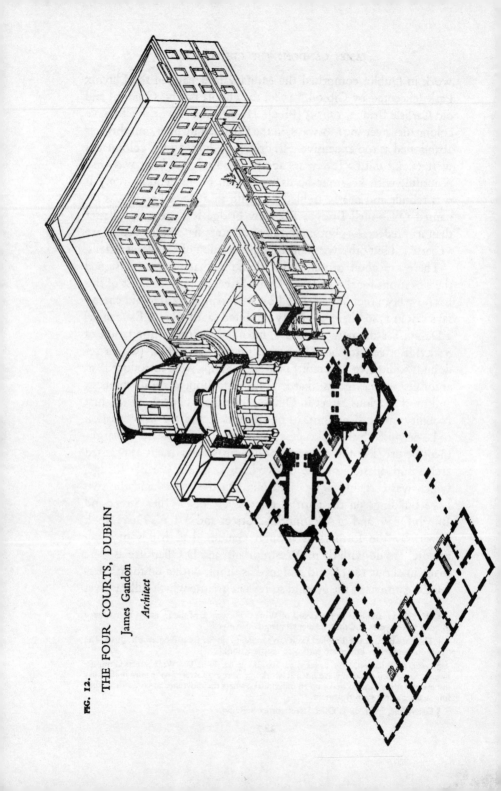

FIG. 12.

THE FOUR COURTS, DUBLIN

James Gandon
Architect

in a good many instances. The replanning of this area by the Wide Streets Commissioners had been mooted since 1782, and if Gandon was working for them, as he appears to have been, the street would have some reason to show his influence. During his long retirement he designed a few villas in the suburbs, notably one at Sandymount

FIG. 13. The Custom House from the South-East.

for his friend William Ashford the painter. His own house at Lucan has, most unfortunately, been changed out of all recognition.

These buildings entitle Gandon to a very high place among architects. His work has that rewarding depth which repays long study with delight and continual refreshment. He was, of course,

FIG. 14. The Four Courts from the South-West.

very fortunate: no man can be a great architect who is not. Very few are given the chance to build two monumental buildings on riverside sites near enough to be interrelated but not near enough to interfere with one another, and so placed that they dominate an entire city. (They are not quite half a mile apart: St Paul's and Somerset House, the nearest parallel in London, are a little over three-quarters of a mile.) Standing on the Metal Bridge, one is half-way between them.

Four Courts and Custom House must be considered together, for they stand for the two aspects of Gandon's mind. The Four Courts is masculine in feeling, built on a cubical if not vertical theme: the Custom House is feminine and predominantly horizontal. The active and the contemplative phases are complementary. This antinomy runs through every aspect of these two buildings: materials and colour (grey granite versus white Portland* in the main fronts), texture (roughness and baroque 'movement' versus smoothness and the purest Palladian clarity), mass (the seventy-six-foot diameter drum-tower as against the thirty-one feet of the Custom House). In the Four Courts drum and dome we see one of those dream-palaces of Poussin or Piranesi in all their Roman grandeur. In that of the Custom House the elements are taken straight from Wren's twin towers at Greenwich, but with the proportions and detail so subtly adjusted as to seem a feminine version of the theme.

The same contrast runs through the use of the orders. In the Four Courts Gandon uses a robust Roman Corinthian, breaking his cornice out over coupled and clustered pilasters to give the bold rich modelling of which that order is capable. In the Custom House he is more daring and uses a Roman Doric, which one might suppose to be the very embodiment of male sturdiness. Yet the effect, by some strange alchemy, is one of grace at least as much as of strength. Stranger still, he has quietly omitted the architrave,† and the frieze rests directly on the capitals. Frieze and capitals are of simple rectangular section: there are no mouldings. But on the necking of the columns there are tiny harps six inches high.‡ On the frieze of the north and south porticoes these harps appear between the swags and boukrania—this time they are in circles two feet high. Finally, in the Arms of Ireland which crown the delicately ornamented blocks on the wings, the same harps re-appear for the last time, five or six feet high. The window-case mouldings of the

---

* Some of the Four Courts detail, *e.g.* columns, capitals &c, is in Portland stone. But much relatively fine detail is in granite.

† He did the same thing in the north lobby of the King's Inns.

‡ Harps and shamrocks in imitation adorn the colonnade which carries the hideous railway-bridge of 1889.

Custom House are delicate as a cabinet-maker's, yet never weak, while those of the Four Courts are suited to the more rugged stone in which they are cut, and to the larger elements in the design.

When we look at the general disposition it is the same story. The beauty of the Custom House is one of surface modelling, that of the Four Courts one of depth and the relationship of masses. The domed hall of the Four Courts is the very hub of the plan: the Custom House dome is set just so far behind the portico as was convenient and effective. Only in the east front of the Custom House

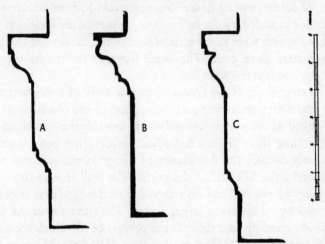

FIG. 15. Custom House and Four Courts, profiles of window-architraves.
A. Custom House, first floor.   B. Custom House, ground floor.
C. Four Courts, first floor.

can the disposition be said to be more than surface modelling. Here a single-storey pavilion, virtually free-standing and recessed one foot—no more—behind the ground-line, once presented its open arcade between the loftier and solider blocks of the wings. On the west front Gandon took a subordinate connecting element from the south front and made it his centre-piece, and here, also, an open arcade once gave greater depth of shadow than can be seen there to-day.

The composition of the south or river front is beyond praise. Arranged A-B-*A*-C-*A*-B-A, where A equals *A* except that *A* has the attic storey and A the sculptured arms, it is a beautiful study in overlapping symmetries as well as in the use of sculpture as a terminal feature. The great fault of the building is, as Professor Richardson has remarked,[19] the disparity in scale between the main order and the order of the drum. This is perhaps more a paper fault than a real one. The critic who looks at the Custom House to-day may feel that the drum and dome are a little slender for so long a façade. But before the fire of 1921 this feature received a good deal of visual 'abutment' from the four statues over the portico, the high roof of the Long Room behind the dome, and the chimney stacks. By then, of course, a great many chimney stacks had grown up which were not intended by the architect to be part of the façade, as well as those which were and which now, like the statues and the Long Room roof, have gone. The north front, in its lengthy severity, remains much as it always was.

The river front of the Four Courts is a study of a different kind. The undulating movements of the massive centre block are gradually stilled as the eye moves outwards towards the wings, so that by the time these are reached visual stability has been achieved. Not only is there the dominance of the great saucer dome to be reckoned with, but behind the portico the wall recedes to make a deep curved porch,* and on either side of this the curve is doubly repeated by niches set in larger niches. The statues over the pediment are standing, but those at the corners of the block are sitting and facing inwards, as though to contain all this curved movement. But the curves are too strong to be so contained: they carry the screen arcade outwards, are checked for a moment while they arch a little higher to support the sculptural groups over the courtyard gates, then they abut against the wings. But here everything is rectilinear. An outward break of fifteen feet makes for strength: the blocking-course has† a large panelled block in the centre, and over it the concealed valley-roof has accomplished the translation of the dome-curve into straight lines. The movement is finally arrested, and the two arm-like wings enfold the square courtyards without any loss of coherence. To achieve this result Gandon carefully retained the necessary elements in the Cooley façade, and as carefully obliterated others.[20] When the wings were reconstructed

---

* Not shown in the earliest Gandon design, 1785.

† Or, alas, more correctly, 'had'. See Appendix II, p. 333.

after the siege of 1922 some of these elements, whether through ignorance, parsimony or laziness, were altered or omitted, the wings were trimmed back flush with the arcade, and this incomparable building remains mutilated and shorn of much of its original power.

Not that the design was entirely faultless. The proportions of the main order, for example, have an unsatisfactory relation to the fenestration of the return walls. Again, this is largely a paper fault, depending on our knowledge that the return walls are sides of a square bearing the same relation to the dome as does the front. A more serious objection can be urged against the balustrading on the arcaded screens, for one can see at a glance that there is no footwalk there, and it is somewhat out of scale with the main balustrade. But one could pick small holes like this in almost any building. It

FIG. 16. The Custom House: North Front, to Beresford Place.

would be less easy to produce a rival to this river front, apart from the Custom House itself.

In the sphere of planning Gandon, like most eighteenth-century architects, lies open to criticism by modern lights. There is no denying that he was fond of pretty patterns, and pretty patterns do not always make for good planning. The lobby-and-staircase systems, for example, in the north and south fronts of the Custom House (which survive almost intact) are charming, but they have no very inevitable relation to necessities either of plan or of elevation. And here, as everywhere else, he was careful to ensure that corridors, not apartments, should have the benefit of south lighting.

The flower-like plan of the Four Courts, with King's Bench, Chancery, Exchequer and Common Pleas* radiating from the great circular hall towards the *corners* of the square, seems at first sight to be open to the charge of pattern-making. But in cold fact it is a very convenient plan. The little octagons and triangles at

* The Rolls Court was originally at the back on the main axis, where the Supreme Court is now.

which the enemy mocks made excellent retiring and robing rooms for judges and the like. In the reconstruction they were retained with some modifications. True, the larger triangles at the corners of the block appear to have been completely unused and unusable at first, except that Curran used the north-western one as his stables when he was Master of the Rolls. The clerestorey lighting of the courts prevented the top storey of the centre block from being used at all at first: in the reconstruction this difficulty was surmounted by skylighting.*

The great central hall (Pl. LVI) of the Four Courts, sixty-four feet in diameter, is, and still more was, an admirable interior. Like St Paul's, it has an inner dome with a round hole through which one sees the under-surface of a higher dome. Gandon intended to vault the inner dome in brick,[21] and the immense prism-shaped buttresses round the outside show the preparation for this vaulting. In fact it was of plaster on timber framing, and very magnificent it must have been, with Edward Smyth's eight colossal statues standing on consoles between the windows, and representing 'Punishment, Eloquence, Mercy, Prudence, Law, Wisdom, Justice and Liberty'. From the heads of these statues a running arabesque enclosed medallions over each window, and these were of 'Moses, Lycurgus, Solon, Numa, Confucius, Alfred, Manco-Capac and Ollamh Fodhla'—a series which ranges literally from China to Peru, and includes ancient Ireland. Beneath the windows, in the attic storey, were eight sunk panels, four of which (those over the Courts†) represented William I instituting Courts of Justice; the signing of Magna Carta; Henry II granting an audience to the Irish chiefs and giving Dublin a charter; and finally James I abolishing the Brehon Laws, tanistry, gavelkind and gossipred; and publishing the Act of Oblivion. An oblivion all too complete has descended on all this work of Edward Smyth's, for all was blasted to fragments in the siege of 1922, but all the rest from the capitals of the order [see pp. 333-4 below] downwards is original work which survived the explosion.‡ In the niches between the columns were statues of

* The entrance apsidal lobby is now lit through floor-lights in the room above.

† The alternate panels were plain: all are now empty.

‡ The wooden partitions at the entrances to the Courts were replaced in the reconstruction by masonry walls harmonising with the old piers. The photograph in Richardson: *Monumental Classic Arch.*, shows the original arrangement.

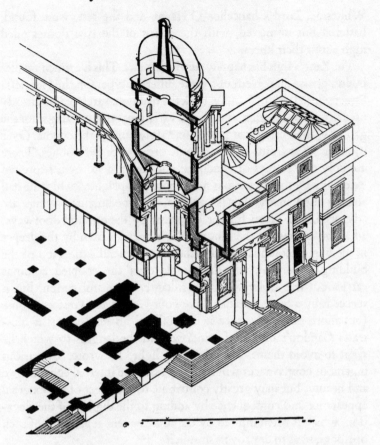

FIG. 17. The Custom House, centre of river front. The roofing arrangements are conjectural restorations. The Long Room is on the first floor behind the dome.

nineteenth-century legal luminaries, sitting in the niches with their feet on great blocks of stone. But, alas,

> ... Time his Northern Sons of Spoil awoke,
> And all the blended Work of Strength and Grace,
> With many a rude repeated Stroke,
> And many a barb'rous Yell, to thousand Fragments broke.

and after the explosion these worthies—Sir Michael O'Loghlen the Master of the Rolls, Lord Chancellor Plunket, Lord Chief Justice

Whiteside, Lord Chancellor O'Hagan and the rest, were found, battered but unmoved, with the debris of the two domes piled high about their knees.

The King's Inns has happily survived intact. This is a much smaller building, and a problem of a quite different type. On the Henrietta Street side (Pl. xlvii) Gandon took the triumphal arch theme already used in the Four Courts, and played variations on it, curving it for the gateway, then using it as the ground storey under the cupola. Over it, in the west front, he set an ionic order with flat volutes. There are only two storeys of windows, but the third storey is expressed externally by the alternating medallions and plaques* which he had already used in the Lords' portico. The pedimented wings are advanced, and given further emphasis by the caryatid doorways: all at the expense of the centre, which holds its own by the deeper modelling of colonnade and niches. The general expression of the building is vertical, and the cupola over the coupled columns carries out this feeling. It is a brilliantly successful design, but it succeeds by a hair's-breadth. Like Four Courts and Custom House (but more obviously since it has suffered no restoration) it illustrates Gandon's dislike of windows and the lengths to which he went to avoid them. 'The admitting light,' he wrote, 'by various ingenious contrivances will not only assist the internal convenience and beauty, but may greatly contribute to the effect of the external appearance and consequence by adding to the dignity of the elevation, which is often injured by the too frequent repetitions of such openings, so as to destroy its simplicity.'†[22]

The spirit of the detail is Greek, even more refined than that of the Custom House,‡ yet never weak. We can hardly call the building 'neo-grec' as a whole, yet it seems that in his last years of practice Gandon's mind went back to his old friendship with 'Athenian' Stuart, who rebuilt the Greenwich Chapel in 1779. Since Gandon's day wings have been added to north and south of the west front:

* By Edward Smyth. They represent various historical scenes, but are really too fidgety to be in scale with the rest of the building.

† The façade of the Courthouse, Philipstown, Co. Offaly, said to be by Gandon, shows a close general resemblance to that of the King's Inns. The elevation has also some points of resemblance to Samuel Wyatt's Trinity House, London.

‡ Apparently the north wing was finished first; the south wing, containing Prerogative Court and records, not until 1816–7. Johnston added the cupola and its colonnade, to the Gandon-Baker design, in 1816–7. These dates, on the Johnston drawings in the Murray Collection, National Library, are confirmed by the Bryan Bolger Papers in P.R.O. Dublin.

this was very tactfully done but it has made the cupola look rather disproportionate to the length of the façade. Though by no means so unfortunate as Soane, all of whose major works have been destroyed or altered out of recognition, Gandon has suffered a good deal. All his major work has been bombarded, burnt, rebuilt or at best added to: the nearest approach to work as he left it is the restored exterior of the Custom House, and the Benchers' Dining-Hall in the King's Inns.

In his private life he was a genial and convivial soul. His friends included Horace Hone the miniature painter, and that bibulous and altogether delightful antiquary Captain Francis Grose, who died while visiting Dublin in 1791, and was buried in Drumcondra Churchyard. When Gandon himself died over thirty years later, he was laid in the same grave. Horace Hone's portrait shows him as a placid but resolute figure, comfortably plump, with the ghost of a smile playing about his mouth. In the distance, the river-front of the Custom House rises, as it does today, over the dappled waters of the Port of Dublin. No man could wish for a finer monument. He was, like Johnston or Soane, first and last the professional man whose life lay entirely in his work. He was not an aristocratic recruit like Burgh or Pearce, nor a rakish adventurer and speculator like Nash. In his dealings with patrons and noblemen he preserved a becoming independence never swamped by deference or gratitude, though of these he had a fitting share. His friends, painters and architects, used to go out to Lucan to visit him, and found him 'in his Bath chair, sitting out under the shade, enjoying his Tivoli, as he called the scene about him; sometimes . . . confined to the parlour suffering from gout, but always cheerful and communicative'. He had a lively interest in Irish antiquities, a study then in its foolish infancy,* and as early as 1783 surveyed Strafford's abandoned palace at Jigginstown.

When George IV came to Ireland in 1821, the first British monarch to land here on a peaceful mission, he was expected to

* He wrote an Essay on Architecture in Ireland, printed in Mulvany's *Life*. From this we gather that Gandon had an admiration for the work of Vanbrugh, by no means characteristic of his own age. Of the attribution of the Royal Hospital to Inigo Jones (apparently in his time the equivalent of the more recent attribution to Wren) he says. '. . . of the truth of this assertion there are strong doubts, inasmuch as Inigo Jones died on the 21st of July, 1651, thirty-two years before the commencement of this building'. Not everyone, at the time, would have been so cautious!

pass through Lucan on his way to the Curragh, and it was believed that the King intended to confer a knighthood on Gandon. The old man was wheeled down to the road in his Bath chair by some friends, but for some reason the royal route was changed, and he was wheeled up the hill again to dinner. Two years later a deputation including Francis Johnston, went out to see him and ask him to become a foundation member of the new Royal Hibernian Academy. He refused on the score of age and infirmity, but kept Johnston and the others entertained with the sketches and designs with which he had been amusing himself; and all the way back to town Johnston could talk of nothing but the old man's liveliness and generosity. The ministers of his peace during his last days were his sketch-book and his Bible. When he died later in the same year his neighbours and tenants followed him to Drumcondra, many of them walking the sixteen miles there and back and refusing to accept any conveyance. In 1942, on the two-hundredth anniversary of his birth, the Royal Institute of Architects of Ireland erected a plaque to his memory in the church. He was a man, in the words of his biographer, 'whose urbanity of heart and blandness of manner converted acquaintances into friends, rendering a long-protracted life one continued exercise of benevolence and affection'. But even these private virtues are as nothing beside his services to architecture and to Dublin.

REFERENCES

[1] New Style. Unless otherwise stated, the biographical information in this chapter is derived from Mulvany's *Life of Gandon*, Dublin, 1846.

[2] *Letters to Parliament* . . . by an Admirer of Necessary Improvements . . . Dublin, 1787, p. 206. This book, which includes also the reprinted *Letters of Publius*, has been attributed to James Malton. Though, as the extracts show, exceedingly malicious, it is not without value as a biographical source.

[3] See the Act 25, Geo III, 49; which is, however, hard to square with the information in Mulvany. Ferns Palace, which still exists, was gutted in 1798.

[4] This very complicated question, which involves James Lewis, an English architect who seems to have settled for a time in or near Limerick, cannot be developed here.

[5] This is confirmed by *Letters to Parliament*, p. 86, which says that twelve gentlemen guaranteed £50 per annum each, making £600.

[6] *I. Commons Journ.* Feb. 22, 26, 28, 1774.

[7] See H. G. Leask in *JRSAI*, LXXV, 187 *sqq.*

[8] Reprinted in *Letters to Parliament*.

[9] All estimates agree on a figure of about £260,000 for the Custom House itself.

[10] *Board of Works Report*, 1928–9, 6, 37.

[11] Curran in *Bank of Ireland*, 1949, 441.

[12] *I. Commons Journ.* April 15, 28, 1762. The actual suggestion was that the Courts should be in the triangle bounded by Longford Street, Aungier Street and Stephen Street.

[13] See his answers in Mulvany, 292 *sqq.*

[14] Author of the *Letters to Parliament* &c.

[15] Gandon, in Mulvany, 107, confirms that the Agar-Ellis family were 'much interested' in the matter.

[16] During the interim the King's Inns were in Townsend Street (Ferrar, *Ancient and Modern Dublin*, 1796, 16). See also Hamilton, *The King's Inns*, Dublin, 1915.

[17] See Chapter XXIII below. It was not finished till 1817 (working drawings in Murray Collection, National Library).

[18] Information of Mr H. G. Leask, who saw them.

[19] *Monumental Classic Architecture*, 1914, 24. This book contains excellent drawings and photographs of public buildings in Dublin.

[20] See the Cooley elevation reproduced in *JRSAI*, LXXIX, Pl. II.

[21] Mulvany, 104.

[22] *ibid.* 270.

PART FOUR

Whose Dublin?

CHAPTER XXII

Two Revolutions

THE LAST TEN years of the eighteenth century are more crowded with incident than any decade in Dublin's history until the present century. The statute book gives a convenient mechanical measure of this acceleration. The years 1791–1800 occupy five and a half volumes against only ten and a half for the preceding ninety. That is to say that the pace of legislation, judged by volume, was more than five times as rapid as it had been; and of course it should also be remembered that a great deal of the pre-1740 legislation consisted of sterile anti-popery laws (even if some of these, like that which established the Registry of Deeds, were inadvertently beneficial),* while much of the later law-making was constructive in its tenor. By 1793 the penal laws had nearly all been repealed, though of course the fabric of the Establishment, with its tithes and glebe-lands, its political functions and its possession of the historic sites, remained intact. Of all these attributes, only the historic sites now remain: 1838 and 1869 got rid of all the rest.

During the same period the Irish National Debt multiplied by ten, owing mainly to the war with France and the Rising of 1798. Private expenditure became ever more hectic: pictures, books, silver and inlaid mantelpieces proliferated. Speculative building, especially in and round Mountjoy and Merrion Squares, went ahead at a prodigious pace, as the dated papers of Bryan Bolger the quantity surveyor testify. The Volunteers were suppressed, and the United Irish Society, republican and egalitarian, arose. Its rather ineffectual competitor was the Whig Club, 'composed of Men of Genuine *Whig Principle*, and consequently ardent Lovers of their Country and its Liberties . . . In this truly respectable Body there are, 1 Duke, 10 Earls, 1 Archbishop, 3 Bishops, 2 Barons, 2 Judges *honorary Members*, 50 Members of the House of Commons, and

---

* The original purpose of this Act was to prevent land from falling into Popish hands, by registering all conveyances.

several Gentlemen, as reputable in Character as Fortune' and the secretary was the Rt. Hon. Thomas Conolly with his £30,000 a year.[1] About the same time the Catholic Committee purged itself of its Earls and Barons and gentlemen of property and emerged as an association of shopkeepers and merchants. Its secretary was a young Protestant coachbuilder's son. His name was Theobald Wolfe Tone, and he was the founder of the United Irishmen.

Earl Fitzwilliam, a liberal Englishman who owned land in Ireland, came as Viceroy in 1795, and the hopes of everyone (except perhaps of Tone and Lord Clare)* rose again. But the Beresfords had him sacked, and when he went back to England every shop in Dublin was shut and the day was observed as one of mourning. His offence had been not so much the proposal of further Catholic relief, but the dismissal of that old rascal John Beresford, whom he had relieved of his post but not, be it noted, of the large salary attaching thereto. Beresford was a lover not of money but of power: his chief motive in building the Custom House seems to have been the typically Irish one of wanting to see if he could get it done in spite of opposition. A little before his death he is found writing to Gandon in a tone of self-congratulation that 'we can most certainly console ourselves with the certain knowledge that, in an expenditure of very great amount, between £200,000 and £300,000, the public lost not a sixpence by either of us'.[2] At about the same time he is found quite altruistically indignant that the Union which he had done so much to contrive was resulting in the giving of jobs to Englishmen. It is not from the corruptible that Ireland has most to fear, but from the corrupters who themselves remain incorrupt.

In his correspondence with the architect the old ruffian sounds quite genial: 'I am just about to set off to dine, five miles from this place and return again; a fine time of the year for such frolics' or '... avoid business, and take exercise, get into Irish post-chaises, and come and visit me, they will give you a good shaking'. Yet this was the man who turned Tyrone House into a torturing barrack in 1798, so that the bareback performances in his riding-school are still remembered to-day. 'Mangling done here by John Beresford & Co' wrote the wags on the stable-gate. The evil that men

* *i.e.*, the extreme right and the extreme left.

do is extraordinarily pertinacious in Irish popular memory: the good, less so.

Kerry or Shelburne House (the site of the present Shelbourne [sic] Hotel) was also used for similar purposes in 1798:* so, as already mentioned, was the Royal Exchange. But perhaps the most startling metamorphosis was that of Carlisle Bridge. Only seven years after Beresford had laid its foundation-stone it was to be seen decorated with rebel corpses, among them that of Dr John Esmonde, the brother of a baronet, who was hanged on the bridge with his coat turned inside out by way of reminder that he had changed sides.

On June 5th Lord Mountjoy was killed at the Battle of New Ross. This was the second and (practically) last Luke Gardiner,† a man who deserved better of his country than to die in a civil war on the wrong side. His Catholic Relief Act of 1778 was a landmark, and he had renewed his efforts with success in 1782. He had developed the North Side estate even more rapidly: at the time of his death it had spread (Fig. 9) along Denmark Street and Gardiner's Place to Mountjoy Square and Great Charles Street, and the half-mile avenue linking the Square with the Custom House had been laid out and partly built. His intention was at first to have the houses on the several sides of the Square composed into grandiose elevations with porticoes, pilasters and central domes, such as one sees in London.[3] But such a scheme was against the sense of the city, and it was abandoned. Most of the square, except the east side, was built by 1798, by such craftsmen as Stapleton, William Pemberton and John Russell.[4] The east side, built in the next year or two, includes houses built by Charles Thorp. Instead of the church originally proposed in the middle of the square, St George's was ultimately built in Hardwicke Place, which was also Gardiner territory. But by this time the Gardiners were losing their long connexion with Dublin.

The promotion of building on the north side was in the hands of such people as the Darley family—Frederick, George, Arthur, John, William and Robert—Graham Myers the architect, Nicholas Kildahl, Alderman John Cash and others, who took plots from Gardiner and others, for speculative building. Some of these people

---

* It was the scene of the exploits of Lt. Heppenstall, the aptly-named 'Walking Gallows'.
† His grandson Luke died at the age of nine.

were connected with the building trade, and others were attorneys or simply men of business. Very often a man who is principal in one building scheme is found as contractor on a scheme of somebody else's. The Darley family, in particular, employed one another wholesale.[5] This method led to the erection of houses in batches of three or four, with no more than an approximate uniformity over a square or street, which is the characteristic beauty of Dublin. It knocked on the head the most grandiose of the Gardiner schemes, the elliptical Royal Circus which was to have been at the northwest end of Eccles Street, and which haunted the Directory Maps for nearly forty years, from 1793 till after 1831!

A word of political commentary may not be out of place here. The Volunteer movement of 1782 had been, very roughly speaking, the English Revolution of 1688 in Ireland. The United Irish movement, culminating in the Rising of 1798, was, again very roughly, the French Revolution of 1789 in Ireland. Some of the Volunteers were later United Irishmen, and some were Yeomanry on the other side. The United Irish movement was a compound of republican-jacobin ideas with Irish nationalism and Catholicism (among Catholics) and religious liberalism (among Protestants). The Union of 1800 was carried through a Parliament of Protestants by a judicious mixture of bribery and threats. It was opposed by the great majority of Protestant opinion, and in general by the manufacturing interests, as well as by a large part of the landed interest. It was supported by the Catholic hierarchy, and acquiesced in by the inarticulate mass of the Catholics. It seems very improbable that it could have been passed by bribery alone: it was necessary that the Unionists should be able to point to a bloody and apparently dangerous rebellion, drawing therefrom the moral that nothing short of an union could secure property and protestantism (but especially property) from the return of a like danger.

It follows that the Rising was not unwelcome to the Unionists; and indeed there is ample evidence that it was nursed, guided and timed by the Castle authorities. Before we conclude too rashly that the members of Grattan's Parliament were, since they could be bought, worthy only of being bought, we should remember the ferocity of the alternative presented to them. Grattan defined Unionists as men 'who make their loyalism a pretence to perpetuate their supremacy, and distract the peace of a country under colour of protecting it', [6] and this definition is as apt to-day as it was then. It is unnecessary to dwell further on this distasteful topic.

Considering that Ireland has since become known as a literary centre of some distinction, it is at first glance remarkable that the culture which began to die at the Act of Union, should have been so weak in its literary aspect. There are several possible explanations, and all should have their weight. A society uncertain of its foundations and its destiny is, as we are now proving, unhappy ground in which to cultivate the art of letters. Architecture and the applied arts generally lend themselves to the celebration of power and prosperity: Percier and Fontaine or Charles Garnier were happier under their respective Empires than Benjamin Constant or Victor Hugo. Literature is more apt to analyse than to celebrate. Differences of tradition mingle more readily in decoration or even music than in the spoken or written word. Most of the inhabitants of the Dublin of Grattan and Gandon were too busy with politics and parties to spare reflexion for literature.

All these considerations go to explain why the two outstanding prose monuments of the period were published, respectively, in Washington in 1826, and in London in 1827: the *Journals* of Theobald Wolfe Tone, and the *Personal Sketches* of Sir Jonah Barrington. Tone was one of the first modern men in Europe, a man of action who happened to be a first-rate diarist: Barrington one of the last of the corrupt and genial old augustans, who filled his pages with extravagant and boisterous action because he thought it was amusing.

Tone was irreverent, boyish, impulsive and idealistic. While an undergraduate at Trinity, he used to go to listen to the debates in the House of Commons, and in the gallery under Pearce's dome he first met his friend Thomas Russell. Tone and his friends were not awed by the splendour of the scene, they revived the old name of the Goose-Pie for the Commons' dome, and proposed to one another going 'to hear what the geese are saying in the pie'. They plotted the destruction of British power in Ireland, and no one knows how near they came to achieving it. Both (and many others) perished in the attempt: Tone committed suicide in prison in 1798, and Russell was hanged in 1803. They and their friends are probably the only

Irishmen of the period to whom we could talk freely if they were suddenly revived from the dead. His *Journal* captivates by its charm and freshness. We see him courting his delicate wife in Grafton Street, and living with her in a 'little box of a house' at Irishtown (where is it now?) to give her the benefit of the sea air. He travelled indefatigably all over Ireland and to America, the Low Countries and France, organising and planning, absorbed in his mission but keeping open a lively eye for landscape and manners and everything entertaining. He was only thirty-five when he died, but he had invented the Irish Republic and he is among his country's immortals.

Jonah Barrington was a very different type. He was much of an age with Tone, but being a prudent man he died in his bed at the age of seventy-three. He was a country gentleman's younger son, and the author of the famous stratification of the Irish gentry:

> *half-mounted gentlemen*
> *gentlemen every inch of them*
> *gentlemen to the backbone*

He himself belonged to the second of these classes. Like most men of any eminence in his time and place, he was a barrister. He had tried soldiering but given it up when he learnt that he would see active service in America. As for the Church 'I could not, in conscience, take charge of the morals of a flock of men, women, and children, when I should have quite enough to do to manage my own'. Medicine was ruled out by 'my horror and disgust of *animal putridity* in all its branches . . . inclusive even of *stinking venison*, which most people admire'. So Jonah (whose father had moved up to town and bought a house in Clare Street) went for the Bar. He sat for the city of Tuam from 1792 till 1798, and from 1799 till the Union for Banagher. His first years of practice were spent on the Western Circuit. He took silk in 1793 and was appointed Clerk of the Ships' Entries in the Port of Dublin, a sinecure office of which the emoluments were payable weekly. In 1798 he became a Judge in the Court of Admiralty. After the Union he stood without success as a Grattanite candidate for Dublin City. He was in France during the Hundred Days, and in 1830 had the distinction of being the only judge ever to be unseated by a unanimous petition of both

Houses of the United Parliament. This was on account of his peculating sums of money paid into his court, in 1805, 1806 and 1810.[7] For years previously he had lived abroad, exercising his functions by proxy, and in Versailles he died on April 8th, 1834. It is asserted that, had he supported the Union, he could have been Solicitor-General. It is asserted also that, though he himself opposed the Union to his own disadvantage, he acted as intermediary for the purchase of other consciences less precious than his own. It has been whispered that the little matter of his peculations had been winked at by the British Government, on condition that he should suspend publication of the book in which he was exposing the methods by which the Union was passed. Certainly the *Historic Memoirs of Ireland* ceased abruptly after five parts had appeared in 1809. Twenty-one years later, emboldened by the success of his *Personal Sketches*, he announced his intention of proceeding with the *Historic Memoirs*,[8] and it was then that the British Government, concluding that the bargain was at an end, had him removed, and Jonah's second volume duly appeared in 1833. These transactions may be largely conjectural, but the dates are certainly suggestive.

His merits are happily independent of these facts. His memoirs are almost unfailingly amusing. They are suffused with what he called 'that glow of well-bred, witty and cordial vinous conviviality which was, I believe, peculiar to high society in Ireland'. This phrase is taken from a description of a dinner-party which he gave in 1793, at which the guests included Foster the Speaker, Sir John Parnell the Chancellor of the Exchequer, and two young men just coming into notice, Captain Wellesley and Mr Stewart, both Members of the Irish Parliament and known to history as Wellington and Castlereagh. Barrington later moved to a new house in Merrion Square East (No 8, now No 42). In his younger days he had been a lodger in a boarding-house in Frederick Street (*i.e.* South Frederick Street, in one of those smallish houses, then about fifty years old). This was kept by an ex-trooper whose nephew later became Provost of Trinity, and whose wife had been companion to Jonah's grandmother, that Mrs French whom Yeats described (stealing the story from Jonah's pages) as 'gifted with so fine an ear'. The other lodgers included Lord Mountmorres, famous for having sent to the newspapers a speech which he should have delivered in a debate which was cancelled, though publication of the speech was not. Lord Mountmorres had a hanger-on called Lieutenant Ham or Gam Johnson, 'one of the ugliest men in Christendom'. Then came Sir John O'Flaherty, Bart, whose brother was murdered by one Lanegan who recovered from being hanged and lived to borrow money from Jonah in London. Two elderly ladies, Lady Barry, widow of a famous doctor, and Mrs Wheeler, grandmother of a baronet who was a cousin of Jonah's, added weight to the party. Both these ladies were of a bibulous disposition—'though we never saw either of them *very* far gone'—and Mrs Wheeler went in for lap-dogs as well. Lady Barry's daughter, also an inmate, took to theatricals and so was lost to virtue. Her weak, dissipated brother, Sir Edward, used to require her late at night 'to come from her chamber to sing, or play, or spout, for the amusement of his inebriated companions'. Though she married a Colonel Baldwin, 'that delicacy of mind which is the best guardian of female conduct, had been irrecoverably lost by her pernicious education, and in a few years she relinquished her station in society, and became a governess'.[9]

Barrington's description of this boarding-house is very instructive in many ways. It shows, incidentally, that some proportion of the enormous acreage of Georgian housing in Dublin was let in lodgings, a fact at which we might guess but which is otherwise badly documented.* It also shows, what again is fairly apparent, that movement up and down the social scale was at this time both rapid and free. It reminds us that nearly everyone in Ireland is related to everyone else. But most of all it demonstrates that there was scarcely a name about which Sir Jonah did not know some scandalous or farcical anecdote.

He has often been sneered at as an untrustworthy source of social information. Undoubtedly he was a master of the tall story, and what his picture of the times lacks in depth it makes up in breadth. He was one of those people— who does not know them?—to whom and within whose ken absurd and improbable events occurred, attracted thereto by his powers of narrative and observation. One of the best stories may be taken as illustration.

* Though this particular house was almost certainly not built as such, much of the speculative housing, especially round Mountjoy Square, probably was. Houses which externally are precisely similar, differ widely in the amount of ornamentation within: it is reasonable to suppose that many of the plainer examples were finished to be let by the floor for the season.

He tells, in Volume I of the *Sketches*, some 'singular anecdotes' of Dr Achmet Borumborad, a tall Turk with an 'immense' black beard who appeared as a refugee from Constantinople with a proposal to set up 'Hot and Cold Sea-Water Baths' in Dublin, together with free medical attention for the poor who attended. With the aid of Parliamentary grants, he set up his baths, and everything went swimmingly. 'Session after session, he petitioned for fresh assistance, and never met with refusal: his profits were good, and he lived well.' Before every Parliamentary session he gave a large party, at which wine and song ministered to the good temper of the Members. On one occasion, hoping for a larger grant for an extension, he gave a particularly grand entertainment to nearly thirty of the leading Members. Unfortunately, while the Turk was in his cellar bringing up another dozen to finish the good work, a comparatively abstemious Member got up to leave. He was pursued by some of the keener drinkers, who with wild cries protested that he must stay to drink the last dozen. He hastened his steps in what he believed to be the direction of the street-entrance, and (since it was dark and the evening well advanced) fell precipitately into the Doctor's great cold bath. His pursuers, having hold of his coat-tails, were involved in his ruin: those behind tripped over those trying to save themselves, and when the Doctor returned with the wine, he found 'a full committee of Irish Parliament-men either floating like so many corks upon the surface, or scrambling to get out like mice who had fallen into a bason!' With brandy and mulled wine, large fires and oriental blankets, the damage was partly repaired and the Members sent home one by one in sedan-chairs. But the Doctor had lost his parliamentary favour, and no more grants were voted. Shortly afterwards, having fallen in love with a Miss Hartigan, he agreed to shave off his beard and turn Christian. It then came out that he was one Patrick Joyce, from Kilkenny, who had spent his youth in the Levant, taking Turkish costume, and attracting the notice of Lord Charlemont when the latter was in Greece.[10] 'The honest fellow', says Jonah, 'had never done any discreditable or improper act'.

What is the truth of this matter? No other writer, that I know of, mentions this excellent anecdote: the Charlemont papers seem to be silent about Borumborad. But in 1771 the *House of Commons*

Journals reveal financial support given to 'Dr Achmet' for his baths, and so for several following years also. To sniff at Barrington as an historical authority seems to me the very nadir of ingratitude.

Some of Jonah's anecdotes, such as that of the countryman who cut off his own head while attempting to spear a salmon with a scythe, have a truly classic grandeur of conception, and admirably exemplify the ruthlessness of Irish humour. His wit is sometimes barely more than facetiousness, as when, under the heading 'Dangers of Reflection' he recounts how Counsellor Conaghty, confronting himself unawares in a mirror, fell down in an apoplectic fit, went off his head and died in three weeks of constipation.[11]

His book is the chief source for the *obiter dicta* of that unforgettable parliamentarian Sir Boyle Roche, member successively for the boroughs of Tralee, Gowran, Portarlington and Old Leighlin (one of the many Irish analogues of Old Sarum) and Gentleman Usher and Master of Ceremonies at Dublin Castle. (He was also, by the way, Tiger Roche's brother.) His famous dictum about posterity has already been quoted in this narrative. It was he, too, who observed that no man could be in two places at once, barring he was a bird. It was his political wisdom which expressed itself thus, in words which have had many an echo since: 'It would surely be better, Mr Speaker, to give up not only a *part*, but, if necessary, even the *whole* of our constitution, to preserve the remainder!' On another occasion he proposed a bill enacting that a quart bottle should hold a quart. He also observed that if French principles should take root in Ireland we should come down to breakfast one morning to find our bleeding heads upon the table staring us in the face.

With such flowers of eloquence did Sir Boyle adorn the debates under the Goose-Pie. It was maliciously asserted that his intellects had been injured by his wife, the daughter of an English baronet, who made him read Gibbon, by whom, says Sir Jonah, 'he was cruelly puzzled without being in the least amused'. He was forever boasting that this baronet had given him his eldest daughter, until one day Curran reassured him, 'Ay, Sir Boyle, and depend upon it, if he had had an older one still, he would have given her to you!' Yet Sir Boyle was not entirely a fool. As Sir Jonah observed, his absurdities usually enshrined a kernel of sound sense ('the best way to avoid danger is to meet it plump'), and he scored nearly as neatly against Curran as Curran against him. Curran boasted in debate that he was the keeper of his own conscience, and quickly Sir Boyle interposed his congratulations to the hon. member on the enjoyment of a sinecure.[12]

'After the Union,' writes Jonah in his *Sketches*, 'my public pursuits were nearly at an end. Ireland lost all charms for me; the parliament (the source of all my pride, ambition, and gratification as a public man) had been bought and sold; I felt myself as if nobody,—became languid, careless, and indifferent to every thing. . . . I neither sought nor would have accepted any other government office in Ireland'. In his more serious work he has a moving description of the day on which the final and fatal division was taken. 'The Houses of Parliament were closely invested by the military, no demonstration of popular feeling was permitted. A British regiment, near the entrance, patrolled through the Ionic colonnades, the chaste architecture of that classic structure seemed as a monument to the falling Irish, to remind them of what they had been, and to tell them what they were. It was a heartrending sight to those who loved their country, it was a sting to those who sold it, and to those who purchased it, a victory, but to none has it been a triumph'.[13] His regrets were not so much political (though that they were) as social. 'The convivial circles', he says, 'of the higher orders of Irish society . . . down to the year 1800, in point of wit, pleasantry, good temper, and friendly feeling, were pre-eminent: while the plentiful luxuries of the table, and rich furniture of the wine-cellar, were never surpassed, if equalled, among the gentry of any country. But everything is now [1832] changed; that class of society is no more; neither men nor manners are the same . . .' He goes on to relate how two old men sat sentimentally over their wine in Jonah's dining-room in Versailles: one, Jonah himself, the disgraced and exiled peculator, the other an Irish peer who had voted for the Union and been fortunate throughout life. 'When we talked over the days we had spent in our own country, his eyes filled, and he confessed to me his bitter repentance as to the *Union*.' But the tears, like Catholic Emancipation, and most other things in Irish history, came thirty years too late.

It has become a commonplace to remark that at the Union

Dublin lost her hundred or so resident peers. This overlooks the fact that *immediately* after the Union Dublin was full of brand-new peers whose patents all bore the same shameful date 1800. But most of these noblemen rapidly took themselves off to the new fountain of advancement, and Dublin was well rid of them. For the most part, however, they had been given Irish peerages which did not carry a seat in the new House of Lords, for the British Government, knowing all too well what they were worth, did not want them at Westminster. The disappearance of the resident peers was gradual: nine years after the Union there were still some forty with addresses in or very near Dublin, but very few of these were 'Union peers'. Many of them, however, like Charles Gardiner the last, Viscount Mountjoy, later Earl of Blessington, were fulfilling only a token occupation.

The lawyers had always been prominent in Dublin, and they now became, together with the established clergy, the doctors and a few of the grander figures in industry, trade and banking, the cream of the capital's society. In the years following the Union there were resident in the town more than 650 barristers and nearly 1,500 attornies, so that more than one person per cent of the *total* population of Dublin was a lawyer: an extraordinary state of affairs. The doctors, though not nearly so numerous, are found living in the best streets and squares,* particularly after the Union: before it they were mostly in second-class streets such as Stephen Street, Bishop Street, Grafton Street, Jervis Street, Suffolk Street or William Street.

The Irish Bar was, and is, famous for wit and conviviality. The following legal dialogue, between a Counsellor Shannon and a Counsellor Whitestone, though it did not actually occur in Dublin, seems worthy to be repeated. Shannon had brought three witnesses into court, he said, 'but Whitestone got up and attempted to say I had brought witnesses into court, but no evidence, upon which I

---

* John Gamble's *Sketches . . . in Dublin and the North of Ireland* (London, 1811) gives a vivid picture of the scene ten years after the Union: 'Dublin physicians do not forget that they are men, and Irishmen—they converse, laugh, and drink, and have thrown aside the grave airs and formal manners, with the large wigs and gold-headed canes of their predecessors: they have a candour and openness of address, an ease and dignity of deportment, far superior to their London brethren—the truth is, a physician here is almost at the pinnacle of greatness: there are few resident nobility or gentry since the Union, and the professors of law and medicine may be said to form the aristocracy of the place.'

addressed his lordship on the slur thrown on my respectable witnesses, and said that if his lordship would give me time, "I would bring a chain of evidence that would reach from the court to the Liffey". On this Whitestone remarked that all the water in the Liffey with the Shannon to back it, would not wash my witnesses clear of perjury. "You think so, Counsellor," said I, "why then, let me tell you, that all the water in the Shannon, with the Liffey to back it, would not wash a Whitestone into a Blackstone. Now, what do you think of that, Counsellor Whitestone?" [14]

Of all legal wits John Philpot Curran is the most famous, the most enigmatic and fiery personality at the Bar. He has political importance, too, for he was in Parliament and he defended in court nearly every United Irishman who came to trial in Dublin: Hamilton Rowan, Drennan, William Jackson, the Sheares brothers, Oliver Bond, Wolfe Tone and Napper Tandy. The ground was honeycombed with treachery: not only were the United Irish ranks themselves full of *agents-provocateurs* and Government spies, but Curran's own associate counsel, Leonard McNally, who wrote *The Lass of Richmond Hill* and defended the prisoners in Court, was an informer in the pay* of the Castle. Curran's daughter Sarah, as all the world knows, was engaged to Robert Emmet at the time of the 1803 Rebellion, and Curran, sickened by years of fruitless support for the middle course, behaved towards her with great inhumanity. His wife had deserted him; his favourite daughter was dead. In 1806 he accepted the Mastership of the Rolls from the Whig Government, resigning it in 1814, and three years later he died in London, melancholy and embittered, at the age of 67. He escaped the supreme indignity which, with brazen cynicism, the British authorities conferred on Grattan by burying him in Westminster Abbey, 'the indiscriminate dormitory', said Jonah Barrington who was furious at it, ' of generals and spies . . . escorted to the grave by the mock pageantry of those whose vices and corruptions ravished from Ireland everything which his talent and integrity had obtained for her'. Curran was buried in Paddington Churchyard, London, but removed in 1834 to Glasnevin, where he has a tomb worthy of him.

Death was a topic on which Curran was not afraid to jest, perhaps

* Extraordinarily poor pay, too! See Lecky VII, 141n.

because he had fought him so often in court. When they told him that Clonmell was dying,* 'I believe', said Curran, 'he is scoundrel enough to live or die just as it suits his own convenience'. When he fought a duel with his friend Egan (from whom he was temporarily estranged), Egan complained that Curran being a small man and himself a large one, he was at a disadvantage. Curran proposed that his own size should be chalked on that of Egan, and that only the shots within the target area should count. On another occasion, pleading before his friend Yelverton (then Chief Baron) to a jury of illiterate shopkeepers, he quoted two lines in Latin from what purported to be the *Phantasmagoria* of Hesiod (a non-existent work by a Greek poet). Yelverton woke up, and a long argument at cross-purposes ensued, Curran insisting that he had been quoting Greek. He finally clinched the matter by pointing out that it was not a point of law but of fact, and that the jury would certainly find it Greek.

Many anecdotes are told of Curran's passages with John Toler, Lord Norbury, one of the worst judges in Ireland, though pleasant enough in company, warbling 'Black-eyed Susan' and 'Admiral Benbow', as well as parts of divers glees and catches, most agreeably, as Barrington relates. Perhaps the best is that of the ass which started to bray in the street when Curran was in the middle of a speech in court. 'One at a time, please, Mr Curran', said the judge. On another occasion the Bar was dining on circuit in a country hotel, when someone complained that the meat was tough, while others held the contrary. 'You try it,' said Curran to Norbury, 'then it will surely be well hung'.

Apart from his patriotism and the power of his personality Curran is best remembered by the one first-rate poem he wrote.

> *If sadly thinking, and spirits sinking,*
> *Could more than drinking our griefs compose—*
> *A cure for sorrow from care I'd borrow*
> *And hope to-morrow might end my woes.*
>
> *But since in wailing there's naught availing,*
> *For Death, unfailing, will strike the blow;*
> *Then, for that reason, and for the season,*
> *Let us be merry before we go!*

* Clonmell died the day the '98 Rising broke out.

A wayworn ranger, to joy a stranger,
Through every danger my course I've run.
Now, death befriending, his last aid lending,
My griefs are ending, my woes are done.

No more a rover, or hapless lover,
Those cares are over, ' my cup runs low; '
Then, for that reason, and for the season,
Let us be merry before we go.*

Curran's house at Rathfarnham has been a ruin these fifty years, the briar and the bramble over-run those hospitable rooms, and even the daughter's grave has been obliterated.

The law bred other poets, notably Pleasant Ned Lysaght, a County Clare man who excelled in the social virtues, a first-rate mimic whose imitations of Grattan and Clare were widely celebrated, a punster and, it must be admitted, but a slight poet, though pleasant. He wrote both in English and in Irish, and though he sang of Grattan and the Volunteers in a stirring ballad, he also wrote a tribute to the memory of Lord Clare:

Cold is thy heart, hushed is thy voice;
Around thy sacred urn
Rapine and fraud and guilt rejoice,
While truth and justice mourn.

There was plenty of rejoicing, certainly, at Lord Clare's funeral, for the populace of Dublin gathered in force and pelted the coffin with dead cats, while old Counsellor Jeremiah Keller, when approached by a deputation of the Bar to know whether he would attend Lord Clare's funeral, replied, 'I shall certainly attend his funeral with the greatest pleasure imaginable'. Why Lysaght should have written as he did is difficult to explain: according to Barrington he had no fixed politics or decided principles of any kind, and was bought by Castlereagh. But perhaps he knew some good of Lord Clare. The editor of the 1811 edition of Lysaght notes that the lines are applied to Lord Clare as a law officer, not a politician, and elsewhere remarks that he has left out a number of Lysaght's patriotic poems, presumably for political reasons.

After the Union, the great domed hall of the Four Courts

---

* Imitated by Byron ('Could Love for Ever').

succeeded to the lobbies of the Parliament House as the centre of Irish political life. Here might be seen such veterans of the Union debates as William Conyngham Plunket, William Saurin the Solicitor-General, and Curran himself, the robes of whose office seemed designed as an extinguisher for the wiry vitality of that figure and the piercing fire of those eyes under the bushy brows. Rubbing shoulders with these was a burly dark young man, rising in his practice, but not yet an evident giant. This was Daniel O'Connell, Curran's equal as a defending counsel, and prototype of many later arrivals from the submerged provinces of the south and west.

The Irish Bar has changed remarkably little. To go to the Four Courts to-day in Law Term is to be transported back to the eighteenth century. Wig and gown seem to endow those figures who flit to and fro and consult in little knots in the Great Hall or the vestibules of the Library, with the features portrayed by a Daumier or a Rowlandson. Perhaps it is the costume, perhaps the lighting. Whatever the cause, the effect is startling and a little unnerving. And once again the Four Courts has become, as it was in Barrington's day, one of the recognised and most promising entrances to political life.

REFERENCES

[1] Advertisement in 1792 *Treble Almanack*.

[2] Mulvany's *Gandon*, 177–8.

[3] Plan and elevation in National Library.

[4] See F. A. Ashe in *DHR*, III, 4, pp. 98 *sqq.*

[5] Bryan Bolger Papers in PRO Dublin.

[6] Quoted by Barrington in *Personal Sketches* (2nd ed. 1830), II, 443.

[7] See W. J. Fitzpatrick, *The Sham Squire*, 1895 ed. 289 *sqq.* and R. O'Flanagan, *History of the Irish Bar*, and *Eighteenth Report on Courts of Justice in Ireland*. (*Reports from Committees*, 1829, II, 293).

[8] See prospectus at end of Vol. II of 2nd ed. (1830) of the *Personal Sketches*, where Barrington protests too much.

[9] *Personal Sketches*, 1827, I, 117 *sqq.*

[10] I found no trace of this among the Charlemont Papers.

[11] This is in Volume III, 1832, into which Jonah put the stories at first deemed too tall for inclusion.

[12] Other stories of Sir Boyle may be found in W. R. LeFanu's *Seventy Years of Irish Life*, Chapter XVI.

[13] *The Rise and Fall of the Irish Nation* (first published as *Historic Memoirs of the Union*) Duffy ed., p. 287.

[14] Herbert, *Varieties*, 1836, p. 154.

CHAPTER XXIII

Francis Johnston and Others

TOWARDS THE END of Gandon's professional life, other figures appear on the architectural scene. The careers of this generation of architects overlap the great political watershed of 1800, which must be ignored in dealing with them.

There were, for example, the Parks or Parkes, Robert and Edward. Robert was responsible for the western extensions of the Parliament House, roughly similar in outline to Gandon's eastern buildings, but with a quadrant colonnade, twelve feet behind which was a wall with niches, and a smaller portico differing somewhat in detail from the rest of the building.* These extensions were complete by 1792, in which year the Goose-Pie fell victim to the ingenuity of a 'smoke-doctor' named Nesbit, who persuaded the House that he could heat the Commons chamber with hot air, and succeeded only in burning down the dome. It was rebuilt in a circular form, in brick, and not so high as it had been. The architect was Vincent Waldré, a painter and stucco-man who had done the great frieze round the dome at Stowe, and was brought over by the Marquis of Buckingham to decorate St Patrick's Hall in Dublin Castle. He and his wife lived at Celbridge, where they were so badly treated by a gang of bandits that they died.

Edward Parke was apparently a younger man. His best-known work is the Commercial Buildings (Pl. LVIII) in Dame Street (1796-9), whose noble three-storeyed astylar elevation in golden granite still imparts some dignity to that commercial thoroughfare. Its beautiful plaster-vaulted vestibule and internal courtyard are still unspoiled. He was Architect to the Dublin Society and the Royal Exchange, and in 1806 designed the Royal College of Surgeons on the corner of York Street and Stephen's Green. Twenty years later the façade was

---

* Mulvany's *Gandon*, 112 *sqq*. Mr Curran (*Bank of Ireland* 1949 p. 446) doubts the claim made in Mulvany, p. 115 n, that Parke used Gandon's design for the west portico. The architectural evidence seems to support Mr Curran.

extended four bays to the northward and re-centred by William Murray, who deprived it of most of its character, but the elevation to York Street and some of the interiors survive of Parke's work.

Henry Aaron Baker, Gandon's pupil and Master of the Architectural School, designed the pleasant little fountain (Pl. LX) in Merrion Square West, with its Coade stone ornaments, in 1791 and rather in the manner of Ivory than of Gandon.[1] As well as working on various churches, he designed Sir Patrick Dun's Hospital in the Artichoke Road (1799–1808), in which, however, George Papworth is said also to have been concerned.[2] This Papworth was brother to John Buonarotti, and settled here, where his son also became an architect. Dun's Hospital is an honest but not outstandingly good building. The Corn Exchange, on Burgh Quay, is another building of some interest. It was built in about 1815, and the architect's name is given[3] as Halpin, presumably the G. Halpin who was Inspector of Works to the Ballast Board. Its spacious interior, with a large rectangular lantern carried on hollow cast-iron columns, is nowadays hardly visible, so much has it been cut up with partitions. The elevation is presentable but, taken by itself, a little grim.

Richard Johnston, elder brother of the more famous Francis, designed in 1784–6 the New Assembly Rooms (now the Gate Theatre &c) in Cavendish Row, Rutland Square. This is a very attractive group, the plan provided by Frederick Trench, an amateur gentleman-architect, but the elevations and execution are by Johnston. It adjoins Ensor's Rotunda, and gave Dublin 19,654 square feet of assembly rooms, only twenty square feet short of the facilities at Bath, as the Rotunda authorities proudly recorded.[4] About the same time an Act of Parliament prevented the Hospital from erecting any more buildings on its pleasure-grounds, the wall was replaced by elegant railings, and the Gardens renamed Rutland Square.[5] Soon afterwards (1790) Frederick Street was made; but this, by making a north-south thoroughfare along the Sackville Street–Carlisle Bridge line, ultimately destroyed the amenities of Square and Mall. Richard Johnston also designed Green Street Courthouse (1792–7), a rather pedestrian building adjoining Newgate, but of some historic interest* and still intact.

Francis Johnston is, after Gandon, the greatest name in Irish

---

* It was the scene of the State Trials of 1848 and 1867.

architecture. Though he never did anything to equal the Parliament House or Castletown,* he left so much work and such evidence of versatility, that his place cannot be disputed. He was born in Co. Armagh in 1760 and, attracting the attention of Primate Robinson, was sent to Dublin at the age of eighteen to work under Cooley and Samuel Sproule, architect to the Wide Streets Commissioners.[6] His first Dublin building is Daly's Club House (Pl. LIX), beside Robert Parke's Commons' extensions on the corner of Foster Place and College Green. Of this only the centre block survives; the wings on Foster Place and Anglesey Street have been rebuilt. With its un-tapered ionic pilasters and its attic pierced by round windows† it makes a pleasant contrast to the Commercial Buildings a few yards away. Its granite is of a pleasant golden colour. The ceiling of the great card-room is now hidden by a false ceiling inserted when the room was cut up for offices. It was described by an English visitor in 1791 as 'the most superb gambling-house in the world'.[7] 'The god of cards and dice,' says another contemporary, 'has a temple, called Daly's, dedicated to his honour in Dublin, much more magnificent than any temple to be found in that city dedicated to the God of the Universe'.[8] It was Johnston himself who redressed the balance.

As Architect to the Board of Works, Johnston was responsible for so many buildings in Dublin and elsewhere, that only his most important work in the capital can be mentioned here. One of his earliest jobs, before his appointment to that post, was the comple-tion of the rebuilding of the Round Church, already begun by a carpenter-architect named Hartwell on the lower part of Dodson's walls.[9] Johnston designed a gothic tower which, as usual in Dublin, was never finished. The interior was galleried and fitted up in what was believed to be 'the Egyptian style' and the windows hung with oiled-silk transparencies. It was destroyed by fire in 1860.

Like most of his generation, Johnston designed in many styles: classic, gothic, classical-gothical and a peculiarly hard and callous manner which can only be called institutional. A certain hardness distinguishes nearly all his work, even when he is at his most human, and seems to have been a part of his temperament. On the whole,

---

* Mainly because nobody ever asked him to.
† They have now been enlarged by squaring off the bottoms.

the richest of his works in Dublin is St George's (see Pls. LXIII and LXVII), Hardwicke Place, 1802–13. It is the focus of three streets, one (in which Johnston lived)* nearly a third of a mile long; and it stands in a place step-shaped behind and crescented in front. No church in Dublin, and few elsewhere, enjoys such a site.

The church itself is neo-grec in feeling, the spire more of the high renaissance. Like so many other designers, Johnston adapted St Martin's-in-the-Fields for his spire, omitting the bottom storey and adding another at the top. The convex silhouette which results is utterly unlike Gibbs's work, and some may feel the effect to be a little precarious. Internally the church is wider than it is long, with galleries on three sides which, cantilevered on an inner wall between which and the outer wall a passage runs round the church, appear to be without supports. Until about 1880 the east end was arranged in the presbyterian fashion, with a three-decker in a shallow apse and the communion-table out in front, the whole surrounded by an elliptical railing. All the wood-carving, decorations and fittings of the church bear the strong impress of Johnston's personality, and of the style of joinery and carving followed, under Johnston's inspiration, by such carvers as Richard Stewart. The curious thing about this style is that it makes the same impression whether it is officially 'classic' as here, or officially 'gothic' as in the Chapel Royal and elsewhere. The flat plaster ceiling which spans the whole church without any support, became dangerous in 1836 because, owing to the Napoleonic wars, Johnston had to use short lengths of timber. But a young engineer named Mallet managed, with the aid of bowstring girders, to make it secure. On Johnston's plans for the church the capacity of the pews is shown in £ s. d. of pew-rent, and the capacity of the vaults in hogsheads.

The Chapel Royal which he built in Dublin Castle was begun in 1807 and finished in 1814. It is of black Dublin calp and adjoins the massive Record Tower which Johnston recased with the same material and adorned with crenellations at the same time. Externally

---

* Johnston also built houses in Eccles Street. His own house, No 64 (next door to that of Sir Boyle Roche, No 63), was apparently already existing before he doubled its width with the part adorned with round-headed windows and plaques emblematic of the Arts. It appears that this addition was later increased in height. The joinery of his house is very Johnstonian in feeling. At the rear is an octagonal room with a lantern roof. Inset in the outer wall of this room, overlooking the garden, are busts of George III and Queen Charlotte. Johnston's politics were very 'loyal'.

it is an interesting example of early Gothic Revival: internally it is an aisled and galleried hall with rich oak carving and fantastic plaster fan-vaulting and figure-sculpture. By a neat coincidence, the last available space in the windows was filled with the arms of the last Viceroy of Ireland, Lord FitzAlan, in 1922. The adaptation of the Chapel for Catholic worship in 1943 was unobtrusively effected, and Smyth's carved heads of St Peter and Jonathan Swift still greet the visitor who enters by the north door. Johnston did two other churches in Dublin which bear a strong family resemblance to this one: the Chapel of the Foundling Hospital (now St Kevin's Hospital) and that of the Female Orphan House on the North Circular Road.*

He did a great deal of adaptation and alteration, in all of which he showed that pious spirit of respect for other men's work which distinguishes the greatest architects. The most striking example is the Parliament House, which he adapted for the Bank of Ireland in the years following 1804. The Bank, founded in 1783, occupied miserable premises in Mary's Abbey, and made various efforts and plans to house itself more suitably, the most important project being that of 1799, when it treated with the Wide Streets Commissioners for the triangle of land bounded by Westmorland, D'Olier and College Streets, and caused Sir John Soane to prepare plans and elevations. On balance, one can only feel grateful that this came to nothing.[10]

In 1802 the Bank bought the Parliament House. The Government, who sold it, had recent memories of buying and selling within those dishonoured walls, and they were afraid of ghosts. They imposed a covenant that both Chambers of Parliament should be completely altered. Happily for us, part of this bargain was not kept, and the House of Lords remains. It was also proposed that external alterations should 'reconcile the citizens' to the change.

Johnston tidied up the exterior in an exemplary manner (Pl. XIII). The Goose-Pie had already gone, and presented no problem. He did the very minimum to Pearce's colonnade, walling up the windows and crowning the central pediment with statues.† He assimilated

---

* The architect of the orphanage itself was Whitmore Davis, protégé of the La Touche family and architect to the Revenue Commissioners.

† By Edward Smyth and his son John. Before the Bank took over, the east pediment was the only one to boast any statuary.

the two wings by taking down Parke's wall and rebuilding it between his columns, and substituting a niched wall with engaged columns and balustrade for Gandon's screen. He lost the prominence which Gandon had given the porticoes, but he gained regularity and reconciled his predecessors by toning one up and the other down. When he had finished with the exterior, there was not a window to be seen. Gandon, who disliked windows, must have been almost pleased, but Parke (if he was alive) would have been furious.

Johnston's great Cash Office, seventy feet by fifty-two feet, immediately behind the colonnade, is a magnificent piece of work in Bath and Portland stone, with a giant order and a cove rising to a huge rectangular lantern, equally successful as a construction and a lighting device. The most important of the other halls he inserted are those which succeeded to the House of Commons, the Accountant-General's Office, the Board Room and the Governor's Room,[11] top-lit apartments with intersecting brick vaults, the extrados of the vault acting as the roof, which looks from above more like a Roman bath than an Irish bank. He did nothing to the House of Lords (the Court of Proprietors) beyond rescuing the tapestries from a junk-room in the Castle where he found them, and hanging them up again. The Bank of Ireland, as we have it now, is the Dublin analogue of Greenwich Hospital: all our greatest names have brought something to it, yet it remains a coherent and satisfactory whole.

Another of Johnston's adaptations was the Viceregal Lodge in the Phœnix Park, a mid-eighteenth-century Ranger's house which now became the chief official residence of the Viceroy. It was this house, which, being in bad repair, the Government had tried to present to Henry Grattan, only that the patriot saw through their manœuvre and refused to accept it. This stroke of bad luck was followed by another, when the Duke of Rutland died in the house a few years later. In 1816 Johnston added wings to it and built the conspicuous south portico. Its popularity with the later Viceroys may have been due in part to Johnston's success in making it look like a Residency or Government House somewhere in the Colonies, thus giving the Viceroy, as he walked between the cypresses, the illusion that he really was abroad. It was from here that on May

6th, 1882, Earl Spencer saw what he thought to be two natives wrestling—Lord Frederick Cavendish and Mr Thomas Burke being assassinated by the Invincibles.

Johnston's most conspicuous Dublin building is the General Post Office (1814–18) (Pl. LXIX), in Lower Sackville (O'Connell) Street. This is a massive block of building some 220 feet long and with a general height of about fifty-six feet. It has a hexastyle Greek ionic portico out over the pavement like that of the House of Lords: the most frequented pavement in Dublin passes under both of them. Unfortunately the G.P.O. photographs badly: nothing but a large-scale measured drawing would do justice to its quality of opulent severity. It suggests that Johnston was thinking along similar lines to Schinkel in Berlin, or Harvey Lonsdale Elmes half a century later in Liverpool. The placing of the perfectly plain voids is subtle and surprising. The coigns at the angles are treated almost as pilasters enriched by channelling to frame the whole mass.

The internal arrangements were greatly hacked about during the nineteenth century: the last re-arrangement was barely completed when, in Easter 1916, the interior was completely gutted by fire and bombardment during the Rising. The main façade however escaped any serious damage.

One of Johnston's more amusing gothic adventures was the grand black limestone gateway which he erected on the quay at Bloody Bridge, to lead to the Royal Hospital. When this gate was taken down in 1846 for removal to Kilmainham where it still stands, the architect's arms were found carved on a stone hidden by a piece of wood painted to match. He doubtless intended that in the course of ages the wood would moulder and drop off; but instead the arms of the Hospital were substituted, and his harmless trick frustrated.[13]

A somewhat more suitable monument to Johnston has met with an even sadder fate. In 1823 the Royal Hibernian Academy of Arts was founded with Gandon's friend Ashford as first President, succeeded in 1824 by Johnston. In the following year he laid the first stone of its building, designed and paid for by himself. It had an elegant little façade, with an inset porch behind slender doric columns, and keystone-heads of Palladio, Raphael and Michael-angelo.[14] It had a top-side-lit gallery, and an octagonal gallery designed by Johnston's nephew William Murray and presented by Johnston's widow. Being on the south side of Lower Abbey Street, it was unfortunately gutted during the Rising of 1916, and was never rebuilt. Its ghost, however, is still to be seen: for the upper part of the elevation is still there. But plate-glass shop-windows have replaced Palladio and the rest.

This was almost his last building. He died at his house in Eccles Street (now No 64) on March 14th, 1829, aged 69, and is buried in St George's burying-ground, Drumcondra. At the back of his house he had built a tower* in which he used to practise his favourite amusement of bell-ringing, until the neighbours complained, when he presented the peal to St George's with a long list of occasions, some public and some private, on which the bells were to be rung.

Johnston profited by the Union, as did all professional men, by the enjoyment of a higher social status than would have been possible for his predecessors. Eccles Street is, and always was, a good deal grander than Mecklenburgh Street. His personal qualities seem to have been appreciated by those who worked under him, for Thomas Humphrey's *Irish Builder's Guide* (1813) and William Stitt's *Practical Architect's Ready Assistant* (1819) were both dedicated to him by their authors, described respectively as 'measurer . . . bred to the study of Mechanism' and 'Architect and Measurer'. Others were no less loud in their praise. Thomas Bell, in his *Gothic Architecture of Ireland*, published in the year of Johnston's death, pays tribute to the architect's genius both in Classic and Gothic, but prizes his generosity above either. Of Johnston's work for the Academy he says: 'Compared with this act of a private individual, the pompous endowments of Princes sink into insignificance. . . . Such an artist—such a patriot—such a man, is

FRANCIS JOHNSTON

the architect of the Castle Chapel; the founder of the Royal Hibernian Academy of Arts; and the restorer of Gothic Architecture in Ireland!' His influence on later Irish architecture, particularly in the provinces, was enormous: but it was his classic manner

* Demolished about 1940.

rather than his gothic which was followed. His institutional manner, too, found innumerable echoes in the vast numbers of workhouses, barracks, gaols, lunatic asylums and orphanages which were built all over the country in the second quarter of the century, and still form such a conspicuous and melancholy feature of the Irish landscape.

Though not strictly the architect, he was concerned with the erection of Dublin's most conspicuous and most discussed monument, the Nelson Pillar in the middle of O'Connell Street. This was undertaken immediately after Trafalgar by a committee of Dublin merchants and bankers who had good reason to be grateful to Nelson for reopening the sea-lanes to mercantile shipping.[15] The Pillar was built in 1808-9, and the stupid statement sometimes made that it was done in imitation of the London example (built half a century later) hardly needs refutation. It is 134 feet to the head of Kirk's admirable statue of Nelson; and though this is much lower than the London example, it is suitable to the site and has the great advantage of containing a stairway to the top, where one stands dizzily on the doric abacus, overlooking the G.P.O. and O'Connell Street (Pl. LXIX).

Johnston certainly acted as consulting architect, though the preliminary design was furnished by Wilkins, who built a very similar Nelson Pillar at Yarmouth ten years later. One of Johnston's drawings shows an eight-oared galley instead of the Nelson statue, and the sarcophagus on the south side of the base (removed about 1860) is also shown. The entrance was originally underground instead of by the present porch by G. P. Beater, 1894.

The Pillar has been attacked on several grounds: as a political anomaly; as an obstruction to traffic; and on the ground that it should be at one end or the other of the street instead of in the middle where it reduces the apparent length. W. B. Yeats did not think it beautiful, thought it was in the wrong place but should be re-erected or left where it was because 'the life and work of the people who erected it is a part of our tradition'. I think it both beautiful and well-placed, for it helps, with the G.P.O., to redeem O'Connell Street, potentially so beautiful, from a squalid disorder almost equal to parts of London.

This is perhaps the place to refer to the other great Napoleonic memorial of Dublin, the Wellington Testimonial in the Phœnix Park. This is the most massive structure in the city, and an important element of interest in the view along the western quays. £26,000 were subscribed after Waterloo, and a competition held, in which Wyatt, Wilkins and Bowden took part, as well as a Dr Hill who proposed a circular temple. Wyatt's scheme was for a corkscrew column on a dome.[16] We were spared this, and spared also, the erection of Robert Smirke's colossus in Stephen's Green or Merrion Square, for both sites were discussed. Smirke's 205-foot obelisk is placed in the only site in Dublin which could stand it. On the faces of its plinth are reliefs cast from the bronze of captured cannon, but an intended equestrian statue of the Duke, on a separate plinth, was abandoned. Gandon, then old and gouty, did a design for a triumphal arch at the Park Gate, but apparently never entered it for the competition. He also wrote to Castlereagh suggesting that Westminster Bridge be embellished as a London Waterloo memorial; but Castlereagh had forgotten Ireland and Gandon, and a curt acknowledgement from a secretary was all he got.

The Liffey was repeatedly bridged during the Johnston period, though not by him; and since these are largely the bridges which remain, they may as well be treated here. The oldest and one of the most beautiful is Queen's Bridge (Pl. LXX), successor to Arran Bridge, which was financed by a loan from the La Touche Bank, and built in 1764–8, it is said from the design of General Charles Vallancey, who was then an Engineer in the Ordnance Office. He later attained an unenviable fame as a speculative and wrong-headed antiquary, but for this bridge with its niches and its judicious rustication we would forgive him much. A year or so later the earliest city canal bridge, the so-called Rialto, was built: but this was destroyed in 1939, a grievous loss. No architect, or rather too many possible 'architects', can claim the credit for it.

Carlisle Bridge (1791) has already been mentioned as Gandon's. At the same time were built the many beautiful canal bridges, presumably designed by the engineers of the Grand and Royal, Mr Jessop, Mr Chapman or Mr Evans, of whom we know nothing.[17] Many of these still survive. Huband Bridge (Pl. LXV), Upper Mount Street (1791), is perhaps the most attractive.

Sarah or Island Bridge (see Pl. LXXII), by a Scotchman named

Alexander Stephens or Stephenson, is coeval with Carlisle Bridge, and has an extraordinarily graceful single arch of 104 feet, with a light wrought-iron balustrade.[18] It carries the South Circular Road over the river to the Phœnix Park wall, and is little seen except by those who go out of their way to look at it. Ringsend Bridge over the Dodder, built after the flood of 1802 by an unknown designer, is also excellent, finely textured and gracefully chamfered on the angle between the face and soffit of the arch. It is momently threatened with demolition, which would be a disaster.

The same flood made havoc of the older bridges in the central area. The Old Bridge of Dublin and Ormonde Bridge, one above and the other below the Four Courts, were ruined. The opportunity was taken to replace them with two bridges harmonising with Gandon's great work, and linked with an open balustrade (Pl. XLIV) along the Inns Quay. It was only now that the Quays were thoroughly cleared of obstruction.

Richmond Bridge, built 1813–6, is slightly west of old Ormonde Bridge: Whitworth Bridge, 1816–7, is successor to the Bridge of Dublin. Richmond was designed by Savage, perhaps the J. Savage who was Superintendent of Mason-work to the Royal Canal, or a later Andrew Savage, Carpenter and Builder.[19] Whitworth was designed by Knowles, probably George Knowles, resident engineer to the Royal Canal, (under Rennie who was not resident).[20] Richmond has carved head keystones and segmental arches, Whitworth console keystones and elliptical arches: otherwise they are very similar. Both are of granite with cast-iron balustrades, and both are lower than Queen's Bridge. Together these three beautiful bridges give an enviable distinction to this reach of the Liffey. At the same time the elegant single-span cast-iron footbridge officially called Wellington Bridge (Pl. LXXI), but in conversation always the Halfpenny or Metal Bridge, was built by a private toll-company. I still stands to make its protest against the philistine hebetude of its rebuilt neighbours.

Two more iron bridges were built, Kingsbridge (1827–8) and Barrack Bridge (successor to Bloody Bridge) in 1863. Kingsbridge, to commemorate the visit of George IV, is an agreeably vulgar affair by George Papworth, encrusted with Greek detail cast by Mr Robinson of the Phœnix Iron Works: of Barrack Bridge, as of

Essex rebuilt as Grattan in 1874, the less said the better. On the whole, and so far, Dublin has been lucky in this respect.*

* The Bridges have more recently been renamed as follows:

Wellington	= Liffey		Queen's	= Queen Maev
Richmond	= O'Donovan Rossa		Barrack	= Rory O'More
Whitworth	= Father Mathew		King's	= Sean Heuston

These names are rarely used in practice.

REFERENCES

[1] The use of Coade Stone was in accordance with Gandon's precepts. He wrote in favour of the use of such materials, and did so himself in his re-casing of the Rotunda, and in Emo, the house he built for Lord Portarlington.

[2] Wright's *Historical Guide*, 2nd ed. 1825, says Baker. Dr T. G. Moorhead, (*History of Sir Patrick Dun's Hospital*) says Papworth.

[3] Wright's *Historical Guide*. The first edition (1821) says 'The design was not given by any particular person, but was composed from different elevations ... Mr Halpen [*sic*] of the Ballast Office, superintended its erection'. But the second edition, in the Architectural Synopsis, assigns it to Halpin without qualification.

[4] Rotunda *Sedan-Chair List*, 1787.

[5] See the Acts 15 & 16 Geo III, 20; 23 & 24 Geo III, 57; 25 Geo III, 43 (see especially the Schedule of the last).

[6] A very useful table of Johnston's life and works was published by John Betjeman in his article on Johnston in *The Pavilion* (ed. Myfanwy Evans [1947]). There are also many most valuable reproductions of Johnston drawings in this publication, as well as photographs, &c.

[7] John Bowden, *Tour in Ireland*, 1791.

[8] Quoted in Gilbert, III, 39–40.

[9] Wheeler & Craig, *op. cit.* Bolger papers. James Lever was also concerned in this building. See also T. Cromwell: *Excursions in Ireland*, 1820, I, 79.

[10] Full details in Curran, *The Bank of Ireland*, 1949, pp. 456–7 and Plates 40–42.

[11] Curran. *loc. cit.* Plates 64–8.

[12] Lecky, IV, 559.

[13] *Irish Builder*, Sept. 15th, 1879, p. 291. See also Childers and Stewart, *RHK*, 1921, p. 53.

[14] See elevation in Betjeman, *loc. cit.*

[15] See paper, "Nelson's Pillar", by P. Henchy, in *DHR*, X, 2.

[16] Untitled volume of competition designs in National Library. See also Wright: *Ireland Illustrated*, 1831, p. 16.

[17] See the Directories and Ferrar's *Ancient and Modern Dublin* 1796, p. 32. Also *DHR*, VII, 4, 153–4.

[18] Ferrar, *ibid.* 32, 46, 135. Wright (*op. cit.* p. 15) calls him Stephenson, apparently in error.

[19] Wright's *Historical Guide*, 1825, Architectural Synopsis, and Directories.

[20] *ibid.* Rennie also designed the Customs Stores in Store Street, demolished 1945–6. There is an interesting description of the interior in Wright's *Historical Guide*.

CHAPTER XXIV

The End of a Tradition

RANCIS JOHNSTON died in the year of Catholic Emancipation. In the next few years there was a spate of Catholic church-building which gave Dublin at least one of its finest buildings. Not that Catholic churches* were lacking before this: that of the Discalced Carmelites in Clarendon Street appears to be, though much enlarged, a work of 1793. SS Michael and John's, on the Blind Quay, by J. Taylor (1815) is the most archaic Catholic church remaining in Dublin: its exterior in the serio-comic gothic of the period, its interior galleried and more like a country church.†

Very different is the Pro-Cathedral (at first known as St Mary's Metropolitan Catholic Chapel), begun in 1816, a massively monumental granite Greek Doric building, with a grand internal colonnade, dome and apse, by John Sweetman,[1] on the site of Annesley House. But, largely for political reasons, it is badly sited. Its huge hexastyle portico is ungainly: far better is the treatment of the return façades.

Passing over various churches now rebuilt, we come to the huge church of the Calced Carmelites in Whitefriar Street, by George Papworth. This has been much enlarged, but Papworth's stucco façade to Whitefriar Place survives. The church is now most remarkable for possessing the beautiful mediæval wooden statue of Our Lady of Dublin, originally from Mary's Abbey.

In the 1830's and 1840's comes a group of Catholic churches with a strong corporate individuality and a strong family resemblance. They are mostly in the older and poorer quarter west of Christchurch: large aisleless churches with transepts but little or no 'eastward' extension, with 'west' galleries which always contain

---

* St Catherine's, Meath Street, an octagonal brick church with galleries, built in about 1780, must have been interesting, but was long ago replaced.

† It had the first Catholic bell to sound in Dublin since the Reformation. Taylor, who designed it, did also the now demolished church of St Michael and All Angels (Established) in 1815.

the organ and sometimes also seating space. The crossing is usually covered by a flat dome: sometimes, as in St Andrew, Westland Row, so flat as hardly to be called a dome. Some have exceptional features: the Franciscan Church on Merchant's Quay (by Patrick Byrne, 1830, always known as Adam and Eve's) has arcaded aisles and a (modern) ambulatory apse behind the altar. St Paul's, Arran Quay, by the same architect (1835–7), has no transepts but instead of a reredos has a large curved wall-painting behind a screen of two giant ionic columns, an idea no doubt borrowed from St Mary Moorfields in London. The Jesuit Church in Upper Gardiner Street (by T. B. Keane, 1832)[2] has a flat coffered ceiling instead of the usual segmental vaults, and the plan is a little more elaborate than usual.

All these churches were designed by their architects to be well lit, and so they still remain, except St Nicholas of Myra, Francis Street, and, to a lesser extent, the Jesuit Church. Being aisleless, and requiring lower wall-space for confessional-boxes and Stations of the Cross, they were treated as being of two internal storeys, with varying degrees of success. Perhaps the least successful interior is the huge St Andrew's, Westland Row (by James Boulger,[3] 1832–7), with its uneasy wall-spaces and unresolved duality, while the finest is undoubtedly Byrne's masterly St Audoen's, High Street (1841–6), which has two internal storeys of niches, detailed with a rich chastity, and is lit only by lunettes which cut into the plaster barrel-vault. The dome over the crossing of this church collapsed in 1884, and the present flat plaster circle is out of character. St Andrew's atones for its ungainly interior by its finely-proportioned corridors to north and south, full of wall-monuments of the Catholic county families, Barnewalls, Nettervilles, Lentaignes, Butlers and others.

The exteriors of these churches vary much more than the interiors. There is a certain hardness about them all, which belongs to the period rather than to the faith. It is not unattractive, once the taste has been acquired. The Jesuit Church and St Andrew's are set with exemplary good-manners into the Georgian façades of their respective streets. Two ancillary buildings, in domestic style, flank the gigantic Doric portico of St Andrew's and tie it to its neighbours. This portico, with a crowning statue of St Andrew, has curious block-like details which make it more impressive than graceful. An octagonal tower with a green copper hat east of the crossing is visible from distant points.

Two of these churches, St Nicholas of Myra (Pl. LXXVI) (by John Leeson, 1832),[4] and Byrne's St Paul's (see Pl. LXXVII), have the classic combination of portico, tower in stages, and cupola. St Paul's, from its riverside situation, is an important element in the shape of Dublin, and is worthy of its position, grouping admirably with the Four Courts dome as one enters the city from the western Quays. St Nicholas was originally intended to have a short spire, but the *Dublin Penny Journal* of December 1832, publishing a note on the church with a view of Leeson's design, objected to the spire as incongruous and remarked: 'As it is not yet too late, we indulge a hope that this error will be corrected'. It was: and the church now has a copper pudding-bowl dome like that of Bowden's St Stephen's.

But, as with interiors, so with exteriors, by far the finest is St Audoen's (Pl. LXXV), that immense black mass which towers over the squalid little dwellings of Cook Street. It looks like some impregnable fortress of the faith, its rugged calp masonry, battered like that of a mediæval castle to its base, pierced only by the windows at the very top, and crowned with the cross which breaks the silhouette against the sky. It is superbly dramatic in the advantage it takes of the falling ground, and dramatic, too, in its relationship to that other great mass, the domed block of the Four Courts, which faces it across the river down the wide vista of Skipper's Alley. Below it is a straggling fragment of the mediæval city wall, and the roofless aisle and chancel of the ancient St Audoen's, whose battlemented tower completes the scene. It is a composition which owes as much, perhaps, to accident as to design; but it is none the less impressive for that.

Who was this Patrick Byrne who so excellently improved this occasion? We know little except that he studied under Baker at the Dublin Society's School, and designed the Turf Gas Co's building in Gt Brunswick Street (Pearse Street),[5] as well as various suburban and country churches, and died in 1864. Byrne is a common name: but it may not be worthless to record that an Edward Byrne, bricklayer, was a subscriber to Aheron's *Architecture* in

1754, while a John Byrne entered a design for the Royal Exchange Competition of 1769.*

This is really the last, as it is the grandest, monument of the classical tradition in Dublin church-building. Ten years later, in 1855-6, Newman had brought John Hungerford Pollen over to build the Catholic University Church in Stephen's Green, a scholarly and delightful building, byzantine and basilican, which is emphatically re-vival rather than sur-vival. Two years after this, the long reign of J. J. MacCarthy began with St Saviour's, Dominick Street, and his French Gothic vies with that of Pugin and Ashlin in the Augustinian Church of 1860.

The *Dublin Penny Journal* observed in 1832 that 'the new Protestant Churches are generally in what is called the Gothic or pointed style of architecture, but those of the Roman Catholics are more usually in the Greek or Italian style—a choice which may be variously accounted for, either from the taste for such a style acquired by the ecclesiastics in their foreign travels, or by the wish to have their places of worship distinguished from those of the Established Church'. A more likely reason than either is the natural conservatism of building tradition.

The last important Classic church of the Establishment is St Stephen's (Pl. LXIV), Upper Mount Street, consecrated in 1824 as a chapel-of-ease to St Peter's. It was designed by John Bowden and completed after his death by Joseph Welland, both of whom held positions under the Board of First Fruits.[6] Like St George's it is effectively sited, with a magnificent vista along Merrion Square South, and a minor but very charming one along Herbert Street (Pl. LXI). It is extremely delicate and scholarly, its main order taken from the Erectheum and those of the tower from the Tower of the Winds and the Monument of Lysicrates—just the sort of thing that the Inwoods and others were doing in London at the same time. It was criticised because, being on an island site, it presented its unornamented side walls indecently to view. But to our eyes these rubble walls with their plain windows and blind coping make a pleasant contrast to the front. Bowden had an extensive provincial practice designing courthouses, and was architect to the Board of

---

* Since this was written I find that Mr C. P. Curran devoted an article to Byrne in *Studies*, June 1944, where further facts are set forth.

Education. He may have been related to the James Bowden, carpenter, who flourished in Dublin about the turn of the century.

The only other classic church of the Establishment which need detain us is St Matthias, Hatch Street, by Daniel Robertson[7] (1843: later enlarged), and this chiefly because of the character of the architect himself, who designed the upper terraces at Powerscourt also in 1843. He 'was wheeled about the place in a wheelbarrow grasping a bottle of Sherry. When the Sherry was finished Mr Robertson ended his designing for the day'.[8]

The gaiety of which we here get a glimpse is, alas, absent from the architecture of St Matthias' church.

The presiding genius of the Board of First Fruits was John Semple. He was their Architect for the Province of Dublin, and he invented his own brand of Gothic which can be identified at longer range than any style I know. There is only one example in Dublin proper; but it is quite enough to demonstrate his originality. This is St Mary's Chapel of Ease (always, in conversation, The Black Church) (Pl. x), built of black Dublin calp in 1830. Semple's architecture is like cubist painting: everything is reduced to the severest geometry: buttresses, pinnacles, mouldings—everything is expressed as a contrast of planes. Scholarship and orthodox notions of scale are flung to the winds.

But not constructional integrity. The Black Church has neither walls nor ceiling: instead it has an unbelievable parabolic vault which takes the place of both. Up to the very crown of the arch this vault is built on the Mycenæan principle, laid in flat courses which oversail one another. Only at the very crown has it six or eight feet of true radial vaulting.* Into this vault the lancet windows penetrate, projecting themselves in an unnerving series of S-curves. Paradoxically, the west gallery, with its enormous Scotch-baronial corbels, is a timber-and-plaster structure imitating stone.

It has been asserted that Archbishop Magee, in his later years, suffered from delusions and refused to consecrate any church which was not capable of being used as a fortress, because he believed that the Protestant population was in danger of being massacred while at worship. Hence, we are told, the extraordinary solidity of these

---

* This is the ancient Irish construction as of the stone-roofed churches of the eleventh century.

Semple churches. But this pleasing legend is unnecessary: we need credit only the architect with this eccentricity. There are a number of other Semple churches near Dublin: Rathmines[9] (which had at its erection a similar vault), Donnybrook, Tallaght, Whitechurch and Kiltiernan, as well as the astonishing example at Monkstown, facing up Monkstown Road, and adorned with towers and turrets for all the world like chessmen, with an elaborate internal plaster vault to simulate masonry, described by contemporaries as 'a mule between the Gothic and Saracens'. He also designed, for the visit of George IV in 1821, the Round Room at the Mansion House with its shapeless conical roof, still one of the most useful large halls in Dublin. His relationship with the other Semples remains obscure, but he was certainly the most remarkable member of a remarkable family.

The Black Church and St George's are little more than a quarter of a mile apart: the explanation is that the former was a 'free' church, no rent being paid for the pews, on a site given free by the absentee Earl of Blessington, Luke Gardiner's son. About the same distance on the other side of St George's is another 'free' church: in Great Charles Street at the head of Upper Rutland Street. This was built as a Methodist church and designed by one Robins in 1800. It was bought by the Establishment and re-consecrated in 1828.

Thomas Cromwell, who toured Ireland in 1820, writes thus of this quarter of the town: 'The spectator placed in front of St George's Church is immediately impressed with the idea of his arrival in a quarter of the city which taste and opulence have united to embellish: the streets in the vicinity are all built on a regular plan: the houses are lofty and elegant; and neither hotels, shops, nor warehouses, obtruding upon the scene, the whole possesses an air of dignified retirement—the tranquillity of ease, affluence and leisure. The inhabitants of this parish are indeed almost exclusively of the upper ranks . . .'[10]

In 1894 Somerville and Ross describe the same quarter of Dublin as follows: 'An August Sunday afternoon in the north side of Dublin. Epitome of all that is hot, arid, and empty. Tall brick houses, browbeating each other in gloomy respectability across the white streets; broad pavements, promenaded mainly by the nomadic cat; stifling squares, where the infant of unfashionable parentage is taken for the daily baking that is substitute for the breezes and the press of perambulators on the Bray Esplanade or the Kingstown pier. Few towns are duller out of the season than Dublin, but the dullness of its north side neither waxes nor wanes ... So at least it appears to the observer whose impressions are only eye-deep, and are derived from the emptiness of the streets, the unvarying dirt of the window panes, and the almost forgotten type of ugliness of the window curtains'.[11]

Such a revolution had the seeing eye undergone in a mere seventy years. In the half-century since then, it has undergone another almost equally complete. To Mr Cromwell, in 1820, Fitzwilliam Square (then brand-new) had 'little to recommend it beyond its air of cheerful neatness. Miss Elizabeth Bowen, writing recently of her childhood near Fitzwilliam Square, recalls how 'Some days, a pink-ish sun-charged gauze hung even over the houses that were in shadow; sunlight marked with its blades the intersections of streets and dissolved over the mews that I saw through archways. On such days, Dublin appeared to seal up sunshine as an unopened orange seals up juice'. To her, walking as a small child to dancing-classes in the Molesworth Hall, 'Everything in this quarter seemed outsize. The width of the streets, the stretch of the squares, the unbroken cliff-like height of the houses made the human idea look to me superhuman. And there was something abstract about this idea, with its built-up planes of shadow and light'.[12] I myself, as a child, going to tea with school-friends in Fitzwilliam Place, remember chiefly the immense spaces behind, where the Grand Canal flows under hump-backed bridges and between tree-planted walks, with the rears of those huge houses, all bowed projections and down-pipes, ranked along the skyline.

Even the purest eye cannot dissociate buildings from their present uses, though one advances always towards that ideal view-point. But there is more than a change of occupancy between the north side of Mr Cromwell and that of Somerville and Ross. We no longer feel the cheerful neatness which drew forth Mr Cromwell's sober approval, nor can we see the dullness and gloom of the tall brick houses which filled them with revulsion. We see, in the same buildings, qualities of drama and associative poetry of which neither the builders nor earlier observers were conscious. Ragged washing, propped on a pitiable contrivance of sticks and wire out of a third-storey window in a decaying crescent, is not architecture, but it would not seem without visual value to a Piranesi or a Méryon. The cult of the dilapidated is no new thing. One may feel that in Dublin it has been carried a little too far, but then in Dublin it is not a cult at all. Our present authorities value 'cheerful neatness' at least as highly as Mr Cromwell ever did.

Theatres are notoriously among the most perishable of buildings, and Dublin to-day can show no theatre of even moderate antiquity. In 1821 Buck Jones, the patentee of the Theatre Royal, Crow Street, was elbowed out of his position and the patent conferred on two of his rivals in association with Harris, the patentee of the Theatre Royal in London. This coincided with a move to the site in Hawkins Street recently vacated by the Dublin Society who had bought Leinster House. The Hawkins Street building was entirely remodelled by Samuel Beazley, the leading English theatre-architect. The auditorium, sumptuously decorated, was a little larger than Crow Street, and the façade to Hawkins Street must have been extremely attractive, to judge by Petrie's drawing, fully the equal of any London theatre.[13] Unfortunately the entire building was destroyed by fire in 1880, and has been twice rebuilt since. Round the corner, in College Street, was the pleasant little building of the Royal Irish Institution (Pl. XLVI), by Frederick Darley (1827-9).* Darley was one of a building, quarry-owning and brewing family, intermarried with the Guinnesses and prominent at this time and a little earlier in speculative building on the north side. George Darley the poet, born in Dublin in 1795, is the most famous of them. Frederick was also responsible for the refined Greek Magnetic Observatory of Trinity College, for the Merchants' Hall (Pl. XLIX) so agreeably sited by the Metal Bridge (1821), and for the bleak and uninspired Library of the King's Inns (1827) as well as for conservatories in the Botanic Gardens at Glasnevin.

The Canals set the seal upon the shape of classical Dublin. The railways, following cruelly soon upon them, came near to marring that shape irreparably, and did in time so mar it in one essential aspect—the view of the Custom House from Carlisle Bridge. The

* Now demolished.

first Irish railway was the Dublin and Kingstown, opened in 1834, which linked the capital with its coastal suburb. Rennie had built his great harbour at the old fishing-village of Dunleary, re-named in honour of George IV's departure, and this, helped by the railway, superseded Ringsend and Howth as the packet-station for England. This brought the iron monster almost to the eastern end of the College Park at Westland Row. To the railway engineers of the thirties, as to the canal-engineers of fifty years before, transport was neither beautiful nor ugly: it was neat and presumably also cheerful. The Railway Commissioners published in 1837 maps of their proposals. The Drogheda Railway was to have a terminus in Sackville Street almost opposite the G.P.O., a general line to the north-west via Armagh was to have a remote terminus on Dorset Street near St George's Church, while another general line to the south and west was to start from Barrack Bridge and follow the valley of the Liffey through Lucan. There is nothing very offensive in all this. But the grand feature of the plan was the cross-town connexion between Westland Row and Barrack Bridge: clattering along the north wall of College Park, crossing Brunswick (Pearse) Street at a long-slanting angle, doing similar violence to D'Olier Street, and so across Westmorland Street on to the Quay immediately west of the Ballast Office. Thence it was to follow the line of the river, on a cast-iron Ionic colonnade, with one foot on the southern quay and the other in the water. But this nightmarish project was happily stillborn, and all the termini were kept at some distance from the centre.

Westland Row need not detain us: it was extensively rebuilt and has no architectural character. But the remaining termini show triumphantly that Dublin, unlike most cities, contrived to turn the railway to good account and emerge richer than before.

Of the other four termini, the earliest, Amiens Street (1844–6, Dublin and Drogheda, later Great Northern) is the least interesting. It was designed by William Deane Butler,[14] and its Italianate tower closes the vista of Talbot Street from the Nelson Pillar. It is a respectable building, but coarse in detail and poorish in conception. Its finest feature, the granite cab-ramp to Store Street, was not added till thirty years later. The line is carried over Sherriff Street on a fine cast-iron Doric colonnade. This railway, it may be noted, was non-political. That is to say, the Bill was piloted through Parliament by O'Connell and the railway opened by the Viceroy just before O'Connell was arrested for sedition. These two men could not appear on the same platform, not even a railway platform, but it was necessary to honour both: so O'Connell made a ceremonial journey with military band and refreshments and speeches on May 23rd, after which, on May 24th, the Queen's birthday, it was the Viceroy's turn. Impartiality was carried to (for Ireland) fantastic lengths: in the foundations His Excellency deposited, as well as the usual coins, copies of both government and opposition newspapers. No doubt he wore gloves.[15]

Kingsbridge (Pl. VI) (Great Southern and Western, by Sancton Wood, 1845–6) is a delightful building, a renaissance palazzo, gay and full-blooded, with fruity swags and little domed towers on the wings, a thoroughgoing formal composition, excellently articulated. It is the fashion nowadays to sniff slightly at it because it is not as good as the Broadstone; but by these standards relatively few buildings would escape whipping. The long south front is much less seen by those who depart on chilly mornings to Limerick or Cork, but it is, in its way, even more praiseworthy than the east front. One of the architect's alternative designs, a less expensive scheme, would have had a fanciful onion-like ball over the east doorway, with taller pilastered wings.[16]

The Broadstone (Pl. LXXX) (Midland Great Western to Galway, by John Skipton Mulvany,[17] 1841–50, the eastern colonnade added 1861) is the last building in Dublin to partake of the sublime. Its lonely grandeur is emphasised now by its disuse as a terminus, and the melancholy quarter of high-and-dry hotels close beside it. It stands on rising ground, and the traveller who sees it for the first time, so unexpected in its massive amplitude, feels a little as he might if he were to stumble unawares upon the monstrous silences of Karnak or Luxor.

This, of course, is a literary judgment, and the Egyptian character of Mulvany's noble design invites and expects it. But in purely architectural terms it is hard to praise it too highly. As one mounts the slope the great pylon-like block of the main building arrests and holds the eye: then to the right the seemingly interminable colonnade carries the imagination towards the flat bogland of the

Central Plain—to the countless sleepy stations, Kilcock, Moyvalley, Killucan, Streamstown, Ballinasloe, Ballyhaunis or Claremorris, to the cattle-pastures of Westmeath and the wide solitudes of Longford and Roscommon. Much of the poetry of travel perished when the Broadstone was abandoned in 1931. This colonnade also served, most conveniently, to accommodate the jarveys and their cabs.

The last of the Dublin termini, Harcourt Street, (Dublin and South-eastern, to Bray and Wexford) was designed by George Wilkinson in 1859. Both Mulvany and Wilkinson were much occupied in designing railway-stations and lunatic-asylums with occasional relief in domestic work. Both of them also wrote,

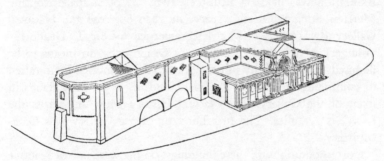

FIG. 18.   Harcourt Street Station, George Wilkinson, 1859.

Mulvany over the signature 'M' in the *Dublin Monthly Magazine*, 1842, and Wilkinson published in 1845 a fascinating book, the *Practical Geology and Ancient Architecture of Ireland*, the work of a man who knew his country, its rocks and ancient buildings, deeply, widely and lovingly.

Harcourt Street Station (see Pl. LXXIX) is a beautiful example of the blending of materials and textures, no less than of forms. The harmony between its rubble calp, brown brick and dressed granite, deserves a better fate than to be plastered with frivolous advertisements and daubed with paint as it is to-day. The planning is ingenious and pleasing, especially the arrangement of the two staircases. If the detail is a little touched with the frost of Victorianism, it is at least free from Victorianism's later and so much more disastrous thaw. As a composition in masses, it is excellent.

The great figure of the Irish Railway Age was William Dargan, who had worked under Telford on the Holyhead Railway, and returned to Ireland to have a finger in every railway scheme which touched Dublin, whether as engineer or financier, for he was both. He was the arch-improver of his time, making and losing several fortunes, the last of which disappeared in the attempt to make Bray, Co. Wicklow, the 'Brighton of Ireland'. He died in 1867. He projected and largely financed the Dublin Exhibition of 1853, a counterblast to the Cork Exhibition of 1852, and his committee included Roe the distiller and Sweetman the brewer.[18] Queen Victoria visited it, and visited also Dargan himself at Mount Annville, Dundrum, offering him a baronetcy, which he refused. This Exhibition was held on Leinster Lawn, the open space fronting Merrion Square. On this space, in 1859–60, rose the National Gallery (by Francis Fowke, later enlarged by Sir T. Deane the younger), of which the long return façade is by no means to be despised. It was built by subscriptions to a Testimonial Fund raised to commemorate Dargan's services, and his statue now stands in front of the Gallery. The Natural History Museum, across the Lawn, is a replica. The first Director of the Gallery was G. F. Mulvany.

Corresponding with these buildings, on the west side of Leinster House, the National Library and the National Museum, replicas of one another (also by Sir T. Deane the younger) were built in the eighties. They began,* respectively, as the Library of the Royal Dublin Society, and the Irish Antiquities Collection of the Royal Irish Academy. Behind the Library is tucked away the National College of Art, successor to the Dublin Society's Drawing School; and so the state establishment of these cultural institutions, begun by the voluntary bodies of the eighteenth century, was almost completed.

All through the nineteenth century Dublin continued to expand, especially to the south and east. Nearly all the expansion was upper-to-middle-class-residential: as the slum families, housed in Georgian times in mud-huts and 'weavers' houses', slowly moved in to the grand streets of the north side, the professional classes moved out to Ballsbridge, Ranelagh and Rathmines. The Pembroke district in

* The collections, not the buildings.

particular, on the Fitzwilliam estate, lying between the Grand Canal and Donnybrook, is a suburb of enviable beauty. Such a street as Wellington Road, with its immense scale of layout, its well-mannered architecture and the granite stable-walls in the lanes behind, well planted and dominated at one end by the Dublin Mountains, is by no means exceptional.

Many squares were laid out in these nineteenth-century suburbs. The earliest and by far the most beautiful is Mount Pleasant Square (about 1830) with three sides, two of which are curved. Belgrave Square, Rathmines, somewhat later, has a handsome array of semi-detached houses on its eastern side.

Nearly all this building, right down to the sixties and even later, is basically 'Georgian' in character. As time wears on, basements rise up out of the ground and the characteristic Dublin front door, at the head of a long flight of steps, makes its appearance. Very often the front door, still with steps, is moved to the sides of a semi-detached pair, giving on to a lateral porch-hall. Fanlights become elliptical, and lose their tracery and grilles. Sash-windows lose their astragals, becoming two sheets of plate-glass. Lintels become slightly cambered, then segmental, coloured brick creeps in for flat arches and door-surrounds. Doorways themselves become Ruskinesque-Venetian, with keystone-heads and rope-mouldings. The standard old Dublin flat granite coping yields to a cornice and blocking-course, still in granite. This in turn is followed by a bolder, stucco cornice and block, built on flags, till the final stage of the built-up brick cornice with a notched course marks the end of the evolution.* But all this happens very slowly, and there are many reversions and anticipations. A block of buildings in Lower Baggot Street would, save for its plate-glass which might pass at first sight as replacement, appear to be of about 1825, till one notices the datestone, 1862.

One of the pleasantest growths is the house of a single apparent storey, often with a stucco lion, eagle or phœnix over the doorway or the coach-arch. These are scattered most thickly in Dalkey and Sandycove, where rosy granite walls ramble over granite outcrops by the sea. But they occur elsewhere, in Rathgar, Harold's Cross, Drumcondra and Marino, and the urban version of the type may be

* Timber eaves with brackets also appear.

seen in Synge Street, Heytesbury Street and other city areas not developed till the fifties. Many Dublin streets and suburbs can be dated by their names: Raglan, Malakoff and Sebastopol tell their own tale (Pl. LXII).

In all this building one principle is constant, whatever the stylistic trimmings. Building associates with building on equal terms: all groupings are free and informal. The formally composed terrace and the geometric layout are almost equally unknown. True, Harcourt Terrace (about 1840) might be in London, with its giant stucco order and its gimcrack version of the Parthenon frieze. In Gloucester (Sean MacDermott) Street Lower, there is a pathetic fragment of such a formal composition, unfinished and long degenerated into slum, and another such fragment, also unfinished, in Morehampton Road. Dublin rejected this kind of building, cold and passionless and grandiose as it is, in favour of something warmer and subtler.

Dublin, like London, has drawn for a century or more on a reservoir of rural and provincial population. To-day, with a population of 600,000,* her life is in some danger of being swamped by a preponderance of inhabitants with no urban traditions. Their strength may be guessed at by the enormous numbers of provincial newspapers—*The Skibbereen Eagle*,[19] *The Sligo Champion*, *The Enniscorthy Echo*, in every newsagent's. The great political figures of the nineteenth century were not townsmen, as those of the Grattan period had been. Though O'Connell lived in Merrion Square, and Parnell under the shadow of St George's spire, O'Connell remained to the end the Kerryman, and Parnell, though his great-grandfather had been Chancellor of the Irish Exchequer, was more at home on the bedrizzled hustings of the County Cork than in the drawing-rooms of North Great George's Street. Dublin became, more and more, a step on the road to Westminster for some; to Manchester, Glasgow and Liverpool for others. But the building tradition, being still in the hands of craftsmen and architects trained in Dublin, spoke still with an echo of the old voice.

The great innovation in architecture came from the provinces, when Thomas Deane and Benjamin Woodward, fresh from their work on the Queen's College, Cork (now University College),

* 1949 estimate: including Dunleary, which is technically separate.

came to Dublin to do the Museum Building in Trinity College in 1853–7. Their work is a startling contrast to the adjoining buildings of New Square, barely ten years earlier. The outward glory of the Museum Building is the carvings by the O'Shea brothers: its inward glory is the magnificent domed entrance-and-staircase hall. But as a piece of planning the building is not entirely a success.

Only a few yards away, towering above the trees of the College Park, is the other building in which Deane and Woodward and the O'Sheas collaborated. The Kildare Street Club, for all its Venetian detail, its stilted arches and its plate glass, is a work thoroughly consonant with the spirit of Dublin. It succeeded the old premises of the Club further up the street burned down in 1860, the year in which the Round Church also was destroyed by fire. The Kildare Street building is most distinguished both inside and out: though its inmates have often been the butt of good-natured ridicule, one would think twice before mocking at their premises. Its brickwork, admirable both in colour and texture, gives the bands of carving a much higher value than they have in the Trinity Museum. The composition of the façades, especially the longer side towards Kildare Street, is masterly. The treatment of the plate-glass windows, set far back behind a 'false jamb' or 'inner order' which insulates the glass completely from the wall-surface, is a bold and brilliant solution of the plate-glass problem.

As everybody knows, Ruskin came all the way from England to see the Museum Building, pronounced Woodward the only architect in Europe, and haled the entire team, Woodward, Deane and the O'Sheas, to Oxford to build the Museum there. Woodward died in 1861, at the early age of forty-six, and Deane ten years later. Contemporary with their work was such uninspired leavings of the classical tradition as William Murray's Royal College of Physicians, also in Kildare Street, finished in 1864. It is dangerous nowadays to use such words as 'debased'; but it is legitimate to hold that many minute changes finally add up to a great change, and that therefore the Dublin classical tradition may be said to have run out in the sands somewhere between 1860 and 1870: a time when nothing particular was happening and as good a time as any for us to take our leave.

REFERENCES

[1] Wright's *Hist. Guide*, 2nd ed. Arch. Synopsis, credits it to Morrison and Taylor, R. M. Butler (*Dublin Civic Week Handbook*, 1927), says 'attributed to Sir Arthur [*s c*] Morrison and sometimes to Sweetman'. Raymond McGrath (*RIBA Handbook to Dublin*, 1947) says 'T. B. Keane is said to have collaborated with John Sweetman'. See also story in Wright's *Hist. Guide*, 1825, p. 86.

[2] Fr. Dillon Cosgrave (*North Dublin*, 1932) credits the design to Fr. Bartholomew Esmonde, S.J., but says that Keane 'erected' the church.

[3] Pettigrew and Oulton's *Directory*, Annals, *s.v.* 1834. A 'James Bolger, Surveyor of Buildings' appears in the Directories, at this period.

[4] See Rosalind Elmes: *Catalogue of Irish Topographical Prints*, Dublin, 1943, No 455. The *Dublin Penny Journal* does not give the architect's name.

[5] Drawings in Murray Coll. National Library. Much information about the Catholic churches of this period may be found in Mgr. Donnelly's *Short Histories of Dublin Parishes*, 1911.

[6] Bowden was sole architect to the Board, and died in about 1824. Afterwards the Board had an architect for each ecclesiastical province, of which there were four, roughly corresponding with the political provinces.

[7] See Wheeler and Craig, *op. cit.*

[8] *Powerscourt Gardens*, leaflet, 1948.

[9] See *Dublin Penny Journal*, Sept. 14th, 1833.

[10] T. Cromwell, *Excursions through Ireland*, 1820, I, 163.

[11] Somerville and Ross, *The Real Charlotte*, 1894.

[12] Elizabeth Bowen, *Seven Winters*: London, 1943, 29–30.

[13] The original, with many other beautiful wash drawings by Petrie, hangs in the Secretary's Office of the Royal Irish Academy. The engraving is in Wright's *Hist. Guide*.

[14] Drawing in author's possession.

[15] Kevin Murray, *The Great Northern Railway*, 1944, 25–6.

[16] Drawings in author's possession. It is not signed, but bears a strong stylistic resemblance to Sancton Wood's executed building.

[17] Thomas James Mulvany, painter, biographer of Gandon, Keeper of the Royal Hibernian Academy, had three sons: John Skipton the architect, George F., a painter and first Director of the National Gallery, and William Thomas, an engineer, whose son Thomas Robert was also an artist. John Skipton was a pupil of William Deane Butler. The Royal Irish Yacht Club at Kingstown (now Dunleary) is another of his works in Dublin. He died in 1870, aged 57. See Richardson: *Monumental Classic Arch.* 1914, pp. 87–8.

[18] This particular member of the Sweetman family was in fact a barrister. See Berry's *History of the Royal Dublin Society*, pp. 281 *sqq.*

[19] Strictly speaking, *The Southern Star*, which retains The Eagle as an emblem of its famous predecessor.

CHAPTER XXV

Epilogue

I T IS DIFFICULT to write with patience of the nineteenth century in Ireland. It is an era of slow decay and fitful growth: slow decay of the classical ideal as the chances of repeal of the Union imperceptibly receded: fitful growth of the modern ideal of Irish nationality as the buried seed of Lord Edward and Wolfe Tone sent up pale green shoots—the Emmet Rising of 1803; the Tithe War of the Thirties; Young Ireland and the Rising of 1848; the Fenians and the Rising of 1867; Parnell and Davitt and the Land War of the 'Eighties. One after another the shoots were cut down, but each was a little sturdier than the last and of a more decided shade of green. In the end the phœnix fires of Easter Week showed the true colour of events.

But in truth the era has little discernible shape, divided as it is by nothing but the hideous climax of the Famine, which reduced Ireland's population by one half. For all its mass movements, it is an era of individuals, of occurrences apparently isolated and apparently without meaning. The corporate sense of the classical epoch was dying all the time.

How else but in isolation can we regard the fantastic scenes at the visit of George IV in 1821, when

The good sense of the Roman Catholics caused them to change their intentions
of annoying, with their complaints, the royal ear;
And they propos'd having a public dinner to celebrate the coronation, at which
was expected the very best of good cheer;
Then an unexpected proposal came from the Protestants to the Catholics
so very distinct and clear,
That all hostilities and jealousies should cease, and both parties assemble at
dinner without any doubt or fear
At the celebration, celebration, oh! the wonderful celebration!

when

His Majesty's reception, on landing, was so flattering that he was induced to
extend, on all sides, his royal hand.

307

The people, throng'd and press'd around him, anxious to see their sovereign on
so good a footing in their devoted land.
And, tho' evidently fatigued, he, with the greatest affability, did for several
minutes stand.
At length he gain'd his carriage, which bore him off amidst the proudest
cheers, to his palace in the Phœnix Park, where he was to take the
command.
This was consummation, consummation, oh! 'twas wonderful consummation!

and when finally

His Majesty, having promised relief to the Roman Catholics, fixed upon his
return to England; and on the third of September it accordingly took place
from Kingstown, where some fifty thousand persons had collected.
There was O'Connell on his knee, with a laurel wreath in his hand, and an
address in his mouth. The one was not spoken, nor the other presented,
as his Majesty and the other party were inseparably connected.
The King thus escaped this and many other addresses, by making a most
gracious speech to his affectionate people, whom he visited with pleasure,
and parted from with regret; this was as much as could reasonably be
expected.
The crowd closing and pressing about the King, he hasten'd to the boat, which
convey'd him to the yacht, as it was order'd and directed.
This was embarkation, embarkation; oh! 'twas wonderful embarkation.[1]

The first English king to visit Ireland on a peaceful mission, landed
at Dunleary speechlessly drunk, and suffered for most of his visit
from a distressing looseness. When he went to the Curragh, a
sanitary engine was prepared for his comfort, Lord Mayo observing
that 'the usual dimensions would suffice, as his Majesty, though
corpulent, was finely turned'. But Lord Meath knew better, and
Mr Massey Dawson, the Member for Clonmel, who 'declared his
willingness to contribute by any means in his power', was measured
for the purpose.[2] The King's departure from Dunleary was commemorated by the change of name to Kingstown and, more
lastingly, by the erection of a precarious-looking obelisk supported
on four balls, and itself supporting a crown.

The Protestant grocers and tradesmen, with their country villas
at Bray and Blackrock and Dundrum, so feelingly described by
Maria Edgeworth, were doubtless greatly edified at these proceedings. But the efforts at conciliation had some colourful results. The
following year the Viceroy prevented the annual dressing-up of

King William's statue on the 12th of July, as offensive to the Catholics. The Orangemen demonstrated their loyalty by packing the pit of Crow Street Theatre and pelting His Majesty's representative with whiskey-bottles. This Viceroy, it may be noted, was no less a person than the Marquis Wellesley, the Duke's brother and a former Governor-General of India. He was an admirable Viceroy, liberal, humane, upright and strong-minded: he combated bigotry as forcefully as he fought against the 1822 famine.

But this famine was a mere rehearsal for the Great Famine of 1847-9. Dublin became a gigantic refugee camp. Soyer, the famous French chef, came over, and immense kitchens in Merrion Square dispensed his soup. But the rumour got about that Soyer's brew contained no meat but only vegetables (as was indeed the case), and the unfortunate man, pursued by a famished and half-crazed populace which thought his was an elaborate attempt to poison them, had to be smuggled out of the country. Thus ended, in disastrous irony, this latest embodiment of the perennial Irish hope of help from France. Grim scenes were enacted on the esplanade before the Royal Barracks, where the starving people lined up in their thousands to drink at a 'national model soup-kitchen', gaily beflagged and fitted with chained spoons, while the scene was surveyed by 'military officers, braided with public braid, and padded with public padding'. 'And all this time,' as John Mitchel observed with savage contempt, 'the genteel persons chatted and simpered as pleasantly as if the clothes they wore, and the carriages they drove in, were their own—as if Royal Barracks, Castle and soup-kitchen were to last for ever'.[3] The distress which the Famine caused among Irish Landlords was very great. Lady Blessington, for example, the widow of the last Charles Gardiner, found her jointure unpaid. She had, as Countess of Blessington, spent a few days in Dublin in 1818, when Mountjoy House was redecorated at vast expense to receive her. The Gardiners, overcome with great wealth, had in the end gone mad. They should have remembered Voltaire's maxim in favour of cultivation.

During those long and terrible years of famine did anyone, I wonder, go down to Custom House Quay to consult the Edward Smyth sculptures in the pediment of the south portico? Did any telescope or spy-glass scrutinise the stone faces of Britannia and

Hibernia in friendly union, or (still more to the point) that of 'Neptune, with his trident, driving away Famine and Despair?' Can anyone now be sure that none of those faces either winked or wept?

There were so many of these magic-lantern scenes in Victorian Dublin: Liszt playing in the Rotunda, Father Mathew administering the pledge to kneeling thousands in Beresford Place: O'Connell holding meetings in Conciliation Hall, that temporary building of 1843 which became a corn store and the Tivoli Music-Hall and now houses the *Irish Press*; O'Connell's body returning from Genoa for burial in Glasnevin, the coffin landing at the Custom House Quay from the *Duchess of Kent* for one of the most magnificent of the long series of magnificent funerals for which Dublin is renowned; and of course the visits of Queen Victoria in 1849, 1853 and 1861, when stones were thrown through the windows of the Kildare Street Club to express disapproval of the Prince Consort. There is not much order about these lantern-slides: some of them would look as well, or better, upside-down.

As the public and ceremonial life of Dublin sank into provincialism, the intellectual life slowly gathered cohesion and strength. For the first time, a serious Irish literature in English makes its appearance.

The literary scene in the years following the Union was no great improvement on the eighteenth century. Its best-known figures are Lady Morgan and Charles Robert Maturin, Lady Morgan, (Sydney Owenson), an actor's daughter who married a doctor, was an insipid enough writer, with her *Wild Irish Girl*, her *France* and her *Italy*, her *Life of Salvator Rosa* and other fashionable undertakings, together with innumerable novels with such names as *O'Donnell*, *Florence MacCarthy* and the like. But she is not entirely to be despised, and, more important, she kept things going with her literary salon in Kildare Street from 1821 till 1839. Though herself a nationalist in politics, she welcomed all opinions; and, of course, distinguished expatriate men of letters such as Tom Moore were attracted there when in Dublin.

Maturin is a much more interesting figure. He was of Huguenot family, the son of a postal official, and a remote relative of Lady Wilde (and hence of Oscar). He was the curate of St Peter's, and lived in No 37 York Street, where he died in 1824, aged forty-two. He was so fond of dancing that it is said that he used to keep the shutters of his house closed and dance during the daytime by artificial light. He was also in the habit of pasting a wafer on his forehead when he was in the throes of composition, as a sign to his family that he was not to be disturbed. In his last years he became very eccentric: Mangan describes him walking along York Street in an 'extraordinary double-belted and treble-caped rug of an old garment'; another time he saw him with a boot on one foot and a shoe on the other.[4] When Walter Scott came to Dublin in 1825, he intended to visit Maturin for whom he had a great admiration, but it was too late. In spite of his eccentricities he was a good clergyman and universally loved.

His early novels and tragedies are tiresome—*Bertram* deserves most of what Coleridge said of it in *Biographia Literaria*. He lives, of course, by *Melmoth the Wanderer*, the European culmination of the Novel of Terror, a work which had the respect of Balzac and of Baudelaire. *Melmoth*, which was reprinted in 1892, remains, in its kind, a masterpiece. If tackled with determination, it is still readable with pleasure, and will probably remain a favourite with specialists. *Women*, the novel which preceded it, has received less attention. It is set in the Dublin of 1814, with an interlude in Paris, and it shows Maturin in a surprisingly sophisticated vein of social comedy, aiming his satire at Calvinists and Methodists within a framework which is still, basically, that of the 'terror' novel of mysterious hags, concealed identities and tragic endings. At last we see the beginnings of a realistic literature about Ireland.

For the last four years of her life the poet Felicia Hemans lived in Dublin, and is buried in St Ann's. But she had few Irish friends: among them were the Graves and Perceval families, and William Hamilton the mathematician.

A new generation of writers appeared in the thirties: Carleton, Mangan and Charles Lever, differing widely in their origins but alike in their unlikeness to anything the eighteenth century had seen. Carleton was a Co. Tyrone peasant who turned Protestant and wrote pioneer fiction about rural Ireland; Mangan, the son of an unsuccessful publican, a poet of great, if somewhat febrile genius. Lever's father was a building contractor (sometimes called an 'architect') and Lever himself was a doctor. He began to write his novels only after 1840, under the inspiration of William Hamilton Maxwell, but from 1830 till 1845 he was intermittently in Dublin literary circles, and even after his final settlement on the Continent he continually visited Dublin to keep himself supplied with materials for his books. He was not a true expatriate in the same sense as Burke or Bernard Shaw.

There was, in the eighteen-thirties, such a rebirth of intellectual life as had not been seen in Dublin since the seventeenth century. As in the earlier period, there is an alliance between nationalist politics and the study of Irish antiquities: including, of course, the Irish language. The third element now added was poetry, and for the rest of the nineteenth century there is little Irish poetry of any consequence which is not inspired by politics or by the study of antiquities, language or folklore. The work of Yeats and of some living poets is still a stem from this tradition. It had begun, of course, in the eighteenth century, with the Royal Irish Academy and Charlotte Brooke. Now it was a movement simultaneously serious and popular.

It may be seen in the pages of the *Dublin Penny Journal*, begun by George Petrie and Caesar Otway in 1832, and continued by Philip Dixon Hardy till 1834. It contained poetry by Mangan and Sir Aubrey de Vere, historical and topographical articles by John O'Donovan and Petrie, and illustrations of ancient and modern buildings. The tone is refreshingly didactic: an excellent example of the 'Steam Intellect' outlook at its best. The fact was that Lord Brougham's *Penny Magazine*, lately started, was unsuited to Ireland: 'The subjects were, in fact, too useful to attract a person unacquainted with the practical value of arts and manufactures—too foreign or too British for Irish sympathies . . . Had they been better adapted to Ireland, the *Dublin Penny Journal* would not have been thought of . . .' Such was the opinion of its conductors. The Irish version of Steam Intellect would probably have pleased Peacock better than the British version did.

The real focus of the movement was the Ordnance Survey, The Irish Six-Inch Survey was the first in these islands, and the Director, Thomas Larcom, decided to extend it as a survey of antiquities, folklore, nomenclature and architecture. The staff included Petrie,

Wakeman, O'Donovan, O'Curry, Dunoyer, and, in a minor capacity, Mangan. But, after a few years and the publication of one volume, the Survey was scotched by a mixture of parsimony and political suspicion. Its social centre was Petrie's house in Great Charles Street, where might be seen 'O'Curry with his hungry horse-face, tall, lean figure, and long, unkempt white hair; O'Donovan, a plump, dapper, pleasant-faced man, as he stood shaking his snuff-box or taking a pinch from it, while he paused from his beautiful Gaelic script to answer our ... questions';[5] or Mangan, with his 'odd little cloak and wonderful hat ... his flax-coloured wig and false teeth and the inevitable bottle of tar-water ... wearing a huge pair of dark green spectacles'.[6] O'Donovan and O'Curry supplied Mangan with prose versions from the Gaelic, on which he constructed his incomparable paraphrases. Poor Mangan, he lived in squalid rooms in the laneways behind York Street, or in Bride Street, and died in the cholera epidemic of 1849.

George Petrie, draughtsman, antiquary, linguist, and musician, was the most versatile of the group. The son of a Scotch miniature-painter who settled in Dublin, he put Irish Christian archæology on its feet as a serious study; recorded Irish folk-music; and left pictorial records of Irish buildings of all periods, which have never been surpassed. He is the best embodiment of an era which had a deep and serious interest in everything Irish, of whatever period or racial origin, a movement of thought which was the best hope for the future.

'This country of ours', wrote Thomas Davis (who was half an Englishman), 'is no sand bank, thrown up by some recent caprice of earth. It is an ancient land, honoured in the archives of civilisation, traceable into antiquity by its piety, its valour, and its sufferings. Every great European race has sent its stream to the river of Irish mind ... If we live influenced by wind and sun and tree, and not by the passions and deeds of the past, we are a thriftless and a hopeless People'. Davis was the brightest star in the Young Ireland constellation: others were Charles Gavan Duffy, William Smith O'Brien (one of the great clan of the protestant O'Briens), John Blake Dillon and John Mitchel.

These, the men of 1848, seem to me to have had all the virtues of the eighteenth century and very few of its failings. They had the eighteenth-century idealism, its common sense and freedom from bigotry, but they had also a breadth of historical perspective, a quickening imagination and a scholarship unknown in the Ireland of fifty years before. Though many of them were of provincial origin, they had the urbane habits of the true townsman: they sat under trees in the Phœnix Park and plotted revolution, or they sat up late at night discussing life and its problems in top floors in Baggot Street. Davis died young in 1845, but some of those who were left celebrated the fiftieth anniversary of the United Irish Rising in a startlingly practical fashion, by organising a rising themselves in the County Tipperary. For their pains they were sentenced to death, commuted to transportation.

Among the convicts of that year were John Blake Dillon and Charles Gavan Duffy. The grandson of one is a Cabinet Minister to-day, and the son of the other is President of the High Court. Gavan Duffy's crime was publishing in *The Nation* a leading article by Jane Francesca Elgee, Maturin's niece. Three years later this lady married William Wilde, antiquary and ophthalmologist, traveller, topographer and medical pioneer, 'Dear Wilde', as Samuel Ferguson called him, of 199 Great Brunswick Street, 15 and 21 Westland Row, and Number One Merrion Square. His addresses show to a nicety the stages in a successful medical career: they give no hint of how much more Wilde was than a mere successful doctor. He founded two medical journals which still survive, his two best travel-books are still in print, there is no aspect of his versatile activity without some value, even now. His wife's poems are unreadable, but her *Legends and Charms of Ireland* was a pioneer study in folklore. Their son, born at 21 Westland Row in 1856, was the celebrated Oscar.[6a]

The *Dublin University Magazine*, which ran from 1833 till 1877, was of much wider interest than its title suggests. In the words of a modern English authority, 'although it hardly ever ceased to put Irish affairs, personalities and interest in the very forefront of its programme, [it] soon established itself on equal terms with the best London reviews, was supported increasingly by English advertisers, and was respected all over the world for its literary quality'.[7] It was edited by a number of hands, the most important being Isaac Butt (1834–8), Charles Lever (1842–5) and Joseph Sheridan Le Fanu, who both owned and edited it for some years after 1861. Its contributors included Caesar Otway, John Anster the translator of Goethe, Samuel Ferguson, Samuel Lover, W. H. Maxwell, Carleton, Mangan and Kenealy, as well as British authors such as James Hogg, Trollope and George Gilfillan. Butt was responsible, as editor, for discovering both Lever and Le Fanu, and in its last years of existence the magazine saw the first appearances in print of Oscar Wilde. Its politics were Irish, but not nationalist: it began by representing the young conservatives of Trinity College, and was very protestant in outlook. Its rival, the *Dublin University Review*, soon dropped part of its title and, as the *Dublin Review*, still exists though it has long ceased to have any connexion with that city.

The most interesting literary figures of mid-Victorian Dublin are Ferguson and Le Fanu. They were much of an age: Ferguson a Belfast man born in 1810, Le Fanu a Dubliner four years younger. Both were barristers, but neither persisted in that calling. The outward calm of their lives cloaked, in the one case, the barbaric splendour and passionate lyricism of *Congal* and *Cashel of Munster*; in the other the sinister whisperings of *The House by the Churchyard*, the macabre imagination of *Carmilla*.

Ferguson was an antiquary, a sketcher of architecture, a student of the Gaelic sagas, a Petrie with the element of poetry added. He was friendly with the men of 1848—his *Lament for Thomas Davis* is a much better poem than Davis ever wrote—but his politics were milder than theirs. He founded the Protestant Repeal [of the Union] Association. He married one of the Guinnesses, became Deputy-Keeper of the Records, was knighted and in his last years was President of the Royal Irish Academy. His face, like Petrie's, shows great gentleness and depth of character;[8] but the life of his poetry was largely a hidden life. It is related that Standish James O'Grady who, like many others, frequented Ferguson's evenings at 20 North Great George's Street, remained for long unaware that his cultivated host had ever written any poetry!

Le Fanu was the son of a Dean. Like three other people known to literature, Helen Selina Lady Dufferin, The Hon. Mrs Caroline Norton, and James Sheridan Knowles, he had a share of the brilliant blood of the Sheridans. His mother, when a young woman of the emotional rebel type, stole Lord Edward Fitzgerald's dagger from the house of Major Swan who had helped Major Sirr to capture Lord Edward. Le Fanu bought and edited a number of journals and papers, including the *D.U.M.* and the still-existing *Dublin Evening Mail*. His early ghost-stories and novels were published in Dublin: later, when he was better-known, he re-wrote them with English settings and as such some of them have become famous. To this day I can never pass down Aungier Street but a particular house reminds me of *Mr Justice Harbottle*, for I am morally certain that the original version of the story was written about it.[9] When his wife died in 1858 he shut himself up in No 70 Merrion Square (then 18 Merrion Square South), and there he wrote and dreamed his strange dreams, appearing infrequently in the half-light of the evenings under the trees. In society he had been renowned for his wit: in politics a moderate, his romantic nationalism more than a little tempered by the experiences of a country clergyman's son during the Tithe War.

At the other end of Town, lived Le Fanu's predecessor in the editorial chair, the last great political figure before the cold, bitter wind came with Parnell to blow the cobwebs out of Irish politics for many a long year. Isaac Butt's career bears a curious and wholly superficial resemblance to that of Gladstone, for he, too, began on the extreme right as an Orange Unionist, and ended on the left as founder of the Irish Party. More than that, he had, like Gladstone, all sorts of outside interests. He was a Professor of Political Economy (imagine Parnell as a Professor of anything!) and he translated the *Georgics*. But there the resemblance ends. Butt was a genial and improvident figure: he lived, characteristically, in a rented house—it was in fact Francis Johnston's house in Eccles Street. In the back parlour was an organ supposed to have belonged to Handel. The wits remarked that it must be a regular fixture or the bailiffs would have had it out long ago. Butt was perpetually in debt, he gave wonderful parties in Johnston's Octagon Room, and his repertoire of parlour tricks and convivial foolery was endless. The house however was sold over his head, young Parnell ousted him from the leadership of the party, and Isaac Butt, uncomplaining as ever, was swept down the stream of history, commemorated only by the last bridge over the Liffey on its way to the Irish Sea.[10]

Let us leave these men in their lamp-lit studies and hospitable dining-rooms, oblivious that a little boy called Shaw is surveying his world through a window in Synge Street, or that another little boy called Yeats will soon be born in Sandymount. For the city in which they live is, for our purpose, a finished article. The pleasant aroma of freshly-cut timber and damp mortar is a rare occurrence now, except in the outermost suburbs. The sharp edge of newness is hardly ever seen, the want of it perhaps not felt. The capital has begun to take on an air of mild melancholy: after sixty years the loss of political status is beginning to induce an unmistakable feeling of provincialism. The earliest photographs of Dublin date from about this time: to our eyes they have an extreme air of remoteness, infinitely more remote than the bright and cheerful aquatints of James Malton, taken in the closing years of Grattan's Parliament. The personality of mid-Victorian Dublin is mysterious to our eyes: so much, we know, was stirring there: so little of it was apparent, or so it seems to us. It is only a few years till the performance of *The Countess Cathleen* in the Antient Concert Rooms, till Douglas Hyde, so lately dead as I am writing, founds the Gaelic League; till George Moore takes a cab and drives round the squares and suburbs looking for a house, coming to rest at last in Ely Place, for 'The sceptre of intelligence,' in the words of Edward Martyn's telegram, 'has passed from London to Dublin'.[11]

The sceptre, we may feel, has melted in our grasp, unable perhaps to endure the fires of revolution. Perhaps George Moore was dreaming, and it was no sceptre but only an old blackthorn stick, a Donnybrook Fair shillelagh. Perhaps one day we shall wake to find it bursting into miraculous flower, like the rod of Tannhäuser or the blest Mosaic thorn. The Mosaic analogue is the more fitting, for it is Moses who, carved by Edward Smyth, stands on the pediment of the Four Courts holding the Tables of the Law, with the great dome behind him, and below the Liffey with its quays and bridges and the swans drifting on the stream.

October 18th, 1949.

REFERENCES

[1] Herbert, *Irish Varieties*, 1836, 269 *sqq.* The 'poem' is well worth reading in full.

[2] Lady Glengall to Thomas Creevey, quoted in M. J. MacManus, *Irish Cavalcade*, 1939, pp. 261-3.

³ John Mitchel, Open Letter to Lord John Russell, also quoted by MacManus.

⁴ *C. R. Maturin*, by Niilo Idman, 1923, p. 308.

⁵ The description is by A. P. Graves, quoted in p. 12 of *Standish James O'Grady*.

⁶ W. F. Wakeman, quoted in Whitley Stokes, *Life of George Petrie*, 1868, p. 97.

⁶ᵃ There is a good modern life of Wilde: *Victorian Doctor*, by T. G. Wilson.

⁷ Michael Sadleir, 'Dublin University Magazine', *Bibl. Soc. of Ire.* 1938, from which I have derived most of the information given in the text.

⁸ There is a good photograph of Ferguson as frontispiece to the 1888 edition of *Lays of the Western Gael*.

⁹ The story was certainly about a house in Aungier Street: the only doubt is which house. See *Madam Crowl's Ghost* (ed. M. R. James), p. 102.

¹⁰ There is a good modern life of Butt: *The Road of Excess*, by Terence de Vere White.

¹¹ George Moore, *Hail and Farewell*, 2-vol.-ed. of 1925, I, 83.

LIST OF STREETS AND BUILDINGS*

(as at 1 January, 1950)

REGION I

North-East City, bounded by the River, Capel Street, Dorset Street and the Royal Canal.

ABBEY STREET. An old street widened and straightened at its eastern end by the Wide Streets Commissioners. Dublin Savings Bank, by Isaac Farrell, 1839. Abbey Theatre, northern portion, formerly Mechanics' Institute, built about 1830. Remains of Royal Hibernian Academy, see pp. 285-6. Some houses of *c.* 1740-60 in Middle Abbey Street. Good shop-fronts, *e.g.* 43 (Middle) and 4 and 146 (Upper) (D6 and D7). No. 10 (upper) has a good rococo ceiling.

ALDBOROUGH HOUSE, Portland Row, see pp. 231-3 (C8).

AMIENS STREET Station, see p. 299. The street called after the Earl of Aldborough, Viscount Amiens (D8).

BATCHELOR'S WALK, Nos. 6 and 7 are good houses of *c.* 1740 (D7).

BELVEDERE HOUSE, Great Denmark Street, see pp. 229-31 (C7).

BERESFORD PLACE, *c.* 1795-1800, ? Gandon, architect (D8).

BUCKINGHAM STREET has a few good houses of *c.* 1795 (C8).

CAVENDISH ROW, Nos. 6, 7, and 8, 1756-7, see pp. 141-2 (C7).

CHARLEMONT HOUSE, Parnell Square, now the Municipal Gallery of Modern Art. Sir William Chambers, architect, see pp. 223-4 (C6).

CUMBERLAND STREET SOUTH, middle-sized houses of *c.* 1760, very dilapidated (C7).

CUSTOM HOUSE, see pp. 239 *sqq.* and 250 *sqq.* (D8).

DENMARK STREET, GREAT, begun as Gardiner's Row *c.* 1775-80. No. 5, Killeen House, now part of Belvedere College (C7).

DENMARK STREET, LITTLE, Fortick's Asylum with date-stone, 1755 (D6).

DOMINICK STREET, LOWER, mostly 1755-70. No. 4, a large house, appears to be about 1740. For No. 20, see p. 168. No. 13 was the town house of the Dukes of Leinster after the sale of Leinster House in 1815. At No. 36, as the tablet records, Sir William Rowan Hamilton was born in 1805. No. 41, belonging to the Earl of Howth but lived in by Lady Clanricarde, figured prominently in the Tichborne Trial. St Saviour's Church, by J. J. McCarthy, 1858 (C6 and D6).

DORSET STREET, the ancient highway from the North to Dublin Bridge. Some very large houses of *c.* 1750-60. At No. 12 Dorset Street Upper Richard Brinsley Sheridan was born in 1751, as the tablet records (C6).

GARDINER STREET, laid out *c.* 1787. Middle Gardiner Street is the oldest part. Beginning at the north (upper) end: Jesuit Church, see p. 292. Opposite are some houses of *c.* 1810, perhaps by Francis Johnston. Middle Gardiner Street has some magnificent houses, see Pl. xxxvii. Part of this section has recently been reconditioned as working-class flats by the Dublin Corporation. In Lower

* Index figures after entries refer to the street map at the end of the book.

Gardiner Street, near the Railway Bridge, is the former Trinity Church (C. of I.) by Frederick Darley, 1838, now an Employment Exchange (O7).

GARDINER'S ROW and GARDINER'S PLACE are extensions of Great Denmark Street. Gardiner's Row laid out 1769, Gardiner's Place 1790 (C7).

GLOUCESTER STREET, see Sean MacDermott Street (C7 and C8).

GRANBY ROW has mostly been re-named Parnell (formerly Rutland) Square (C6).

GREAT CHARLES STREET, c. 1800. For the Free Church, see p. 296. No. 21 was the home of George Petrie (C7).

GRENVILLE STREET, c. 1785-90. Large houses, now greatly decayed (O7).

HARDWICKE STREET, laid out c. 1802, but the Hall on the north side was there at least fifty years earlier. It was originally a Convent of Poor Clares, later a Catholic Chapel-of-Ease, then in 1816 a Jesuit chapel. It became a Jesuit school, then a Presbyterian school, was the scene of early productions of the Irish Theatre Movement, and is now the factory of the Dun Emer Guild of craft-workers, cognate with Yeats's Cuala Press. The houses in the street are smallish (C6 and C7).

HILL STREET, formerly Lower Temple Street, see Temple Street (C7).

JERVIS STREET, made by Sir Humphrey Jervis c. 1675, see p. 27, 73. A few houses of the early eighteenth century survive north of Mary Street, in great decay (D6).

MARLBOROUGH STREET has many medium-sized houses of c. 1740-60. For the Pro-Cathedral, see p. 291, and for Tyrone House see p. 131. The main entrance of the Abbey Theatre, in this street, was built c. 1830, occupied in 1850 by an 'Emigration Agent', later by the Morgue. Adapted for the Theatre by Joseph Holloway, architect. The original building looks not unlike the work of Frederick Darley, architect (D7).

MARY STREET, made by Sir Humphrey Jervis c. 1675. Langford House, one of the earliest town houses, stood here until about twenty years ago. See St Mary's Church (D6).

MECKLENBURGH STREET (now called Waterford Street (western part) and Railway Street (eastern part)). Mostly demolished, including the house where Gandon lived. St Thomas's Almshouse, 1768, near the Cumberland Street corner, has a doorway with plaque over, worth notice. Forty years ago this was the heart of the brothel quarter, hence the changes of name (C7 and C8).

MOUNTJOY SQUARE, 1792-1818, see p. 265. Houses by Charles Thorp, Michael Stapleton and others. The second-smallest of the city Squares. The four-acre garden was acquired by the Corporation from the Commissioners in 1938. The Square has deteriorated in recent years, especially towards the south-west corner. No. 61, formerly Annesley House, has a particularly fine doorway (C7).

NORTH GREAT GEORGE'S STREET, mostly c. 1785 onwards. Vista to Belvedere House. The southern end is now rather slummy. At No. 22 lived Major Swan, and at No. 20 Sir Samuel Ferguson, at No. 35 Lord Kenmare, and at No. 38 Sir J. P. Mahaffy. No. 2 was till recently the town house of the Dillon family (C7).

O'CONNELL STREET (formerly Sackville Street) see pp. 104 and 173. The upper portion laid out by Luke Gardiner I in 1750, the lower portion, slightly wider, by the Wide Streets Commissioners in 1782-4. Little now remains but a few houses on the west side of Upper O'Connell Street. For the General Post Office, see p. 285, and for Nelson's Pillar, p. 287. The trees in Upper

O'Connell Street are in the winter full of wagtails at night, giving the illusion of foliage (D7).

ORMONDE QUAY LOWER, laid out by Sir Humphrey Jervis, see p. 26. A handsome stucco-fronted house of c. 1790 on the Capel Street corner (D6).

PARNELL SQUARE (formerly Rutland Square) the earliest of the Squares, after Stephen's Green. See pp. 141-2. Houses by Ensor, Vierpyl and others, the east side being the earliest and most magnificent. Charlemont House, by Sir William Chambers, c. 1764, much modified, is now the Municipal Gallery of Modern Art. The temples at the two northern corners of the Gardens, originally shelters for the sedan-chair-men, were destroyed in 1942 (C6 and C7).

PARNELL STREET (formerly Great Britain Street) an ancient thoroughfare. Off it, to the south, a few of the characteristic old Dublin markets, with hooded shop-fronts, still survive (D6 and C7).

RAILWAY STREET, see Mecklenburgh Street.

ROTUNDA HOSPITAL complex, by Richard Cassels, John Ensor, Richard Johnston and James Gandon, 1749-1786. See pp. 143-5 and see especially the Chapel ceiling (C7).

RUTLAND SQUARE, see Parnell Square.

ST GEORGE'S CHURCH, see p. 282 (C7).

ST MARY'S CHURCH, Mary Street, soon after 1697, architect unknown, see pp. 73 *sqq.* (D6).

SACKVILLE STREET, see O'Connell Street.

SEAN MACDERMOTT STREET, formerly Gloucester Street, laid out c. 1772. Large fine houses, many with granite-faced ground storeys and varied doorways, at present in process of renovation and conversion as working-class flats. The direct access from O'Connell Street was made after 1922. The Gloucester Diamond, at the intersection of Gloucester Place, was never fully built up. Further east is an uncompleted ' regency' terrace, and opposite it a very accomplished neo-grec Presbyterian church of c. 1835, now used as a corn-store (C7 and C8).

SHERRARD STREET, called after Thomas Sherrard, surveyor to the Wide Streets Commissioners. Date-stone, 1825 (B7).

STORE STREET, the old Custom House Stables, c. 1810? now a dairy (D8).

SUMMERHILL, the ancient thoroughfare to Howth and Malahide. Very tall houses of about the 1780s, now in bad condition. The backs, from Sean MacDermott Street, are very spectacular (C7 and C8).

TEMPLE STREET, Little St. George's Church (tower only), see pp. 84, 112 (C7).

TYRONE HOUSE, Marlborough Street, see p. 131 (D7).

WATERFORD STREET, see Mecklenburgh Street.

REGION II

South-East City, bounded by the River, Aungier and Camden Streets, and the Grand Canal.

ADELAIDE ROAD: Presbyterian Church, 1840, porticoed on a high podium (G7).

ANGLESEA STREET, see p. 42. Has some smallish houses of c. 1740-60 (F7).

ASTON'S QUAY, first laid out about 1700, see pp. 42-3 (D7).

AUNGIER STREET (east side) see p. 40. Has a few houses apparently of *c.* 1735–50. Thomas Moore's birthplace, No. 12, was originally gable-fronted (E6 and F7).

BAGGOT STREET, the ancient Baggotrath Lane or Gallows Lane, widened and straightened by Lord Fitzwilliam, 1791. The brothers Sheares, 1798 rebels, lived at No. 128, and Thomas Davis at No. 67, marked by plaque. No. 134 was for many years the premises of the Cuala Press, run by the sisters of W. B. Yeats (F8).

BANK OF IRELAND (formerly the Parliament House) see pp. 124 *sqq.*, 283–4 (E7).

CHARLEMONT MALL and CHARLEMONT PLACE, canal-side streets of about 1800. George Petrie lived at No. 7 Charlemont Place from 1858 to 1864 (G7).

CHARLEMONT STREET contains a number of large old houses, apparently about 1770. It is the ancient road to Cullenswood, built up much earlier than any other street so far south (G7).

CHARLOTTE STREET, also part of the old Cullenswood road. Some of the old houses in this street are very English in character, not unlike some old houses in Cork (G6).

CLARE STREET, see pp. 190, 191 (E8).

CLARENDON STREET still has some middling mid-eighteenth-century houses. The Municipal School of Music occupies the site of Sproule's Clarendon Market, built for Sir John Allen Johnston, 1783. For St. Teresa's Church, see p. 291 (E7).

COLLEGE GREEN, formerly Hoggen Green. See also Bank of Ireland. For Daly's Club House (now the Yorkshire Insurance Co.) see p. 281. The National Bank, by William Barnes and Isaac Farrell, 1842 (E7).

CRAMPTON COURT, doorways probably about 1740 (E6).

CUFFE STREET, see p. 43. Some early eighteenth-century houses still survive, in bad condition (F6).

DAME STREET, most of the work of the Wide Streets Commissioners in the 1780s has been rebuilt or refronted since. But No. 53 (corner of Temple Lane) survives, with its oval stucco panels. The house Nos. 18–19 is a handsome stone front of *c.* 1840. For the Commercial Buildings, see p. 279. The Munster & Leinster Bank (corner of Palace Street), is by Sir Thomas Deane the elder (E6 and E7).

DAWSON STREET, see pp. 106, 107 and 108. Mostly refronted or rebuilt, but some houses still retain plaster decoration. For St Ann's Church, see p. 113; for Mansion House, see pp. 110–1; for Royal Irish Academy, see pp. 224–5 (E7).

DIGGES STREET, early eighteenth century. Some gabled houses, some with good doorways, survive in very bad condition (F6).

D'OLIER STREET, projected by Wide Streets Commissioners about 1785, carried out about 1800. Some of the original uniform shop-fronts still survive. Carlisle Building, on the Burgh Quay corner, stripped of its stucco embellishments 1949–50 (D7).

ELY PLACE, fine large houses of 1775–85 period. At No. 3 lived Barry Yelverton, Lord Avonmore; at No. 4 John Philpot Curran; at No. 5 Charles Kendal Bushe; No. 6 was the palatial and stoutly barricaded house of John Fitzgibbon, Earl of Clare (now the Valuation Office); No. 8 was Ely House. There is some excellent ironwork in this street (F7 and F8).

EUSTACE STREET, for the Presbyterian Church (now Brindley's printing-house), see p. 115 (E6).

FITZWILLIAM SQUARE, STREET and PLACE, see pp. 191, 297. Pre-eminently the doctors' quarter of Dublin (F8).

FLEET STREET, see p. 43. Mostly rebuilt, but some good doorways survive on the northern side near the east end. Note the stucco group on No. 30 (near the D'Olier Street end) (E6 and E7).

FOSTER PLACE, made 1787–94 when the Parliament House was enlarged. The trophy of arms over the Central Bank gateway (formerly the Bank of Ireland guard-house, by Francis Johnston) is by Thomas Kirk, c. 1811. The Royal Bank of Ireland building (interior completely modernised) was originally the Hibernian United Service Club, probably early nineteenth century (E7).

FOWNES STREET: Nos. 3 and 4 are fine houses of c. 1740 (E6).

FREDERICK STREET SOUTH: small houses of c. 1740, with very varied doorways, see pp. 108 and 269–70 (E7).

GRAND CANAL STREET, was originally part of the Artichoke Road to Merrion. For Sir Patrick Dun's Hospital, see p. 280. Some of the houses are by Samuel Sproule (F9).

GREAT BRUNSWICK STREET, see Pearse Street.

HARCOURT STREET, see p. 228. No. 17. Clonmell House, see pp. 226–9. No. 40 (now part of the High School) has good ironwork. The houses opposite, with ruskinesque doors, are post-1850. For the Station, see p. 301 (F7).

HARCOURT TERRACE, see p. 304 (G7).

HATCH STREET, 1810 onwards. St Matthias' Church, by Daniel Robertson, 1843 (G7).

HERBERT STREET, built about 1830, houses very regularly arranged in pairs with adjacent doors. No. 21 is much later (F8).

HUME STREET, large houses of 1775 onwards (date-stone 1768) (F7).

KILDARE STREET, 1745 onwards, see p. 109. For Leinster House, see pp. 132–4; for the Kildare Street Club, see p. 305. The College of Physicians, by W. G. Murray, 1860–4, with later additions. No. 45, originally Doneraile House, has particularly fine ironwork, doorway, staircase and joinery. Nos. 43 and 44 are also good houses. No. 20 is an early house, much altered, perhaps by Cassels, c. 1748. Nos. 4 and 5 by Edward Nicholson (No. 4 now refronted) 1748 (E7).

KING STREET SOUTH contains one attractive double-bowed shop-front (E7).

LEESON STREET, LOWER: an ancient road straightened. Nos. 10 and 11, c. 1730, with stone skewbacks flanking flat arches as in many Limerick houses. No. 13 also early. Nos. 6 and 7 (the Magdalen Asylum) c. 1760, (the asylum founded 1766). The Chapel of the Asylum is basically early nineteenth-century. The south-east end of the street, c. 1820, very large houses (F7, G7, G8).

LEINSTER HOUSE, see pp. 132–4 (E7).

LEINSTER STREET, made about 1760. The house (No. 5) with the decorated coigns and the statue of Hibernia was once the home of Archibald Hamilton Rowan, who erected the statue and another now destroyed. It was previously the house of Lord Kilwarden, 'the justest judge in Ireland', unfortunately killed in the Emmet Rising of 1803 (E8).

LINCOLN PLACE, formerly Park Street, has the remains of Sir William Wilde's eye-hospital and of the Turkish Baths (E8).

MERCHANT'S HALL, Wellington Quay, by Frederick Darley, 1821 (E7)

MERRION SQUARE, see pp. 187–91. For the Rutland Fountain, see p. 280. The houses on the south side have, in general, much less decoration than those on north or east. No. 42 was Sir Jonah Barrington's, No. 58 Daniel O'Connell's, No. 70 Joseph Sheridan Lefanu's, and No. 82 W. B. Yeats's (E8 and F8).

MERRION STREET, UPPER, see pp. 188–9. Mornington House, see p. 159 (F8).

MOLESWORTH STREET, 1727 onwards, see pp. 107–8. Nos. 3 and 5, the latter by Thomas Quin, c. 1735, are panelled. No. 12 has a good hall and staircase. Nos. 15 and 16 are gabled houses, pre-1740. Nos. 20 and 21, the former with an unusual and beautiful doorway, are similar in plan, built by George Spring. No. 33 (' Lisle House ') 1738, has a fine interior. The Molesworth Hall and the Diocesan School were built soon after 1850 (E7).

MOUNT STREETS UPPER and LOWER were gradually built up after about 1820. Nos. 58–62 Upper Mount Street are somewhat earlier. St Stephen's Church, see p. 294. Date-stone on Lower Mount Street, 1814 (F8 and F9).

NASSAU STREET, formerly St Patrick's Well Lane, widened 1834, renamed earlier (E7).

PEARSE STREET, formerly Great Brunswick street, made about 1810. The Antient (sic) Concert Rooms (now a cinema), built as the Dublin Oil Gas Station, 1824, J. Cooke, Architect. St Mark's Church, 1729 (E8).

PEMBROKE STREETS UPPER AND LOWER, about 1820 (F7 and F8).

PETER PLACE, about 1800 (G7).

SIR JOHN ROGERSON'S QUAY, see p. 90. Tropical Fruit Co's building contains the keystones of Old Carlisle Bridge. Hibernian Marine School (now an ice-factory) see pp. 197, 218 (D9).

ST STEPHEN'S GREEN, laid out 1663, see pp. 19 sqq. It was farmed out to the Earl of Meath in 1702, but reverted to the City on his death in 1709, and was administered as a municipal park. At this time it was surrounded by a ditch and formally planted. By an Act of 1814 it was vested in Commissioners, from whom it was bought in 1877 by Sir Arthur Edward Guinness, Lord Ardilaun, who in 1880 had it ' landscaped ' with winding paths, lakes and a cascade, and presented it to the nation, on whose behalf it is administered by the Board of Works. There is a statue of Lord Ardilaun on the West side.

North side: No. 8, the United Services Club, c. 1754, and No. 9, the Stephen's Green Club, c. 1756. Both refronted, but both possess good eighteenth-century plasterwork, that in No. 9 being the earlier. No. 9 altered in 1844 by Michael Mullins, architect. Nos. 14 and 15 are very large, with similar door-ways to Nos. 16 and 17, which are larger still. All four date from the 1770s. No. 16, at first a La Touche house, was long the Archbishop's Palace. No 17, originally Miltown House (Leeson) has been the University Club since 1850. No. 18 is of stucco, in regency style, with pilasters and garlands, c. 1830. No. 21 has a good doorway of c. 1770. No. 22, of similar period, is the Clubhouse of the Friendly Brothers of St Patrick. Nos. 32, 33 and 34 are a triplet of 1770, containing much interesting plaster (No. 32 has been raised by two stories). No. 35, 1748.

East side: No. 41, by Benjamin Rudd, has a good door of 1745 (window-cases much altered). No. 42 has a late fanlight over an early door. No. 44 has an early door, very provincial in style. Nos. 46–50 are good mid-eighteenth-century houses. No. 47 is by John Ensor, 1769. The present Office of Public Works, an agreeable building, much remodelled, was the Museum of Irish Industry and later the Royal College of Science. Nos. 52 and 53 are a pair,

52 (now the Representative Church Body of the Church of Ireland) was a La Touche house, 53 is now the Loreto School. St Vincent's Hospital, founded 1834, embodies interesting plasterwork of 1760. No. 56 was Lord Meath's house.

South side: Nos. 74 (early doorway) and 77 (ironwork and moulded coping as elsewhere in the Green) are worth notice. Nos. 80–1, Iveagh House, now the Department of External Affairs, remodelled and partly built for the Guinness family by Young of London, 1863 onwards, has some Georgian work and a great deal of *le style Rothschild*. Nos. 78–9 were the guest-wing. See p. 130. Nos. 82, 83 and 84 are early houses, partly remodelled in late eighteenth century. No. 82 was the home of Francis Higgins, the notorious secret service agent and underworld boss, and now houses the Irish Folklore Commission. The Aula Maxima of University College, 1878. For Clanwilliam House and No. 86, see pages 130, 221–3. For the University Church, see p. 294. Nos. 87 and 88 are about 1730, with string courses and good doorways. The masking of the gable in No. 87 is not original. The Wesleyan Centenary Church, 1843, by Isaac Farrell, has a classical portico. Nos. 97–8 are gable-fronts, not originally masked, No. 97 with lunette. No. 101, of *c.* 1790. has interesting doorway.

West side: Nos. 119–20 are a formally composed pair, of 1761, probably based on a Cassels design. A blind venetian window unites four bays as at Bellamont Forest, Co. Cavan. Main cornice below attic story. also as at Bellamont, unusual in Dublin. First floor sills have probably been lowered. For the College of Surgeons (E. Parke, 1806, and W. Murray, 1827) see p. 279. Interiors by both men survive (F7).

TOWNSEND STREET. St Margaret's Hospital, 1753 and 1792. See p. 168.

TRINITY COLLEGE, see pp. 180 *sqq.* The Library (Burgh, 1712–32, staircase by Cassels, 1750). The 'Rubrics' (*c.* 1720, much mutilated 1894). The Printing-House (Cassels, 1734. unusually charming). The Dining-Hall (1759–61, possibly following Cassels's design of 1745). The West Front and Parliament Square (Keene and Sanderson, 1752 onwards, Hugh Darley supervising). The Provost's House (John Smyth, after Lord Burlington, 1760). The Chapel and Examination Hall, (Sir William Chambers, Graham Myers, plaster by Michael Stapleton, *c.* 1779–90). The elevations, especially of the return sides, are excellent, and the Chapel interior creditable enough, but the Examination Hall is very ungainly. 'Botany Bay', grimly institutional building of *c.* 1810. Magnetic Observatory, by Frederick Darley, 1837, very good. New Square (1838–44) chilly late-classic. The Campanile, by Sir Charles Lanyon, 1852. The Museum Building (Woodward and Deane, 1857). Other later buildings (E7).

WESTLAND ROW: The Royal Irish Academy of Music was the town house of Lord Conyngham. Oscar Wilde was born in No. 21 (E8).

WESTMORLAND STREET, made by Wide Streets Commissioners about 1800, uniform with D'Olier Street. Still partly original (D7 and E7).

WEXFORD STREET, No. 12, about 1800, has attractive 'gothick' venetian windows (F6).

WILLIAM STREET, SOUTH. A narrow street of middling mid-eighteenth-century houses. For Powerscourt House (now Ferrier, Pollock & Co.) see pp. 225–6. The City Assembly House, 1765 -71 (E7).

YORK STREET, a narrowish street of large mid-eighteenth-century houses, now mostly decayed. Part of the South side is at present (1949) under conversion as working-class flats. No. 37 was the house of C. R. Maturin, and Edward Henry Carson, architect of St Peter's Church and father of Lord Carson, lived at No. 14 (F6 and F7).

REGION III

North-West City, bounded by the River, Capel Street and Dorset Street, and the North Circular Road.

ARBOUR HILL has some grim specimens of mid-nineteenth century barrack architecture (D4).

ARRAN QUAY, laid out *c.* 1680. For St Paul's Church, by Patrick Byrne, 1835–7, see pp. 292–3. Edmund Burke was born at No. 12 in 1728 (demolished 1950). Behind it is the eighteenth-century Arran Quay (Catholic) Chapel, now disused (D5).

BARRACKS, BENBURB STREET (formerly Barrack Street). Formerly the Royal Barracks, now Collins Barracks. By Thomas Burgh, 1704, much enlarged (D5).

BLACK CHURCH, see St Mary's Chapel-of-Ease.

BLACKHALL STREET, large houses of *c.* 1775, now rather decayed (D5).

BLUECOAT SCHOOL (properly King's Hospital), see pp. 218 *sqq.* (D5).

BROADSTONE RAILWAY STATION, see pp. 300–1 (C5).

BROWN STREET, off North King Street, contains the remains of the Bridewell, opened in 1801 'for the correction of young criminals' (D5).

BRUNSWICK VILLA, off North Brunswick Street, is a curious little model village with a green, long since engulfed by the city (D5).

ECCLES STREET: southern end *c.* 1750 (No. 18–19 was Tyrawley House), northern end about 1820. No. 59 was the house of Cardinal Cullen, No. 63 of Sir Boyle Roche, No. 64 of Francis Johnston and later of Isaac Butt. No. 64 and other houses by Francis Johnston, see p. 282. Mater Misericordiae Hospital, 1860 onwards, on the site where the elliptical Circus was long intended (B6).

FOSTER AQUEDUCT (Broadstone), by 'Mr Millar', *c.* 1800, later widened (C6).

FOUR COURTS, see pp. 243 *sqq.*, and Appendix II, p. 333 (D5 and D6).

GRANGEGORMAN MENTAL HOSPITAL. The main building by Francis Johnston. 1812, originally the Richmond General Penitentiary. 'The general appearance of this façade is very imposing, and calculated to produce in the mind of the approaching criminal, an impression of hopeless incarceration, and compel him at once to resign every idea of liberty, unless deserved by a reformation of manners.' (G. N. Wright, 1825) (C5).

GREEN STREET COURTHOUSE, by R. Johnston, 1792–7 (D6).

HENDRICK STREET still has half a dozen gable-fronts of *c.* 1710–40, some with good doorways. Three were demolished in 1949 (D5).

HENRIETTA STREET, see pp. 102–3. The King's Inns Library, by Frederick Darley, 1827 (C6).

KING'S HOSPITAL (Bluecoat School) see pp. 218 *sqq.* (D5).

KING'S INNS, see pp. 256–7. The statue facing the west front, in the park, stood originally in the centre of the Great Hall of the Four Courts, bearing aloft a gas-jet (C6).

MONTPELIER HILL has some varied and interesting houses of the eighteenth century (D3 and D4).

MOUNTJOY JAIL, *c.* 1850. Impressive (B6).

PRUSSIA STREET, called after Frederick the Great, has some oldish small houses, and the City Arms Hotel, No. 54, a large georgian house which in the mid-nineteenth century was the town house of the Jameson family, the whiskey-distillers. Nearly opposite are two early eighteenth-century houses (C4).

ST MARY'S CHAPEL-OF-EASE (C. of I.) (The Black Church), see p. 295 (C6).

ST MICHAN'S CHURCH, CHURCH STREET (C. of I.): see pp. 10 and 40–1 (D5).

ST MICHAN'S CATHOLIC CHURCH, Halston Street and Anne Street. By O'Brien and Gorman, 1811–14. Halston Street front by G. C. Ashlin, 1893 (D6).

ST PAUL'S CHURCH, North King Street, (C. of I.), 1821–4, replacing the church of 1702 in which George Berkeley was consecrated Bishop of Cloyne in 1734. A wide gothic church, formerly galleried on three sides, tower over sanctuary. The Trevor vault in the churchyard is one of the more likely of many possible burial-places of Robert Emmet (D5).

ST PAUL'S, Arran Quay (Cath.), see pp. 292–3 (D5).

SMITHFIELD AND HAYMARKET, both of seventeenth-century layout, contain a few eighteenth-century houses (D5).

STONEYBATTER (the stony *bothar* or road) is an ancient thoroughfare (D5).

REGION IV

South-West City, bounded by the River, Aungier and Camden Streets, the Grand Canal and the Islandbridge section of the South Circular Road.

ARDEE STREET has one good house of *c.* 1780 (F5).

BACK LANE contains the Tailors' Hall, for which see pp. 77 *sqq.* (E5 and E6).

BISHOP STREET has many middle-sized eighteenth-century houses, and the Moravian Church, of 1753. The houses in the courtyard to the south of the street are very English in style, and very unusual for Dublin (F6).

BRAITHWAITE STREET contains a few very dilapidated weavers' houses (E5 and F5).

BRIDE STREET; the East side still has a few old houses, but most of this street and Kevin and Patrick Streets have been rebuilt by the Iveagh Housing Trust since 1900 (E6 and F6).

BRIDGE STREET still contains a few old houses, especially the Brazen Head Hotel (E5).

BRIDGEFOOT STREET, leading to Queen's Bridge. The west side still contains a number of old houses (E5).

CAMDEN STREET, (formerly Kevin's Port). A fine wide street containing Pleasants' Asylum, *c.* 1785 (see also Stove Tenter House), with plaque (1818). No. 70, McDonnell's grocers' shop, is a particularly good shop-front (F6 and G6).

CASTLE, THE: see pp. 164, 167. Upper Castle Yard, mostly before 1753, probably by John Ensor and Joseph Jarratt. The statues on the gates by Van Nost. The State Apartments include St Patrick's Hall, decorated by Vincent Waldré, *c.* 1788, the Throne Room (formerly the Dinleaxe Hall) redecorated *c.* 1820, and the old Presence Chamber (more recently the Drawing Room) damaged in a recent fire. The Bermingham Tower was rebuilt in 1777, and a small polygonal tower in the centre of the south front occupies the site of an old tower and contains a gothic mirror-room, probably by Francis Johnston. The Bedford Tower, c. 1763, perhaps by Thomas Ivory. The elevation of the State Apartments to south, overlooking 'The Pound', is mid-eighteenth-century work of some merit. The buildings in Lower Castle Yard are mostly early nineteenth century, the Chapel Royal (see p. 282) and the remodelling of the Record Tower by Francis Johnston, 1807–14 (E6).

CASTLE STEPS, terroristic architecture of about 1810. See Pl. XLII (E6).

CASTLE STREET contains the entrance to St Werburgh's Church (through Bristol Buildings), and the remains of the ground storey of La Touche's Bank, before 1735. The Municipal Buildings (formerly Newcomen's Bank) by Thomas Ivory, 1781, duplicated to northwards and porch added to Cork Hill, 1856–8 (E6). Good painted ceiling in elliptical room on first floor.

CHAMBER STREET (rectius Chambré) still has a good many weavers' houses, now very dilapidated (F5).

CITY HALL (formerly Royal Exchange) by Thomas Cooley, see pp. 195–7. The interior altered by Hugh Byrne, City Architect and son of Patrick Byrne, in about 1852 (E6).

CLANBRASSIL STREET, the centre of the modern Jewish quarter, still has a few old houses (F5 and G5).

COOMBE, THE, retains few evidences of antiquity except sinuous narrowness and the Weavers' Hall (see p. 164) now a factory. St Luke's Church (see p. 112) has pleasant approaches. No. 124 has some fanciful woodwork of indeterminate period (F5).

CORK HILL, so called from the Earl of Cork's house which stood here in the sixteenth century, on the site of the City Hall. For the Municipal Buildings, see Castle Street (E6).

CORK STREET was formerly the heart of the weaving quarter, but little evidence of this now remains. The Fever Hospital dates from 1802, much enlarged (F4 and F5).

CROMWELL'S QUARTERS has no connexion with the Lord Protector (E3).

DOLPHIN'S BARN still has a few old houses (G4).

EUSTACE STREET is late seventeenth century in origin. For the Presbyterian Meeting-House, probably about 1717, and now a printing-works, see p. 115. (E6).

FISHAMBLE STREET still shows the entrance to the Music-Hall in which the Messiah was first performed in 1743. It is now an ironworks (E6).

GRAND CANAL HARBOUR (Echlin Street) is a fine commercial layout of c. 1780, still in use and little changed. Close by is the now disused City Basin, a reservoir which was also a fashionable promenade (E4).

GUINNESS'S BREWERY contains some agreeable late eighteenth and early nineteenth-century building, notably the main gate and the houses on either side of it. The present Visitors' Entrance was originally the Catholic Church of St James. The gateway further west on the same side of the street was that of a Military Infirmary in the eighteenth century (E4).

IRWIN STREET, of early eighteenth-century houses, has now mostly fallen down (E3).

JAMES'S STREET, see Guinness's Brewery and St James's Church. See also St Patrick's Hospital (E4).

KEVIN STREET still contains a few old houses of interest. The Guards' Barracks, formerly St Sepulchre's Palace, has magnificent gate-piers, perhaps late seventeenth century, a seventeenth-century internal doorcase, and a sixteenth-century external window, as well as some mediæval remains (F6).

KILMAINHAM, for the Royal Hospital, see pp. 58 *sqq*. The small garden-house is probably contemporary, the Deputy Adjutant-General's house (at the east end of the terrace) probably about 1700. The Adjutant-General's Office by Francis Johnston, *c*. 1808. For west gate, see p. 285. Kilmainham Gaol, *c*. 1800, architect unknown, later enlarged (about 1848). The sculptor of the chained serpents in the tympanum is unknown. The building, in which Parnell was imprisoned and fourteen of the 1916 leaders shot, is disused and derelict. The Courthouse is reputedly by G. Papworth (E2 and E3).

KINGSBRIDGE STATION, see p. 300 (D4).

LONGFORD STREET has the last unaltered curvilinear gabled houses in Dublin. See Fig. 3, p. 87 (E6).

MALPAS STREET has an old pedimented house (F6).

MARROWBONE LANE still has a small group of triangular-gabled houses on its south side (E4 and F4).

MARSHALSEA, the Four Courts, in Marshalsea Lane off Thomas Street, is an eighteenth-century debtors' prison now occupied as tenements, and has some architectural features (E5).

MARSH'S LIBRARY, Guinness Street, by Sir William Robinson, *c*. 1707. See pp. 66–7. It was refronted in the Guinness restoration of St Patrick's Cathedral, 1863–9 (F6).

MERCHANT'S QUAY, for the Franciscan Church, see p. 292 (E5).

MILL STREET contains a fine house of *c*. 1700, made hideous by modern alterations (F5).

MOIRA HOUSE, Usher's Island (now the Mendicity Institution). Built in 1752 for the first Earl of Moira, but gutted and deprived of its top storey in 1826, to fit it for its present purpose (D5).

MOUNT BROWN has one handsome early eighteenth-century house, recently reconditioned (E3).

NEWMARKET, a large open space created at the end of the seventeenth century, has no longer any architectural character (F5).

NICHOLAS STREET has the ground-floor façade of St Nicholas Within, 1797 (E6).

PORTOBELLO has the former Grand Canal Hotel, *c*. 1810. The Portobello Gardens, on the site of the present Victoria Street, were opened in 1839 and succeeded the Coburg Gardens in popular favour. They disappeared about 1865 (G6).

ST AUDOEN's (C. of I.) Church. The tower restored by H. A. Baker, 1824, has now lost its cast-iron pinnacles. For St Audoen's (Cath.) Church, see pp. 292–3. The portico, added in 1898, is greatly inferior to Byrne's work (E5).

ST CATHERINE's (C. of I.) Church, see p. 179 (E5).

ST JAMES's (C. of I.) Church, by J.Welland, 1861. Spire removed, 1949 (E4).

ST KEVIN's HOSPITAL (successively the City Workhouse, the Foundling Hospital, and the South Dublin Union) Great Hall, 1703, cupola and wings and Catholic Chapel by Francis Johnston, *c*. 1800 (E3).

ST KEVIN's CHURCH (Old) Camden Row. A quasi-country church of *c*. 1780, now roofless (F6).

ST LUKE's (C. of I.) Church, The Coombe, 1707 (F5).

ST MICHAEL'S HILL is a crescent of houses with Wyatt windows, of *c.* 1800. See Pl. I (E6).

ST NICHOLAS OF MYRA, Francis Street, see pp. 292–3. The portico and tower were added in 1860, presumably by Byrne who was still alive (E5).

ST PATRICK'S DEANERY, 1781, has a fine staircase-hall and good rooms. The cellars may date from Swift's Deanery, and a few Swift relics are kept in the house (F6).

ST PATRICK'S HOSPITAL (Swift's), James's Street. By George Semple, 1749–1757, enlarged by Thomas Cooley, 1778, and others. The Hospital has a good collection of Swiftiana (E3 and E4).

ST SEPULCHRE'S PALACE, see Kevin Street.

ST WERBURGH'S CHURCH, see pp. 96 and 178–9 (E6).

SHIP STREET is a corruption from Sheep Street, and has a fine gate into the Castle (E6).

SOUTH DUBLIN UNION, see St Kevin's Hospital.

STEEVENS'S HOSPITAL, see pp. 96–8 (E4).

STOVE TENTER HOUSE, Weaver Square, was built by Thomas Pleasants (see also Camden Street) in 1815, to enable the weavers to dry their materials indoors, and thus avoid hardship. It is now part of a school (F5).

SWIFT'S HOSPITAL, see St Patrick's Hospital.

TAILORS' HALL, see pp. 77 *sqq.* (E6).

THOMAS STREET: Halpin's (No. 20) is a particularly fine early-nineteenth-century shop-front. See also St Catherine's Church (E5).

USHER'S ISLAND, has some old houses, especially Moira House, which see. The large stucco building (Ganly's) was originally Home's Hotel, *c.* 1820, and had a colonnade over the pavement, now represented only by its respond pilasters (D5).

WEAVER SQUARE has now nearly lost the architectural character which still survives in Chamber Street adjoining (F5).

WINETAVERN STREET: the old houses at the south-east end were demolished late in 1949 (E6).

REGION V

The Phœnix Park.

ARUS AN UACHTARAIN (the President's official residence, formerly the Viceregal Lodge). Central portion, built 1750 for the Rt. Hon. Nathaniel Clements, now masked by later work, but some ceilings etc. survive, notably the 'Aesop' ceiling. South portico, wings and stucco refronting by Francis Johnston, 1816. The formal garden is very fine indeed (B1).

ARMY G.H.Q. (formerly the Military Infirmary). Designed by Gandon, but carried out by W. Gibson, 1787 onwards. The cupola by Gibson. The centre portion of the façade has suffered a modern remodelling (D3).

CHIEF SECRETARY'S OFFICE, see U.S. Embassy.

CIVIC GUARD DEPOT, a fine severe building of *c.* 1845 (C3).

HIBERNIAN MILITARY SCHOOL (now St Mary's Chest Hospital). Main building 1766, enlarged by Francis Johnston, 1808–13. The Chapel (C. of I.) by Thomas Cooley, 1771, chancel added later: one of the least-known and most charming of Dublin buildings.

LODGES: several of these are by Decimus Burton.

MAGAZINE FORT, apparently the building of 1734, frequently adapted (D1). Celebrated in a famous quatrain by Swift:

> Lo, here's a proof of Irish sense,
> Here Irish wit is seen.
> Where nothing's left that's worth defence
> They build a magazine.

MILITARY INFIRMARY, see Army G.H.Q.

MOUNTJOY BARRACKS, now Ordnance Survey Office. Kernel built by Luke Gardiner I as his private lodge.

PAPAL NUNCIATURE, formerly the Under-Secretary's Office.

ST MARY'S CHEST HOSPITAL, see Hibernian Military School.

U.S. EMBASSY, formerly the Chief Secretary's Lodge, enlarged for Sir John Blacquiere, c. 1775.

VICEREGAL LODGE, see Arus an Uachtarain.

WELLINGTON TESTIMONIAL, by Sir Robert Smirke, 1817 onwards. See p. 288 (D2).

ZOO, opened 1830. The *cottage-ornée* gate-lodge is contemporary (C2).

SELECT OBJECTS IN THE SUBURBS

NORTH SUBURBS*

CABRA: The Dominican Nunnery has inhabited Much Cabra House, the eighteenth-century red-brick seat of the Arthur family, since 1819.

DRUMCONDRA: the (C. of I.) Church, an unpretentious building of 1743, contains the grandiose tomb of Marmaduke Coghill (d. 1738) by Scheemakers, and in the churchyard the grave of Gandon and Francis Grose. All Hallows College occupies Drumcondra House, built by Coghill in about 1720, with two contrasting fronts. The pilastered feature is probably later. In the ground is a 'Temple'. St Patrick's Training College occupies Belvedere House, a red brick house, also of the Coghills. Clonturk House has, in the garden, part of the balustrade of Old Carlisle Bridge.

GLASNEVIN: the village contains a number of small early-eighteenth-century houses. The (C. of I.) Church, 1707, adjoins the demesne of Delville (see p. 119). The Botanic Gardens, 1795 onwards. Prospect Cemetery, founded in 1832 by O'Connell, the Père Lachaise of Dublin, containing monuments of many national worthies. The O'Connell Tower, an outsize version of the Irish Round Tower theme, from a design supplied by Petrie in 1851, but much modified in the execution.

MARINO: The Casino, by Sir William Chambers, c. 1762 onwards, for the first Earl of Charlemont. Now a National Monument.

* None of the objects listed under 'North Suburbs' are on the map, nor is Sandymount.

SOUTH SUBURBS

HAROLD'S CROSS: a village with some pleasant old houses, now embedded in Dublin. Mount Jerome Cemetery: the office is an eighteenth-century house. Parnell Place has good small eighteenth-century houses (H5).

PEMBROKE: Mespil House, Mespil Road, built 1751, has superb plaster ceilings. Pembroke Road, Wellington Road, Morehampton Road, Lansdowne Road and others are excellently planned and built streets of 1830–60 (G8 and G9).

RANELAGH: Mount Pleasant Square, c. 1830–40. Belgrave Square, East side, is finely-articulated building of a little later (H7).

RATHMINES: Leinster Road, good Victorian-residential. Rathmines Road spoiled by building on front-gardens, but Rathgar Road still virtually intact. Rathmines (Cath.) Church, by Patrick Byrne, 1850, the dome modern, after a fire. Rathmines (C. of I.) Church, by John Semple, 1833. Leinster Square (really T-shaped) is well laid out, c. 1840 (H6).

SANDYMOUNT: contains a number of agreeable villas of the early nineteenth century.

ADDITIONAL NOTES ON THE RESTORATION OF THE FOUR COURTS AND THE CUSTOM HOUSE

I. *The Four Courts*

In the closing days of June, 1922, the Four Courts was held by Republican forces under Rory O'Connor, and bombarded by field artillery, fired by Free State forces on the Southern Quays. The garrison mined the building before evacuating it, and in the resulting explosions both the inner and outer domes were destroyed, the south-east and south-west wings, and the south-west portion of the arcaded screen, were badly ruined. The entire building was also burnt. Various shell-holes also pierced the outer walls, notably one immediately east of the main portico.

The restoration was completed in 1932. The east and west ranges were each shortened by some ten feet, the new front walls being almost flush with the arcaded screen. The panelled blocks in the centres of the blocking-courses of these wings were also omitted. The valley-roofs of the wings were replaced by single-span roofs which have an entirely different silhouette. No mention of these changes was made in the official report, which asserts that 'care was taken, by retaining the architectural character of the façades, to preserve an outstanding example of the work of a master architect. . . .'

The adjoining north ranges were re-planned internally to provide corridors to north instead of to south as in Gandon's design. This expedient, reasonable in itself, meant that the open arcades to the fore-courts were closed and turned into windows.

The centre block has suffered very little external alteration. But four out of the nine niches at first-floor level were opened and turned into windows. The report does not mention this. On the east and west walls a number of dummy windows, especially on the second floor, were made real. The drum of the dome also escaped modification, except that the prism-shaped buttresses to north-east and north-west were replaced by stepped buttresses of cement, which catch the eye in certain views. The capitals of the dome colonnade, which were fully worked on all sides, were each turned through 180 degrees. The lowest member of the entablature was apparently renewed in cement-concrete, and so were the stepped blocking-courses above the cornice. The outer dome, in ferro-concrete, is both a little narrower and a little higher than the original, and gives a subtly different impression.

The original planning of the central block was to a very large extent retained. The visible work in the Great Hall, up to and including the capitals, is almost entirely original: only a few damaged stones being renewed. The four entrances to the courts, however, which had originally each two pairs of whole columns, with (? later) timber partitions, have now only two single columns, each with a masonry wall behind. This change is on the whole an improvement. It is worth noting, however, that Gandon's other designs for courthouses, Waterford and Nottingham, seem to envisage courts with their backs wide open to the concourse hall, as the Four Courts would have been, and perhaps originally was, without the partitions. The part of the centre block north of the Great Hall has been completely re-planned, though the Supreme Court is approximately on the site of the original Rolls Court.

A piece of original detail which survived the siege but is not often noticed may be found in the two plaques over the north and south doors of the ante-hall immediately north of the main portico. All the external sculpture survived practically intact, save that the trophies of arms over the gates in the arcade screen were originally surmounted with crowns but are now, in deference to political changes, surmounted by balls.

The extreme west wall of the building appears to date from Cooley's Public Offices, as the window-cases are of a different character from all the rest.

The space between the inner and outer domes was originally intended as a library, and was at one time used for the storage of records. It is now not used at all. Gandon's sectional drawings show it surrounded by twenty-four pilasters. If these pilasters ever existed, they were not structural. Instead, a series of twelve vertical channels, worked in the stone, appear a few feet to the left of each of the windows, each with a stone corbel at the bottom, just above the floor, and each with iron bolts, some still bearing nuts, at intervals of five or six feet in the centre of the channel. Mr H. G. Leask, to whom I put the question, suggests that wall-posts, bolted in these channels, carried the thrust of the timber-and-copper dome as far down the wall as was practicable. He suggests that their position slightly to the left of each window was designed to carry the weight clear of the centres of the enormous flat-arches underneath, over the eight windows which pierce the inner dome. I am convinced that this explanation is correct. It is, of course, possible that these timbers were masked by plaster pilasters, but there is no evidence of this.

II. *The Custom House*

The Custom House, being at the time the headquarters of the Local Government Board and therefore a military objective, was burned by the Republican forces on the morning of May 25th, 1921. It continued to blaze merrily for five days, and even five months later cracks were still appearing as the building cooled down. At the height of the fire the temperature within was at least 1,850 degrees Fahrenheit. As the wind was blowing from the south-west, the greatest damage occurred on the north and east fronts, where Portland stone window-cases were split and calcined. 'Most of the original work above the cornice level' in the words of the official report, 'was either missing or dangerously defective'. The cornice in fact, Mr Leask tells me, was barely stable, owing to loss of tail-weight.

The timber-and-copper dome perished in the fire, exposing the intersecting diagonal arches carrying the tapered shaft on which stood the statue of Commerce. Later it was found that the entire drum and peristyle was insecure and had to be taken down. This included the statue which, a good deal the worse for wear but unconquered in spirit, was replaced on the top of the new structure.

The exterior of the building suffered very little alteration. The open arcades of the east and west fronts had long ago been closed: to re-open them would have been an extravagant concession to purism. But the eastern arcade of the south front, which had more recently and with inexcusable barbarity been closed, was re-opened. Immediately above these arcades were, until the fire, alternating niches and windows, three niches and four windows on each side. These, as in the Four Courts, were all opened as windows (the fire had in fact opened them); and as in that building, southern corridors were transferred to the north.

All the sculptures survived the fire except the four statues (two of them by Smyth) over the south portico. The remains of these may be seen in the two internal courtyards, where there is a permanent open-air exhibition of interesting debris, including capitals from the peristyle and the Long Room colonnade.

The new dome was built with a granite base (above general roof level), but the peristyle, etc., which had been in Portland stone, is now of Ardbraccan, which is gradually turning dark. Otherwise it is a faithful enough reproduction, except that the small square windows over the coupled columns at the angles, formerly blind, are now open.

The internal planning was greatly changed. Only the outer walls of the centre block, which measured over 130 ft. from east to west and contained the Long Room, 70 ft. by 66 ft., were retained. On part of the site of the Long Room a large light-well was created. The new Long Room occupies the east pavilion. The famous flying-arch staircase, behind the centre of the north front, vanished.

But the general disposition of halls and lobbies in the centres of both north and south fronts, survived with very little alteration. In particular the first-floor lobby immediately under the dome survived intact except for its decorative plaster dome, now renewed in plain plaster. In the centre of this lobby there was formerly an octagonal railed opening, so that the whole thing was visible immediately inside the main

335

entrance. The elimination of this feature was unnecessary and most unfortunate.

The east and west internal courts were cleared of the shacks which almost filled them, and excavated to basement level. At the same time the centre blocks were reduced one storey in height, but in 1939-40 they were increased by one storey, and are now the same height as originally, less the additional height of the Long Room roof on the main axis.

In the restoration, the Custom House lost all its chimneys, both those which were designed as formal elements and those which were not. It now has a single massive chimney-stack on the main axis, the casing of which is an old chimney-stack from Kildare Place, designed by Deane for the boiler-house of the National Museum–National Library complex.

In compiling these notes much information has been derived from the Annual Reports of the Commissioners of Public Works, 97th Report, for year 1928-9 (Custom House) and 100th Report, for year 1931-2 (Four Courts). The remaining information is from personal observation, photographs, documents and conversations.

SOME CHARACTERISTICS OF THE DUBLIN HOUSE

The commonest width of frontage in the best streets is about 28 to 30 ft. The depth of the main block may be anything up to 55 ft., roofed usually in two ranges, parallel to the street. The back walls are frequently curved outwards, for better lighting and internal effect. Return projections, which are almost universal, are often later additions. Five storeys including basement are almost invariable, the total height from ground to parapet being from 40 to 55 ft. Roofs are low-pitched and unobtrusive; visible dormers are rarely found, nor is the top of the party-wall made a visible feature as in London. Chimney-stacks are often reduced in bulk by a sloped step inwards half-way up their visible height. String-courses are unusual, and practically never found after 1740: a granite band at threshold level is, except for doorway and flat parapet, the only external stonework. Steps and dwarf-walls are granite. In some houses, especially in St Stephen's Green, the simple parapet is replaced by a slight cavetto cornice in granite, with blocking-course. Red brick laid in flemish bond predominates, though grey and yellow are also found in later streets. Semicircular relieving arches disappear about 1740, and granite coigns are occasionally found towards the end of the century, according to situation. The Dublin flat arch over a window-opening has a skewback more nearly vertical than is usual in London.

Wrought-iron open-work newels are frequent, flanking steps. In addition, vertical or elaborate bracket-shaped lamp standards are fairly common. Occasionally a single lamp-holder is carried on a semi-elliptical or ogival wrought-iron arch over the approach. The later fanlights have occasionally a hexagonal glass-sided lamp-box, inset in the middle.

The earliest doorways are tall and narrow, segmental-headed and bordered with a stone architrave with a bold keystone. These were soon followed by a round-headed type with blocked architrave, and, from about 1755, the pedimented and pillared type with the necking carried across to form the lintel. Fanlights of this period vary greatly in design, sometimes of lead with an inner protector of simpler and contrasting design, in wrought-iron. Fanlights of the 1775 vintage are semicircular, sometimes as much as twice the width of the door, which is flanked by semi-columns or pilasters, sometimes enclosing narrow side-lights, the whole embraced within an arched recess in the wall.

Balconies are a late feature, more commonly of cast than of wrought iron. Sometimes they are bowed outwards in a sinuous S-curve: in a few cases this curve is repeated in a continuous stone sill-cum-string-course on which the balconies rest (Gardiner Street). First-floor windows, only a little taller than those above and below them in the mid-century, become gradually taller and taller until in about 1800 they approach 'Queen Anne' proportions. The grandiose canopied balconies of Merrion Square North are of Victorian date.

Plans vary enormously. Entrances in three-bay houses are nearly always to one side, except in a few early examples in Molesworth Street. In the larger houses the entrance-halls are wide, usually stone-flagged, sometimes with a small corner-fireplace. The brass rail, at dado-level, inside the front door, nine inches or a foot out from the wall, is still the subject of much speculation. It certainly protects the wall from the greasy shoulders of loungers in the hall. It occurs in other Irish cities besides Dublin. There is often an elaborate fanlight between entrance-hall and staircase-hall. The main staircase usually stops at the second floor, a smaller staircase continuing at right-angles to the top floors. The larger houses have a service staircase also: in Henrietta Street the main staircases have mostly been taken out and sold, and the space used for additional tenement-rooms. In the later houses, *e.g.*, Fitzwilliam Square, front and back drawing-rooms are separated by folding doors, so that a large L-shaped apartment can be created. This feature has been inserted into many earlier houses. Door-saddles are universal, as throughout Ireland.

The construction of these houses was not always very robust. Hand-cock, in his *History of Tallaght*, tells the story of some of the houses in Harcourt Street, built by George Wildridge, that 'The walls of these houses were so thin, that . . . a gentleman sleeping in one of them was wakened by a hammering in the next house, and presently the point of a twelvepenny nail drove into his head through the wall'. I have been told myself in Harcourt Street that some of the internal walls were built of blocks of turf (peat).

Houses were often built in pairs or groups of three, always with a rough, but never with an exact, correspondence with neighbouring houses. End walls were sometimes left blank, as though by a convention not seen. But at other times the treatment of corner houses shows much resource: good examples are in Upper Pembroke Street, Ely Place, Grenville Street and—most striking of all—the corner of Parnell Square North and Granby Row.

From a bill of quantities in the possession of Mr H. G. Leask, it appears that the cost of building a medium-sized house in Merrion Row in 1795 was approximately £1,200, including internal joinery. This document is a treasury of obsolete and curiously-spelt building terms. The second Lord Cloncurry relates that his father bought

Mornington House (a very large house indeed) for £8,000 in 1791, and says it was sold in 1801 for £2,500. He thinks that at the time of writing (1848) it would barely fetch £500!

For further observations the reader is referred to 'Notes on XVIIIth Century Houses', by J. A. Geoghegan, in *Dublin Historical Record*, VII. 2. (1945).

APPENDIX IV

THE ARCHITECTURAL SUCCESSION

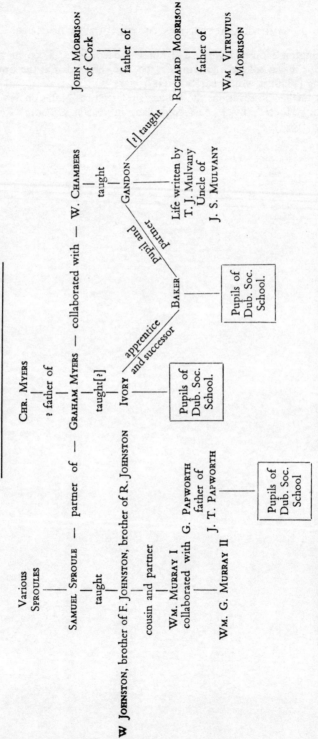

Note.—This simplified table necessarily leaves out much. If we knew more, for example, of the Cooley-Ivory relationship, and of the departmental history of the Barrack Board, the pattern could be amplified.

GRAPH OF DUBLIN POPULATION

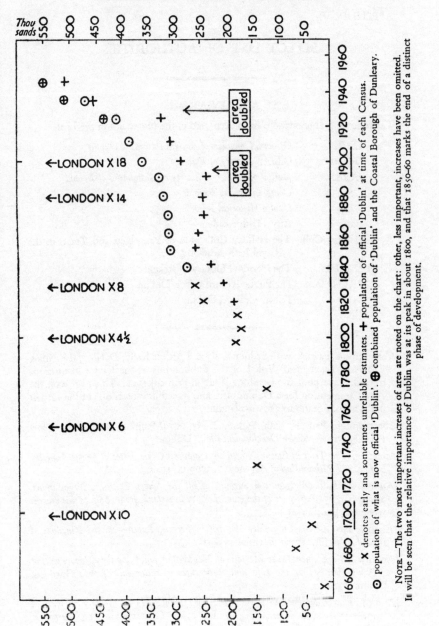

NOTE.—The two most important increases of area are noted on the chart: other, less important, increases have been omitted. If will be seen that the relative importance of Dublin was at its peak in about 1800, and that 1850-60 marks the end of a distinct phase of development.

X denotes early and sometimes unreliable estimates. + population of official 'Dublin' at time of each Census. ⊙ population of what is now official 'Dublin'. ⊕ combined population of 'Dublin' and the Coastal Borough of Dunleary.

APPENDIX VI

SELECT LIST OF AUTHORITIES

ABBREVIATIONS

The following abbreviations have been used in the Notes and in the List:

CARD	Gilbert, *Calendars of Ancient Records of Dublin*
Gilbert	Gilbert, *History of Dublin*
JRSAI	*Journal of the Royal Society of Antiquaries of Ireland*
GS	*Georgian Society Records*
DHR	*Dublin Historical Record*
RIA	Royal Irish Academy
Haliday Coll.	The Haliday Collection of Pamphlets and Tracts in the Royal Irish Academy
Nat. Lib.	The National Library of Ireland
PRO Dub.	The Public Record Office, Dublin
TCD	Trinity College, Dublin

Abercrombie, Patrick, with Sydney Kelly and Arthur Kelly, *Dublin of the Future, The New Town Plan.* Vol. I of the Publications of the Civics Institute of Ireland. Liverpool and London. [Dublin printed] 1922. This plan won the 1914 Competition for a Dublin plan, and its publication is one of the earliest in the history of modern town-planning.

Abercrombie, Patrick, with Sydney Kelly and Manning Robertson, *Town Planning Report, Sketch Development Plan.* Dublin. 1941.

Annesley, *The Trial in Ejectment between Campbell Craig, lessee of James Annesley Esq ... and Richard Earl of Anglesey ...* Dublin. 1744.

[Anon.] *A Full and Impartial Account of all the Secret Consults, Negotiations, Stratagems, and Intriegues of the Romish Party in Ireland, from 1660, to this present year 1689.* London. 1690.

[Anon.] *Four Letters Originally Written in French, Relating to the Kingdom of Ireland.* Dublin. 1739. Written 1734-5.

[Anon.] *A Supplement to the Memoirs of Mrs Woffington, being the Achievements of a Pickle-Herring; or the Life and Adventures of Butter-milk Jack.* Third ed. Dublin. 1760.

[Anon.] *Letters addressed to Parliament, and to the Public in General on Various Improvements in the Metropolis.* Dublin. 1787. Contains also the 'Letters of Publius'. Supposed by some to be by James Malton.

Anthologia Hibernica, or Monthly Collections of Science, Belles-lettres, and History Dublin. 1793-4.

Antiques. The Magazine Antiques. Vol. LVII, No. 3. March 1950. Philadelphia, U.S.A. Number devoted to Irish arts and crafts, mainly of the eighteenth century.

Ashe, F. A., ' Mountjoy Square ', in *DHR*, III, 4. [1942].

Ball, Francis Elrington, *A History of the County Dublin to the close of the XVIIIth Century.* 6 vols. Dublin. 1902-20.

—— [editor], *The Correspondence of Jonathan Swift.* 6 vols. London. 1910-14.

—— *The Judges in Ireland, 1221-1921.* 2 vols. London. 1926. See also Dineley, below.

Barrington, Sir Jonah, *Personal Sketches of his Own Times.* Vols. I & II, London. 1827. Vol III, *ibid.* 1832.

—— *Historic Anecdotes and Secret Memoirs of the Union.* 5 Parts. London. 1809-[15]. No more published. The complete work was finally republished as *Historic Memoirs of Ireland.* 2 vols. London. 1833, and as *The Rise and Fall of the Irish Nation.* Paris. 1833. It was re-issued in London in 1835, as *Historic Memoirs of Ireland,* and frequently reprinted in Dublin as *The Rise and Fall* etc. The London editions are illustrated with excellent portraits of the chief actors. See also Parliamentary *Accounts and Papers.* 1829 (5). xiii. 195., 1829 (293). iv. 1., 1830 (382). iv. 749.

Bell, Thomas, *The Origin and Progress of Gothic Architecture in Ireland.* Dublin. 1829. The last chapter deals with the Gothic Revival.

Berry, Henry F. [alias H. F. Twiss], *A History of the Royal Dublin Society.* London. 1915.

—— ' The Merchant Tailors' Guild', in *JRSAI,* XLVIII, 19. [1918]

Betjeman, John, ' Francis Johnston, Irish Architect', in *The Pavilion* [ed. M. Evans]. London. [1947] Lavishly illustrated and equipped with a chronological table of Johnston's works and life.

Bibliographical Society of Ireland, *Publications,* 1918-38.

Bodkin, M., S.J., ' Notes on the Irish Parliament in 1773 ', in *Procs. of RIA,* XLVIII, C, 4. [1942] See also Hunt,W.

Bolger, Bryan. The Papers of Bryan Bolger, Quantity Surveyor, in the *PRO Dub.* [Manuscript] See *DHR,* III, 1.

Bowen, B. P., ' John Rocque's Maps of Dublin ', in *DHR,* IX, 3. [1947]

Brewer, J. N., *The Beauties of Ireland.* 2 vols. London. 1825. Brewer derived much of his information from Francis Johnston.

Brocas, Samuel Frederick, *Topography of Ireland.* Dublin. 1820. A volume of coloured views. Only Dublin was covered before the series (of twelve prints) ceased.

Brooking, Charles, *A Map of the City and Suburbs of Dublin.* London. 1728. The first detailed map of Dublin, surrounded by small prints of the principal buildings then existing.

Burton, Rev. Nathanael, *The Royal Hospital, Kilmainham*. Dublin. 1843.

—— *Oxmantown and its Environs*. Dublin. 1845.

Bush, J., *Hibernia Curiosa. A Letter from a Gentleman in Dublin to his Friend at Dover*. Dublin. 1769.

Butler, Eleanor, ' The Georgian Squares of Dublin ', in *Country Life*, Oct. 25, 1946 and Nov. 1, 1946. Very informative and well illustrated.

—— ' An Introduction to Dublin Architecture ', in *RIBA Dublin Handbook*. London. [Dublin printed] 1947.

Butler, R. M., ' Dublin; Past and Present ', in *Dublin Civic Week Handbook* [ed. Bulmer Hobson]. Dublin. 1927.

—— ' Irish Architecture ', in *Saorstat Eireann Official Handbook* [ed. Bulmer Hobson]. Dublin. 1932.

—— ' The Dublin Custom House ', in *The Architect*, July 15 and Aug. 12, 1921.

—— 'Dublin: its Arts, Trade and Commerce ', in *Journal of the Royal Society of Arts*, May 19, 1933.

Caldwell, Andrew, with Frederick Trench and Sackville Hamilton] *Observations on the Appropriation of the Parliament House for the National Bank* [*i.e.* the Bank of Ireland]. Dublin. 1803.

Carte, Thomas, *An History of the Life of James Duke of Ormonde*. 2 vols. London. 1736, also 1 vol. of *Letters, ibid*. 1735. See also Historical MSS Commission.

Castle, Richard [*i.e.* Richard Cassels], *An Essay Towards Supplying the City o, Dublin with Water*. Dublin. 1736.

Chart, D. A. *The Story of Dublin*. London. 1907, revised éd. *ibid*. 1932. Arranged in two sections, the first historical, the second topographical. Well indexed and illustrated.

Childers, E. S. E., and Robert Stewart, *The Story of the Royal Hospital, Kilmainham*. Amplified and republished by Captain R. F. Nation. London. 1921. Scrappy but well illustrated.

Clonmell, John Scott, first Earl of, *Diary*. [No title-page, no place, no date. Privately printed.] Copy in TCD.

[Colley, Richard, later Wesley] *An Account of the Foundation of the Royal Hospital of King Charles II, &c. near Dublin*. Dublin. 1725.

Collins, James. *Life in Old Dublin*. Dublin. 1913. Chaotically arranged but has an index.

Cosgrave, Dillon, O. Carm., *North Dublin, City and Environs*. Dublin. 1909, second ed. *ibid*. [1909] a useful complement to Gilbert's City, and Ball's County, neither of which is complete as to the North side.

Cosgrave, E. MacDowel, and Leonard R. Strangways, *The Dictionary of Dublin*. Dublin. 1897. Reprinted with alterations [1907]. Alphabetically arranged, and illustrated. Very useful, though not always accurate.

—— ' A Contribution towards a Catalogue of Engravings of Dublin up to

1800 ', continued as ' A Contribution towards a Catalogue of Nineteenth-Century Engravings of Dublin ', in *JRSAI*, XXXV, Parts 2 and 4, XXXVI, Part 4 and XXXVII, Part 1. [1905-7] Very full and informative. Should be used together with Elmes, below.

Craig, Maurice James [editor and part author], *The Legacy of Swift, a Bi-Centenary Record of St Patrick's Hospital, Dublin*. Dublin. 1948. Illustrated. Contains excerpts from a 1749 specification for the building.

Cromwell, Thomas, *Excursions through Ireland*. 3 vols. London. 1820. Illustrated with beautiful engravings after George Petrie. Vol. I deals entirely with Dublin.

Crone, John S. *A Concise Dictionary of Irish Biography*. Dublin. 1928. An essential supplement to the British *DNB*, but suffers from a too narrow definition and a restricted field of interest. No person not actually born in Ireland is included, and representation of the arts, especially architecture, is weak and patchy.

Curran, Constantine P., *Nos. 85 & 86 St Stephen's Green*. Dublin. [1939] An 18-page pamphlet.

—— ' Dublin Plaster Work ', in *JRSAI*, LXX, Part 1. [1940] Authoritative and indispensable.

—— ' Michael Stapleton, Dublin Stuccodore ', in *Studies*, Sept., 1939.

—— ' Benjamin Woodward, Ruskin and the O'Sheas ', in *Studies*, June, 1940.

—— ' Patrick Byrne, Architect ', in *Studies*, June, 1944.

—— *The Rotunda Hospital, its Architects and Craftsmen*. Dublin. 1945. Definitive and well illustrated.

—— ' The Architecture of the Bank ', in *The Bank of Ireland*, by F. G. Hall. Dublin. [London printed] 1949. The definitive account of this great building. Lavishly illustrated.

—— ' Cooley, Gandon and the Four Courts ', in *JRSAI*, LXXIX, 20 *sqq.* [Centenary Volume, 1949] Illustrated by Gandon and Cooley drawings.

D'Alton, John, *The History of the County of Dublin*. Dublin. 1838.

Directories and Almanacks. The Almanacks, by various publishers, run from *c.* 1700 onwards; the Directories begin with *Wilson's Dublin Directory*, 1752, 1753 and 1755 onwards. After about 1760 the *Almanack* (Watson's) and the *Directory* (Wilson's) were frequently bound up with the Dublin-printed *English Registry* (Exshaw's), under the title *The Treble Almanack*, which ceased in 1837. *The Post-Office Directory* begins in 1832, lasting till 1851, and *Pettigrew & Oulton's* runs 1834-1850. *Thom's Directory*, still current, began in 1844. For further details, see paper by Joseph Dennan in *Pubs. of Bibl. Soc. of I.* Vol. I, No. 7, 1920. See also below under Shaw.

Delany, Mrs (Mary Granville), *Autobiography and Correspondence*, ed. by Lady Llanover. 6 vols. London. 1861-2.

Dineley or Dingley, Thomas, Journal of his visit to Ireland, 1680-1, MS in Nat. Lib. Extracts and reproductions of drawings, ed. by F. Elrington Ball in *JRSAI*, XLIII, Part 4. [1913]

Donnelly, Most Rev. Nicholas, Bishop of Canea, *Short Histories of Dublin Parishes*. Dublin, in parts. [190?–1917] Mainly concerned with the Catholic parish organisation.

Dublin Builder, The, 1859–66, continued from 1867 onwards as *The Irish Builder*, contains innumerable articles on buildings, mostly by Edward Evans. As well as these, which are retrospective or antiquarian, it carries full notices, often illustrated, of contemporary buildings.

Dublin Historical Record, The, 1939– [in progress]. Vol. X, No. 4. [1949] contains an index by contributors to vols. I–X. The papers vary greatly in merit. See also above, under Ashe and Bowen, and below, under Geoghegan, Henchy, Hughes (James L. J.), Kelly, Lovett, McCall, Meehan, Murray, Stephenson.

Dublin University Magazine, 1833–77. The number for June 1847 contains a long review of Gandon's Life by Samuel Ferguson.

Dublin Penny Journal, 1832–5.

Duhigg, Bartholomew Thomas, *History of the King's Inns*. Dublin. 1806.

Dunton, John, *The Dublin Scuffle*. London. 1699. Reprinted in *The Life & Errors of John Dunton*. London. 1818. See also MacLysaght, below.

Eachard, Laurence, *An Exact Description of Ireland*. London. 1691.

Elmes, Rosalind M., *Catalogue of Irish Topographical Prints and Original Drawings*, [in Nat. Lib.]. Dublin. 1943. Of very great value, especially when used with Cosgrave ,above.

Evans, Edward, many topographical and historical articles in *The Irish Builder*, in the period 1885 onwards.

Falkiner, Caesar Litton, *Studies in Irish History and Biography, mainly of the Eighteenth Century*. London. 1902. Deals mainly with political history.

———— *Illustrations of Irish History and Topography, mainly of the Seventeenth Century*. Of great value. The second half of the book consists of useful reprints of seventeenth-century sources. It contains also a useful map ' Dublin in the 17th Century ' by L. R. Strangways.

———— *Essays Relating to Ireland*. London. 1909. Valuable especially for the article on the first Duke of Ormonde.

Falkiner, Sir Frederick R., *The Foundation of the Hospital and Free School of King Charles II., Oxmantown, Dublin*. Dublin. 1906. Of wider scope than the title would suggest. Contains also useful maps etc.

Ferrar, John, *A View of Ancient and Modern Dublin*. Dublin. 1796. Contains more architectural information than the generality of such books, also some good plates.

Fitzpatrick, Samuel A. Ossory, *Dublin, a Historical and Topographical Account of the City*. London. 1907. Comparatively detailed and attractively illustrated with drawings, many of unusual subjects.

Fitzpatrick, William John, *Lady Morgan*. London. 1860.

———— *Ireland Before the Union*. Dublin. 1867. Frequently reprinted.

Fitzpatrick, William John, *The Sham Squire.* Dublin. 1866. Frequently reprinted.

—— *The Life of Charles Lever.* 2 vols. London. 1879. Reprinted 1901.

—— *Secret Service Under Pitt.* London. 1892. Fitzpatrick's books are specially valuable for the light they throw on the political underworld of Dublin in the last ten years of the eighteenth century.

[Gamble, J.] *Sketches of History, Politics and Manners, taken in Dublin and the North of Ireland, in the Autumn of* 1810. London. 1811.

Gandon, James, *The Life of James Gandon Esq... from materials collected and arranged by his son, James Gandon, Esq., prepared for publication by the late Thomas J. Mulvany.* Dublin. 1846. An inadequate but essential book. The MS materials from which it was compiled have vanished. The only illustration is a portrait frontispiece.

Geoghegan, Joseph A., 'Notes on XVIIIth Century Houses', in *DHR*, VII, 2. [1945]

Georgian Society, *The Georgian Society Records of Eighteenth-Century Domestic Architecture and Decoration in Dublin.* 5 vols. Dublin. 1909–13. Copiously illustrated, with architectural and historical articles by J. P. Mahaffy, E. MacDowel Cosgrave, Page L. Dickinson, T. U. Sadleir, H. G. Leask and others. The survey suffers from an unequal scale of treatment, and from poor quality in many of the reproductions. But as a whole it is a praiseworthy achievement, providentially timed. Hardly any public buildings are included.

Gilbert, Sir John, *A History of the City of Dublin.* 3 vols. Dublin. 1854–9. Topographically arranged. Covers little more than the area within the mediæval walls and a comparable area to the east. Though full of learning and generally reliable, it suppresses its authorities and is thus difficult to follow up.

—— [editor, followed by Lady Gilbert] *Calendar of Ancient Records of Dublin.* 19 vols. Dublin. 1889–1944. Transcripts of municipal transactions, charters and associated material. This important primary source is without any sort of index. Some of the volumes contain useful illustrations, *e.g.* the maps in vols. V and VII.

—— *The Parliament House, Dublin.* Dublin. 1896. An expansion of a chapter of the author's *History of Dublin.* Fully illustrated, especially with all five of Bernard Scalé's prints. Now superseded, as to the architectural part, by Curran (see above).

Grattan, Henry. *Memoirs of the Life and Times of the Rt. Hon. Henry Grattan,* by his son. 5 vols. London. 1839–46.

Haliday, Charles, *The Scandinavian Kingdom of Dublin.* Dublin. 1881. Conceived originally as a history of the Port of Dublin, this volume, published long after its author's death in 1866, is an important topographical authority and contains valuable maps. 'A leading Irish figure of the high noon of individualistic liberalism' (Joseph Hone's description), Charles Haliday was one of a most remarkable family. He was a Governor of the Bank of Ireland and also formed the famous Haliday Collection of pamphlets, now in the RIA.

Hall, F. G., *The Bank of Ireland, 1783-1946*. Dublin & Oxford. [London printed] 1949. Reprinted, without the contributions by C. P. Curran and Joseph Hone, 1950.

Harris, Walter, *The History and Antiquities of the City of Dublin*. Dublin & London. 1766. The first substantive history of Dublin, but unworthy of its position. Based on the collections of Sir James Ware. Illustrated.

Harrison, Wilmot, *Memorable Dublin Houses*. Dublin. 1890. Illustrated with thumbnail sketches.

Harvey, John, *Dublin, a Study in Environment*. London. 1949. Accurate and well illustrated. The first short book to treat seriously of Dublin architecture.

Haughton, Joseph P., ' The Social Geography of Dublin ', in *The Geographical Review* (USA), XXXIX, No. 2. [1949] A brief modern historio-geographical survey, illustrated and with excellent maps.

Henchy, Patrick, ' Nelson's Pillar ', in *DHR*, X, 2. [1948] Clarifies Johnston's part in the scheme.

—— ' Francis Johnston, Architect ', in *DHR*, XI, 1. [1950] Draws on unpublished Johnston MSS. Important.

Herbert, J. D., *Irish Varieties, for the Last Fifty Years . . . The First Series* [no more published]. London. 1836. The author was an architectural student in Dublin and later an actor.

Historical MSS Commission: *Ormonde MSS* contained in *HMC* 4th Report, App. 719–780; 6th Report, App. 719–780; 7th Report, App. 737–834; and in *Calendar of Ormonde MSS*. New Series, Vol. I, 1902; Vol. II, 1903; Vol. III, 1904; Vol. IV, 1906; Vol. V, 1908; Vol. VI, 1911; Vol. VII, 1912; Vol. VIII, 1920. *Charlemont MSS* contained in 12th Report, App. 10, 1891; and 13th Report, App. 8, 1892.

Hughes, James L. J., ' Dublin Castle in the XVIIth Century ', in *DHR*, II, 3. [1940]

Hughes, Rev. Samuel Carlyle, *The Church of St Werburgh*. Dublin. 1889.

—— *The Church of St John, Fishamble Street*. Dublin. 1889.

Hunt, William (editor), *The Irish Parliament 1775, from an Official and Contemporary Manuscript*. London and Dublin. 1907. A somewhat similar document to that edited by Bodkin, noted above.

Incumbered Estates Court. Printed *Rentals* of sales from 1850, now in PRO Dub., together with *Rental* of the Blesinton [*sic*] sales, 1846 and 1848.

Irish House of Commons, *Journals, 1613–1800*. Dublin, various dates. Reprinted with new index, 1796–1802.

Irish House of Lords, *Journals, 1634–1800*. 8 vols. Dublin. 1783–1800.

Joyce, James, *Ulysses*. Paris. 1922.

Joyce, Weston St John, *The Neighbourhood of Dublin*. Dublin. 1912. Topographically arranged. Frequently reprinted.

Kelly, Thomas, 'Papers of Bryan Bolger, 1792–1834', in *DHR*, III, 1. [1940]

Kirkpatrick, T. Percy C., with H. Jellett, *The Book of the Rotunda Hospital.* Dublin. 1913. Mainly a medical history.

—— *History of Dr Steevens' Hospital.* Dublin. 1920. Contains much source material.

Lancaster, Osbert, ' The Seventh City of Christendom ', in *The Cornhill Magazine.* No. 962. [May 1944] Impressions of a sapient visitor. Illustrated, in the author's best manner.

Leask, Harold G., *Dublin Castle, A Short Guide.* Dublin. n.d. Authoritative. Illustrated.

—— ' Dublin Custom House; The Riverine Sculptures ', in *JRSAI,* LXXV, 4. [1945] An illustrated account of Smyth's masterworks, with identifications. See also under Georgian Society.

Lewis, Samuel, *Topographical Dictionary of Ireland.* 2 vols. London. 1837.

Lewis, R., *The Dublin Guide.* Dublin. 1787.

Longfield Maps. Three volumes of maps made by the surveying firms of Brownrigg and Longfield. In National Library, Dublin.

Longford, Christine [Countess of], *A Biography of Dublin.* London. 1936. A masterpiece of selection and compression. By far the best short account of Dublin.

Lovett, Rt. Rev. E. Neville, ' Mr Lovett out of Iorland ', in *DHR*, III, 3. [1941]

Luckombe, Philip, *A Tour Through Ireland.* Dublin. 1780.

McCall, P. J., *In the Shadow of St Patrick's.* Dublin. 1894. Folklore of the Liberties. Contains a useful map of the area before the rebuilding by the Iveagh Trust.

—— ' In the Shadow of Christchurch ', in *DHR*, II, 1; 2; and 3. [1939–40]

McCready, Rev. C. T., *Dublin Street Names Dated and Explained.* Dublin. 1892. Contains also details of bridges, statues, etc.

McDowell, R. B., *Irish Public Opinion, 1750–1800.* London. 1944. An important modern analysis of political trends.

McGrath, Raymond, ' Dublin Panorama ', in *The Bell.* Vol. 2, No. 5. [Aug., 1941] An appreciation by a distinguished modern architect, illustrated by seven of the author's drawings.

—— Notes to the Plates in *RIBA Dublin Handbook.* London. 1947.

McGregor, John James, *New Picture of Dublin.* Dublin. 1821. Contains many illustrations and a map. One of many such books published in the period. See also G. N. Wright, below.

MacLysaght, Edward, *Irish Life in the Seventeenth Century.* Dublin. 1939. Contains a long unpublished MS by John Dunton (see above). The chapter on town life deals largely with Dublin. New (enlarged) edition. 1950.

MacManus, M. J., *Irish Cavalcade, 1550–1850.* London and Dublin. 1939. An anthology of original sources, some very rare and curious.

Madden, Richard Robert, *History of Irish Periodical Literature*. 2 vols. London. 1867.

Malton, James, *A Picturesque and Descriptive View of the City of Dublin*. London. 1792–99. 25 plates. Deservedly celebrated as the essence of Dublin at the height of her splendour.

Maxwell, Constantia, *Dublin under the Georges*. London. 1936. 3rd. ed. Dublin. 1946. The standard work.

―――― *A History of Trinity College, Dublin, 1591-1892*. Dublin. 1946.

Meehan, Patrick, with Francis O'Kelley, ' The Assembly House, South William Street ', in *DHR*, I, 1. [1939].

Moorhead, Thomas Gillman, *A Short History of Sir Patrick Dun's Hospital*. Dublin. 1942.

Morgan, Francis, *Rental of the Estates of the [Corporation] of Dublin*. Dublin. 1867. Revised ed. by Edmund W. Eyre. Dublin. 1884. Contains a useful map.

Murray, Kevin, ' Dublin's First Railway ', in *DHR*, I, 1 and 2. [1939]

―――― *The Great Northern Railway*. Dublin. 1944.

Office of Public Works, Ireland, *Annual Reports*. Dublin. 1832. [in progress]

O'Lochlainn, Colm [editor], *Irish Street Ballads*. Dublin. 1939. Revised ed. 1946. Mainly eighteenth and nineteenth century.

O'Rourke, Horace T., *The Dublin Civic Survey*. Liverpool. [Dublin printed] 1925. A sequel to Abercrombie, 1922.

Pakenham-Walsh, W. P. ' Lieutenant-Colonel Thomas Burgh ', in *Royal Engineers' Journal*, Aug.-Sep., 1907.

Pasquin, Anthony [i.e. John Williams], *An Authentic History of the Professors o, Painting, Sculpture and Architecture who have practised in Ireland*. Dublin. 1796. A disappointing work.

Pembroke [formerly Fitzwilliam] Estate. Original leases and maps in the Pembroke Estate Office, Wilton Terrace, Dublin.

Peter, Ada, *Sketches of Old Dublin*. Dublin. 1907. Well illustrated.

Petrie, George, *The Life of George Petrie*, by William Stokes. London. 1868.

Petty, Sir William, *The Political Anatomy of Ireland, 1672*. London. 1691. Reprinted in *Ireland, Tracts and Treatises*. Vol. II, Dublin. 1861.

Phillips, Charles, *Curran and his Contemporaries*. London. 1818. Frequently reprinted.

Place, Francis. Drawings of Dublin Buildings in 1698–9, illustrating ' Francis Place in Dublin ', by John Maher, in *JRSAI*, LXII, Part 1. [1932]

Pool, Robert, and John Cash, *Views of the most Remarkable Public Buildings, Monuments and other Edifices in the City of Dublin*. Dublin. 1780. The first serious architectural survey of the city.

Richardson, Albert Edward, *Monumental Classic Architecture in Great Britain and Ireland*. London. 1914. Still the fullest treatment of the more important public buildings of Dublin.

[Robertson, Manning] *Cautionary Guide to Dublin, with 64 Illustrations*. Dublin. 1933. A witty and trenchant assault on commercial philistinism. Some of its criticisms were later acted upon. See also Abercrombie's *Town Planning Report*, 1941, above.

Rocque, John, *An Exact Survey of the City and Suburbs of Dublin*. Dublin. 1756. Frequently reprinted with additions. A very detailed and valuable map, in four sheets.

Rotunda Hospital, *A List of the Proprietors of Licenses on Private Sedan Chairs*. Dublin. [1787] Illustrated with architectural plans etc. A valuable source for both social and architectural history. The Hospital profited by the tax on private chairs.

Royal Archaeological Institute of Gt. Britain and Ireland, *Descriptive Programme of the Summer Meeting in Dublin 1931*. [1931] Reprinted in *The Archaeological Iournal*. Vol. LXXXVIII. Contains useful maps and plans.

Sadleir, Thomas Ulick, ' Richard Castle ' [=Cassels], Architect ', in *JRSAI*, XLI, Part III. [1911]

―――― ' Sir Edward Lovett Pearce ', in *Journal of the Kildare Archaeological Society*, X, No. 5. [1927] Illustrated. See also under Georgian Society.

Semple, George, *A Treatise on the Art of Building in Water*. Dublin. 1776. Reprinted in 1780 as *Hibernia's Free Trade*.

Shaw, Henry, *New City Pictorial Directory*. Dublin. 1850. Appeared only once. It contains elevations of many of the principal streets.

Statutes, *The Statutes at Large, 1310–1800*. Dublin, various dates.

Stephenson, P. J., ' Sean McDermott [= Gloucester] Street ', in *DHR*, X, 3 and 4. [1948–9]

Strickland, W. G., *Dictionary of Irish Artists*. 2 vols. Dublin. 1913. Does not deal with architects as such.

Sullivan, Sir Edward, *Decorative Bookbinding in Ireland*. London. Ye Sette of Odde Volumes. *Opusculum*. LXVII. 1914. Illustrated.

―――― illustrated articles on ' Irish Bookbinding ' in *The Studio*. Vol. 36 [October, 1905], and in *Country Life*, Sept. 5th, 1908.

Tone, Theobald Wolfe, *The Life of Theobald Wolfe Tone &c. written by himself and continued by his son &c.* 2 vols. Washington 1826. Reprinted London, 1827.

Twiss, Richard, *A Tour in Ireland in 1775*. Dublin. 1776.

Wakeman, W. F., *Old Dublin*. First and second series. Reprinted from the *Evening Telegraph*. Dublin. [1887]

Walsh, John Edward, *Ireland Sixty Years Ago*. Dublin. 1847. Reprinted in 1877 as *Ireland Ninety Years Ago*, and in 1911 [ed. Dillon Cosgrave] as *Ireland One Hundred and Twenty Years Ago*.

Warburton, John, and Rev. James Whitelaw and Rev. Robert Walsh, *History of the City of Dublin*. 2 vols. London. 1818. Unsatisfactory.

Webb, J. J., *Industrial Dublin since 1698, and The Silk Industry in Dublin*. Dublin. 1913.

Webb, J. J., *The Guilds of Dublin*. Dublin. 1929.

Westropp, M. S. Dudley, *Metal Work. Gold and Silver*. National Museum of Ireland Guide. Dublin. Fifth edition. 1934.

—— *Irish Pottery and Porcelain*. National Museum of Ireland Guide. Dublin. 1935.

—— *Irish Glass . . . from the XVIth Century to the Present Day*. London. [1930]

Wheeler, H. A. and M. J. Craig, *The Dublin City Churches of the Church oj Ireland*. Dublin. [Edinburgh printed] 1948. Illustrated.

Whitelaw, James, *An Essay on the Population of Dublin, 1798*. Dublin. 1805. Extremely valuable, especially since the MS. of Whitelaw's full Census was destroyed in the Public Record Office. See also under Warburton.

Wide Streets Commissioners: *Extract from the Minutes of the Commissioners . . . for making Wide and Convenient . . . Streets . . . 1757–1802*. Dublin. 1802.

Wilkinson, George, *Practical Geology and Ancient Architecture of Ireland*. London and Dublin. 1845. Contains valuable notes on building materials.

Wright, G. N., *An Historical Guide to Ancient and Modern Dublin*. London. 1821. Second ed., *ibid.* 1825. Illustrated. The second edition contains an ' architectural synopsis '.

—— *Ireland Illustrated, from Original Drawings, by G. Petrie, W. H. Bartlett, & T. M. Baynes*. London. 1831. Most of the Dublin plates appear also in *Dublin Delineated*. Dublin. [c. 1831]

Young, Arthur, *A Tour in Ireland*. 2 vols. Dublin. 1780.

I. ST MICHAEL'S HILL, Winetavern Street, *c.* 1800.

II. UPPER MERRION STREET, from Merrion Square. Mostly *c.* 1765.

III. WINETAVERN STREET

IV. THE ROYAL HOSPITAL, KILMAINHAM: the Courtyard, looking north.
Sir William Robinson, architect, 1680. Tower and spire, 1701.

V. PAIR OF DOORWAYS IN CRAMPTON COURT, *c.* 1750.

VI. KINGSBRIDGE STATION: the east front. Sancton Wood, architect, 1845.

VII. THE OLD CUSTOM HOUSE. Thomas Burgh, architect, 1707. From a print
by Joseph Tudor, 1753.

VIII. THE THOLSEL (now demolished). From a drawing by
Thomas Dingley, 1680.

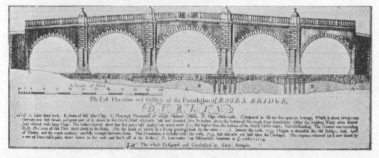

IX. ESSEX BRIDGE. From a print by George Semple, architect, in Harris's *History and Antiquities of Dublin*, 1766.

XI. ST MARY'S, Mary Street: the East Window. Architect unknown, 1702.

X. THE BLACK CHURCH (St Mary's Chapel-of-Ease). John Semple, architect, 1830.

XII. TRINITY COLLEGE LIBRARY. Thomas Burgh, architect, 1712–32. Roof raised in mid-nineteenth century.

XIII. THE BANK OF IRELAND (formerly Parliament House), from the south-east, showing Pearce's colonnade, Gandon's House of Lords portico, and Johnston's remodelled screen-walls.

XIV. TRINITY COLLEGE LIBRARY. Thomas Burgh, architect, 1712-32.
The barrel-vault by Benjamin Woodward, 1857.

XV. THE PROVOST'S HOUSE. John Smyth, architect (after Lord Burlington), 1769.

XVI. THE TAILORS' HALL. Richard Mills, architect, 1706.

XVII. THE PARLIAMENT HOUSE (now Bank of Ireland). Sir Edward Lovett
Pearce, architect, 1729.

XVIII. THE PARLIAMENT HOUSE: the Colonnade, looking towards Trinity College.
From an etching by James Malton, 1793.

XIX. THE ROYAL EXCHANGE (now City Hall). Thomas Cooley, architect, 1769.
From a water-colour by Patrick Byrne. This interior has since been altered.

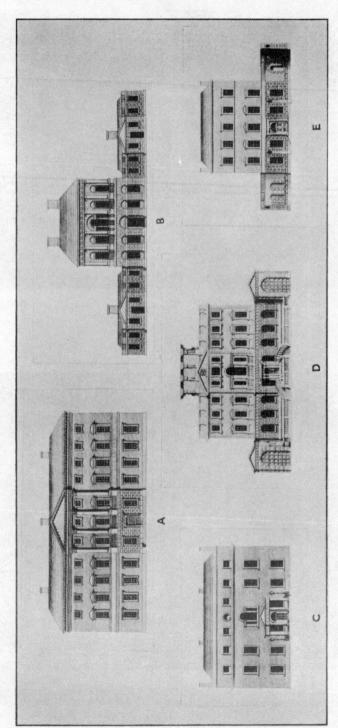

XX. STONE HOUSES OF DUBLIN: (a) Leinster, 1745; (b) Provost's, 1759; (c) Tyrone, 1742; (d) Powerscourt, 1771; (e) Charlemont, 1767.

XXI. DUBLIN CASTLE: the north side of Upper Castle Yard, architects uncertain, c. 1750–63.

XXII. DUBLIN CASTLE: the (dummy) Gate of Mars.
The statue by Van Nost, c. 1753.

XXIII. DUBLIN CASTLE: the Gate of Justice. Architect uncertain, c. 1753. The
statue by Van Nost. In the background is Newcomen's Bank, by Thomas Ivory, 1781.

XXIV. KILMAINHAM GAOL, the doorway, c. 1800. Architect and
sculptor unknown.

XXV. 20 DOMINICK STREET: detail of interior. Robert West, builder and
stuccodore, 1755.

XXVI. ST WERBURGH'S: the west front (now mostly demolished).
The lower part by Thomas Burgh, 1715; the tower and spire 1768,
architect unknown but possibly John Smyth. From Pool and Cash, 1780.

XXVII. ST WERBURGH'S: the interior. Upper gallery (and probably organ-case)
by John Smyth, 1767, pulpit by Francis Johnston, carved by Richard Stewart.

XXVIII. VIEW FROM CAPEL STREET TOWARDS THE ROYAL EXCHANGE.
From the etching by James Malton, 1797.

XXIX. ST CATHERINE'S CHURCH. John Smyth, architect, 1769. From the
etching by James Malton, 1797. This view is hardly changed today.

XXX. TRINITY COLLEGE, from the air.

XXXI. THE MARINE SCHOOL, Sir John Rogerson's Quay (now almost destroyed).
By Thomas Cooley or Thomas Ivory, 1768–73.

XXXII. THE BLUE-COAT SCHOOL. Thomas Ivory, architect, 1773–80. Engraving
by Pool and Cash, showing the central cupola as designed but never executed.

XXXIII. NEWGATE GAOL: centre feature. From an old photograph. Thomas Cooley, architect, 1773. The hanging-apparatus is visible over the main door, as in most Irish gaols.

XXXV. POWERSCOURT HOUSE. Robert Mack, architect, 1771.

XXXIV. NEWCOMEN'S BANK (now Municipal Buildings). Thomas Ivory, architect, 1781. Right-hand half of façade, and porch, added 1856-8.

XXXVII. MIDDLE GARDINER STREET: doorway, c. 1790.

XXXVI. NORTH GREAT GEORGE'S STREET: doorway, c. 1785.

XXXVIII. THE CUSTOM HOUSE, from across the river.

XXXIX. THE CUSTOM HOUSE: detail of window in south-west pavilion. The keystone-head, carved by Edward Smyth, probably represents the river Slaney.

XL. THE CUSTOM HOUSE: central keystone-head of north front, representing the river Lee. Carved by Edward Smyth.

XLI. THE CUSTOM HOUSE STABLES, Store Street (now a bakery). Architect unknown, *c.* 1810.

XLII. THE CASTLE STEPS. Architect unknown, *c.* 1810. Note how the recessed panels emphasise the thickness and impenetrability of the seat of government.

XLIII. THE CUSTOM HOUSE: south-east pavilion. From a photograph taken before the fire of 1921.

XLIV. THE FOUR COURTS. From a photograph taken before the bombardment of 1922. In the middle distance i
St Paul's, Arran Quay, and beyond it the Wellington Testimonial.

XLV. THE KING'S INNS AND ROYAL CANAL HARBOUR. From an engraving
after George Petrie, 1821.

XLVI. COLLEGE STREET, looking towards the House of Lords portico. On the
right, the Royal Irish Institution (now demolished). Frederick Darley, architect, 1827.
From an engraving after George Petrie, 1828.

XLVII. THE KING'S INNS, from Henrietta Street.

XLVIII. THE KING'S INNS: west front. James Gandon and Henry Aaron Baker, architects, 1795–1808, completed by Francis Johnston, 1816. The wings added in mid-nineteenth century. Sculptures by Edward Smyth.

XLIX. THE MERCHANTS' HALL, seen across the Metal Bridge. Frederick Darley, architect, 1821.

L. OLD CARLISLE BRIDGE. James Gandon, architect, 1791. Replaced by the present O'Connell Bridge, 1880.

LI. KILMAINHAM GAOL. Architect of original part (*c.* 1800) unknown.

LII. GRAND CANAL HARBOUR, *c.* 1780.

LIII. BARRACK BRIDGE (now replaced), QUEEN'S BRIDGE, and THE RICHMOND TOWER (now moved). From an engraving after George Petrie, 1819.

LIV. SACKVILLE (NOW O'CONNELL) STREET. From an engraving after George Petrie, 1821.

LV. THE ROYAL EXCHANGE: section from east to west. From an engraving by
Pool and Cash, 1780.

LVI. THE FOUR COURTS: section from south to north. From an undated
engraving after James Gandon, not exactly as executed.

LVII. POWERSCOURT HOUSE: detail of interior. Carving by Ignatius McDonagh.

LVIII. THE COMMERCIAL BUILDINGS, Dame Street. Edward Parke, architect, 1796–9.

LIX. DALY'S CLUBHOUSE, College Green. Francis Johnston, architect, 1790. This is the centre portion only: the wings have disappeared, and the attic storey has been remodelled.

LX. THE RUTLAND FOUNTAIN, Merrion Square. Henry Aaron Baker, architect, *c.* 1787.

LXI. HERBERT STREET, *c.* 1830, looking towards St Stephen's, 1825.

LXII. HOUSE IN RATHGAR AVENUE, *c.* 1860.

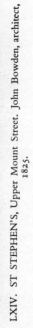

LXIV. ST STEPHEN'S, Upper Mount Street. John Bowden, architect, 1825.

LXIII. ST GEORGE'S, Hardwicke Place. Francis Johnston, architect, 1803–13.

LXV. HUBAND BRIDGE (1791) and ST STEPHEN'S
CHURCH (1825).

LXVI. ECCLES STREET, with St George's in the distance.

LXVII. HARDWICKE PLACE, with St George's Church, *c.* 1805.

LXVIII. TRINITY COLLEGE CHAPEL. Sir William Chambers and Graham Myers, architects. Michael Stapleton, stuccodore. *c.* 1779–90.

LXIX. O'CONNELL (SACKVILLE) STREET, THE NELSON PILLAR and THE G.P.O. From a photograph taken before the destruction of Easter, 1916.

LXX. QUEEN'S BRIDGE. Charles Vallancey, architect, 1764–8.

LXXI. THE METAL BRIDGE. Designer unknown 1816.

LXXII. SARAH BRIDGE (Islandbridge). Alexander Stephens or Stephenson, architect, 1791.

LXXIII. RINGSEND BRIDGE, over the Dodder. Architect unknown, 1803.

LXXIV. THE QUAYS, looking west from the Ballast Office.

LXXV. COOK STREET, with St Audoen's Catholic Church. Patrick Byrne, architect, 1841–6. On the right are some remains of the walls of Dublin.

LXXVI. ST NICHOLAS OF MYRA, Francis Street. Body of church, 1832, by John Leeson; west front (shown here), 1860, perhaps by Patrick Byrne.

LXXVII. ARRAN QUAY, with St Paul's, the Four Courts and Whitworth Bridge (1816).

LXXVIII. ORMONDE QUAY UPPER, with the Four Courts.

LXXIX. HARCOURT STREET STATION. George Wilkinson, architect, 1859.

LXXX. THE BROADSTONE. John Skipton Mulvany, architect, 1841–50.

Index

353

INDEX

INDEX

INDEX